W9-ASD-132

MERCHANTS
AND
MASTERPIECES

MERCHANTS AND MASTERPIECES

THE STORY OF THE METROPOLITAN MUSEUM OF ART

CALVIN TOMKINS

E. P. DUTTON & CO., INC. | NEW YORK | 1970

For My Mother and Father

First Edition

Published simultaneously in Canada by
Clarke, Irwin & Company Limited, Toronto and Vancouver

Library of Congress Catalog Card Number: 75-95484

A02402   [04]

The contemporary photographs between pages 128 and 129 were taken for this book by Judy Johnston unless otherwise credited. The others in that section, except for the photographs of the Kevin Roche, John Dinkeloo & Associates architectural models taken by Ezra Stoller, are from The Metropolitan Museum of Art's archives.

The portraits on pages 366–370 are also from Museum archives unless otherwise credited.

ACKNOWLEDGMENTS

This book began another way. Albert Ten Eyck Gardner had planned for nearly twenty years to write the Metropolitan's centennial history. Having served the museum since 1941 in several different capacities—as librarian, archivist, and associate curator of American Art—his personal knowledge of persons and events extended back over many years; he died without getting any of this down on paper, though, and one can only guess at what was lost. In the absence of firsthand knowledge I have had the unstinting cooperation of nearly all of Mr. Gardner's former associates, members of a brilliant staff too large to list here individually. Unjust as it may be to single out a few among the generous many, I would like nevertheless to pay special thanks to those within the museum whose time and patience I have tried most sorely.

Of the curators emeritus, A. Hyatt Mayor, Charles K. Wilkinson, Stephen C. Grancsay, and Lydia Bond Powel have provided me with invaluable insights as well as many delightful hours in their company. Claus Virch, Guy-Philippe de Montebello, Elizabeth E. Gardner, Margaretta M. Salinger, and Hubert F. von Sonnenburg of the European Paintings Department have been much more than helpful, as has Theodore Rousseau, who was curator of European Paintings when I began the book and vice-director and curator in chief of the museum when I finished. John G. Phillips, William H. Forsyth, Thomas Pelham Miller, Emanuel Winternitz, Fong Chow, Henry Fischer, Nora Scott, John K. Howat, Berry B. Tracy, Jacob Bean, Dietrich von Bothmer, John J. McKendry, and Henry Geldzahler have

5

guided and enlightened me on curatorial matters, while Harry S. Parker III, Joseph V. Noble, Dudley T. Easby, Jr., Richard R. Morsches, Kate C. Lefferts, Thomas M. Folds, Louise Condit, Polaire Weissman, Robert Chapman, Arthur Klein, and Leon Wilson have helped me to grasp some of the million-and-one other aspects of the museum colossus. The entire staff of the Metropolitan's Centennial Committee has borne with me faithfully throughout the writing; I am particularly grateful to George Trescher, the centennial secretary, for assistance of all kinds and at all levels, and to Linda R. Hyman, who ably carried out much of the research for this book, an enterprise in which neither she nor I could possibly have managed without the help of archivist John Buchanan and his colleague Patricia Finlay. Many trustees have shared ideas, and countless others outside the museum have contributed reminiscences—most notably Mrs. Herbert E. Winlock, Mrs. Francis Henry Taylor, and Mrs. James J. Rorimer.

Perhaps the greatest debt is due to Arthur A. Houghton, Jr., the Metropolitan's chairman, and to Thomas P. F. Hoving, its director, who encouraged me in every way possible without attempting to influence my approach. Whatever interpretation may be made of these pages, the book reflects an independent view of the museum's history, and its flaws are the author's alone.

C.T.

"What's to do? Shall we go see
the reliques of this town?"

—*Twelfth Night,*
III:iii.19

CONTENTS

PREFACE

Like all successful institutions, the Metropolitan Museum of Art is a mirror of its times. The ideas, ambitions, and tastes that have shaped its growth during the last century have been those of particular men and women living in a city, New York, which has lent its own peculiar coloration to the background, and it is largely in terms of these individuals—collectors and curators, benefactors and trustees, establishmentarians and eccentrics— that I have tried to tell this story. If the tale has a recurrent motif, it is that for a hundred years those who guided the Metropolitan have sought to make it something more than a treasury of great art.

That it is such a treasury—the greatest museum in the Western hemisphere and one of the half dozen greatest in the world—goes without saying. The Metropolitan's vast collections are surpassed in certain areas by those of the leading museums of Europe, whose riches accumulated during centuries of royal patronage and plunder; Italian paintings may be seen to better advantage in the Uffizi or the Louvre, Spanish art in the Prado, Greek sculpture in the British Museum or the Vatican. No other museum can match the Metropolitan's encyclopedic survey of five thousand years of man's art, however, and no other museum attracts such a huge and avid public.

Curators abhor the numbers game, of course. It is a sign of cultural naïveté to boast of six million visitors a year when what matters is the private quality of the museum experience—and what kind of privacy is possible on Sunday afternoons at the Metropolitan, when the concentration of sixty or seventy or eighty thousand people in the galleries makes it nearly impossible to view the works of art? Critics, artists, and some Metropolitan trustees have been heard to mourn the passing of the museum as a place of quiet contemplation, a temple and shrine of art. After a hundred years of seeking to attract the public, the museum is now criticized for succeeding too well.

And yet the mass public has always been the implicit justification for art museums in this country. Founded on the assumption that art was insepa-rable from education, American museums have addressed their primary ap-peal to the man in the street—rather than to the artist, the scholar, or the connoisseur, who are nevertheless welcomed on their own terms—and it is for this reason that they have prospered and proliferated on a scale almost unknown in Europe. Far from becoming mausoleums or "dungeons of the ideal" as European galleries are often accused of being, the best American museums have played a continuously active role in the life of the commun-ity, and they have influenced our lives in a number of ways unforeseen by their founders.

There have been stagnant periods in the Metropolitan's history, to be sure, whole decades when the trustees and the staff seemed content to savor the exclusive joys of acquisition and when the museum itself took on something of the aura of a private club, but sooner or later a new genera-tion would sound once again the tocsin of education and social action. Now that the mass public has been drawn into the temple, not even the elitist critics expect it to go away. Its presence, in fact, may be the clearest sign that the Metropolitan's real work has only just begun.

PART I
MEN OF FORTUNE AND ESTATE

ONE

A crowd had been gathering since noon in front of the raw, rather ugly red-brick building in the park. By three o'clock a line of fashionable broughams, landaus, clarences, coupés, and livery hacks extended down Fifth Avenue as far as the eye could see, while inside the building, in the large exhibition hall on the main floor, every inch of available floor space was occupied by frock-coated gentlemen and ladies in bright afternoon silks. There was an audible fluttering of fans and programs; although the weather was cool, the ventilation was rudimentary. Downstairs, in their boardroom on the ground floor, the trustees waited nervously for the arrival of Rutherford B. Hayes. The President of the United States had agreed to preside over the formal dedication of the Metropolitan Museum of Art, which, after an uncertain infancy in makeshift quarters, was established at last—in March, 1880—in its new Central Park home.

The President's carriage drove up promptly at three thirty, and a few minutes later, as the band played "Hail, Columbia," Hayes and his honor guard of trustees and dignitaries took their places on the raised speakers' platform. The Reverend Dr. Henry C. Potter of Grace Church read the opening prayer. He was followed by the president of the Department of Public Parks, who formally presented the museum to its trustees, and by John Taylor Johnston, the Metropolitan's first president, who formally accepted it. Joseph C. Choate then rose to deliver the principal address, and the large audience settled back in pleased anticipation.

Choate was younger than most of the other trustees. Tall and slender, with a massive head of reddish-brown hair that he frequently rumpled with both hands, he had been born in Salem, Massachusetts, in 1832, had graduated from Harvard College and Harvard Law School, and was now well launched on a great career as a trial lawyer, a career distinguished by dramatic victories on behalf of wealthy clients and powerful corporations. He was active in Republican politics, had played a leading role in arousing New Yorkers against the iniquities of the Tweed Ring, and would go on in later life to become ambassador to the Court of St. James's and a famous international statesman. Choate was also a great wit, and the most popular after-dinner speaker of his day. Although he came from one of New England's oldest families, he had taken on the easier and more genial manners of a born New Yorker, and he was not above an occasional jibe at his own rockbound ancestors—such as his remark, at a dinner of the New England Society, that the Pilgrim mothers deserved even more respect than the Pilgrim fathers because they had endured all the same hardships and had also been obliged to endure the Pilgrim fathers. Asked at another dinner whom he would like to be if he could not be himself, Choate shot a glance at his wife across the table and said gallantly, "I should like to be Mrs. Choate's second husband." His wit sometimes got him into difficulties. He once suggested to the audience at a St. Patrick's Day dinner that the solution to Irish Home Rule was for the Irish in New York to go back home and rule Ireland, inasmuch as they had mastered the political art so completely that they now ruled New York. His hosts were outraged, and Choate was violently attacked in the newspapers the next day. Choate's speech at the opening day ceremonies for the museum was by no means irreverent. In fact, it was an almost perfect summation of the animating ideas that had brought the Metropolitan into being, and which, although they would undergo many metamorphoses over the years, would largely shape the institution's first quarter century.

The founders of the Metropolitan, Choate said, "believed that the diffusion of a knowledge of art in its higher forms of beauty would tend directly to humanize, to educate and refine a practical and laborious people; that though the great masterpieces of painting and sculpture . . . could never be within their reach, yet it might be possible in the progress of time to gather together a collection of works of merit, which should impart some knowledge of art and its history to a people who were yet to take almost their first steps in that department of knowledge." Here, indeed, was the crux of the matter. The basis and justification for the museum's existence lay in its educational role. The accumulation of masterpieces was specifically ruled out (such an endeavor being considered impossible in any case), and the trustees, at least in their public statements, placed their profound trust in art conceived as a "department of knowledge." Once the toy of the idle rich, art now belonged to the people as a whole—"has become their best resource and most efficient educator," as Choate said, and could thus be seen as "the vital and practical interest of the working millions."

This striking and still rather original notion told more, perhaps, about the founders than about the working millions whose aesthetic sensibilities were to be refined and educated. The Metropolitan, which in 1880 was exactly ten years old, had been founded and conceived, as Choate said, "by a very small number of persons." Most of them belonged to that extraordinary group of liberal-minded reformers who came to prominence in New York during and soon after the Civil War—leading abolitionists like Frederick Law Olmsted and Henry Tilden Blodgett, moral idealists like William Cullen Bryant, enlightened clergymen like the Reverend Henry Bellows, the popular pastor of All Souls Unitarian Church. These men believed in art without knowing very much about it. Bellows himself had said that it would be difficult to find men qualified to administer an art museum in New York, because "men of affairs and enterprise and executive ability are seldom interested in art, or marked with a taste and appreciation of the delicate interests of the Beautiful," while "artists, a brooding, dreamy, meditative class, closed to the world by their intensity of passion for their coy mistress, are seldom men of practical wisdom, push, and enterprise." Bellows had also warned that little support could be expected from the public. If the public had been given a choice in the matter, he said, they would never have voted the funds for Olmsted and his partner, Calvert Vaux, to lay out Central Park. In Bellows' opinion it was essential to find the men of push and enterprise who *were* interested in art, and for them in their turn to secure the money and confidence of the general public—to secure it "long enough to allow the few who know their wants to perfect the plan, against the protest of their poorer taste and judgement."

If the argument sounds patronizing today, it must be remembered that in the immediate post-Civil War period New York struck most of its educated citizens as an appalling sink of ignorance and depravity. Even the energetic and self-confident business class was finding it harder and harder to ignore the seamy underside of New York life. The bloody draft riots of 1863, which claimed twelve hundred dead and more than a hundred buildings destroyed by fire, had shaken confidence in the city's ability to control its restless and rapidly expanding population. Nearly half of the city's inhabitants were foreign-born, and far too many of them were packed into slums more miserable than those of London or Calcutta. By 1873, according to a contemporary article in *Harper's*, an estimated ten thousand homeless children prowled the streets of New York, singly or in gangs. Girls of poor families drifted inexorably into the one profession open to them: an official report in 1866 stated that the city had six hundred and twenty-one houses of prostitution, ninety-nine houses of assignation, and seventy-five concert saloons where "waiter girls" doubled as whores.

Residents of the brownstone and brick mansions on Washington Square and the new palaces then being built along Fifth Avenue as far north as the fifties could shut their eyes to conditions in the Tenth Ward (known to health officers as the "typhus ward," and to the Bureau of Vital Statistics as the "suicide ward"), but they could not so easily ignore the city's visible filth and deterioration or the virtual paralysis into which its transportation system had fallen. The old horse-drawn omnibuses were hopelessly overcrowded. The *Evening Post* reported in 1867 that the average workman spent more than four hours commuting to and from his job. Efforts to deal with the crisis were consistently blocked by the Tweed Ring, which had control of municipal transit and nearly everything else in New York, and which, before its melodramatic collapse in 1871, would manage to cheat and extort the city of sums estimated variously from $30,000,000 up to $200,000,000.

Public and private scandals filled the newspapers. Their readers seemed to take a cynical delight in each new outrage against decency, somewhat in the spirit of William Marcy Tweed's famous reply, when confronted with the published reports of his crooked deals, "Well, what are you going to do about it?" For a time it looked as though nothing could be done. The nation's largest city—the ninth census in 1870 gave Manhattan's population as just under a million—was firmly in the grip of the most corrupt political machine yet developed in America. Tweed owned the mayor, Abraham Oakey ("Elegant Oakey") Hall, the city chamberlain, Peter Barr Sweeny, the comptroller, Richard B. Connolly, and at least three important judges including State Supreme Court Justice Albert Cardozo (the father of a future Associate Justice of the Supreme Court). Even the governor of the state, John T. Hoffman, was a creature of Tweed. Anyone who wanted to do business with the city had to pay Tweed and his cronies a percentage, and the percentage kept going up. Tweed had reportedly spent more than a million dollars to get his new city charter passed in 1870. He would get it back, with interest. "A politician coming forward takes things as they are," Tweed explained. "This population is too hopelessly split up into races and factions to govern it under universal suffrage, except by the bribery of patronage and corruption." George Templeton Strong, the diarist and barometer of his time, concluded during this period that "to be a citizen of New York is a disgrace."

Worse still, New York seemed to be merely a reflection of the entire nation's moral and spiritual decay. President Ulysses S. Grant (Hayes's predecessor in office) had associated openly with Jay Gould and Jim Fisk, and when those two notorious speculators tried to corner the gold market in 1869 and precipitated the "Black Friday" panic on Wall Street, many thought that Grant was at least indirectly implicated. The extent of corruption in the federal government emerged during the Crédit Mobilier scandal of 1873—White House aides, congressmen, and even the out-going Vice-President Schuyler Colfax were shown to have stock for which they had not paid in the company that built the Union Pacific Railroad. The worship of Mammon was everywhere in ascendance, although usually it was carried on under a cloud of suffocating hypocrisy. Walt Whitman, the Brooklyn-born poet who had taken all America for his province, looked about him and saw evidence of a disease infecting not only the worst elements of society but many of those who considered themselves the best. "The depravity of the business classes of our country is not less than has been supposed, but infinitely greater," Whitman wrote in *Democratic Vistas*, published in 1871. "The official services of America, national, state, and municipal, in all their branches and departments, except the judiciary, are

saturated in corruption, bribery, falsehood, maladministration; and the judiciary is tainted. The great cities reek with respectable as much as non-re-
spectable robbery and scoundrelism. In fashionable life, flippancy, tepid
amours, weak infidelism, small aims, or no aims at all. . . . I say that our
New World democracy, however great a success in uplifting the masses
from their sloughs, in materialistic development, products, and in a certain
highly-deceptive superficial popular intellectuality, is, so far, an almost
complete failure in its social aspects, and in really grand religious, moral,
literary, and esthetic results . . . It is as though we were somehow being
endow'd with a vast and more and more thoroughly-appointed body, and
then left with little or no soul."

The Metropolitan's founding trustees consigned problems of the soul to
organized religion, preferably Presbyterian. Any basic weakening of the
church's influence would have been inconceivable to them, in spite of such
amazing events as the revelation, in 1872, that Henry Ward Beecher, rector
of Plymouth Church in Brooklyn and the most famous preacher in America, had been involved in not one but several adulterous liaisons with
members of his flock. If the church had lost little of its hold on the upper
middle class, however, it was nonetheless a declining factor in the lives of
a great many Americans. In its place, consciously or unconsciously, liberal
thinkers and idealists had developed a boundless faith in education. Although successful men of the time still preached the Puritan gospel of self-
help and tended to look upon poverty as an avoidable sin, most of them
supported the movement to add public high schools and state universities
to the national system of free education. Popular education shone forth like
a beacon as the answer to all the country's major ills. Tamed by twelve
years of schooling, the rude and previously unlettered masses would learn
not to vote for Tweed and his kind. They would also become gentler and
more civilized—all the more so if they could be exposed to the refining
touch of the fine arts. Just as Andrew Jackson Downing, the landscape architect largely responsible for the movement to build Central Park, had
argued for years that city parks would "civilize and refine the national
character," the influential art critic James Jackson Jarves insisted that "We
cannot make the world more beautiful without making it better, morally
and socially." Heavy emphasis was placed on the moral appeal of art and

beauty, and more than one social historian has seen a relationship between the decline of organized religion and the spectacular growth of the museum movement in America.

The country's first three major art museums—in Boston, in Washington, D.C., and in New York—were all incorporated in 1870.° Before the century was out these three would have served as models for at least twenty-five art museums in other cities, virtually all of which would place primary emphasis on education, moral uplift, and social betterment. It was this that made the American museums so different from the great museums of Europe, where centuries of royal patronage and plunder had set the prevailing tone of aristocratic connoisseurship, and it was this that Choate stressed again and again in his speech to the fashionable audience at the Metropolitan's formal dedication. Rejecting all snobbish distinctions between fine and applied arts, rejecting also the trivial accumulation of "a mere cabinet of curiosities which should serve to kill time for the idle," the Metropolitan's founders had decreed that the museum, in Choate's words, would "gather together a more or less complete collection of objects illustrative of the history of art in all its branches, from the earliest beginnings to the present time, which should serve not only for the instruction and entertainment of the people, but should also show to the students and artisans of every branch of industry, in the high and acknowledged standards of form and color, what the past has accomplished for them to imitate and excel."

Choate and his fellow trustees knew very well that the Metropolitan would not be able to achieve any of these idealistic goals unless it had the support of those whom Choate called "men of fortune and estate"—the New York bankers and businessmen whose wealth was compounding just then at an incredible ratio. New York, already established as the financial and trading hub of the continent, was feeling at this time the invigorating stimulus of new money—vast sums of it, in fact, pouring in on an unprece-

° Boston's Museum of Fine Arts, chartered that February, opened for the first time in 1876. In Washington, D.C., the banker William Wilson Corcoran had given his art collection and funds for a museum to house it before the Civil War; the building, however, was commandeered as an arsenal during the war, and the Corcoran Gallery was not incorporated until May 14, 1870.

dented scale from the development of the railroads. "Probably no age and
no city has ever seen such gigantic fortunes accumulated out of nothing as
have here been piled up within the last five years," Choate observed in
passing. The city was growing chaotically, real estate was pushing farther
and farther uptown, and cultural ambitions were rising as well. New York's
theaters and music halls paid the highest fees and attracted the leading
stage and concert performers of Europe. Its dignified Academy of Music on
Fourteenth Street rivaled Boston's Music Hall (the ancestor of Symphony
Hall) as an operatic and social mecca, and in recent years even the literary
men seemed to prefer New York. Thoreau had died in 1862, Hawthorne in
1864. Emerson's voice still lectured to the national oversoul, but the long
reign of New England's literary pantheon was drawing to a close. In the
eyes of most Americans the country's greatest living man of letters was
William Cullen Bryant, a transplanted Bostonian who now dominated the
New York intellectual landscape from his position as editor of the influential *Evening Post,* and from 1860 on it was New York, with its publishers
and its magazines, its theaters and restaurants and quickening tempo of
life, that drew the young writers. The combination of new wealth and cultural yearnings had also led, naturally enough, to a growing interest in art
among the business classes.

A few New York magnates—the railroad men William H. Aspinwall and
John Taylor Johnston, the financier August Belmont, the retail merchant
Alexander T. Stewart—had begun even before the Civil War to amass sizable collections. "It has become the mode to have taste," James Jackson
Jarves had written in 1864. "Private galleries in New York are becoming as
common as private stables." An increasing number of postwar art auctions
and exhibitions, together with booming sales of inexpensive prints and the
rise in European travel, had greatly enhanced what one New York journalist called "the mercantile and social importance of art." Enlightened merchants did not need to be persuaded that a museum of art deserved their
support and encouragement. Not every businessman was sufficiently enlightened, however, and it was to these individuals—pragmatic money-
makers not yet initiated into the delicate interests of the Beautiful—that
Choate presumably addressed himself when he stressed the practical and
even *commercial* advantages of art museums.

Europe's great art centers, Choate pointed out, had long been aware of these advantages. "The wealth and prosperity of Dresden rest largely upon the throngs that report to its vast galleries, and whole cities in Italy live upon their inherited treasures in art," he said. But even more important than the pilgrimages of art lovers were the benefits that *manufacturers* would reap from the development of museums. Choate cited as evidence the South Kensington Museum in London, established in 1852 with the primary goal of raising the quality of British manufacturers. Its departments had been organized according to materials—textiles, metals, ceramics, wood—and its appeal was directed to artisans who might come there and find inspiration and guidance in their respective trades. There was even a room of bad design, with garish pajamas and other examples to be avoided. Embedded in this notion, of course, was the idea that by improving the level of the native artisan's taste, design, and workmanship one also stood a good chance of improving the retailer's profits. This, Choate said, was precisely what had happened in England during the ten years after the foundation of the South Kensington Museum. In fact, according to Choate, "every nation that has tried it has found that every wise investment in the development of art pays more than compound interest." Choate made it clear that the trustees of the Metropolitan were deeply interested in the "artisans of every branch of industry," whom they burned to provide with edifying exhibits of "what the past had accomplished for them to imitate and excel."

Museums of art were not only socially desirable, then, they were also good business. And the good businessmen who had made their fortunes in New York could do no better, for their city or for themselves, than by helping the Metropolitan Museum to acquire what, at the moment, it needed most—money. "These trustees are too proud to beg a dollar," Choate said genially in conclusion, "but they freely proffer their services in relieving these distended and apoplectic pockets. Think of it, ye millionaires of many markets—what glory may yet be yours, if you only listen to our advice, to convert pork into porcelain, grain and produce into priceless pottery, the rude ores of commerce into sculptured marble, and railroad shares and mining stocks—things which perish without the using, and which in the next financial panic shall surely shrivel like parched scrolls—into the glorified canvas of the world's masters, that shall adorn these walls for centuries. The rage of Wall Street is to hunt the philosopher's stone, to convert all baser things into gold, which is but dross; but ours is the higher ambition to convert your useless gold into things of living beauty that shall be a joy to a whole people for a thousand years."

The next and final speaker was Rutherford B. Hayes, who in a single sentence declared the museum open to the public, and promptly sat down. Cheers and applause broke out, the band blared and banged its way into a march, General Louis P. di Cesnola, the Italian-born director of the Metropolitan, took the President off on a tour of the premises, and Choate, flushed and smiling, accepted the congratulations of the assembled and not at all apoplectic millionaires.

TWO

The civilizing lessons of art and beauty had not seemed particularly urgent to America's founding fathers. John Adams had looked upon the glories of French art and seen in them a threat to democratic liberties; painting and sculpture were essentially antidemocratic and "on the side of Despotism and Superstition," said Adams, who added that he "would not give six-pence for a picture by Raphael or a statue of Phidias." A few small, pioneer-ing art galleries had been founded since Adams' time—the gallery of the Pennsylvania Academy of Fine Arts in 1805; the Wadsworth Atheneum in Hartford, the nation's first real art museum, in 1842. To most nineteenth century Americans, though, art remained something suspicious and Euro-pean, and the word *museum* connoted natural science, not painting and sculpture.

Nearly every town of any consequence had its natural science museum, where science served as a pretext for catering to the national appetite for anything bizarre or grotesque, and where one could usually find, along with the bones of the woolly mammoth and the miniature steam engine carved from a cherry pit, the most lifelike waxwork tableau of some cele-brated criminal in the act of committing his most celebrated crime, with the very hatchet or the very knife. These "dime museums," as they were called, reached their apogee in 1841 when Phineas T. Barnum opened his famous New York establishment at the corner of Broadway and Ann Street. Barnum had bought out the natural science collections of several earlier museums, including the original one started by the artist Charles Willson

Peale in Philadelphia in 1805, but his principal asset was showmanship. His American Museum offered everything from "roaring baboons" to "interesting relics from the Holy Land," and Barnum claimed that it outdrew the British Museum. In his autobiography he tells of a Fourth of July holiday when the premises were so crowded that he was forced to stop selling tickets. "I pushed through the throng until I reached the roof of the building," Barnum wrote, "hoping to find room for a few more, but it was in vain. Looking down into the street it was a sad sight to see the thousands of people who stood with their money ready to enter the Museum, but who were actually turned away. It was exceedingly harrowing to my feelings."

The boisterous, commercial spirit of Barnum's New York had not kept the city from becoming a magnet for American artists, whose numbers were steadily increasing in spite of the absence of art museums. The New York Academy of Fine Arts, founded in 1802, was the country's first formally organized art institution. It had quickly ossified into a narrowly exclusive club dominated by the painter John Trumbull, whose idea of encouraging American art was to procure government commissions for himself. Trumbull's arrogance finally induced several of his associates to break away in 1826 and form the National Academy of Design; although this group soon became as exclusive and reactionary as the New York Academy, it in turn gave rise to more open-minded art schools and artist societies. New York's rapid growth, moreover, held out the promise of rich patronage. "The more I think of making a push at New York as a permanent place of residence in my profession, the more proper it seems to me that it should be pretty soon," the Massachusetts-born painter Samuel F. B. Morse (who would become better known as the inventor of the telegraph) confided to his diary in 1832. "New York does not yet feel the influx of wealth from the Western Canal but in a year or two she will feel it, and it will be advantageous for me to be previously identified among the citizens as a painter."

Morse's reasoning was sound, although at the time few New Yorkers were giving much thought to art. A single dealer, Michael Paff (known as "Old Paff") supplied the limited demand for "Old Masters"—usually with atrocious copies of dubious originals. The only significant collector of the period was Luman Reed, a wholesale grocery merchant who bought and commissioned paintings directly from the New York artists of his day, and who had converted the third floor of his house on Greenwich Street into a picture gallery to which the public was invited one day a week. After Reed's death in 1841 his collection became the nucleus of the New York Gallery of Fine Arts, one of the earliest efforts to establish an art museum in the city. The New York Gallery closed in 1854, plagued by chronic debts, but by this time the artists whom Reed had befriended and helped to support were receiving encouragement from other sources. Asher B. Durand, Thomas Cole, John F. Kensett, and other painters of what came to be called the Hudson River School were accepted and even lionized by upper-class New York society, more and more of whose members had come to feel that paintings and sculpture were a necessity for the well-appointed home.

These same artists were also beneficiaries of the American Art Union, whose astonishing success disclosed an unsuspected taste for art among the socially ambitious middle classes. The American Art Union began in 1838 as the Apollo Gallery, a nonprofit organization at 410 Broadway where artists could show their latest work and where the public paid a small entrance fee. It soon broadened its scope, becoming a cooperative association on a national scale. Subscribers to the Union paid an annual fee of $5.00, in return for which they received a steel engraving of an American painting, several issues of the Art Union *Bulletin*, and—the big attraction—a chance to win an original oil painting at the annual prize drawing in New York. Subscriptions poured in from every part of the country, more each year, until in the peak year 1849 cash receipts from 18,960 subscribers totaled more than $96,000—enough to buy four hundred and sixty paintings for distribution. Three years later the American Art Union was defunct, closed down by the courts as an illegal lottery. In its brief and spectacular career, though, it had distributed twenty-four hundred paintings (including such fine works as George Caleb Bingham's *Fur Traders Descending the Missouri*, now in the Metropolitan), and established New York as the marketplace and center of American art.

The public's growing interest in art was demonstrated anew in 1864 by the success of the Metropolitan Art Fair. This event was conceived as a benefit for the United States Sanitary Commission, a volunteer organization formed in 1861 to help care for sick and wounded Civil War soldiers. (Twenty years later its example would lead to the formation of the American Red Cross.) To raise money for the Sanitary Commission, several of its members evolved the idea of holding an auction of paintings and other works of art from New York private collections. One hundred and ninety-six paintings were donated, and more than a million dollars were raised for the Sanitary Commission. Never before had the "social and mercantile" advantages of art been so clearly demonstrated, and it is not surprising that several of the men who played an active part in the Metropolitan Fair should become, six years later, the prime movers on the Metropolitan Museum's founding board.

Like many of New York's more pleasant amenities, the idea for the Metropolitan Museum was first conceived in Paris. In the course of an after-dinner speech to a group of Americans celebrating their Fourth of July at the Pré Catalan, the fashionable garden restaurant in the Bois de Boulogne, John Jay, an eminent lawyer and a grandson of the first chief justice, remarked that it was "time for the American people to lay the foundations of a National Institution and Gallery of Art," and suggested that the American gentlemen then in Paris were the ones to inaugurate the plan. Among the Americans present that day were a number of New York citizens for whom Jay's proposal—coming at such a moment, and in a city that has traditionally stirred cultural longings in the mercantile soul—had the ring of a moral imperative. Before the evening was over, a group of these gentlemen approached Jay and pledged themselves to work toward such a goal.

The next steps took place inside the Union League Club, which at first blush might have seemed an inappropriate setting. The club had been established in 1863 to provide a focus for Unionist, pro-Lincoln sentiment in New York, and was thus politically rather than socially oriented. Its membership included most of the prominent men of the city, however, including Jay himself, William Cullen Bryant, Frederick Law Olmsted, William T. Blodgett, Joseph H. Choate, John Taylor Johnston, and the Reverend Henry W. Bellows. Bellows and Olmsted had been the principal organizers of the Sanitary Commission during the Civil War. Blodgett, Johnston, and others were largely responsible for the success of the Metropolitan Art Fair in 1864. These were all men of strong social conscience, so that when the little group that had responded so enthusiastically to Jay's speech in Paris (several of them were naturally Union Leaguers) returned from Europe and proposed that the Union League Club "might properly institute the best means for promoting this great object" of a major art museum, the social and moral advantages of the plan received a sympathetic hearing. By coincidence, John Jay was elected president of the club that fall, so that the proposal he had inspired came to him for action. Jay referred it to the club's art committee, which consisted of the publisher George P. Putnam, the painters John F. Kensett, Worthington Whittredge, Vincent Colyer, and George Baker, the sculptor J. Q. A. Ward, and Samuel P. Avery, an engraver who had branched out as a dealer in European paintings. Avery was instrumental in forming the collections of William H. Vanderbilt, August Belmont, and several other New York millionaires, and for more than twenty years he would function as the Metropolitan trustees' principal adviser and expert on all art matters.

The committee took its time deliberating. In fact, nearly three years elapsed before it reported to a meeting of the full membership that an art institution, provided it were "free alike from bungling government officials and from the control of a single individual," was surely worth the members' consideration. Events moved more quickly after that. Another meeting at the Union League Club was scheduled for November 23, 1869, with invitations going out to all those in the city who might be thought to have an active interest in the plan. A heavy downpour kept some potential sponsors from attending, but more than three hundred people showed up nonetheless, among them virtually the entire artist community, the leaders of most of the city's cultural and educational institutions, a sprinkling of municipal officials, and a liberal assortment of bankers, businessmen, and lawyers. John Jay was not there—he had become the United States ambassador to Austria in the meanwhile. In his absence William Cullen Bryant, the city's white-maned and white-bearded first citizen and its most elevated symbol of culture, had agreed to serve as presiding officer.

Bryant's opening address, which reverberated with organ tones and trumpet calls, played on the keys of civic and national pride. "Our city is the third great city of the civilized world," Bryant said. "Our republic has already taken its place among the great powers of the earth; it is great in extent, great in population, great in the activity and enterprise of her people. It is the richest nation in the world." And yet, Bryant added, its riches were too often diverted to mean or uncouth ends. "My friends, if a tenth part of what is every year stolen from us . . . in the city where we live, under the pretence of the public service, and poured profusely into the coffers of political rogues, were expended on a Museum of Art, we might have, reposited in spacious and stately buildings, collections formed of works left by the world's greatest artists, which would be the pride of the country."

In his austere and dignified voice, Bryant went on to state that virtually every country of Europe had its museums of fine arts, even Spain, "a third-rate power of Europe and poor besides." In America, however—and here he touched a sensitive nerve—"when the owner of a private gallery of art desires to leave his treasures where they can be seen by the public, he looks in vain for any institution to which he can send them." Great collections came on the market in Europe from time to time and could easily be acquired, but where, in America, could they be housed? American artists were growing in numbers and skills, but they still were obliged to go abroad to study because nowhere in their own country could they see the great works of the past. Bryant also mentioned "another view of the subject, and a most important one." New York was growing with unparalleled and chaotic speed, and attracting not only those who were "eminent in talent" but also the more sinister elements—those "most dexterous in villainy" and "most foul in guilt." "My friends," Bryant said gravely, "it is important that we should encounter the temptations to vice in this great and too rapidly growing capital by attractive entertainments of an innocent and improving character." Art, the great moral teacher, would redeem the wicked while refining the good.

Most of the other speakers provided glosses of one sort or another on Bryant's evangelical text. One speaker, however, presented a number of clear and concrete suggestions. This was George Fiske Comfort, a young lecturer at Princeton. Comfort had visited most of the major European museums, and for some time he had been urging the establishment in this country of art museums that differed essentially from the European model. "A great museum—one worthy of New York City and of our country— should represent the History of Art in all countries and in all ages, of art both pure and applied," Comfort told the audience at the Union League Club. He went on to discuss practically every aspect of museum work that would later be adopted by the Metropolitan and other museums—loan exhibitions, display techniques, the use of decorative and applied arts, museum lectures, and programs for schoolchildren. In each instance the underlying principle was clear: the museum must be an instrument of popular education. Its function was basically social and moral—aesthetics were secondary.

Comfort's ideas were really rooted in the revolutionary origins of Europe's museums. Art museums as we know them today are recent developments in Western society. They appeared at the same historical moment as the first encyclopedias, toward the end of the eighteenth century, and like the encyclopedias they were strongly influenced by the radical currents of French thought that helped to bring on the French Revolution. The first public museum was born in 1793, when the Louvre Palace with all its treasures, confiscated by the republican regime, was declared open to the people. In Europe, however, where centuries of private connoisseurship, royal patronage, and bourgeois family pride had gone into the accumulation of works of art, the Jacobin notion that art belonged to the people did not take firm hold. With a few important exceptions such as the South Kensington Museum in London, European museums had remained wedded to aristocratic ideals of connoisseurship. Even the Louvre, when it was opened to the public in 1793, limited admission on five days out of every ten to professional artists; as a result it has served ever since as the great laboratory for French art, but the majority of its visitors have been foreign tourists. Until well into the nineteenth century the British Museum, which was officially opened to the public in 1759, could be visited only by written appointment and by those who were able to qualify as "gentlemen." Today most European museums, the Louvre included, consider that their chief obligations are to the artist, the scholar, and the connoisseur. They tolerate but do not cultivate the public, and only in recent years have they given much thought to education.

The November meeting at the Union League Club was widely reported in the press, which saw evidence of high enthusiasm and sober purpose in the proceedings. A period of feverish activity now ensued. Legal documents were drawn and redrawn (mostly by Choate), potential trustees were sounded out, and advice was solicited. On January 31, 1870, the first board of trustees was elected. The ingredients of this twenty-seven-man founding board were predictable—a pomposity of businessmen and financiers, a clutch of lawyers, a nod of city officials, and a scintillation of writers and architects; less predictable, perhaps, was the inclusion of four practicing artists—the painters John F. Kensett, Frederick E. Church, and Eastman Johnson, and the sculptor J. Q. A. Ward. Choate, Comfort, Blodgett, Putnam, and the other "working trustees" were concentrated in the twelve-man executive committee. Bryant, who was seventy-six, had little time to give to the project, and soon resigned from the board. For president, the members selected a man who could be expected to give a great deal of his time, and who fitted almost ideally into that rare category of businessmen who were actively interested in art. He was John Taylor Johnston, the railroad executive and art collector whose private gallery, installed on the second floor of the stable behind his house at 8 Fifth Avenue, was considered one of the finest in the city.

Johnston had found that his presence was no longer continuously required by his railroad interests. In fact, on the evening his colleagues elected him the first president of the Metropolitan Museum, he happened to be in Egypt with his wife and daughter, drifting comfortably down the Nile. The Johnstons had rented a Nile steamer at Cairo and sailed up the river to Luxor, where Johnston negotiated with several native dealers for a collection of antiquities. The negotiation had ended abruptly when a dispute broke out among the dealers, a quarrel so loud and unseemly that Johnston felt obliged to hurry his family back on board the boat. The following day, docking at Gizeh, Johnston found a large packet of mail waiting for him. In it was a cablegram from New York offering him the presidency of the prospective Metropolitan Museum of Art. As his daughter recalled the moment later, "He was very much pleased, sent an immediate acceptance, and made arrangements for hastening our return home."

THREE

New York has no enduring aristocratic traditions. Inherited money brings only its face value there, and defects of breeding have never kept an ambitious New York hostess from using her husband's spoils to establish her sway. In the absence of dynasties on the order of Boston's Lowells or Philadelphia's Biddles, however, there was once a social infrastructure known as Old New York, which managed to exert an influence on the behavior of those members of the wealthy class who were not quite rich or nervy enough to ignore it and do as they pleased. Old New York was upright, pious, hard-working, and smug, but at the same time it was more worldly than Boston, more interested in food and comfort and European travel. The Old New York families lent their names to the Manhattan topography and the Manhattan telephone book—Rhinelander and Schuyler, Beekman and Wickersham and Stuyvesant—and they did the work of founding its major institutions. They vanished about 1920, taking their cozy brownstone world with them.

John Taylor Johnston, while not Old New York himself, was a personification of the Old New York influence. His father was a Scot from the River Dee, who had come to America as a young man in 1804 and gone to work in the counting house of a fellow Scot named James Lenox (*his* son would one day found the Lenox Library). The elder Johnston had prospered gradually, built a brownstone house on Washington Square, and raised his four children in strict accordance with the requirements of Presbyterian conduct —requirements so unbending that the old gentleman, on a visit to Rome in

33

his later years, declined to meet the Pope because his audience had been scheduled on a Sunday. Young John Taylor Johnston studied law at Yale and was admitted to the bar, but his interest soon shifted to the development of two small railroads, the Lehigh and Susquehanna and the Central of New Jersey. He devoted the next thirty years to the presidency of these lines, making in the process a substantial but not unseemly fortune. Johnston was no railroad buccaneer like E. H. Harriman or Jay Gould. His business methods were cautious, and he cared deeply about such matters as railroad safety, the cleanliness of terminals, and the churchgoing habits of his employees.

Johnston also came to care deeply about art. He began buying paintings before the Civil War, and like most of the collectors of the day he bought "modern," which meant, for the most part, pictures by contemporary French academicians. A discreet Bouguereau, historical scenes by Meissonier and Gleyre, genre studies, landscapes, anecdotal pictures ("a most painful story in a picture by Hubner"), paintings of cattle—these were all very much to his taste, although Johnston sometimes showed more daring: Turner's great, impressionistic *The Slave Ship* entered his collection in 1872, and became one of his favorites. He was also the most active buyer of American paintings since Luman Reed. Other wealthy American collectors of this period looked almost exclusively to Europe for the cultural traditions that they had decided were their due, but Johnston also believed in encouraging native traditions. Frederick Church's huge *Niagara* and Winslow Homer's *Prisoners from the Front* hung prominently in his gallery, along with representative works by Kensett, Cole, Durand, and most of the New York painters of the time, all of whom were invited once a year to a reception at the Johnston home. The collection had long since overflowed the house that he had built in 1856 at the corner of Fifth Avenue and Eighth Street (the first private house in the city to be built of marble; people used to go out of their way to see it). Johnston displayed his pictures in a gallery built over the stable in back, and because he felt morally obligated to share the pleasure his collection gave him he opened his gallery to the public every Thursday afternoon, setting a precedent that was soon followed by August Belmont, William H. Vanderbilt, and several others. The diarist George Templeton Strong, who went by invitation in 1869, agreed with the general view that no collection in the city outshone the

Johnston gallery, not even Belmont's. "How superb it is," Strong wrote, "how rich he must be, and how much wiser of him to spend his money this way than on race horses, four-in-hands, and great ostentatious parties."

When Johnston returned from Egypt to assume the presidency of the Metropolitan, he found much accumulated enthusiasm and goodwill but very little else. So far the museum existed only on paper. The New York Legislature voted an act of incorporation in the name of the Metropolitan Museum of Art on April 13, 1870. The museum thus had a charter, which gave its purpose as "encouraging and developing the study of the fine arts, and the application of the arts to manufacture, of advancing the general knowledge of kindred subjects, and, to that end, of furnishing popular instruction and recreation." It also had a constitution and a board of twenty-one elective and six ex-officio trustees (among them the mayor, the governor, and the head of the Department of Public Parks). Unlike the Boston Museum of Fine Arts or the Corcoran Gallery, however, the Metropolitan did not own a single work of art, nor did it have any space in which to exhibit future gifts or purchases.

Various remedies were suggested. "Order immediately from each middle-aged contemporary artist a masterpiece," one middle-aged enthusiast urged the trustees. Masterpieces cost money, however, and so far as most of the trustees were concerned they were only painted in Europe. That spring, Johnston and his colleagues addressed their major problem by launching a public subscription campaign for funds. They established three classes of membership in the museum corporation: one could become a Patron for $1,000, a Fellow in Perpetuity for $500, or a Fellow for Life for $200. The campaign goal was $250,000—remarkably modest even then—and the results were extremely discouraging. John Jacob Astor, August Belmont, and several other men of fortune and estate flatly refused to subscribe; they believed the new institution stood little chance of surviving without massive state aid. One year later only $110,000 had been raised, and in a city of millionaires the largest contribution was $10,000—it came from John Taylor Johnston. One year later, the fund raisers were still $24,000 short of their goal. "This state of things is very disappointing," the trustees conceded in the museum's second annual report, "and what makes it more surprising and more sad is that in a much shorter period than that during which these appeals have been pending here, $210,000 have been raised in Philadelphia *from twenty-one persons,* and $300,000 have been raised in Boston, in each case for a kindred purpose."

The stinginess of their fellow citizens helped to establish a pattern of forced generosity on the part of the Metropolitan trustees. Most of the founding trustees contributed at least $1,000 to the subscription campaign. William T. Blodgett and Alexander T. Stewart each gave $5,000—the largest gifts after Johnston's. In the summer of 1871, moreover, Blodgett single-handedly provided the opportunity for the museum on paper to become a museum in fact. Blodgett had made his money in the varnish business, and doubled it by shrewd investments in New York real estate. Although he was what the *New York Tribune* described as "a gentleman and a capitalist, and never pretended to palliate or deny either offense," Blodgett had distinguished himself by liberal good works. He was a fiery abolitionist, a founder of *The Nation* magazine, an active patron of the Sanitary Commission and the Metropolitan Art Fair, a popular member of the Century Club and the Union League Club, and, for these and other reasons, a natural choice for chairman of the Metropolitan's first executive committee. Unfortunately, his health broke down in 1870, and his doctors advised prolonged residence abroad. He resigned from the executive committee (the trustees immediately made him a vice-president) and went to live in Europe. Blodgett had been collecting pictures for several years— European "moderns," and, like his friend Johnston, works by American artists of that period; his purchase of Church's *Heart of the Andes* in 1859, for $10,000, had marked the beginning of really high prices for American pictures. When Blodgett arrived in Europe this time, the Franco-Prussian War was just beginning. "Mr. Blodgett writes from Paris that there never was such a time as now and therefore great bargains in works of art," Joseph Choate reported to his wife. "Those Germans who by the recent order are being expelled from the city are many of them very wealthy and old inhabitants of Paris, but are compelled to flee, and sacrifice, in order to do so, pretty much all their household goods and Gods—so that many fine pictures, etc., old masters even, that are almost never for sale, change hands for a fifth of their ordinary value. It is a great pity that our Metropolitan Museum is not yet far advanced enough to go into the market." Blodgett thought it was too great a pity. Acting entirely on his own initiative, he secured the services of M. Etienne Leroy, art expert of the Royal

Museum in Belgium, and through him negotiated for and bought in the summer of 1870 three important private collections of paintings—none of the owners were Germans, incidentally—which he then offered to the trustees of the Metropolitan for exactly what they had cost him.

One hundred and seventy-four pictures were involved, mostly Dutch and Flemish seventeenth century paintings, with a few Italian, French, English, and Spanish works ranging from the sixteenth to the nineteenth century. The cost, including expenses, came to $116,180.27. President Johnston thought the purchase "somewhat rash," but his confidence in Blodgett's judgment was so firm that he volunteered to assume half the cost, borrowing $100,000 from the Bank of America on joint account with Blodgett. The proposal was transmitted to the trustees at their quarterly meeting in November, with the understanding that if the museum did not want the paintings Blodgett and Johnston would divide and keep them for their own collections. There was a good deal of opposition among the trustees, several of whom felt that Blodgett had been unmercifully swindled. The Old Master boom was just beginning in 1870. Throughout the first three quarters of the nineteenth century, as indeed in almost every other period of history, the predominant taste was for contemporary art; of the Old Masters only Raphael and a handful of others had retained the esteem and the high value placed on them by *their* contemporaries, and as a result a great many old paintings, provided they were sufficiently dark and either mythological or religious in subject, were attributed without the slightest evidence to the best-known masters of the Renaissance. Blodgett, to be sure, had had each picture examined by an expert, but experts were not always to be trusted, and swindles did take place—particularly when honest Americans went traipsing about Europe. Besides, what with the subscription campaign lagging so badly, where was the money to come from? In the end, though, Johnston and a few others won over the doubters, and the trustees voted in March 1871 to accept Blodgett's offer. The first shipment of paintings arrived in New York soon afterward. "I am simply delighted," Johnston wrote to Blodgett. "The quality of the collection as a whole is superior to anything I had dared to hope, while the number of masterpieces is very great . . . If the other half come up to the ones I have seen, the Metropolitan Museum will make a splendid start in life."

All this while, intricate and complex negotiations were in progress with the city in regard to a museum building. The trustees wanted no "bungling government officials" involved with their museum, but they did want municipal support in acquiring land and municipal funds for construction (the city officials, it was assumed, should be duly impressed by the heavy emphasis on public education as the museum's main purpose). The American Museum of Natural History, which had been chartered a few months before the Metropolitan in 1869, was also seeking city land and city funds at this time, and so was the New York Historical Society. The latter institution, in fact, came very close to rendering the Metropolitan superfluous.

Founded in 1804 "to collect and preserve whatever may relate to the natural, civil, or ecclesiastical history of the United States in general and this state in particular," the Historical Society had during its first fifty years acquired, more or less inadvertently, a sizable collection of paintings, mostly portraits of prominent citizens. To these had been added the collection of the New York Gallery of Fine Arts, which went out of business in 1858, and, there being no other institution capable of receiving them, deposited with the Historical Society the American paintings originally brought together by Luman Reed. The society had received various other art objects, including a collection of Egyptian antiquities, and in 1860 its officers drew up a plan to establish "a museum of antiquities, science, and art" in the old New York State arsenal building near the southeast corner of Central Park. The legislature approved the plan, but the society was unable to raise the necessary funds. In 1868, having just received a new collection of some two hundred and fifty European paintings from the collection of Thomas J. Bryan, the Historical Society tried again; it petitioned and secured from the legislature permission to build on another site in Central Park, just off Fifth Avenue from Eighty-first to Eighty-fourth streets—the same site now occupied by the Metropolitan. Again it tried and failed to raise the money. The society had always been and was still at that time a rather exclusive organization, devoted to the pleasures of bibliography and genealogy and to the celebration of Federalist holidays and heroes; if it had been able to attract a few more men of practical wisdom, push, and enterprise the history of New York's cultural institutions might have been quite different.

The Metropolitan's trustees were not by any means convinced, in 1870, that their museum should be built in Central Park. The park was a long way out of town so far as most of them were concerned, and they doubted whether people could ever be persuaded to travel such a distance to see works of art. A majority on the executive committee favored another site, known then as Reservoir Square because it adjoined the site of the old city reservoir—it is now Bryant Park, the home of the New York Public Library. Johnston, the painter Frederick Church, and a few other trustees argued spiritedly for Central Park, but it was Andrew Haswell Green, the president of the Central Park Commission, who was primarily responsible for the final decision.

Green was a highly untypical city official. A popular and sophisticated clubman, known around town as "one who converses easily and fluently, and is an excellent essayist," he was also unimpeachably honest and devoted to the improvement of municipal affairs. The idea of locating an art museum in Central Park had originated with Green, who had long wanted to see the park developed as a cultural center. He had taken an active part in the organization of both the American Museum of Natural History and the Metropolitan, and in 1869 he had been instrumental in getting the legislature to pass a bill authorizing the Central Park Commission "to erect, establish, conduct, and maintain in the Central Park . . . a meteorological and astronomical observatory, and a museum of natural history and a gallery of art, and the buildings therefor, and to provide the necessary instruments, furniture, and equipments for the same." This act seemed to suggest that the enabling funds, which the Historical Society had been unable to raise, would be provided out of the city treasury, and it was thus of considerable interest to the trustees of both the American Museum (as that institution prefers to be called) and the Metropolitan.

The trustees of the two prospective museums, working closely together, formulated a plan under which both institutions would occupy a building or buildings on what was known then as Manhattan Square—the present location of the American Museum. Joseph Choate, who served on both boards, framed a legal petition asking that the city be authorized to tax itself to the amount of $500,000 for this purpose. In the spring of 1871, having secured the signatures of a large number of prominent New Yorkers, the young Princeton professor George Fiske Comfort and a representative of the American Museum took the petition up to Albany and paid a call on the man himself—William Marcy Tweed.

"We arrived there and we were placed in seats behind Mr. Tweed as he sat at a table," Comfort recalled some years later, "and he said: 'We will see what the New York papers say about us today.'" The New York papers, led by *The Times,* had been attacking Tweed openly since early in 1870. The Boss had begun to feel a little uneasy, although he did not mind the press attacks as much as he did the vitriolic cartoons of Thomas Nast in *Harper's Weekly,* which even his nonliterate constituents had no trouble understanding. As Comfort sat watching, Tweed glanced at the newspapers and then his eye fell on the petition. He "looked at it a moment, saw the heading and instantly, with that celerity of action for which he was noted, he took it to a room, and said, 'You will see Mr. Sweeny. He will take charge of this.'" Peter Barr Sweeny, the city chamberlain, was known to be the brains of the Tweed Ring. He received the two petitioners without delay. Sweeny "took the paper and skipped the heading, and looked at the names, and when he saw the names attached to it, then he turned back and read the heading. And as I watched his face there was not the quiver of an eye, or twitch of the muscles, but he turned quickly and said: 'Please inform these gentlemen that we are the servants of the people. This is New York. New York wishes this and please inform them and say that they can see us on two or three details of the matter, and then this will go through.'"

There was no mystery about Tweed's sudden espousal of high culture. The names on the petition represented more than half the real estate of New York City, and a great many prominent businesses as well. Tweed needed the support of this element (curiously enough, six eminent New York citizens, including John Jacob Astor III and Moses Taylor, had examined the city's finances the previous year, at Tweed's invitation, and had returned Tweed's administration a clean bill of health), and he undoubtedly saw in the project new opportunities for the well-established shakedown. Tweed sought to persuade the trustees of the two museums that what they really needed was a huge, multimillion dollar structure—something on the order, perhaps, of the new County Court House, which had cost $3,000,000 to build but for which the city had actually paid $12,-000,000, Tweed and his cronies pocketing the difference. The trustees made

it clear that they would be quite satisfied with the $500,000 building origi-
nally proposed. On the prickly question of ownership—one of the "two or
three details" Sweeny had mentioned—the trustees and the Tweed Ring
settled for an ingenious compromise. Sweeny had said that if the city gave
the money to build a museum on city property, then the city must control
the building. Choate, the architect of the compromise, conceded the point;
the city would retain legal ownership of the museum building. In return,
Sweeny agreed to Choate's insistence that the trustees retain ownership
and control of the contents of the building—i.e., the collections. This was
an entirely new idea in municipal government, and it became the pattern
followed by most of the major art museums in America (although not in
Boston, where the Museum of Fine Arts neither solicited nor received any
public funds at all).

Tweed's approval brought swift results. On April 5, 1871, the legislature
passed an act enabling the Central Park Commissioners to authorize construction of a museum building on Manhattan Square, and to raise funds to
the sum of $500,000 toward this end. The trustees had hoped to get funds
from the city so that they could build for themselves; what they got, with
Tweed's blessing, was a partnership with the city, under which the city
was responsible for the construction and maintenance of the buildings and
the trustees were responsible for everything else.

The following year a change of site was agreed upon. The American Museum would build separately on Manhattan Square; the Metropolitan's
building, designed by the firm of Calvert Vaux and Jacob Wrey Mould,
would be situated in the "Deer Park," the area between Seventy-ninth and
Eighty-fourth streets, extending from Fifth Avenue west to the Park Drive.
A number of trustees had argued up to the last in favor of Reservoir
Square downtown, but Andrew Green and his fellow Park Commissioners
wanted the museum in the park, and, since they held the purse strings, that
is where it would be.

Long before the new building was even begun, however, Blodgett's one
hundred and seventy-four Old Masters and a number of gifts and loans
had made some sort of temporary exhibition space necessary. The Metropolitan's first home was at 681 Fifth Avenue, between Fifty-third and Fifty-fourth streets, in a house formerly known to New York matrons and their
reluctant offspring as Allen Dodworth's Dancing Academy. Minor renova-

tions were carried out ("A skylight let into the ceiling of the large hall where the poetry of motion had been taught to so many young men and maidens of New York," as one trustee phrased it), and early in 1872 the Blodgett pictures were installed there along with paintings and statuary lent by Johnston, Blodgett and other well-wishers, and a six-thousand-pound Roman sarcophagus, the first gift accepted by the museum, which had been dug up and donated by a Turkish citizen named J. Abdo Debbas who served as the American vice-consul in Tarsus and was a fervent admirer of all things American. The trustees themselves did most of the installing. Blodgett, who was in Europe at the time, wrote Johnston to suggest that he could easily pick up more Dutch and Flemish pictures, but Johnston advised caution. "Personally I should like to follow up that school and make the Gallery *strong* in one thing, and it may be found judicious to do so," Johnston wrote in reply. "Much will depend, however, on how our pictures take with the public. Unless they are a decided success, it may be well to branch out into some other line before going deeper into pictures, the more so as our space is limited."

Three formal openings were scheduled. The first, on February 17, was a punch-and-oyster party for artists and the press, and to Johnston's great relief it went off smoothly. Some of the New York artists had let it be known that in their opinion the museum should be buying American rather than European pictures. "Personally, I felt very apprehensive of the effect of inviting the disaffected artist element and the gentlemen of the Press, but it worked *very* well," Johnston wrote to Blodgett. Trustees and their friends were invited on the nineteenth, and the following day the museum opened its doors to the public. Johnston by this time was positively jubilant. "No one imagined that we could make such a show," he told Blodgett, "and the disposition to praise is now as general as the former disposition to depreciate. We have now something to point to as the Museum, something tangible and something good."

George Templeton Strong paid his first visit to the new museum in September. He found the collection larger than he had expected ("nearly an acre of high art"), but not especially impressive; "in very few of these pictures did my unskilled eye detect anything to admire," he wrote in his diary. Another early visitor to what he called "the charming little academy in the Fifth Avenue" was Henry James, who found it promising. "It is not indeed to be termed a brilliant collection," James observed, "for it contains no first-rate example of a first-rate genius; but it may claim within its limits a unity and a continuity which cannot fail to make it a source of profit to students debarred from European opportunities." There was no doubt that the gamble on the Blodgett pictures had paid off handsomely. The Dutch canvases appealed to the New York merchants, many of whom were not too far removed in spirit from the early Dutch settlers of Nieuw Amsterdam, and the taste for these realistic, earthy pictures was soon reflected in an increasing number of private collections throughout the city. Some of Blodgett's pictures have since succumbed to the rigors of art scholarship, but by and large the museum's first purchase has stood up surprisingly well. The paintings were for many years the heart and core of the museum, and several of them—most notably Franz Hals's boisterous *Malle Babbe* —have remained continuously on exhibition, along with J. Abdo Debbas' sarcophagus, for a hundred years.

The Metropolitan was less fortunate in some of its other early acquisitions. A larger-than-life-size bronze *Dancing Girl* by the now-forgotten German sculptor Ludwig Michael von Schwanthaler, a gift of New York banker Griffith Rowe, led Johnston to observe that in the future "we must curb the exuberance of our donors except in the article of money, of which they may give as much as they please." Eight feet of dance, Johnston said, was a trial to the feelings. Soon afterward an "association of gentlemen" bought and presented to the museum the portraits of nine reigning belles of New York society, whom the currently fashionable Italian portraitist Guiseppe Fagnani had chosen to depict as the Nine Muses of classical mythology. The group as a whole was intended to represent American Beauty Personified, but one of the belles said later that she thought they all looked "like ladies on prune boxes."

The truth was that in those days the trustees took what they could get. For more than twenty-five years after the museum was founded, money for acquisitions remained pitifully scarce. The original $250,000 subscription, finally realized in 1873, was exhausted almost immediately by the Blodgett and other purchases. That fall, moreover, a severe financial panic cast a pall over further fund raising. Reckless speculation, the chaotic and savagely competitive development of the railroads, and the overexpansion of credit throughout the country had led to the failure of Jay Cooke & Company and several other leading Wall Street firms, which precipitated the Panic of 1873. In the long depression that followed, one of the worst in U.S. history, some fifty thousand commercial enterprises went bankrupt, including a majority of the railroads. John Taylor Johnston's Central of New Jersey lapsed into receivership, and Johnston, who was hard hit financially, had to sell most of his art collection at auction—as a result, the great Turner *Slave Ship* that had been on loan to the Metropolitan is today in the Boston Museum of Fine Arts. Unemployment, strikes, and business failures continued with little relief until 1878.

In the midst of this unparalleled economic disaster, the Metropolitan's founding trustees somehow managed to maintain a serenely optimistic outlook. "The Museum is now completely established as the leading institution of its kind in the country, and its permanence and future success are entirely assured," the museum's third annual report stated in 1873. Throughout the dismal period that followed, the annual reports continued cheerily to stress the Metropolitan's preeminence among American museums, its "visible influence for good on the public mind," and its steady progress toward the goal "kept constantly in mind by the Trustees . . . the education of the public and the cultivation in our Country of a high standard of artistic taste."

As though to prove the truth of these brave assertions, the museum moved at the end of 1873 into larger quarters and embarked on a program of expanded activities. What had made the move imperative was the purchase of the Cesnola Collection, an extensive group of antiquities excavated on the island of Cyprus by the American consul there, General Luigi Palma di Cesnola. Johnston had negotiated for and bought the collection for $60,000, in the hope that the trustees could raise the money to pay him back—as eventually, somewhat to their surprise, they did. There being no space in Dodworth's Dancing Academy to exhibit the more than six thousand stone sculptures, terracottas, glass, and other ancient objects that made up the collection, the trustees took a lease on a larger building on West Fourteenth Street, then a fashionable residential section. The Douglas Mansion, as it was formerly known, had five times as much wall space as the dancing academy, and the rent was lower—$8,000 a year instead of

$9,000. Once again, a group of the trustees did most of the packing and un-packing. General Cesnola came over from Europe to supervise the installation of his antiquities, and stayed for the opening day ceremonies in May 1873, during which, the *World* reported, he was "courteously attentive and kept up a peripatetic lecture to all who sought information or manifested special interest."

The move to larger quarters entailed larger expenses, and the museum's appeals for money took on about this time a somewhat querulous ring. "There is no community in the world which boasts so much of its public schools, which spends so much money for dwelling houses, equipages, furniture, social entertainments, and for personal adornment, as that of New York," the annual report for 1873 pointed out. "There is no community more generous in its support of churches, hospitals, and colleges, or, even in its expenditure for works of art, provided they are bought for private use." And yet, in contributions to its "completely established" public art museum, "New York is less liberal than other smaller places in this country, notably Boston and Philadelphia." This the trustees found hard to understand, particularly in view of the fact that art museums had been shown to be "agencies for increasing the commercial manufacturing wealth of the community."

After a good deal of discussion, the city government had agreed in 1873 to appropriate $30,000 a year for the Metropolitan and the American museums—$15,000 to each—to help pay their rent and other pressing expenses. This helped, but not enough. When the Metropolitan moved into the Douglas Mansion, therefore, it began the delicate experiment of charging admission. At first the fee was fifty cents; it was reduced three months later to twenty-five cents, with Monday declared a free day. The attendance varied accordingly. Night openings were tried again in 1874, in response to appeals from art lovers whose business duties prevented them from attending during the day. The number of such citizens proved to be distressingly small—the average evening attendance was thirty-two souls —and the evening hours were discontinued. Now and then a voice was heard to suggest that the Metropolitan should be open on Sunday. The founding trustees had made their position on that point eminently clear, however, with the firm announcement in 1871 that they did not intend to open the museum on the Lord's day "as a place of amusement."

Disappointed but not disheartened by what seemed rather lukewarm support on the part of their fellow citizens, the trustees paid the deficits out of their own pockets and redoubled their efforts to refine and educate the public taste. The first loan exhibition of paintings at the Douglas Mansion was held in the fall of 1873. Most of the city's major collectors were represented, and the catalogue (the first one issued by the museum) provides a good indication of how the wealthier tastes were tending. Of the one hundred and twelve pictures listed, there were relatively few by Americans, a large number of "modern" European paintings, and a sizable group of heavily varnished canvases attributed with blithe optimism to Titian, Tintoretto, Ghirlandaio, Andrea del Sarto, and other Old Masters. Rather than ask embarrassing questions, the cataloguers described a loan from Mrs. C. L. Derby as "One Oil Painting, Leonardo da Vinci."

Education, the rock on which the museum had elected to build, received substantial attention in the annual reports, although the museum's educational effort at this point consisted mainly of admitting art students free on pay days and sponsoring an occasional lecture to what the trustees referred to as "large and appreciative audiences." The trustees also stressed that "mechanics and artisans" were "among our most steady and studious visitors," and they did not hesitate to draw from this the conclusion that American tastes were changing for the better. Embedded in the annual report for 1876 is the remarkable statement that "the Museum today is not surpassed as an educational power among the people by any university, college, or seminary of learning in the metropolis." It is doubtful whether the Metropolitan during its first decade had as much influence on public taste as the Philadelphia Centennial Exhibition of 1876, the biggest international exhibition ever held up to that time (it cost six times as much as the famous Crystal Palace Exhibition of 1851 in London). Optimistic statements by trustees did no harm, though, and might help to influence public opinion and private subscribers.

There were also some legitimate causes for optimism. Ground had been broken in 1874 for the new building in Central Park, and the work was proceeding on schedule. Relations with the city authorities, moreover, had become considerably more regular since the downfall of Boss Tweed. Indicted by a grand jury in December 1871, Tweed had eventually been convicted on one hundred and two counts, with most of the legal case against him being assembled by Joseph Choate. He had escaped from jail and fled to Spain, only to be arrested there, extradited back to New York, and clapped into jail where he died, a broken man, in 1878. The Tweed Ring's successors in Albany and City Hall were not exactly paragons of civic virtue, but municipal graft no longer took place on such a massive scale.

Meanwhile, private business had started to pick up a little—by 1878 there would be a real upturn—and confidence was returning. New York's rich and fashionable society, moreover, had clasped the Metropolitan to its bosom. Most of the millionaire collectors were now willing to lend their support or at least their pictures—even August Belmont, as Johnston reported to Blodgett, had "forgotten his insulting note declining a post on the Museum board." The Metropolitan was developing an aura of respectability and success. George Templeton Strong, who remained unimpressed by the "alleged" Old Masters, conceded that "Twenty years hence it will probably have grown into a really instructive museum." In addition to these hopeful signs, the trustees had acquired in 1876 a second large collection of antiquities unearthed on the island of Cyprus by the "indefatigable and accomplished explorer," General Cesnola.

The indefatigable explorer came over in 1877, as he had done four years earlier, to supervise the unpacking, cataloguing, and placement of some ten thousand new objects that he had sold to the Metropolitan. Cesnola's boundless energy and military dash evidently made a strong impression on the trustees, some of whom had begun to feel that museum administration was a job for younger men. Several of the founding trustees had died— Putnam and Kensett in 1872, Blodgett in 1875. George Fiske Comfort had resigned to accept a teaching post at Syracuse University. As in most institutions, the board was made up of a minority of trustees who did the work and a majority who said yes, and the active minority—President Johnston, Frederick W. Rhinelander, who had succeeded the banker Robert Gordon as treasurer in 1871, Samuel Avery, Russell Sturgis, Jr., and William C. Prime, the editor of the *New York Journal of Commerce* and a trustee since 1871—had become increasingly aware that the museum was growing beyond their capacity to run it. Someone was needed, someone with practical wisdom and push and enterprise, who could give to the museum his full time and attention. The position of secretary to the board had recently become vacant when William J. Hoppin was appointed to the United States Legation in London. Could Cesnola be persuaded to take his place?

He could and was. Two years later, in 1879, Cesnola became the Metropolitan's first paid director, and the museum became a very different sort of place.

FOUR

Emanuele Pietro Paolo Maria Luigi Palma di Cesnola was born in 1832 at Rivarolo, a small Piedmontese town near Turin in northern Italy. A Palma di Cesnola had been granted feudal authority over this region in the eleventh century, and the family, though somewhat impoverished, could list among its ancestors many distinguished magistrates, diplomats, and warriors. Cesnola's father served under Bonaparte in the Russian campaign; his uncle, condemned to death for his part in the revolutionary movement to unite Italy, fled to Athens where he helped to write the Greek Constitution. The martial and impetuous side of the family nature was inherited by young Luigi, who entered the Royal Military School at Turin when he was thirteen and three years later volunteered for service in the Army of Sardinia for the war against Austria (Piedmont belonged then to the Kingdom of Sardinia). Cesnola was promoted to lieutenant on the battlefield of Novara, and his valor in that losing engagement also earned him a medal from the King. Further decorations honored his exploits in the Crimean War, during which he served as aide-de-camp to General Ansaldi and fought at the battle of Balaklava. Returning home again in 1856, Cesnola soon grew bored with peacetime military life. He resigned from the army, and in 1860, like so many other ambitious young Italians, sailed to seek his fortune in America.

He landed in New York. For the first year and a half he lived in a boardinghouse on Houston Street and earned a meager living by giving private lessons in French and Italian. His pupils were mostly young ladies of good family, and one of them, Miss Mary Isabel Reid, consented in 1861 to become Madame Cesnola. When the Civil War broke out that spring, Cesnola found a more suitable use for his talents than language lessons. He rented space in the Hotel St. Germaine, at the corner of Broadway and Twenty-second Street, and opened a private military school where during the next few months he taught more than seven hundred young New York bloods the rudiments of infantry, artillery, and cavalry warfare (in the absence of horses, Cesnola's pupils practiced astride wooden barrels). Teaching only whetted his appetite for action. In the fall of 1861, Cesnola accepted a commission as major in the Eleventh New York Cavalry Regiment, known then as "Scott's 900," which was in the process of forming on Staten Island. He advanced immediately to lieutenant colonel, and as second in command of the regiment he did most of the recruiting and training. To the recruits, Cesnola must have seemed the cavalryman's beau ideal—handsome, dashing, battle wise, with flowing moustaches and a charming accent. He was intensely disappointed when the regiment was posted in 1862 to Washington, D.C., to perform guard duty for President Lincoln. Someone pulled wires, and Cesnola was soon on his way to the front as a full colonel in command of his own regiment, the Fourth New York Cavalry.

Few regiments of Union cavalry saw more action or lost more men than the Fourth New York. Campaigning in Virginia in the spring of 1863, Colonel Cesnola's men fought with distinction at the battles of Chantilly, Berryville, and at Aldie, where on June 17 they lost their commander. The story goes that on the morning of the battle of Aldie, angered by the promotion over him of a junior officer, Cesnola had complained so vehemently to the commanding general that the general had him placed under arrest. When the order came down for a cavalry charge on the enemy artillery, which was situated on high ground and well protected, the entire regiment refused to obey it without Cesnola in command. Rather than see the regiment dishonored, Cesnola mounted his horse and led the troopers in four valiant, bloody, but unsuccessful assaults on the rebel position. After the fourth charge, the general commended him for bravery, released him from arrest, and told him to try again. On the fifth charge (which Cesnola later referred to as a "senseless order" and a "foolhardy and reckless act"), Cesnola's horse was shot dead under him and he himself took a sabre cut on the head and a rifle bullet in the left arm. He lay for several hours on the field, pinned beneath his horse, until the victorious Confederate troops picked him up.

Cesnola spent the next few months in Libby Prison. In letters to his wife he expressed melodramatic doubts that he would ever "go out of this prison alive," but it does not appear that he was badly treated. One letter home asks for bologna sausage and "plenty of small macaroni for soup." Released in 1864 in an exchange of prisoners, he rejoined his regiment which was then fighting under General Sheridan in the Shenandoah Valley Campaign. He served until the war ended, taking part in many battles, and received in 1865, from Lincoln's hand, the brevet rank of brigadier general. Cesnola had been looking ahead, though, and he used his meeting with Lincoln, which took place only a few days before the President's assassination, to secure for himself the trappings of a diplomatic career—specifically, the post of United States consul at Cyprus.

Cesnola, his wife, and their baby daughter sailed soon afterward. They reached Cyprus on Christmas Day, 1865, and took up an eleven-year residence on that small island whose diplomatic affairs would prove far less absorbing than its ancient buried tombs.

The nineteenth century was the great age of the amateur archaeologist. Winckelmann's books on Pompeii and Herculaneum, Austin Layard's finding of Nineveh, Belzoni's and Mariette's Egyptian excavations (spurred by the opening up of Egypt by Napoleon's armies) had fired the public imagination and induced countless adventurers, romantics, and dilettantes to join in the hunt for lost cities and buried antiquities. Cyprus, the legendary birthplace of Aphrodite and a center of Mediterranean trade since earliest times, was an especially rich field for exploration. Successive waves of Phoenician, Egyptian, Greek, and Roman conquerors had left their mark on the style of native artisans, and Cypriote art thus provided a running history of aesthetic development in the ancient world. The growing interest in archaeology, which had made tomb robbing a thriving profession among the native peasantry, had also led several of the foreign diplomats in Larnaca, the coastal city to which Cesnola was assigned, to enliven the boredom of the consular routine by conducting excavations. Cesnola soon learned that the diplomatic duties of a consul took up practically no time at all. He had an early brush with the Turkish authorities (Cyprus in those days belonged to the Ottoman Empire) when they arrested one of his consular guards; Cesnola appealed to the American consul-general in Beirut, and the affair ended in the arrival of two U.S. warships in the Bay of Larnaca and the hasty return of the arrested guard. After that victory Cesnola took no pains to conceal his withering contempt for the Turk, and this made it somewhat easier for him later on to dig wherever and whenever he pleased. He began in 1866, "in a mere amateur way," as he put it, "the explorations which were afterwards to expand into very serious undertakings, and to extend to every part of the island." *

For a man of Cesnola's energetic temperament, it did not take long for archaeology to become an absorbing passion. At first he limited his excavations to the hundreds of hillside tombs in the vicinity of Larnaca, but by 1867 he was operating farther afield and spending much of his time away from home. At night he read voraciously everything he could find on the subject, including the works of Pliny, Strabo, and Ptolemy who had visited Cyprus in ancient times. Having tried and failed to get financial backing for his excavations, he soon ran through his own and his wife's savings. Now and then he sold a few objects, which helped to pay for further digging, and in 1869 he managed to get a loan from the Paris firm of Rollin & Feuardent, the leading European dealers in antiquities. Early in 1870 he made his first major discovery. Cesnola's native diggers had just started to work on a site near the ancient town of Golgoi (mentioned by Pliny as the center of the worship of Aphrodite on the island) when they uncovered a colossal limestone head. The crew sent a message to Cesnola, who dropped everything and rode out on muleback in the middle of the night. A large crowd of excited villagers had gathered at the site by the time he arrived. The diggers had unearthed several more large stone sculptures, and in the darkness and confusion there was danger that they might be damaged or, more likely, diminished by theft. Acting with military aplomb, Cesnola dispersed the villagers, loaded the colossal head and the other statues on oxcarts and sent them back to Larnaca—"Thus I may say," as he wrote later, "that I rather captured than discovered these stone treasures."

The Golgoi dig yielded a great many more monumental sculptures and

* The above and other quotations in this chapter are from *Cyprus: Its Ancient Cities, Tombs, and Temples,* by General Louis Palma di Cesnola, Harper & Bros., New York, 1878.

smaller objects of all kinds. Cesnola succeeded in buying the property for £20 from the farmer who owned it, and for a month, despite orders from the Turkish authorities to desist, he kept more than a hundred diggers busy on the site. News of the discovery soon spread to Europe, and Cesnola's house in Larnaca, which he had transformed into a virtual museum, became the chief tourist attraction on the island—so much so that the consul found himself "at times not a little annoyed." He did not mind having his treasures admired, but it irked him when elderly English ladies "with the proverbial ringlets" insisted that he explain to them the mysteries of the rites of Venus, and he was shocked to discover that there were some people, "apparently respectable, who think nothing of pocketing antiquities not belonging to them."

Cesnola never doubted for a moment that these antiquities belonged to *him,* were in fact "as thoroughly my property as anything could ever be the property of anyone." He had dug them up, after all, usually (though not always) under an official firman, or permit, from the Turkish governor-general, and there were no laws at that time against the export of such treasures. All his savings and a great deal of prodigious labor had gone into the excavations, and he felt fully entitled to his just reward. Cesnola took up photography, and sent pictures of the most important objects to the leading museums of Europe. He had been advised that he would probably do better to keep the collection together and dispose of it as a whole, rather than to sell it piecemeal. According to Cesnola, the French Emperor, Napoleon III, wanted to purchase the entire collection and present it to the Louvre, but the Franco-Prussian War broke out just then and the plan fell through. In the spring of 1870, the Russian archaeologist Johannes Doell came all the way from St. Petersburg to see Cesnola's collection with a view to its purchase by the Hermitage. (It was the custom at that time for consular officials in out-of-the-way posts to represent more than one government; Cesnola had agreed to represent Russian interests in Cyprus, and was therefore in close touch with the Czarist government.) Dr. Doell stayed several months and made the first scientific catalogue of the collection, but in the end the Hermitage decided not to buy it.

Soon after Doell's visit, Cesnola heard some alarming news. His treasures had aroused "the cupidity of the Turk," as he put it, and the Grand Vizier in Constantinople had given orders to prevent their exportation.

Cesnola decided to pack and ship the collection immediately, if necessary by force. He wrote a letter to the Secretary of War in Washington, who very obligingly agreed to send a Navy man-of-war to Cyprus to pick up the collection. In the meanwhile, though, Cesnola found that he could charter a schooner that had called at Larnaca, and he decided to seize this opportunity rather than wait for the U.S. Navy. While the schooner was unloading at the dock, he hastily finished packing up his collection in three hundred and sixty large wooden crates. He also sent a note to the Turkish governor-general asking bluntly whether he intended to interfere with the shipment. The governor-general replied with great ceremony, saying that he hoped Cesnola would not place him in so disagreeable a position. Just at this juncture, a Turkish naval corvette steamed into the harbor and dropped anchor directly in front of Cesnola's house.

Somewhat disconcerted, Cesnola had his "confidential dragoman, Besbes," pay a call on the chief customs officer of the port. Besbes returned shortly, to say that the officer had shown him two telegrams from his superiors, both expressly forbidding the American consul to export any antiquities from the island. While Cesnola pondered the situation, the wily Besbes ("one of the ugliest men I think I ever saw, but at the same time one of the most faithful") watched him carefully. Let Cesnola describe what ensued: "Suddenly I saw a sort of twinkle in his eyes, and a curious expression dawned on his lips as he said, looking very meekly at me, 'Effendi, those telegrams are to prevent the American Consul from shipping antiquities,' and then he stopped. I replied with some heat, 'You seem to take pleasure in repeating the information to me—I should think I ought to be aware of it by this time.' Besbes did not lose a particle of his equanimity, but only said meekly, 'There was nothing in those orders about the *Russian* Consul.' I understood then what he meant, though my Western civilization would never have arrived at this truly oriental solution of the difficulty." The three hundred and sixty packing cases left Larnaca that day as the property of the Russian consul, accompanied by the indispensable Besbes who saw them safely to Port Said, where he arranged for transshipment. When the Turkish governor-general learned of the subterfuge, he was more impressed than angry. According to Cesnola, "he declared that the whole thing had been most cleverly managed, and that it was a pity I had not been born a Turk."

Acting on Cesnola's orders, Besbes divided the collection at Port Said and shipped one large consignment to New York in care of Hiram Hitchcock, who had lectured at the Metropolitan in 1871 on Cesnola's archaeological discoveries. Cesnola had learned about the new museum in 1870 when he read an article on its founding in *Putnam's* magazine. Early in 1872 he had written to John Taylor Johnston, offering to sell his entire collection to the Metropolitan on very favorable terms—the price would be determined by arbitrators for both sides, and payment could be made over a period of time. The New York consignment was intended to further this negotiation. Unfortunately, the vessel carrying it ran into a violent storm off the coast of Syria and sank with all its cargo. The remainder, some six thousand objects including all the monumental statues found at Golgoi, reached London safely in the fall of 1872. It was received by an agent for the Paris firm of Rollin & Feuardent, which had recently established a branch in London, and negotiations began in earnest with the British Museum and various other institutions, including the Metropolitan. The British Museum offered £10,000 for all the sculptures and inscriptions from Golgoi. Cesnola refused, insisting that the collection must remain together as a whole. Into the breach stepped Johnston, who had not yet suffered the financial reverses that would decimate his fortune. The Metropolitan's president offered to buy the collection for $60,000 of his own money, in the hope that his fellow trustees would raise that sum by public subscription. Cesnola accepted the offer. "What I desire above all," he had said, in words that would become all too familiar to Metropolitan trustees over the years, "is that my collection should remain all *together* and be known as the Cesnola Collection. . . . I have the pride of my race, and that of a Discoverer who wants his name perpetuated with his work if possible."

When Cesnola had seen to the installation of his treasures in the Douglas Mansion, he took back with him to Cyprus a contract under which the Metropolitan trustees agreed to help finance his new excavations, in return for the right to first refusal of any objects found. The financial crisis of 1873 cut off whatever funds Cesnola might have received from this source—the contract was quietly suspended—but nothing could deter the discoverer. Spending without restraint the money he had received for his first collection, he plunged into excavations on a vastly increased scale, scouring sites in every part of the island and often staying away from his house and family for months at a time. In all, during his eleven years on Cyprus, Cesnola explored and identified the sites of sixteen ancient cities, excavated fifteen temples, sixty-five necropoli, and 60,932 tombs; he collected a grand total of 35,573 objects, including more than two thousand statues, four thousand fragmentary busts and heads, some fourteen thousand pottery vases, one thousand engraved gems, cylinders, and scarabs, and nearly four thousand glass objects. His richest strike after Golgoi was at Curium, the site of an ancient city on the western coast, where in 1876 he claimed to have found intact, under an excavated temple, a royal treasury of gold, silver, and bronze objects dating from the sixth century B.C. The "Treasure of Curium" was the climax of Cesnola's archaeological career, and the source of great controversy later on. Archaeological scholars have pointed out that the objects supposedly found as an intact group under the temple were of many different periods, and subsequent excavations by later, more scientific archaeologists could find no trace of the treasure chamber that Cesnola described in his book. The whole incident, in the words of a later Metropolitan handbook on the Cesnola Collection, "is a mystery which cannot be cleared up." At the time, however, and for some years afterward, the Curium find was hailed as a unique marvel (Johnston called it "the most precious single discovery of ancient art ever made"), and Cesnola's work as a whole was compared favorably to the work being done at the same time by Heinrich Schliemann on the site of Homer's Troy.

Aside from a small group of gold objects and engraved gems purchased by Johnston in 1874, the Metropolitan had been too poor to acquire any of the fruits of Cesnola's excavations from 1873 to 1876. Soon after the Curium find, Cesnola offered to sell his entire second collection to the museum on the same favorable terms as before; having no funds at their disposal, the trustees declined. Cesnola then reopened negotiations with European museums. The British Museum agreed to pay him the equivalent of $50,000 in gold for the Curium treasure. The Louvre offered $60,000, also in gold, for the Curium treasure and a selection of other objects. Cesnola decided to give the Metropolitan one more chance. He sent a wire to Johnston offering the entire collection for $60,000, which he said could be paid in three installments. Johnston called a special meeting of the board. Stirred to action, the trustees organized a last-minute subscription campaign and man-

aged within three days to raise $40,000, with "ladies who are known as lov-
ers of art leading the subscription lists." Johnston sent a wire to Cesnola in
London, saying "We accept entire collection." "All right!" Cesnola cabled
back. "Three hearty cheers for our dear New York Museum."

No exportation problems arose this time. Cesnola had foresightedly presented a large group of objects from his second collection to the Ottoman
government, and had also made several judicious smaller gifts, including
one to the museum in his native Turin. The bulk of the new collection—
more than ten thousand objects—reached New York without incident in
1877, and with it came Cesnola. There is reason to believe that some form
of permanent association with "our dear New York Museum" may already
have entered his mind. Mrs. Cesnola, understandably enough, had grown
weary of life in Larnaca and pined to return home to New York. Her husband was now an American citizen (he had shortened his name accordingly, to Louis P. di Cesnola), and he had reached, at forty-five, an age at
which the adventurous soldier of fortune begins to yearn for the more solid
comforts of home and career. Cesnola had impressed the Metropolitan trustees when he came to New York in 1873, and the reaction had been recip-
rocal; the general considered Johnston, Prime, Rhinelander, and others of
the inner circle to be the highest type of American gentlemen, simpler and
less sophisticated than Europeans of their social standing, perhaps, but ad-
mirable in character, and in matters of aesthetic taste willing, even eager,
to learn. Cesnola may conceivably have overestimated the financial
strength of the Metropolitan Museum. As Samuel P. Avery noted in a letter
to Johnston, written in 1877 from Berne, the Blodgett purchase and the acquisition of the two Cesnola collections had given Europeans "the idea
that we have boundless wealth. 'You Americans are so rich you can do
what you like,' is often said to me." It would be many years before the
Metropolitan had the funds to buy what the trustees liked (which may
have been just as well), but there was no doubt that the museum had established itself on a solid basis and that it would continue to grow
stronger. In addition, Cesnola felt genuinely attached to his collection,
which at this point, after the installation of the new objects, took up about
one quarter of the space in the Douglas Mansion. For a variety of reasons,
then, Cesnola looked kindly upon the trustees' invitation to join their
board.

He became secretary and trustee ex-officio in 1877, and promptly turned the secretary's position into a full-time job. Cesnola had an office fitted up for himself in the museum, with curtains "to render opaque the lower part of the glass windows to keep curious people from looking inside," and began devoting to the Metropolitan the same phenomenal energy and vigor that he had devoted to his Cypriote excavations. The trustees showed their gratitude early in 1879 by voting to make him the museum's first professional director, at a salary that fell somewhat short of $1,000 a year.

The new building in Central Park was nearly finished by this time, and the transfer of the collections soon began. Cesnola and two other paid attendants packed up the thousands of items in the Douglas Mansion, which was closed to the public early in February, 1879. At the other end, trustees William Prime and William Loring Andrews spent two months in the new building personally unpacking every item, and were proud to report that not a single work of art had been damaged.

The new director presumably took a hand in writing the ninth annual report, a touching document that summed up, with slightly wounded pride, the first decade of struggle and achievement. The museum's collections, "purchased without a dollar in public aid," had been seen by a total of 353,421 visitors since the opening of the Douglas Mansion in 1873, the report noted. It went on to point out that during this same period there had been "abundant evidences of the civilizing, refining, and ennobling influences which have been introduced into homes," not only in New York but throughout the nation. As an educational force, the museum had clearly demonstrated that art paid. In fact, the report observed, "The Metropolitan Museum of Art has already paid. It has paid during the past six years many hundred thousand dollars into the hands of workmen, women and children in decorative employments unknown a few years ago and in increased art industries, many hundred thousand into the pockets of importers, merchants, manufacturers and real estate owners." And yet, in all dignity, the trustees felt obliged to state that the museum's achievements had been made with money "contributed by a few," that the board had no funds on hand, and that the "thankless task" of soliciting contributions "has invariably ended in a private subscription among the Trustees and a few members to supplement the insufficient contributions obtained." The lack of "proper support" from the public, moreover, was reflected in the indifferent attitude of the municipal authorities, who had thus far failed to comprehend what the Metropolitan trustees were doing for the city of New York. "It is certainly time," the report stated, "for the City and the State to recognize the value of institutions like this."

Not too surprisingly, the trustees' lofty evaluation of their efforts and achievements was not shared by all sectors of the populace. To some, the rather patronizing statements about educational influence, moral uplift, and the refinement of crude tastes did not appear to have much basis in fact, and the whole enterprise smacked annoyingly of *noblesse oblige*. "From the very beginning it has been an exclusive social toy, not a great instrument of education," the *New York Tribune* stated in 1880, in a snappish editorial on the museum's forthcoming move to Central Park, "and all its failure to secure a more generous endowment from the State, all the popular lukewarmness, the restless demonstrations of opposition . . . have sprung from the conviction that this radical fault existed." The charge that the museum was being run as a sort of private, rich man's club—a charge that has persisted to this day—was not really accurate at this point in its development. A strong current of idealism governed the thinking of most well-bred people of the era, and if the trustees' rhetoric sometimes irked the cynics, the trustees themselves were nevertheless entirely sincere in their educational ideals—the same ideals, incidentally, that sustained the founders of the Museum of Fine Arts in Boston, which was described at its opening by the mayor of that city as "the crown of our educational system."

During the next two decades, at any rate, the Metropolitan trustees would no longer have to assume sole responsibility for the museum's relative success or failure. The new director, although staunchly loyal, would also prove to be a volatile and highly autocratic administrator, and the role of the trustees from now on would accordingly be somewhat diminished. As Cesnola wrote in his private diary some years later, "Remember that when *two* men put themselves at the head of an enterprise, there is always *one* too many."

FIVE

Even the trustees agreed that the new building, designed by Calvert Vaux and Jacob Wrey Mould, was not a thing of beauty. A barnlike, red-brick structure in the style known as Ruskin Gothic, it stood inelegantly on its raw patch of park in what was then a semirural suburb. Open fields stretched away to the north and west, and only a few scattered frame houses could be seen on nearby Fifth Avenue. The ends of the rectangular museum building faced east and west. Visitors followed a boardwalk from Fifth Avenue to the main entrance at the west end, where they climbed a flight of wooden steps and entered by a door situated in what is today the sculpture court behind the large medieval hall. James Jackson Jarves, although sympathetic to the Metropolitan and its trustees, wrote in 1882 that both inside and out the building was "a forcible example of architectural ugliness, out of harmony and keeping with its avowed purpose" and "fit only for a winter-garden or a railway depot." As the trustees pointed out, though, this first building was part of a much larger architectural plan, and as the museum expanded each new addition would tend to "harmonize" the structure. Later additions, in fact, have nearly obliterated it.

Just inside the main entrance, visitors walked through a vestibule and into the Statuary Hall, where during the early years one could see Hiram Powers' *California* and other monotonously idealized contemporary works. From there they passed into the main exhibition hall, whose space was given over primarily to the Cesnola Collection. The large stone sculptures from Golgoi lined the far wall. In the middle of the long room were glass-covered cases containing smaller objects from Cyprus and various loans of decorative art. Whenever it rained, the cases were covered with rubber tarpaulins and visitors were obliged to step around pails set out to catch the water that dripped from leaks in the glass roof. During one snowstorm in 1880, Cesnola counted forty-two leaks in the center of the hall and thirty-seven more in a gallery at the north end.

The paintings were on the floor above—two galleries of "Old Masters" and two others temporarily devoted to a loan show in which the usual nineteenth century storytelling canvases predominated. William H. Vanderbilt, who was rapidly establishing himself as the premier New York collector in this field, had sent word from Europe that the trustees were welcome to choose any ten pictures from his house. "You may be sure we took the best he had," Samuel Avery said, referring to a list that included such gems as Van Marcke's *Cattle* and a work by Erskine Nicol, subject matter unknown, called *Looking for a Safe Investment*. The paintings hung one above the other almost to the ceiling, as was the custom then, on wood-paneled walls that were lined with red billiard cloth and shrouded by valances, canopies, and curtains of twilled garnet serge. The floors were heavily shellacked, adding immeasurably to the fire hazard.

Under the terms of its lease with the city, drawn up by Choate and the Parks Department and signed in 1878, the museum was obligated to admit the public free of charge on four days each week, and on all holidays except Sunday. Hoping to recoup some of the revenue lost on four free days, the trustees experimented endlessly with pay days. They began by charging fifty cents on Monday and Tuesday, but soon found that approximately two thirds of the prospective visitors went away rather than pay the fee. Fashionably dressed ladies who had spent a dollar or more for a hired carriage would turn right around and drive off indignantly. The fee was reduced to twenty-five cents, and various combinations of pay days were tried, with no effect. Barely a dozen people a week were willing to pay for the privilege of having their tastes refined. Free days were another story. During the first month in the park, from March 30 to April 30, an attendance of 145,118 was recorded—more than the total for any year of the first decade.

All this time the museum's operating expenses rose steadily. Guards and maintenance men had to be hired, and the beginnings of a professional

staff assembled. In addition, the trustees had pledged themselves to acquire and exhibit a collection of industrial art—the large hall on the
ground floor, under the main exhibition area, had been set aside for this
purpose—and to establish schools for artists and craftsmen. The industrial
art collection never materialized, but by the end of 1880, aided by a grant
from a Massachusetts squire named Gideon F. T. Reed, the museum had
set up two schools in rented quarters downtown, one in woodwork and one
in metalwork, and the following year classes were inaugurated in drawing
and design, modeling and carving, carriage drafting, decorating in distem-
per (practical fresco work), and also, interestingly, in plumbing. The expenses of these and other innovations were met in large part by a highly
successful membership drive conceived by Cesnola and Henry G. Marquand, a trustee who was becoming increasingly active and influential on
the board. Over the next ten years the Metropolitan enlisted more than a
thousand Annual Members, a newly created class of modest subscribers
who paid $10.00 a year but who received the same benefits as Patrons
($1,000) or Fellows for Life ($200). The resulting income, plus timely contributions from a few trustees, kept the museum free of debt for many
years, as Cesnola noted proudly at the close of each annual report.

The trustees' deep satisfaction in this regard was somewhat overshadowed, however, by their director's entanglement in a most distressing and
all-too-public controversy. The origin of the dispute, whose repercussions
would be felt for many years and which would result in protracted litigation and a sensational trial, was an article in the August 1880 issue of *Art
Amateur,* one of the leading New York art journals. The author of the article was Gaston Feuardent, the son of the well-known French art and antiquities dealer, and the agent to whom Cesnola had consigned his first
collection when it went to London in 1872. Cesnola and Feuardent had
quarreled over the sale of the collection, each one accusing the other of
bad faith. Feuardent had subsequently moved to New York, and now he
was questioning the authenticity of some of the articles in the Cesnola
Collection—specifically of a small limestone statuette of a female figure
holding a mirror in her left hand. Feuardent said he had studied this same
statuette in London in 1872, that he had studied it again in 1878 in New
York, and that on neither of those occasions had there been any sign of a
mirror in her left hand. The mirror, he implied, "had been added to this

statue by carving it in stone," in order to permit the identification of the figure as Aphrodite and thus to increase its interest and value (a mirror being the usual attribute of that vain goddess). The piece, in other words, was a fraud.

Feuardent's article might have passed more or less unnoticed, had it not been picked up by several New York newspapers. Interviewed by reporters, Feuardent obligingly broadened his charges to include at least seven other objects, including some of the large statues from Golgoi, and the next day the papers broke the summer news doldrums by running the story under prominent headlines. Cesnola was out of town at the time, undergoing treatments for rheumatism in Richfield Springs, New York. Most of the trustees had been away since early June, estivating in Newport or elsewhere. Prime, who happened to be in town, wired Cesnola to pay no attention, and followed this up a few days later with a letter from his summer place in New Hampshire. "Take it cooly," Prime advised. "Bathe and be patient. It is this ignorance that we are seeking to enlighten, but in summer time I don't care a farthing whether all the land perishes in its ignorance." Cesnola, however, was not taking it coolly at all. From the baths at Richfield Springs he raged to Johnston of the "dastardly attack" made upon him by "the French Jew dealer Feuardent in an obscure monthly paper edited by a Jew." He denied all the charges, found evidence of a dire conspiracy against him, and demanded that the trustees appoint a committee to investigate the whole affair. "I have been attacked by an obscure dealer and accused of purposely doing things which only a crazy man would have done," he wrote to Johnston, "not a man whose whole life has been pure and honorable and his fame hardly won. . . . This is hard to bear!"

Cesnola was forced to bear it until the trustees returned from their summer vacations. In due time, however, an investigating committee was appointed, consisting of trustees Prime and J. Q. A. Ward, the sculptor, and three eminent citizens who were not trustees: Frederick A. P. Barnard, the president of Columbia; Charles P. Daly, president of the American Geographical Society; and Roswell D. Hitchcock, president of Union Theological Seminary. The committee began its investigation toward the end of the year. Cesnola, appearing before them early in January 1881, replied in detail to the charges and denied them all. The statuette of Aphrodite, he said, had been so encrusted with centuries-old dirt that its mirror had not shown up at first; before going on exhibition in Central Park, the stone objects had been cleaned by soaking them in water, and during this process the dirt had loosened and revealed the outlines of the mirror. The committee found Cesnola an excellent and plausible witness; its unanimous report, made public on January 28, stated that "each and all the charges are without foundation." The trustees congratulated their director, and told him to consider the matter closed.

Unfortunately, the matter was far from closed. Feuardent had refused to appear before the committee because the committee had declined to let him appoint an additional member with archaeological training. No sooner had the verdict been announced, though, than the dealer sent up a new barrage of accusations in *Art Amateur* and in *The Times*. Feuardent seemed to be trying to goad Cesnola into a libel suit. Cesnola ached to oblige him, but Choate and the rest of the trustees had insisted that he contain his wrath and say nothing. A lawsuit, Choate said, would only serve to call attention to Feuardent and his charges—besides, Choate added, "It is no remedy for a gentleman." Late in May, just as Cesnola was leaving for a trip to Europe, Feuardent filed suit against *him*. Referring to Cesnola's original statement of denial from Richfield Springs, some of which had gotten into the papers, Feuardent charged libel and defamation of character.

The New York papers kept the issue simmering until the trial began, two and a half years later. *The Times* described Feuardent's accusations as "cumulative, convincing, apparently unanswerable," and called again and again for a new investigation. Clarence Cook, the influential art critic and editor of *The Studio,* joined the attack with a series of articles entitled "Our Mismanaged Museum," in which he ridiculed the Metropolitan's claims to be an educational force. Cook supported Feuardent's charges, and in March 1882 he published a vitriolic pamphlet called "Transformations and Migrations in Certain Statues in the Cesnola Collection" in which he went a good deal further. Most of the large statues in the Cesnola Collection, he wrote, were made up of unrelated fragments stuck together by clumsy means—in fact "few examples can be found that have not been repaired, restored, altered, added to, scraped and painted." By his crude and unscientific methods, Cook added, Cesnola had destroyed any possible archaeological value that the objects might have had, while "As for artistic value, they never had any."

Cesnola told the executive committee of the museum that, if Cook's charges were believed, then "the usefulness of the Museum would be at an end." He begged for a chance to disprove them, and at length the trustees reluctantly agreed. A series of extremely odd happenings now ensued. Cesnola had two large statues and the head of another, all of which Cook had attacked, removed from their glass cases and placed out in the middle of the main exhibition hall, on a small platform within easy reach of anyone, and invited members of the museum, the general public, "and especially editors of public journals, sculptors, workers in stone, and all persons interested in the truthfulness of archaeological objects . . . to make most careful examination" of them. The sculptures remained out on the floor from March 28 to May 2, and were examined, rubbed, scraped with wire brushes, pounded, and even dug into by hundreds of amateur sleuths. Cesnola was willing to let the statues be sawn in half if anyone suggested that. "Let us lose the two statues entirely if necessary," he wrote to one of the trustees, "but let the scoundrel be proved a liar." One of the statues, a large headless votary that Cook had called a fraudulent "patchwork of unrelated parts," bears to this day a white streak running from the neck to the knee, the result of acid spilled accidentally during a test by a group of prominent American sculptors. The sculptors pronounced the pieces to be solid stone, and therefore authentic. Still Feuardent and *Art Amateur* (which Cesnola had taken to calling *Art Defamateur*) were unsatisfied; they claimed that inviting everybody to examine them was the same as inviting nobody, and they demanded "real" tests that employed heat treatments and immersion in chemical baths. The trustees refused, feeling they had gone far enough.

As the date of the trial drew near, the trustees gave Cesnola every assurance of their support. "I will be in New York on the day fixed for the trial," Prime wrote him, "and we will whip the scoundrels out of their boots." Choate, who had tried so hard to prevent a lawsuit, had consented to serve as chief defense counsel, and the museum had assumed all Cesnola's legal expenses. The trial began on the last day of October 1883. Every New York newspaper featured the story prominently, and the early sessions were attended by trustees, ladies of fashion, and notables of all kinds. They soon lost interest. Day after day, week after week, the arguments bogged down in a morass of archaeological detail. There were interminable discussions about the difference between a repair and a restoration—a repair being a simple joining together of fragments belonging to the same object, while a restoration involved the re-creation of missing parts on the basis of theory or guesswork as to the original form. Cesnola denied having made any restorations, but he conceded that an inexperienced workman named Feodor Gehlen, a carpenter who had worked for the museum while it was in the Douglas Mansion, had made some improper restorations to the objects with plaster of Paris. Cesnola said that prior to the move to Central Park he had given orders for all the pieces that Gehlen had worked on to be soaked apart in water, and then repaired correctly without plaster restorations of any kind, but that in the rush and confusion of moving the collections one or two pieces with Gehlen restorations had escaped his notice. Gehlen himself took the stand at one point. Under questioning by Feuardent's counsel, Francis N. Bangs, he said that he had made noses for some of the noseless statues. "Who told you how to make noses?" Bangs inquired. Gehlen said, in his thick German accent, that General Cesnola had told him how—"If the fragments were of a Greek figure, I put on a Greek nose." There were not many light moments, though, and as the tedium mounted the papers began referring to the "Wearisome Trial" and asking "When Will It End?"

Choate had appeared to be in rather a bad humor throughout the trial and had frequently goaded Bangs into angry outbursts. When it came at last to the summation, though, the defense counsel was at the top of his form. Relaxed and informal, strolling loose-jointedly about the courtroom with his hands in his pockets, pausing now and then to put one foot up on a chair, he took the jury into his confidence and made each member feel like an old and valued friend. "Certainly there was never a case that required more patience at the hands of a court jury," Choate told them. "If it had lasted a little longer we should all of us have become part of the antiquities we were employed to discuss. I have felt for some time the corroding surface of antiquity gather over me, and I have observed the same encrustation gather upon his Honor and upon each of you—upon your faces, and especially upon your drapery. It would not have taken much longer to make us all worthy of being gathered into the Museum as a third

Cesnola Collection. I have no doubt that the Trustees of the Metropolitan Museum of Art, with their usual liberality, would have purchased us at our own figure . . ."

He referred to Clarence Cook, the critic, who was absent from New York throughout the trial, as "the false and fleeting but not quite perjured Clarence," a quip that quickly made the rounds and convulsed those who knew their Shakespeare as well as others who did not. Beneath the genial wit, though, a shrewd and steely contempt for the plaintiff ran through all Choate's arguments. The undertone was never clearly anti-Semitic— Cesnola and Prime showed their sentiments more or less openly in this regard, but the other trustees, and especially Choate, were more careful. It was rather an unspoken distaste for the wily foreigner, and especially for the *dealer*, who sullied works of art by his unclean touch and who sought also to sully the pure motives of the museum. "What is the use of living, of eating the bread of carefulness, and being good citizens," Choate asked the jury, "if men whose characters are the treasures of the city can be struck down by a man like this?"

Choate's summation took a day and a half and lasted for more than nine hours. Bangs's lasted even longer. Although he was suffering from a bad cold and had difficulty making himself heard, Bangs spoke almost continuously for two days, pausing every hour or so to drink a glass of ice water. The jury, which had listened for a grand total of ninety-two days, spent one night and all the next day deliberating. Their verdict was a complete vindication of Cesnola. A note from Avery to Cesnola the next day summed up the attitude of the trustees: "Hooray! Hooray! for our beloved Museum and for our devoted and *tried* Director."

Actually the long trial had accomplished very little, for attacks on Cesnola and the Cesnola Collection continued for years in art and archaeological circles. The problem was partly that Cypriote pottery and sculpture, being a mixed style compounded of many foreign influences, simply did not look authentic to some observers, but it must also be conceded that Cesnola himself, an amateur archaeologist at a time when scientific methods of excavation were just beginning, had made some honest mistakes. Several headless torsos in the collection had perhaps acquired heads that did not belong to them, or vice versa, and the material had been excavated without careful attention to exact locations or to the relationship between objects. The controversy did not really die down until 1910, when Prof. J. L. Myres of Oxford University, a leading authority on Cypriote art, examined the collection in detail and pronounced it unquestionably authentic. Although not many people today would be prepared to argue that its artistic value is very great, it can hardly be said that the museum has not had its money's worth. Cesnola sold a large batch of Cypriote objects—mostly duplicates—to Leland Stanford in 1885 for $10,000, with which the museum made its first purchase of ancient Egyptian material, and in 1928 the Metropolitan realized $120,000 from an auction of surplus Cypriote material to other museums, colleges, and to lamp manufacturers for stands. Having paid only $120,000 in all for the collection, the museum thus earned better than a hundred percent on its investment and kept the investment.

In a certain sense, however, the trial was really an attack on the Old New York establishment. As Horace Greeley's *New York Tribune* put it in a post-trial editorial, the libel suit "was the culmination of a series of wanton assaults upon the public character of the Metropolitan Museum of Art, and the private character of the directors, and trustees." The *Tribune* had been one of the few papers to support Cesnola, or to report the trial with any degree of objectivity. A new kind of journalism was gaining strength in New York, where more than eighteen dailies fought for circulation among the city's fast-growing working class population. Scandals and sensations sold newspapers, and so did the doings of the rich; if the scandals involved the rich, the gain was double. There was no doubt that wealthy New York society had adopted the Metropolitan Museum (Choate, who also served on the board of the Natural History Museum, said that from the beginning it was much easier to raise money for the Metropolitan). From now on the Metropolitan and its Old New York trustees would come in for a good deal of journalistic sniping that was aimed at the rich in general, and one effect would be a slight cooling of the trustees' democratic and educational fervor. "Public service in this country does not reward us," Prime wrote sadly to Cesnola after the trial. "However, one need not be discouraged."

SIX

A golden shower of gifts was descending upon the museum, and threatening at any moment to become a downpour.

Almost overnight, it seemed, giving or bequeathing one's treasures to the Metropolitan had become fashionable. Cornelius Vanderbilt, the son of William H. and the grandson and namesake of the rough old Staten Island ferryman who had amassed the largest fortune in America without managing to make himself socially acceptable, signalized his election in 1880 as a Metropolitan trustee by presenting a collection of nearly seven hundred Italian drawings. The collection had been put together in Florence (rather hastily, it would appear) by James Jackson Jarves, who needed money. The attributions included nine Michelangelos, two Raphaels, eleven Titians, twelve Tintorettos, nine Rembrandts, and two Leonardos, and the critic Clarence Cook lost no time in attacking them. If there had been even one scholar among the Metropolitan trustees, Cook said, the collection "would never have been accepted." Although Cook was right this time—there was not a single genuine Old Master in the lot, just copies and school studies —the Vanderbilt gift hung prominently for many years and helped to create new interest in the field of drawings.

Jarves' collection of one hundred and thirty Italian trecento and quattrocento paintings, which he had formed in Florence between 1850 and 1860, had been turned down almost contemptuously, twenty years earlier, by the city fathers of Boston and New York ("pre-Giottoesque ligneous daubs," one prominent critic called the pictures). He had eventually placed them in the Yale University Art Gallery as security for a loan, and when he was unable to make the interest payments Yale had bought the entire collection —now worth millions—for $22,000. Since then the reputations of Jarves and the Italian primitives had risen sharply. Jarves was acting as art adviser to Vanderbilt, Marquand, and several other collectors. In 1881 he offered to give the Metropolitan a fine collection of Venetian glass, in honor of his father Deming Jackson Jarves, the founder of the famous American glassworks at Sandwich, Massachusetts. Cesnola hesitated at first to accept it, suspicious that Jarves might be "of the same stamp as Mr. Feuardent wishing to make use of our Museum as a *lever* to make money for themselves." The trustees did accept it, however, and a few months later Henry Marquand purchased and presented the Charvet collection of Roman and Etruscan glass, which the museum had coveted for several years. Together with Samuel Avery's collection of porcelain, purchased by subscription in 1880, these gifts provided a creditable showing in the decorative arts, with plenty of examples for local artisans to imitate, if not to excel.

The first big bequest of money—more than $100,000 from the New York businessman Levi Hale Willard—came in 1883 with instructions that it be applied to the purchase of architectural casts. Three years later, Henry Marquand added to his steady procession of gifts a fund of $10,000, to be spent for casts of antique, Renaissance, and modern sculpture. A few critics argued even then against the exhibition of plaster casts in a museum of art. Jarves said that they were of interest only to art students, and that they should not be shown to the general public because "they affect the mind differently from real art, and are no more to be mistaken for it than the face in the mirror for the true person." On the other hand, the South Kensington Museum in London, always a strong influence on the Metropolitan trustees, had assembled a large collection of sculptural and architectural casts, and the Boston Museum of Fine Arts was doing the same. A great many people were convinced, moreover, that American museums could never hope to rival the European collections of original art. Europe's museums and private collectors already owned most of the important landmarks of ancient and Renaissance art, it was said, and they would never dream of selling them—a remarkably naive supposition, as it turned out. Although the Metropolitan itself had already scooped up some of the spoils of the Franco-Prussian War, most of the trustees agreed that such occasions would rarely if ever arise again. The only alternative, it appeared, was to build up a collection of casts.

The Metropolitan's sculptural and architectural casts, purchased in Europe, were the finest that could be obtained. They were exhibited on the ground floor of the museum in the area originally planned for industrial art, and proved to be immensely popular with the public, a good part of which took them for the real thing. They were also scrutinized and sketched by some two hundred students in the museum's art school, which from 1889 on conducted its classes in the museum.

The growth of the painting collection continued to reflect the tastes of the period. Since the trustees could not afford to be choosy, the annual reports show them accepting, in 1883, a painting that was listed as "by Caravaggio or Carlo Dolci" (it was by neither), and, the following year, an "Oil Painting, artist and subject unknown." In 1887 Cornelius Vanderbilt gave Rosa Bonheur's *The Horse Fair*, which he had just bought from the estate of the department store magnate (and Metropolitan trustee) A. T. Stewart for $53,000; the huge canvas immediately became and has remained one of the most popular in the museum. Meissonier's *Friedland, 1807,* also from Stewart's collection, arrived the same year, a gift from carpet manufacturer Henry Hilton, and so did Sir Joshua Reynolds' group portrait of *Hon. Henry Fane, with His Guardians,* presented by the London banker Junius S. Morgan whose son would loom so large in the Metropolitan's future affairs. The American millionaires had not yet developed their full-blown passion for portraits of eighteenth century Englishmen. Marquand and one or two others had dipped into this field, which the dealer Joseph Duveen would soon turn to such lucrative account, but the majority still clung to the sentimental and sugary Salon paintings of the Continental "moderns." This taste reached its most luxuriant bloom in the Catharine Lorillard Wolfe Collection, which came to the Metropolitan upon her death in 1887.

Catharine Lorillard Wolfe was an only child. Her father, John David Wolfe, had made a fortune in the hardware business; her mother, born Dorothea Ann Lorillard, was an heiress to tobacco millions. Catharine gathered in the full harvest when her father died in 1872 (her mother had predeceased him), and it was estimated at the time that she was the richest unmarried woman in the world. Marriage failed to interest her. She devoted most of her time to charity, giving away more than $4,000,000 to schools, churches, and ameliorative societies of all kinds. Miss Wolfe also approved of the fine arts. She had been the only woman to subscribe to the Metropolitan's first fund drive in 1870, giving $2,500. Soon after this, she commissioned her young cousin, John Wolfe, who was considered to be a connoisseur, to collect a gallery of paintings for her large house on Madison Avenue, and from then on she was a frequent lender to the museum's exhibitions.

Her collection eventually came to number one hundred and forty-three pictures. It included virtually all the fashionable French Salon painters of the time—Bouguereau, Desgoffes, Bonnat, Detaille, Bargue, Cot, Cabanel (who painted Miss Wolfe's portrait)—and also a few of the more "advanced" canvases by Corot, Daubigny, Théodore Rousseau, and others of the Barbizon School, which Samuel Avery had done much to popularize in America. *The Storm,* painted to order for her by Pierre A. Cot, is a fairly typical example of what she and her contemporaries admired; it shows a lightly garbed young couple running for shelter from a fortuitous shower, and gallery lecturers at the Metropolitan now refer to it as an example of academic art at its most insipid. Miss Wolfe's bequest of paintings came with an endowment of $200,000, the income from which was to be used for the preservation and increase of the collection. It was the first self-sufficient bequest of this kind (the museum has used the income to buy some of its most important pictures, including Renoir's *Madame Charpentier and Her Children,* Goya's *The Bullfight,* Delacroix's *The Abduction of Rebecca,* Daumier's *Don Quixote,* and Winslow Homer's *The Gulf Stream,* none of which Miss Wolfe would have much cared for), and it was also one of the first to come with restrictive strings attached. According to her will, the gift was made "upon express condition that the trustees and managers . . . shall provide and set apart exclusively for said collection a suitable, well-lighted fire-proof apartment, gallery or separate space, where the paintings and water color drawings herein mentioned shall be properly arranged and displayed; and provided also, that said collection shall be designated and continue to be known as 'the Catherine Lorillard Wolfe Collection.' "

The Wolfe bequest set a pattern and a problem that has endured for a century. Art collecting, after all, is a complex pursuit. Immortality, social status, vanity, and other motives both psychological and economic enter into it in varying degrees, and many art dealers are convinced that the pure and selfless love of works of art for their own sake is so rare as to be considered almost nonexistent. The Metropolitan has had its share of benefactors who have sought to make their benefactions reflect "in perpetuity" their illustrious names and matchless taste. Perhaps the trustees could have held out firmly against all such conditions from the beginning, and thus saved themselves a lot of trouble later on, but at this period and for some time to come they did not feel wealthy or secure enough to hold out. They took what they could get, and passed on the problems of restrictive bequests to their successors, who have often managed adroitly, it must be noted, to circumvent the conditions.

In one exceptional case, though, the museum was blessed by a collector whose benefactions were almost as remarkable for the spirit that accompanied them as for the gifts themselves. Henry Gurdon Marquand was without a doubt the most discriminating collector and art patron of his time. A New Yorker by birth, he had left school at the age of sixteen and gone to work in his older brother's jewelry firm (called Marquand and Company then, it eventually became Black, Starr and Gorham). Later on he went into real estate, and then into banking and brokerage on Wall Street. Railroad financing made him wealthy. With his brother and several other investors, he bought the St. Louis, Iron Mountain and Southern Railroad in 1874, and ran it successfully until 1882, when control was wrested away from them by the unspeakable Jay Gould. The clash with Gould must have been deeply offensive to a man of Marquand's refined and pacific sensibilities. He more or less withdrew from business after that, and devoted the remainder of his life to art and good works.

Having started out as a patron of American art, Marquand soon began to collect in a great number of different fields. His house on Madison Avenue at Sixty-eighth Street, a large red sandstone-and-brick mansion designed in late French Renaissance style by Richard Morris Hunt (who also built the Fifth Avenue palaces of William K. Vanderbilt and John Jacob Astor), was almost a museum in itself; the elegant, classic severity of his grey and gold Greek drawing room, the exoticism of his Japanese cabinet and his Moorish smoking room, the furniture and fittings that had been made to order by European craftsmen—all this struck Marquand's contemporaries as marks of a unique and exalted taste. The time and expense that went into his private collecting were soon outstripped, however, by his efforts on behalf of the Metropolitan. Beginning in 1870, when he subscribed $1,000 to the initial fund drive, Marquand continued to give not only regularly and lavishly but thoughtfully, with a constant view to the museum's comprehensive and educational goals. He contributed to the library, to the collection of casts, to the art schools, and to the general endowment. His gifts in the field of decorative arts—glass, metalwork, enamels, bronzes, ceramics—were keyed precisely to the museum's current needs. But it was the Paintings Department that profited most spectacularly from his taste. Early in 1888, Marquand placed on loan at the museum a group of thirty-seven pictures that he had recently purchased abroad. The quality of the group as a whole was extraordinary, and in it were several masterpieces whose reputation has grown steadily ever since: Van Dyck's full-length portrait of *James Stuart, Duke of Richmond and Lennox*, the epitome of English aristocratic hauteur; two magnificent Rembrandts, *Portrait of a Man* and *Man with a Beard;* and, most miraculous of all, Vermeer's *Young Woman With a Water Jug*, the first Vermeer to enter an American museum and one of the first ever brought to this country, a magical, still world of pearly light and exquisitely modulated color. There were in addition three fine Franz Hals portraits, two works by Petrus Christus, a Ruisdael, a Cuyp, a Turner, and a Gainsborough.

The Marquand loan transformed the picture galleries and went a long way toward placing the Metropolitan among the important museums of the world. Newspapers across the country reported the event. In Boston, where the tradition of cultural superiority died hard, there were cries of near-anguish. The *Boston Herald* conceded mournfully that "in the matter of generous patronage of art New York is ahead of us," while the *Advertiser*, biting hard on the nail, said that the Metropolitan now possessed "far and away the finest collection of painting to be seen in this country." Marquand's eye for quality may even have influenced the future trend of collecting in America. The taste for French Salon painting waned rapidly after 1890, although, curiously enough, Marquand himself had a large number of Salon pictures in his house, and would almost certainly have given them to the Metropolitan if financial reverses in later years had not obliged him, like Johnston earlier, to sell his private collection at auction. The paintings in the 1888 loan never even entered Marquand's house. Immediately upon their arrival from Europe they went to the Metropolitan, and the following year, noting the great interest that had been shown to them by critics and the public, Marquand gave them outright to the museum. He gave them without conditions of any kind, beyond a mild request that they be kept together "as much as practicable."

Marquand had been a trustee of the Metropolitan since 1871. His gifts, his superb taste, and his increasingly active part in museum activities—he served on the executive committee from 1872 on, and was elected treasurer in 1883—placed him among the inner circle of "working" trustees, along with Prime, Rhinelander, Choate, and a few others. By the mid-1880s this circle no longer included John Taylor Johnston. The first president, afflicted by age and declining health, had been prevented from resigning in 1887 by a petition signed by all of his fellow trustees begging him to stay on. Two years later, though, the trustees voted to make Johnston honorary president for life, and elected Henry Marquand as the Metropolitan's second president.

In public, at least, the leaders of large cultural enterprises like to look on the bright side of things. The opening in 1888 of the Metropolitan's new south wing, which doubled the amount of exhibition space, had moved William C. Prime, the museum's vice-president and a man who never shrank from hyperbole, to observe that "There has been no hesitation, no pause, no shadow or cloud, not an hour of doubt or discouragement in all our history." At that very moment, however, a cloud considerably bigger than a man's hand darkened the museum's horizon, and Marquand soon found himself at the epicenter of a gathering storm. The issue was whether or not to open the museum on Sundays. Choate and some of the younger trustees were in favor of it, and so was Cesnola. Pressure from the outside had been building up since 1881, when ten thousand people signed a petition urging the Department of Parks to make the Metropolitan and the Natural History museums open their doors on Sundays. Almost every newspaper in the city had demanded that the step be taken, and several politicians had also decided to embrace the cause; in 1885, the Board of Estimate threatened to cut off its annual $50,000 appropriation to both museums unless they instituted Sunday hours. Boston's Museum of Fine Arts had admitted the public on Sundays since it opened in 1876; most of the newer American museums had done the same, and in London, where a similar controversy had been simmering for years, the House of Lords had voted in 1886 to open the British Museum on Sundays. If the Metropolitan's trustees meant what they said about educating and refining the humble artisan, it was argued, how could they refuse to admit him on the only day of the week when he was free to visit? The working classes did not stay at home on Sundays, nor did they go to church. "Where do they go?" another petition abjured the museums. "Frequently to immoral places. Are you ready to assume this responsibility? . . . Will you refuse with such a noble power in your hands to be the ally of this community in its struggle against gigantic vices?"

On the boards of both museums, however, the men of conservative and Presbyterian temper could conceive of no more gigantic vice than breaking the Sabbath. They also had more concrete arguments. Morris K. Jesup, the president of the American Museum of Natural History, summarized the opposition viewpoint when he appeared before the Board of Estimate in 1885: By opening on Sunday, Jesup said, the museums would not only incur heavy additional expenses, but they would almost certainly forfeit the active support of a great many wealthy, churchgoing benefactors upon whom such cultural institutions depended; moreover, opening on Sunday would in fact rob the workingman of his rest day, because, once the fatal step had been taken, other enterprises—theaters, music halls, sideshows of all kinds—would also demand the right to do business on that day; the end result would be that dreadful bacchanal, the "French Sunday," and the workingman's right to rest from labor would vanish forever. The two museums managed to stave off the loss of their city funds by agreeing to stay open two nights a week, a temporary expedient that pleased no one. The press, the labor unions, and various citizens groups clamored more and more vociferously for the Sunday opening. Counterpetitions were circulated by the American Sabbath Union, the Presbytery of New York, and the Ladies Christian Union. The trustees wavered, fearful that a decision either way could prove costly and perhaps ruinous.

The doughtiest opponent of Sunday opening on either board was William Cowper Prime. The son of a Presbyterian minister, Prime had taught school and been headmaster of a boys' academy in his earlier years, before becoming a lawyer. He had left the law for journalism, serving as editor of the *New York Journal of Commerce* and president of the Associated Press, but nothing had blurred the sharp outlines of his religious scruples; even Prime's interest in art and art history had grown out of his lifelong Biblical studies. As a founding trustee, one of the most consistently active members of the Metropolitan board and its first vice-president since 1874, Prime exercised considerable influence on his fellow trustees—he had more or less run the museum during Johnston's declining years—and his arguments, expressed in terms of no uncertainty, carried great weight. His outspoken and somewhat royalist views on such matters as property and private versus public ownership were also shared by a number of other trustees.

Prime objected strongly to the way the public had been led to think about the Metropolitan. "*Now* they think the Museum is a public institution, in the management of which the public has a voice," he wrote to Johnston in 1885. "They must be *forced* to think of it as a private institution. . . . They must stop thinking they support the Museum, and be compelled to see that *we* own and support the Museum and give it in pure charity for public education." One of the things that Prime opposed most vigorously was any closer ties with the city administration. By accepting an annual appropriation from the city, he maintained, the museum had already compromised its virtue; any additional "entangling alliances" with City Hall—such as bowing to the pressure to open on Sundays in exchange for a larger appropriation—would destroy its independence forever and drag the institution down into the mire of municipal corruption. Fundamentally, though, Prime's opposition to Sunday opening was on religious and moral grounds. "I am no Puritan, but I *will* have one day in seven for rest," he wrote to Cesnola. ". . . I *will* have that day as the immovable centre of Christian faith, Christian intelligence, Christian civilization. I will have nothing to do with making it a day of *labor* for one class of people to *amuse* another class. I will not employ fifty men on Sunday to make a show for ten thousand." Prime made it plain that he would resign if the trustees voted to open the museum on Sundays.

Marquand tried his best to soothe and moderate the increasing bitterness over the Sunday question. Characteristically, he saw and understood both sides of the argument. "Every word of Mr. Prime is true and it is cutting to me," he wrote Cesnola. And yet, he added, "Must a man who walks in Central Park shut his eyes when he comes to a statue or a work of art? . . . New York has a great mixed population and we cannot expect those who have been differently brought up to agree with the early New England notions." A few years later Marquand himself would be fighting a desperate rearguard action; now, however, he sided with the liberals. In 1890 a bill was introduced in the state legislature to compel both museums to open on Sundays. The bill was shelved in committee, but time was clearly running out. A few months later, in the spring of 1891, the trustees met at the house of Robert Hoe—Prime and John S. Kennedy, another strong opponent, did not attend—and voted to open the museum on Sunday afternoons, "as an experiment only," from one P.M. until dusk.

The first open Sunday—May 31, 1891—an estimated twelve thousand people pressed through the doors. "It was a good-natured crowd, as became the occasion," the *Boston Herald* reported to its readers. "A good part of it brought big baskets of lunch, but was not a bit disturbed that the baskets could not pass the turnstiles. . . . An integral part of it brought a small baby, which yelled vehemently." By the end of the year, Cesnola was able to report that in spite of a certain "turbulence and disorder" evident on the first few Sundays, when the visitors handled, scratched, and even broke a few objects and some "brought with them peculiar habits which were repulsive and unclean," matters had improved to the point that Sunday attendance was "respectable, law-abiding and intelligent." The experiment also proved less costly than some of the more conservative trustees had predicted. Mrs. Robert L. Stuart, a wealthy widow who had pledged $50,000 apiece to the Metropolitan and the American Museum in her will, revoked both benefactions because of the Sunday openings (the American Museum started having Sunday hours in 1892). Prime resigned from the board as he had threatened to do, and retired to his home in New Hampshire, from which he wrote regularly to Cesnola regarding the impending ruin of the Metropolitan. On the other hand, the Board of Estimate increased its annual appropriation for the Metropolitan from $25,000 to $50,000 (later increased again to $70,000) to help pay the additional costs of Sunday openings, and the Metropolitan's membership stayed loyal in spite of a rather drastic boost in fees, the following year, for all classes above the $10.00 a year Annual Members.* Although Sunday has remained

* Fellows in Perpetuity went up from $500 to $5,000 a year, Fellows for Life from $200 to $1,000, and a new class of Benfactor was created for the escalating fortunes that permitted gifts of $50,000 and over. Patrons (formerly $1,000) were merged with

ever since the most popular day of the week for visiting the Metropolitan, the large attendance has had no discernible effect one way or the other on the struggle against gigantic vice.

For someone who readily admitted that he was "not a man for a contest," poor Marquand had his share of troubles as president. Increasingly over the years, although Marquand would never admit it, the main irritant and source of contention was Louis P. di Cesnola. The president and the director liked and admired one another without reservation. "On *you* the *whole fabric* hangs and few *realise* it," Marquand wrote to the director during the height of the Sunday crisis. Cesnola, who often addressed himself to the president in somewhat fulsome terms ("You are one of the noblest, and most generous of men, and this institution owes to you more than to all the other Trustees and Patrons put together!"), made no secret of his lack of admiration for others on the board, and this was the root of the problem. The director had a genius for antagonizing people. His subordinates thought him a martinet, forever striding about the halls in his military boots to check up on them or sending off stiff memos about getting to work on time. The first curator, William Henry Goodyear, who was hired in 1882 to look after *all* the works of art in the museum, complained continually about his inadequate salary ($2,000 a year) and left in 1888 under strained circumstances. By 1889 there were three curators—George Henry Story for paintings, drawings, and prints; Isaac B. Hall for sculptures, antiquities, and other objets d'art; John Alsop Paine for casts and reproductions —and the total museum staff had grown to fifty-four. Cesnola made them work on holidays, and when the Sunday openings began he made them work seven days a week, with no increase in pay. Their resentment occasionally took concrete form. The museum's first bookkeeper spent months assembling a dossier in support of his accusation that Cesnola had diverted museum funds to his private use. He sent it to the trustees, who investigated but found no trace of wrongdoing; the problem lay in Cesnola's rudimentary system of accounting (the director's cash balance "was never proved to be correct in the whole course of ten years"), but his honesty

---

Fellows in Perpetuity at $5,000, and a few years later the title of Patron was dropped. All the Metropolitan's members are "patrons," and all receive the same benefits, whether they give $10.00 or $50,000—a true democracy of largesse.

emerged without a blot. The bookkeeper, of course, was dismissed.

Cesnola's high-handed methods were not restricted to his subordinates. One of his conditions on accepting the directorship was that he also remain on the board of trustees as its secretary, which placed him in a somewhat equivocal position so far as the other trustees were concerned. To make the situation even touchier, he took offense as readily as he gave it. His private diary and his letters reveal a man permanently smarting under what he considered unjust and malicious criticism. They are full of outbursts against "assinine" art critics and self-serving artists who "have always considered our Museum to have been established for their own pecuniary benefit, a kind of market place where their works were to be sold at exorbitant prices and permanently exhibited as their professional advertisement." Soon after becoming director, Cesnola had suggested that the museum start a collection of early American paintings, but his sympathy evidently did not extend to contemporary artists ("The New York artist in general is *vain*," he concluded), and it most certainly did not extend to the artist or art-scholarly members of the Metropolitan board of trustees. These gentlemen, he argued (referring to J. Q. A. Ward, Samuel Avery, and one or two others) had long wanted to seize control of the museum from the "successful and experienced business men" who were solely responsible for the institution's successful growth. From 1890 on, Cesnola lashed out more and more angrily at what he called the improper interference of some trustees in museum affairs, and at the apathy and dereliction of certain others. With one or two exceptions, he said, "the chairmen of our important Committees do not do *their own work,* but *delegate* it (not to other Members of Their Committee, as they should) but to *irresponsible* parties of their own choice." Cesnola felt that his authority as director was being undermined. His suspicions, as it turned out, were justified.

Opposition to Cesnola on the board had been gathering momentum for several years. One or two trustees had never forgiven him for getting the museum into its embarrassing lawsuit with Feuardent. During the late 1880s and 1890s, moreover, a number of vacancies on the board had been filled by younger men who were at first astonished and then increasingly aggravated by the director's all-too-obvious disinclination to listen to their views, or for that matter to any views that did not coincide with his own. Cesnola was continually being attacked in the press and the art journals as an ignoramus, an unscholarly charlatan who knew nothing about art and cared only for his own dubious collection of Cypriote antiques. He attributed all such attacks to a conspiracy of dishonest critics and dealers, but some of the younger trustees had begun to wonder about this; it pained them that the Metropolitan was so often and unfavorably compared to the Boston Museum of Fine Arts, whose scholarly and professional development under Martin Rimmer, its first president, was universally admired.

The accumulated resentment came to a head in 1895, during a meeting of the special committee on casts. This was one of the groups that Cesnola had railed against with particular fervor. Appointed by Marquand in 1890 to enlarge the museum's cast collection, its members had raised $79,-867 which, instead of turning over to the museum's treasurer, they had retained control of themselves, buying what Cesnola maintained was five times more casts than the museum had space to exhibit. The chairman of this committee was Robert de Forest, a lawyer who also happened to be John Taylor Johnston's son-in-law, and the youngest trustee on the board. In the course of the meeting that night, de Forest, John S. Kennedy, Edward D. Adams, William R. Ware, Howard Mansfield, and Samuel Avery began to discuss frankly their feelings about Cesnola, and found themselves in general agreement that the director's continued presence in that office was undesirable. The following week, summoned by telegrams sent out from de Forest's office downtown, a larger group of trustees met at the Fifty-seventh Street home of John S. Kennedy, the wealthy banker and railroad financier. The subject of the meeting was Cesnola. Hiram Hitchcock, Cesnola's old friend and sole defender on this occasion, reported afterward that de Forest had been in charge of the proceedings, during which several trustees, including Choate, had made the accusations "that Cesnola was not the man for the place, hindered progress, prevented gifts, was deceptive, brusque, insulting, domineering, unjust to subordinates, not a good manager, not in touch with art here and in Europe, does not fairly represent us, is a martinet, owns the Museum, controlled Mr. Johnston and now controls Mr. Marquand."

Marquand had not been invited to the special meeting. Ill and deeply grieved by the recent death of his wife, he was shocked by the letter he received a few days later, signed by trustees Ward, Avery, Ware, Choate, Kennedy, Adams, and de Forest, stating that in their considered opinion

Cesnola should cease to be connected with the Metropolitan Museum. To Marquand (and of course to Cesnola) the whole affair appeared to be a crass attempt by some of the younger trustees to seize power from the older and more conservative members of the board. When de Forest and Kennedy called on the president at his home to explain their views, Marquand more or less accused them of timing the move to coincide with the absence in Europe of Rhinelander and William E. Dodge, two older trustees who would presumably have sided with Cesnola. He urged them to wait until those two returned before pressing the matter further. De Forest and Kennedy respectfully declined, saying the decision would have to be made the following Monday when the trustees met at the museum for the annual election of officers. Marquand was profoundly disturbed. "I am sorry to say that it looks like a contest coming on Monday at the Museum," he wrote to another trustee. "The plan is an adroit one by the youngest of the trustees to put Cesnola out. If they succeed the conservative force will go and the Museum will be run by the impressionists."

The climactic meeting took place on the afternoon of February 18. Marquand had made the issue painfully personal by announcing that he would resign forthwith unless all the presently incumbent officers were reelected. It soon became clear that the "impressionists" did not have a majority. One very telling factor was Marquand's reading of a letter from J. P. Morgan, a trustee since 1888 and already a powerful voice in Metropolitan affairs, stating that "Any change which does not meet with your approval will not meet with mine." Realizing they would be beaten, Kennedy moved that the vote for officers be postponed. Choate and de Forest seconded the motion, but before it could be voted on Marquand rose once again to say that he would resign if the postponement carried. Choate turned on the president at this point and demanded angrily whether "this board was to be bulldozed." Marquand sat staring straight ahead, his mouth firm and set. The vote for postponement resulted in a tie, and the motion was therefore declared to have failed. In the subsequent voting for officers, all were elected unanimously except for Cesnola, who received ten out of seventeen votes, and E. D. Adams, one of the insurgents, who got only seven.

Temporarily, at least, the old guard remained in control, but the board was badly split. De Forest made a statement to *The Times* that March, after the story had leaked out, saying that the opposition to Cesnola had nothing to do with the old Feuardent charges or any "personal difficulties," but that it was based on the belief of certain trustees that so long as he remained director the museum could not "maintain those relations with other Museums at home and abroad, and with the art and scientific, not to speak of the general public, which are important to its growth and influence." For a time there was talk of expelling the dissidents from the board. "We will be ruined unless the youthful element be kept quiet," Marquand wrote gloomily to Dodge.

In the end, Choate and Dodge persuaded both sides to accept a patched-up truce. De Forest resigned from the executive committee but remained on the board. The special committee on casts was abolished. A year later, Marquand told Dodge that he felt "as if a great weight had been moved from my shoulders." The problem, however, was far from being resolved. Universal respect for Marquand had probably kept Cesnola from being ousted, but this knowledge did nothing to chasten the director's intractable nature. If the museum was on its way to ruin—and Cesnola felt sure that it was—the fault lay solely with the cabal of trustees who were "conspiring" to seize control of it "for their own selfish ends." "With our present divided Board it will be impossible to continue to run the Museum as successfully as before," he wrote to Dodge. "To bring back harmony to the Board is impossible, to get rid all at once of the de Forest faction is also impossible, because none will resign, and the terms of some extend to 1901. What will happen to the Museum between now and then God only knows! I am heartily sick of all this—."

Not sick enough, however, to retire from the field of battle.

SEVEN

Like an antique Roman besieged by Visigoths, Cesnola stood fast through the final years of the expiring century. The press would not leave him alone. When a plumber wearing overalls was denied entrance to the museum on a weekday afternoon in 1897, banner headlines proclaimed the injustice:

SOBER WORKMAN HAS TO LEAVE ART GALLERIES
ART FOR THE WELL DRESSED
SENSITIVE AND REFINED PLUMBER AFFRONTED

Cesnola replied in his usual tone of barely suppressed indignation. The Metropolitan was "a closed corporation," he told reporters. "We do not want, nor will we permit a person who has been digging in a filthy sewer or working among grease and oil to come in here, and, by offensive odors emitted from the dirt on their apparel, make the surroundings uncomfortable for others." The president of the Department of Parks wrote to inquire into the case of the sensitive plumber, and received from Cesnola an impassioned defense of the Metropolitan's uplifting influence on public manners. "You do not see any more persons in the picture galleries blowing their nose with their fingers," he wrote back; "no more dogs brought into the Museum openly or concealed in baskets. There is no more spitting tobacco juice on the gallery floors, to the disgust of all other visitors. There are no more nurses taking children to some corner to defile the floors of the Museum. No persons come now with 'Kodaks' to take 'snap views' of things and visitors. No more whistling, singing, or calling aloud to people from one gallery to another . . ." The barbarian hordes were learning to tread timorously in the muses' shrine.

Not long afterward the director was attacked for debauching public morality. Cesnola had placed on exhibition in the great hall of the new Fifth Avenue wing a colossal bronze group by the Italian sculptor Ernesto Biondi. The piece, which was twenty-two feet long and weighed more than three tons, represented an episode of the ancient Roman Saturnalia—"a night of orgies," as the sculptor described it; "a group of plebeians have met their intoxicated priests on the ancient sacred roadway." *The Times* led the attack, calling the Biondi group "uncommonly offensive," "disgusting in subject," and "a scandal and an outrage," and citing its exhibition as proof of Cesnola's utter unfitness for his job. Several of the trustees agreed with *The Times'* criticism (Robert de Forest found the sculpture "revolting"), and they prevailed upon their colleagues to make Cesnola remove it from the floor. Biondi promptly filed suit for breach of contract. The suit was eventually settled out of court, but the incident did nothing to enhance Cesnola's prestige among artists, critics, or upholders of public morals. Even the conservative *Evening Post*, which had long been sympathetic to the Metropolitan and its trustees, treated the Saturnalia controversy as evidence that "the Metropolitan Museum is in miserable odor." As a result of its unprofessional management, the *Post* said, the museum "would suffer not only in comparison with the provincial museums of Germany, say, but also with the Boston Museum of Art."

The attacks never failed to amaze Cesnola. "I have made in my life some few dear and sincere friends," he confided to his diary, "but I have also made an astonishing number of enemies." He consoled himself with the thought that his work would be better appreciated by the next generation. "If I had not this connection *continually before me*," he wrote to Marquand, "I could not have borne so patiently, as I have done, injustice, contumely, injury, and insult, as varied and cruel as devilish ingenuity could devise—borne them, though the muscles ached for a foe on whom it were possible to avenge the wrong, and the brain reeled at the degradation!"

Cesnola could also find comfort in the museum's steady material growth. Important collections continued to come in by gift or bequest. John Jacob Astor joined the donors in 1888, giving his late wife's extraordinarily fine collection of lace. Mrs. John Crosby Brown, whose husband was a partner in the investment banking firm of Brown Brothers, donated her collection of two hundred and seventy musical instruments in 1889, and then spent the next eighteen years adding to it; by 1906, the collection numbered thirty-five hundred instruments from every continent and culture (including forty-three presented earlier by the widow of trustee Joseph W. Drexel), and had become world famous. Edward C. Moore, the president of Tiffany & Company, died in 1891 and left a great number of objets d'art—Greek and Etruscan vases, Tanagra figures, glass, jewelry, porcelain, metalwork, and a reference library of several hundred illustrated volumes. Most of the bequests in these years had strings attached. The Moore objects were to be kept together and preserved as a separate collection in the museum. The Heber R. Bishop Collection of more than a thousand Chinese jades, which arrived in 1902, was subject to the stipulation in Bishop's will that their installation in the museum should exactly duplicate the former installation in the ballroom of his house (he left a sum of $55,000 for this purpose). Some rather meretricious works arrived with great fanfare, such as Emanuel Leutze's gigantic *Washington Crossing the Delaware*, presented in 1896 by John S. Kennedy, "a work of art," as Mark Twain put it, "which would have made Washington hesitate about crossing, if he could have foreseen what advantage was going to be taken of it." * Conversely, some first-rate things arrived with little or no fanfare, and were only "discovered" later. In 1889—the same year the museum took in Catharine Wolfe's Salon pictures —it also received Manet's *Boy With a Sword* and *Woman With a Parrot*, the first two Manets to enter any museum. Erwin Davis, a discerning New York collector, had bought them in at an auction rather than see them go "at meagre figures into the mansions on Fifth Avenue"; he presented them immediately to the Metropolitan, along with Bastien-Lepage's *Joan of Arc*. Although Lepage's picture of The Maid listening to her supernatural advisors was and still is far more popular with the public, the reaction to the two Manets, both extremely advanced paintings at that time, was surprisingly favorable. In a period when French critics were subjecting the Im-

* Twain visited the Metropolitan once, and was told by an attendant that he would have to leave his cane in the cloakroom. "Leave my cane!" the author thundered. "Leave my cane! Then how do you expect me to poke holes through the oil paintings?"

pressionists to the most ferocious attacks, New York accepted the Manets without a murmur of protest.

Contrary to Prime's dire predictions, the entangling alliance with New York City had not undermined the museum's independence. In fact, it sometimes appeared to be the other way around. A letter from President Jesup of the American Museum to President Marquand of the Metropolitan in 1895 gave the surprising assurance that "no appointments will be made to the Park Department *that will not be agreeable to our Museums.*" Jesup said the Mayor had sent him the list of candidates, "which I will show you when I see you." The political influence of museum trustees also showed in the gradually rising appropriations. In 1893 the city's annual grant to the Metropolitan for maintenance rose from $70,000 to $95,000; in 1901 it rose again, to $150,000, and five years later it reached $200,000. The city continued to pay all the costs of new construction. Three new wings were added during Cesnola's time. The south wing (1888) and the north wing (1894) provided space without grandeur, both being designed in the same red brick Ruskin Gothic style as the original building. The new Fifth Avenue wing, completed in 1902, spoke another language entirely. Designed by Richard Morris Hunt, a Metropolitan trustee and the most fashionable architect of his day, and finished after his death by his son Richard Howland Hunt, the Fifth Avenue wing cost one million dollars in city funds and concealed the museum's relatively humble origins behind a monumental limestone facade. At last New York had a neoclassical palace of art, "the most noteworthy building of its kind in the city," the *Evening Post* proudly observed, "one of the finest in the world, and the only public building in recent years which approaches in dignity and grandeur the museums of the old world."

The Fifth Avenue wing announced the opening of a new and grandiose era for the Metropolitan, but that era had really begun a year earlier with the amazing bequest of Jacob S. Rogers. Oddly enough, the man whose gift catapulted the museum into its affluent future was himself a relic of much earlier modes, an eccentric whose iron whims seemed totally out of place in the expanding business world of Morgan and Rockefeller. "His character was anything but lovable," one of the few men who ever gained the slightest entry into Rogers' confidence said of him. "His principal aim in life was to do something wholly unexpected of him." In this he succeeded remarkably.

Rogers made locomotives. The Rogers Locomotive Works in Paterson, New Jersey, manufactured the finest product on the market, and in this period of frantically competitive railroad-building the product was in considerable demand. The richer Rogers got, the more irascible, choleric, and disagreeable he seemed to others. He infuriated his competitors by paying very high wages and telling his workers that he would be glad to pay them even more if only the other firms would do the same. He held a lifelong grudge against the city of Paterson because the city authorities had once blocked his acquisition of a plot of land near his factory; Rogers lost no opportunity to show the town what he thought of it, and upon his death the Paterson *Guardian* described its wealthiest citizen as "a pure animal man, with no sentiments born of human love or human sympathy." Rogers never married, and of course there was no end of stories about him. One of the favorites was that he had been spurned in his youth by a Paterson girl, and that the wound had marked him for life. It was known that in 1873, when the financial panic temporarily slowed new orders for locomotives, Rogers had closed down the factory and gone to Paris, where he indulged an unsuspected side of his nature by throwing lavish parties for the belles of the city. One such diversion, during the height of the Franco-Prussian War when prices were sky-high, allegedly cost him $15,000, another one $20,000. In Paris, so the hometown fraus whispered, he fell in love with another Paterson girl (or maybe the same one), followed her back home, bought her a house in Waterbury, Connecticut, and gave her $40,000 to invest; some said she, too, refused to marry him, others maintained that they had a common law marriage and a child together.

The one certainty in everyone's mind was that Jacob Rogers was the meanest man in Paterson. He flatly refused all requests from local charities. Once, when some neighborhood boys asked to play baseball on a field he owned, Rogers said he would give them a five-year lease provided that they agreed to put up a fence and a grandstand, both of which would revert to him at the end of five years, and as for the annual rental . . . at this point the boys fled. Another time, a miraculously unwarned lady came to his door. "I am engaged in a very important religious movement," she said, "and I need money for it. I prayed fervently for money and God Almighty appeared to me and told me to go to Mr. Rogers and ask him for five thousand dollars, and God Almighty said that you would give it to me."

Rogers eyed her thoughtfully. "By God Almighty," he said, "you mean the Being who created these trees and all this around here?"

"Certainly," she agreed.

"Then go back to your God Almighty," Rogers said, "and tell Him that for once He made a mistake."

Rogers had two nieces and a nephew who were not without hopes, although the old curmudgeon had expressed himself plainly on the subject of inheritances. It was not right to give people money, he often said. Every man ought to work for a living, and if he used common sense he could not help but make a fortune. To give people money destroyed their value as human beings. "If I could convert all my possessions into paper and provide that this paper should be burned after my death I should do so," he once boasted. Luckily he had a better idea. Rogers read in the newspaper about a wealthy man in Chicago who had ignored all his relatives and left his entire estate to educational institutions. The will had been contested but upheld, and Rogers sent for and received a copy of it. He also made, about this time, the first of several yearly visits to the Metropolitan Museum.

Up to this point there had been no indication that Rogers had any interest whatsoever in art. He owned no art objects of any value, and the only pictures in his house were a few mediocre paintings by unknown artists—mostly miniatures of young girls. In 1883, however, Jacob S. Rogers became an annual member of the Metropolitan, and each year after that he paid $10.00 to renew the membership. As a result he received the museum's annual reports, which throughout this period, at the end of the yearly listing of accomplishments, added a poignant appeal for substantial endowment funds whose income could be used to purchase works of art. (New York millionaires did not like to give endowment funds, Cesnola complained. "They will give money for buying collections, and for building purposes, because both remain visible monuments of their generosity . . . while endowment funds are invisible and remain unknown to the general public.")

Rogers used to deliver his $10.00 membership check in person to Cesnola, who apparently received him cordially. In 1891, during the annual visit, he asked Cesnola for a copy of the Metropolitan's charter, constitution, lease, and by-laws. Cesnola obliged him. From then on his visits became more frequent. He asked a great many questions, Cesnola said, most of which had to do with the museum's financial resources, its costs, the amount of its appropriations from the city, and the amount of work done by the trustees. Cesnola did not know whether Mr. Rogers ever visited the art galleries when he came to the museum. Quite suddenly, in 1899, the visits ceased. Cesnola thought no more about it. The man had said something about remembering the Metropolitan in his will, but Cesnola knew nothing about him, and no ten-dollar Annual Member had ever left the museum more than one or two thousand dollars.

When Rogers died in the summer of 1901—felled by heat prostration in the Union League Club, where no one knew him—he left annuities of $1,000 each to two nieces and a legacy of $250,000 to his nephew, who had apparently expected much more. The remainder of his estate, which was believed at first to total $8,000,000, he left to the Metropolitan Museum of Art as an endowment fund, the income from which was to be used "for the purchase of rare and desirable art objects, and in the purchase of books for the Library of said Museum, and for such purposes exclusively."

The trustees could scarcely believe it. "The wonderful will of Jacob Rogers with its splendid possibilities for the museum has astonished us all greatly," Dodge wrote to Marquand. "It seems like a golden dream." From Washington, D.C., Secretary of the Interior J. Edwards Clark wrote to Cesnola that "It is an event on which the whole United States are to be congratulated; for it gives pecuniary independence to the chief art power of the country." The news made headlines everywhere, and utterly unhinged some citizens. A cheerful elderly lady turned up in Paterson to claim the money, saying that she was the Metropolitan Museum of Art. She showed everyone a newspaper photo of the museum and said, "That's my picture. That's me. Jake Rogers left me all his money, and I'm going to have it, too." On being committed to a rest home, she gave her name as Mary Martha Paterson, but insisted that Mary Martha really stood for Metropolitan Museum.

Rogers' heirs contested the will, as the trustees had expected they would. Robert de Forest and Elihu Root handled the case during two years of delicate litigation, which ended in a settlement out of court. The family abandoned all claims to the estate, and received in return the sum of $250,000. The museum's share came to just under $5,000,000, which in 1904, one year after the settlement, yielded an annual income of about $200,000. Through merest chance and the quirks of human personality, a respectable but still struggling institution had been transformed into a powerful and independent force in the markets of art. The founders, God rest them, could sleep content.

Not many of the founding trustees would live to see the vast changes that lay ahead. A mortuary pall darkens the annual reports for the years 1899 to 1904, during which the deaths of nine trustees were recorded. John Taylor Johnston had died in 1893. Henry Marquand, increasingly enfeebled as the years drew on but still lavish in his benefactions, slipped away quietly in 1902. His successor was Frederick Rhinelander, a scion of old New York who had already given thirty years of his life to the Metropolitan. "He is a conservative man," Cesnola said of him when he was elected president, "and under his administration there will probably be no change of policy." Rhinelander's administration lasted only a little more than two years, ending with his death in 1904. Before the year was out, the seemingly indestructible director had followed him to the grave.

Cesnola worked right up to the end. He put in a full and busy week at the museum, went home on Friday night to his apartment in the Hotel Seymour, and died there the next morning, of acute indigestion, at the age of seventy-two. The shocked trustees offered up a handsome valedictory for his twenty-seven years of devotion to the museum. "His fidelity, his minute attention to his duties, and his capacity for work during his long career of service, merit great praise," they stated. "Whoever shall become his successor, and with whatever gifts he shall be endowed, the martial, independent figure of General di Cesnola—somewhat restive in opposition and somewhat impetuous in speech and action, but at all times devoted to duty and winning the affection of his subordinates and associates—will long remain a kindly and grateful memory." Choate, who had defended Cesnola so skillfully in the Feuardent trial and then joined the forces seeking to oust him in 1895, paid his own tribute a few years later. "He was a tremendous driving machine," Choate said of him. "He kept the ball constantly rolling, and the Museum owes him more than some of us have been willing to admit, to his tremendous energy and interest in it."

The day after Cesnola died, J. P. Morgan was elected president of the Metropolitan and the new era began in earnest.

PART II
A CLIMATE
FOR
ACQUISITION

EIGHT

By the turn of the century, the concentration of gigantic wealth in the hands of the new industrial entrepreneurs had begun to worry some Americans. Feeling was building up against the financiers and business overlords whom Thorstein Veblen dubbed "malefactors of great wealth," and whose power sometimes seemed limitless. Had they not made a mockery of the Sherman Anti-Trust Act, passed in 1890 to prevent just such monopolistic practices as those in which they engaged every day? Had they not succeeded in 1895 in having the income tax declared unconstitutional? Even Henry Cabot Lodge, long regarded as the leading spokesman of the wealthy class in the Senate, expressed anxiety over "the gigantic modern plutocracy and its lawless way," and warned that the "darkest sign" of the age was "the way in which money and the acquisition of money . . . seems in the last analysis rampant in every portion of the community."

To most Americans of this period, John Pierpont Morgan was the personification of arrogant and overbearing plutocracy. Morgan's imposing bulk, his swollen and livid nose (permanently disfigured by the *acne rosacea* from which he had suffered since childhood), and his terrifying gaze—the photographer Edward Steichen said that meeting his black eyes was like confronting the headlights of an express train bearing down on you—all served to overawe those who had to deal with him. The financial genius that he applied to his business affairs was not something that the general public could readily admire. The public took note of the impressive fees charged by the firm of Drexel, Morgan and Company for reorganizing bankrupt or overextended railroads; it did not see that these reorganizations were gradually bringing stability into the chaotic and self-destructive competition of the rival entrepreneurs, whose short-term profiteering had been in large part responsible for the wave of financial panics and depressions during the previous decades. Morgan's most spectacular achievements in the financial field—the loan that saved the credit of the United States Government during the 1895 run on gold; the formation in 1901 of the United States Steel Corporation, the first billion-dollar trust; his leadership during the catastrophic panic of 1907, when Morgan and a few other private bankers narrowly prevented the failure of the Stock Exchange by an incredibly skillful diversion of funds to critical areas—these triumphs were scarcely understood outside the world of high finance in which Morgan moved, and in which his authority was without parallel. That his genius might be misunderstood and his motives maligned by outsiders did not appear to trouble Morgan at all. Few men in any field have ever been granted such supreme self-confidence, and with such cause.

Pierpont Morgan conformed to very few of the popular stereotypes regarding rich Americans. He had been educated largely abroad, at a private school in Switzerland and later at the University of Göttingen, where he showed such a talent for mathematics that he was urged to stay on and teach it. His father, Junius Spencer Morgan, a well-to-do banker first in Hartford and then in Boston, had moved to London before the Civil War and established himself there as a power in international finance. Although the younger Morgan decided to make his own career and his home in New York, he retained from his youth an outlook and a style of life that were in some ways more European than American, and throughout his life he was as much at home in London or Paris as he was in New York. Other New York millionaires might build themselves ostentatious replicas of French chateaux or Renaissance palazzi—by 1900, Fifth Avenue from Forty-second Street to Seventy-second Street was lined with these competitive piles; Morgan, content for the moment with his comfortable but relatively inconspicuous brownstone house on Murray Hill, was the only one among his wealthy contemporaries who actually lived on a scale befitting a Renaissance prince. He refused to follow the tides of fashion by taking his family to Newport in the summer, preferring the solid and rather somber country house, Cragston, that he had bought in 1871, overlooking the Hudson

River just south of West Point. Morgan set his own style in everything he undertook, whether in banking, or in yachts, or in the breeding of championship collies. When he began, therefore, to build up what many scholars consider the greatest private art collection ever assembled, it is not surprising that he did so with the assurance of a Medici prince, and according to the methods that he had followed throughout his adult life.

As a child in Switzerland, Morgan collected fragments of stained glass that he found outside the walls of ruined churches. He had picked up various objets d'art over the next few decades, and during the 1880s he acquired some typically mediocre pictures by the French Salon artists. It was not until 1891 that he began to show a serious interest in books and manuscripts, his first passion as a collector, and not until the very end of the century, when he was in his sixties, that he began buying art objects on a large scale. Why did he start so late? It may have been out of deference to his father, who collected pictures and art objects on a relatively modest scale. Morgan admired and revered his father, and he might have felt an old-fashioned reluctance to enter a field where the older man held first claim. A simpler explanation is that he did not have the money. Until Junius Morgan died in 1890, Pierpont was still very much the son of a rich man. In spite of his vast influence and his high fees, the income of a merchant banker did not begin to match the earnings of some of the industrialists he helped to underwrite. Morgan's real wealth was never as boundless as people assumed, and the astonishing fact is that from 1890 on a major proportion of it—more than fifty percent—went into works of art. Having become the greatest financier of his day, Morgan would settle for nothing less than total victory on the battlefields of art.

Morgan made a practice of collecting other men's collections. "What's the use of bothering about one little piece when I might get them all?" he said more than once, as he went about Europe snapping up one after another of the major collections brought together during the time of Napoleon III. His methods were brusque and a little frightening. "I've heard enough," he would tell a dealer. "I'll take it for what you paid, plus ten percent. What did you pay?" He was accused of driving the prices of works of art beyond the reach of ordinary collectors, and he was castigated for buying quantities of fakes and passing them off on the Metropolitan Museum. It is true that the prices for certain classes of art objects rose

threefold during the twenty years of Morgan's active buying. "No price," he
used to say, "is too high for an object of unquestioned beauty and known
authenticity." It is also true that he acquired some fakes. He could hardly
have avoided it, buying on such a tremendous scale. On the other hand,
very few collectors have ever managed to combine quantity with such
a high level of quality in so many different fields of art. Paintings, furniture, bronzes, porcelains, enamels, ivories, tapestries, miniatures, armor,
antiquities—there is hardly a class of objects that Morgan did not collect,
and what he sought in every case were the finest works obtainable, the
masterpieces. Like many large and powerful men, he loved small things.
Exquisitely carved ivories, medieval reliquaries inset with precious stones,
illuminated manuscripts, champlevé enamels—these were his particular
delights, and the surest evidence of his own taste. That he had taste, and a
keen eye for craftsmanship if not always for the subtler workings of the artist's mind, seems beyond question. There is for example the often-told story
of young Joseph Duveen's first brush with him. Feeling that his uncle,
Henry Duveen, with whom Morgan usually dealt, was not getting as much
as he should from the great man, Joseph put together a collection of thirty
miniatures in which six were very rare and the rest relatively undistin-
guished. Morgan took a quick look, and asked the price of the lot. Duveen
named a figure. Morgan unhesitatingly picked out the six best, put them in
his pocket, divided Duveen's figure by thirty, multiplied by six, and announced what his purchase had cost. "You're only a boy, Joe," Uncle
Henry chortled afterward. "It takes a man to deal with Morgan." Another
tale, possibly apocryphal, is that shortly after Morgan had bought six Early
Christian silver plates that had been dug up on Cyprus, a dealer informed
him that they were forgeries, manufactured quite recently by a Naples silversmith. "Anything else this gentleman created I should be interested in
purchasing," Morgan unhesitatingly replied. The plates, of course, were
genuine, and they are now in the Metropolitan. Morgan never doubted his
own eye for quality, or his sovereign right to possess it.

Morgan's active connection with the Metropolitan coincided roughly
with his collecting years. Although he had contributed to the museum's initial fund drive and had been listed among the first fifty patrons, he did not
come on the board of trustees until 1889. He was elected to the executive
committee in 1892, but resigned from it two years later because he could

not spare the time. The mere presence of Morgan on any board carried enormous weight, however—his letter to Marquand, as we have seen, was a crucial factor in the defeat of the move to oust Cesnola—and in 1901, when he came back on the executive committee, the Morgan presence soon became dominant. The following year he made what was in effect his first major art purchase in bulk. A collection of more than two thousand Chinese porcelains had been on exhibition at the Metropolitan for several years, as a loan from the banker James A. Garland. The museum had rather hoped to get the collection as a gift, but when Garland died in 1902 he had made no such provision, and they were purchased instead by Henry Duveen for $500,000. Early the next morning, Morgan paid a visit to Duveen's gallery, repurchased the entire collection for presentation to the Metropolitan, and instructed Duveen to fill out the missing sequences. The Garland Collection never even left the museum; from then on, however, it was known as the Morgan Collection. Morgan was elected first vice-president of the museum in February 1904, and when Rhinelander died that fall he was the inevitable choice to succeed him.

With Morgan's assumption of the presidency, the concept of the museum underwent a fundamental change. No longer would the Metropolitan defer to European institutions, or limit itself to the utilitarian and educational ideals of the South Kensington Museum. Casts, reproductions, and second-rate works of art might still retain some usefulness for artisans and students, but the emphasis had shifted unmistakably to the great and original masterpieces, the treasures that old Europe proved only too willing, after all, to relinquish. All this was spelled out clearly in the museum's thirty-fifth annual report, covering the year 1905. In the past, the report stated, the museum had accepted many gifts, "which may sometimes have included objects hardly worthy of permanent display." From now on, however, it would "rigorously exclude all which do not attain to acknowledged standards." The trustees' principal aim for the future was "not merely to assemble beautiful objects and display them harmoniously, still less to amass a collection of unrelated curios, but to group together the masterpieces of different countries and times in such relation and sequence as to illustrate the history of art in the broadest sense, to make plain its teaching and to inspire and direct its national development." To a sensitive observer, the change could be felt in the very atmosphere of the place. "Acquisition—

acquisition if need be on the highest terms—may, during the years to come, bask here as in a climate it has never before enjoyed," Henry James wrote in 1907, in the section of *The American Scene* that dealt with the Metropolitan. "There was money in the air, ever so much money—that was, grossly expressed, the sense of the whole intimation. And the money was to be all for the most exquisite things—for *all* the most exquisite things except creation, which was to be off the scene altogether; for art, selection, criticism, for knowledge, piety, taste. . . . The Museum, in short, was going to be great . . ."

Some idea of what was involved can be gained by comparing the costs of running the Metropolitan at the beginning and at the end of Morgan's presidency. In 1904 the annual operating cost exclusive of purchases of art came to $185,084, and was covered largely by the city's $150,000 appropriation. In 1913, the year Morgan died, operating costs had soared to $362,-948, and—in spite of increased contributions from the city and a very large, unexpected and unrestricted bequest of money in 1908 from Frederick C. Hewitt, an Owego, New York, gentleman of leisure who was not even an Annual Member—there was a deficit of $71,261. Deficits did not concern Morgan. His usual procedure was to announce the figure at a meeting of the board, and then go around the table, his express-train eyes interrogating each trustee in turn, until the deficit had been erased. Morgan's own check was invariably the largest. He had taken pains, however, to fill the vacancies on the board with millionaires of his own choosing—men like Henry Walters, Henry Clay Frick, John G. Johnson, George F. Baker, and Edward S. Harkness—and as a result the Metropolitan's board of trustees was not only the most exclusive club in New York, but also, without a doubt, the richest.

The first test of the new policy on gifts came in 1906 when George A. Hearn, a New York retailer and a Metropolitan trustee who had previously given the museum twenty-four paintings by American artists, offered to present twenty-seven more American pictures together with a fund of $150,000, the income of which was to be used to buy paintings by living American artists. Like most of the early benefactors, Hearn wanted the museum to keep his gift together permanently in a room bearing his name. The trustees explained politely that their new policy made this impossible. A compromise was eventually worked out, with the museum accepting a "moral obligation" to keep the Hearn pictures together in one gallery for not less than twenty-five years, and Hearn himself agreeing that the museum could sell or exchange any of the pictures he had given for better examples. Five years later, Hearn gave fifty-one more pictures and an additional fund of $100,000 in memory of his son, Arthur Hoppock Hearn.

The Hearn Fund struck some of the trustees as a somewhat mixed blessing, for at this period the Metropolitan was not greatly interested in American art. From time to time in the past, efforts had been made to build up a representative American collection. Cesnola had suggested in 1879 that the museum acquire pictures by the early American painters, and a start had been made along these lines: Marquand presented John Trumbull's portrait of Alexander Hamilton in 1881; H. O. Havemeyer, whose later gifts would establish the Metropolitan's greatness in several areas, gave the Gilbert Stuart portrait of Washington known as the *Carroll Washington* in 1888; a full-length Washington portrait by Charles Willson Peale came in 1896 as the gift of Collis P. Huntington; and the following year, Samuel Avery gave Matthew Pratt's famous conversation piece, *The American School,* showing a group of eighteenth century American painters in Benjamin West's studio in London. In 1905 the trustees recorded once again their intention to build up "the evidence of what America has done" in the arts. The trustees of the Morgan era did not really believe, though, that America had done very much. American pictures and statuary might have a certain historical interest, but for the exquisite things, the masterpieces, one looked automatically to the older and richer culture of Europe, and one also looked increasingly to the distant past. As Henry James pointed out, it was the acquisition and not the creation of great art that interested the millionaires.

When it came to choosing a new director to replace Cesnola, the trustees also looked to Europe. There had been a good deal of speculation in the newspapers regarding the appointment. Several candidates had been mentioned, the most likely of whom seemed to be Edward Robinson, the director of the Boston Museum of Fine Arts. But could any American be truly qualified for the job? Robert W. de Forest, who had resurfaced as an active force on the Metropolitan board after Marquand's death, becoming secretary at the same time that Morgan was elected president, spelled out the requirements for the ideal director in a personal memorandum. Accord-

ing to de Forest, he should combine executive ability, the qualities of a
gentleman (Ah, there, Cesnola!), expert knowledge of art, and museum experience. These rare qualities were gloriously met, or so it appeared to
Morgan and his confreres, in Sir Caspar Purdon Clarke, the director of the
South Kensington Museum in London, who greatly disconcerted his coun-
trymen by agreeing, early in 1905, to leave that post for the Metropolitan.
His departure was the occasion for a famous anecdote. The secretary of the
South Kensington Museum, just prior to going on leave of absence, had entered bids on some Chinese porcelains and some tapestries that were com-
ing up for auction in Paris. On his return, he inquired first about the porcelains. "No, sir," an aide replied. "J. P. Morgan bought them." The secretary
asked next about the tapestries. "Mr. Morgan got them," he was told. "Good
God," he said, "I must talk to Sir Purdon." "Sorry, sir," came the reply,
"Mr. Morgan bought him also."

As though sensitive to possible criticism for having chosen another foreigner to run the museum, the trustees took pains to emphasize Clarke's
practical and down-to-earth qualities. "In appearance and manner he is
more American than English," their report stated. "He is essentially a man
of the people, has made his own career by his own activity and energy and
he is thoroughly democratic and approachable." Until he joined the South
Kensington Museum in 1892 as chief keeper, becoming assistant director
and then director in 1896, Clarke had spent most of his life in the British
civil service. Trained as an architect, he had built embassies, consulates,
and other outposts of British pomp in many different countries, had spent a
long time in India, and had acquired a vast knowledge of various European
and Asian arts and crafts. "His willingness to accept the position will undoubtedly create great surprise in Great Britain," the trustees' report stated.
"The attraction to him is evidently the great opportunity of developing our
Museum in New York." An additional and doubtless minor attraction was the
salary, which was exactly double what he had been receiving in England.

Sir Purdon Clarke, who had made only one previous visit to America,
some twenty years before, certainly did not look very American. *The New
York Times,* in the sort of prose it went in for in those days, described him
as a man of medium height with "beautiful gray hair that falls into graceful
little kinks as it falls over his ears," and added the information that his
gray moustache was "a kinky thing also." For once, though, *The Times'*

opinion seemed to coincide with that of the trustees. Clarke was reported to be the most democratic of men, not above taking off his coat and working alongside the lower orders. " 'That's the way to get nice work done,' " he was quoted by *The Times'* interviewer. " 'There's no sense in putting on airs with workmen.' " The workmen and the staff liked him well enough, but it soon became dismally apparent to everyone that Clarke was the wrong man for the job. The Metropolitan needed a complete and professional reorganization. An old civil servant like Sir Purdon had functioned splendidly within the established and well-organized South Kensington Museum, but he seemed utterly incapable of planning or creating such an organization where none existed. Most of the real administrative burden during his brief tenure was carried by Edward Robinson, who had resigned as director of the Boston Museum of Fine Arts in August 1905 and a few months later accepted the assistant directorship of the Metropolitan under Sir Purdon Clarke.

The New York climate affected Clarke's health, which began to decline almost as soon as he arrived. In the summer of 1909 he was granted a year's leave of absence, but his strength did not return. He resigned in June 1910, and Robinson began his long career as the Metropolitan's third director. Morgan, meanwhile, had hired another Englishman whose tenure would be no less brief than Purdon Clarke's, but a great deal more stormy.

Roger Fry was a Quaker, and an intellectual snob of the most prickly sort. He disliked Americans, and he seems to have harbored the simultaneous fascination with and contempt for great wealth that so influenced the life and writings of F. Scott Fitzgerald. Fry's relationship with J. P. Morgan was complex, ambiguous in the extreme, and replete with misunderstandings, and in view of their vastly dissimilar personalities the final disastrous encounter between them was probably unavoidable.

Fry had started out to be a scientist. He became interested in art while he was an undergraduate at Cambridge, and, overriding the objections of his father, an eminent lawyer and a Quaker of stern principle, he threw over a promising scientific career to become a painter. Fry's stubbornness commands respect. As an undergraduate, he refused his father's offer to increase his allowance substantially if he would promise not to study from the nude. He painted doggedly all his life, with little or no encouragement from anyone and in defiance of what he must eventually have realized to be a very limited talent. His real *métier* lay, however, in being able to see and communicate the unique qualities of other artists.

He had taken to lecturing and writing about art as a means of earning a living, and his scholarly yet extremely lucid articles in the *Burlington* and other art journals soon established him as one of the leading art critics of the day. Fry's early articles and monographs dealt mainly with the Italian masters of the quattrocento and the high Renaissance. Following nearly a century of neglect, during which English collectors bought for the most part contemporary English art or very large seventeenth century European paintings, the market for the earlier masters had rather dramatically revived. Quattrocento pictures that had gone for the price of the frame only twenty years before were selling for as much as £20,000, while Raphael, the only Old Master to retain his reputation and his price throughout the nineteenth century, had soared out of range of all but the wealthiest collectors. Increasingly since the 1880s, the wealthiest and most active buyers in the picture market were Americans. William H. Vanderbilt and a few others remained loyal to contemporary Salon painting, but the new trend, inspired in large part by the proselytizing art scholarship of Bernard Berenson, was toward the art of the Italian Renaissance. Isabella Stewart Gardner, Berenson's patron and pupil, paid £4,500 to the Chigi family in 1899 for Botticelli's *Madonna of the Eucharist,* and £20,600 in 1896 for Titian's *The Rape of Europa.* Pierpont Morgan had also entered the lists, paying £100,000 in 1900 for the Raphael *Colonna Altarpiece,* and where Morgan ventured others followed. Because Italian paintings of the fifteenth and sixteenth centuries had been in relative eclipse for so long, and because the American millionaires had grown wary of Continental art dealers, the professional art expert—the scholar whose trained eye could differentiate between authentic quattrocento or cinquecento technique and heavily varnished imitation—was emerging as a new and potent force in the art market. Roger Fry's credentials in this field were nearly as impressive as Berenson's. His monographs on Bellini and Veronese were considered superior to anything yet written on those masters, and his eye was superbly discerning. Several wealthy American collectors had engaged him to buy for them at London sales. In 1904, Fry was introduced to Morgan, who sent him to Liverpool to report on a picture in which the Metropolitan was interested. His first impressions of the great financier were hardly reassuring. Morgan, Fry wrote his wife, was "the most repulsively ugly man . . . with a great strawberry nose." He behaved "like a crowned head"; nevertheless, he was obviously "a very remarkable and powerful man."

Just before Christmas that year, Fry received a cable from Sir Caspar Purdon Clarke in New York, offering him the post of assistant director of the Metropolitan. Fry went to New York and met the trustees. He was very tempted by the offer, considering the great opportunities of a museum "that had more money at its disposal than any other gallery in the world," but he did not like the idea of living in New York or of working for Morgan, whom he described as "all powerful" at the museum. "I don't think he wants anything but flattery," Fry wrote home. "He is quite indifferent to the real value of things. All he wants experts for is to give him a sense of his own wonderful sagacity . . . The man is so swollen with pride and a sense of his own power that it never occurs to him that other people have any rights." Fry decided that he could never put up with that sort of treatment, and he declined the Metropolitan's offer. Morgan, showing no evidence of insensitivity or swollen pride, did not even take offense. In fact, he made Fry the official European buying agent for the Metropolitan, and personally subscribed £1,000 to the *Burlington* magazine in London, which Fry was then helping to revive.

Fry returned to England, where he soon found himself a leading candidate for the top post at the National Gallery, whose director, Sir Edward Poynter, had just died. While the National Gallery trustees were trying to decide between Fry and Sir Charles Holroyd, the Metropolitan's trustees came up with another offer—they would engage Fry as curator of paintings, with the understanding that he could spend a part of his time in Europe. This was a crucial point to Fry. His wife Helen was seriously ill, suffering from a tragic and undiagnosed mental condition that was discovered, after her death in 1937, to be the result of an incurable thickening of the bone in her skull. She could not leave England, and Fry did not want to be away from her for any length of time. The Metropolitan's new offer seemed an ideal solution, providing a steady income to pay his wife's mounting medical bills while leaving him free to live mostly at home.

Fry's tentative acceptance nearly foundered, however, on a shoal of misunderstandings. It appeared that several of the trustees did not know of Fry's verbal agreement with William Laffan, the publisher of the New York *Sun* and Morgan's principal lieutenant on the Metropolitan board; they assumed that he would live in New York and make occasional trips to Europe. Fry on his part had assumed that his appointment was permanent, and he balked when he learned that he was merely "to hold office at the pleasure of the Board." Meanwhile, the National Gallery in London had finally made up *its* mind, and offered him the directorship. After a number of urgent transatlantic cables, Fry made what must have been the fairly agonizing decision to pass up the top museum position in England. Laffan wrote to Sir Purdon Clarke in January 1906 to say that the incident was satisfactorily resolved. "Fry, now that he has made his choice, is happy," Laffan said, "but apprehensive of a storm of criticism of his unpatriotic choice. It will do him good."

For a while the arrangement worked smoothly. Fry found the Metropolitan in a "state of chaos," and threw himself enthusiastically into the task of creating order. One of his first jobs was to remove from exhibition and reclassify the Vanderbilt drawings, lopping away the spurious "Old Master" attributions that had been one of the worst blots on the museum's scholarship. Fry made up for this surgery by several brilliant purchases of authentic Old Master drawings at bargain prices—the top prize being a Leonardo da Vinci *Head of an Old Man* that he picked up at a 1909 sale in London for £110, "with a very stunning Jordaens thrown in" for good measure. He also bought paintings—"heads of pictures," he wrote to his wife, ". . . Lotto, Goya, Guardi, Murillo, Bugiardini and so on, and am getting ready a great gallery, a sort of Salon Carré, where all the real things will be seen in the hopes that it may throw a lurid light on the nameless horrors of modern art which fill the remainder."

Fry's first article in the Metropolitan Museum *Bulletin,* which had started publication in 1905, outlined very frankly the gaps in the picture collection. There was "only one aspect of the art which is adequately represented," he wrote, "and that is the sentimental and anecdotic side of nineteenth century painting . . . We have as yet no Byzantine paintings, no Giotto, no Giottoesque, no Mantegna, no Botticelli, no Leonardo, no Raphael, no Michelangelo. The student of the history of art must either travel in Europe or apply himself to reproductions." The Metropolitan trustees at this point were interested principally in what Fry called "exceptional and spectacular pieces," which made the going rather tough. Fry's own inclination was to supplement the exceptional acquisitions with pictures that were good but not yet fashionable, a category in which he included the still highly controversial French Impressionists. In 1907, at a moment when most of the older trustees were out of town, Fry persuaded Edward Robinson to let him bid at the Charpentier sale in Paris for Renoir's magnificent portrait of *Madame Charpentier and Her Children.* Fry got the picture for just under $20,000, and the conservative trustees, when they learned of it, were nearly speechless with indignation. It is difficult today to understand how this painting, the key work of Renoir's early years and one of the greatest Impressionist pictures in existence, could have caused such consternation and dismay. Both Fry and Bryson Burroughs, his young assistant, nearly lost their jobs as a result of the purchase, and the ill feeling that had been brewing between Fry and Morgan was certainly intensified.

The ill feeling, one gathers, emanated almost entirely from Fry. Although he had discovered by this time that some Americans were "all right even when rich, and a few quite delightful," he had made up his mind that the main obstacle to the Metropolitan's professional development was its president. Morgan's unilateral buying often threw the staff into confusion. He would sometimes buy works of art for the museum when he was abroad without bothering to inform the other trustees or the director, who would then have to scurry about raising the money to pay for them. Fry accompanied the great banker on several of these buying trips. He resented every minute of his time thus spent, and he poured out his resentment in letters which reveal more about Fry than they do about Morgan. The picture drawn from these letters by Fry's great friend and biographer, the novelist Virginia Woolf, is vitriolic to the point of parody. Morgan behaves boorishly, spends money like a *nouveau riche* bourgeois, and shows himself indifferent to everything but flattery. Stopping at the Grand Hotel in Perugia, Fry is accosted by "a little Levantine or Maltese gibbering in broken English and broken Italian," who offers to sell them a seventeenth century crucifix. Fry notes the indifferent workmanship and prepares to get rid of the fellow, who suddenly whips out a stiletto from the shaft of the cross. "This was the *clou* of the piece and I knew Morgan well enough to guess how likely he was to be taken by it," Fry writes. " 'Shows what the fellows

did in those days! Stick a man while he was praying! Yes, very interesting.'
For a crude historical imagination was the only flaw in his otherwise perfect insensibility." Neither Fry nor his biographer makes clear whether
Morgan actually *bought* the crucifix, which does not appear in any inven-
tory of the Morgan collections; the incident simply provided a satisfying
outlet for Fry's venom.

There is no evidence that Morgan was even remotely aware of Fry's
seething resentment toward him. Morgan did not write personal letters, preferring the telegraph or the newly invented telephone (he was one of the
telephone company's first subscribers in New York). He had long been accustomed to giving orders and having them obeyed without question by efficient subordinates, and since 1907, the year he more or less retired from
banking, he had applied his business methods to the full-time pursuit of
art. John G. Johnson, the Philadelphia lawyer and collector whom Morgan
had brought on the Metropolitan board of trustees, agreed with Fry that
the Morgan brand of one-man rule had its drawbacks. "The trouble is," he
wrote Fry, "that everyone is under the coercion of Mr. M.'s dominating
will. No one does, or dares, resist it." Morgan's will was like a force of nature, implacable and impervious to mere human disturbances; his methods
bruised many egos, but his own egoism encompassed an ambition that
went far beyond the simple vanity which was all Fry saw. Morgan probably intended that his own proliferating collections would come eventually
to the Metropolitan. Some of his most fabulous purchases had gone there
directly—the Garland porcelains, the five Sacrament tapestries, the
Hoentschel Collection of decorative arts—and it is quite conceivable that
in making a major acquisition he did not always distinguish clearly in his
own mind between the museum and his private collection. In the summer
of 1909, however, a misunderstanding over this particular distinction
caused Fry's long-simmering wrath to boil over.

Fry was no longer the curator of paintings at this point. He had persuaded the trustees that he could be more useful as the museum's European adviser and purchasing agent, living in England and receiving in addition to his salary a modest fund for acquisitions up to $2,500. Once again
the arrangement seemed eminently sound at first. Fry bought brilliantly,
and on his recommendations the museum filled some of the widest gaps in

its collection, acquiring first-rate paintings by Andrea del Sarto, Palma Vecchio, Giovanni Bellini, Botticelli, Lorenzo di Credi, Gerard David, and other masters. One fine spring day in 1909, Pierpont Morgan, who was passing through London on his way to Paris, stopped in at the dealer Kleinberger's gallery and purchased a painting by Fra Angelico which had formerly belonged to King Leopold of Belgium. A few days later, Morgan received a curt letter from Roger Fry. Referring to the "superb" Fra Angelico he had just acquired, Fry said:

> I think I ought to tell you that I saw it a few days before you did, and considering it of the utmost importance to the Museum and also likely to be snapped up I bought it. I offered it at once to the Museum and received from Mr. de Forest a wire accepting it on behalf of the Museum at £10,000 subject to Mr. Laffan's approval in writing if you were inaccessible. I wrote to Mr. Laffan asking him to confirm in writing his verbal agreement but by that time you had seen it. Mr. Kleinberger believing that you were acquiring it for the Museum and that this merely confirmed my purchase said nothing. I think you should know the exact state of the case and therefore trouble you with this.

The tone and the general inference that Morgan had undercut the museum were all too apparent. "The most remarkable letter I ever received," Morgan scrawled across the top before sending it on to his secretary. "I do not propose to answer it until I see you." Morgan never did answer it, nor did he ever mention the incident to Fry; in fact, he did nothing at all about the matter, but his displeasure was so evident that both Robinson, the acting director, and Bryson Burroughs, who had become acting curator of paintings when Fry relinquished the title, advised Fry to resign. Fry wrote a number of plaintive letters to Burroughs and Robinson soliciting their help and guidance. "I confess I am no match for these people," he told Robinson, "but in my present situation . . . it would be a very serious matter for me to have suddenly to work for a place here again"—i.e., in England, for an English salary. If Morgan felt so bitterly toward him, Fry argued, "he should in common decency recompense me for the loss of opportunity and the work which I have done for him personally entirely without payment." The situation dragged along until the following February, when de Forest notified Fry that the trustees had voted to terminate his appointment. "The blow I expected has fallen," Fry wrote bitterly to his father. "Morgan could not forgive me for trying to get that picture for the Museum ° . . . It is useless to make any fuss about it. I could get no satisfaction from these people and they have behaved vilely."

The story ends happily, more or less. Later that same year, Fry organized the first major exhibition of Postimpressionist paintings, at the Grafton Galleries in London, and published a pioneering article on the importance of Cézanne, Gauguin, Van Gogh, and Seurat. Virtually overnight, he became the *bête noir* of the British art establishment and a hero to the younger generation of artists. His real career as a critic dates from this moment. Years later, all bitterness forgotten, he was able to see that the directorship of the National Gallery would not have suited him, either, and to express a certain gratitude that "the Americans prevented me from having that post which once seemed to me the height of my ambition."

° The picture, Fra Angelico's *Virgin and Child Enthroned*, remained in Morgan's private collection until his death in 1913. Soon afterward it was acquired by the Swiss Baron Heinrich von Thyssen-Bornemisza, and it now hangs in the collection of the Thyssen Foundation in Lugano.

NINE

At the turn of the century New York was already assuming ungovernable dimensions. It had absorbed Brooklyn, Queens, and Staten Island in 1898 to become Greater New York, whose population stood at just under four million. More than a third of the city's inhabitants were foreign born, and seven percent of them were illiterate. The newcomers formed an easily exploitable core of support for Richard Croker, the latest Tammany strong man, who was firmly back in the saddle following a brief reform administration that had lasted from 1893 to 1896.

Immigration patterns were changing, though, with Italians and Jews from Central Europe and Russia taking precdence over the earlier influx from Ireland and northern Europe. The Lower East Side was the largest Jewish community in the world; its inhabitants would soon exert a strong influence on the educational institutions of New York, which had been the last major city in America to build public high schools. The era of the automobile was just starting—Henry Ford went into mass production of the Model T in 1909—and the era of the skyscrapers had begun in earnest. The Times Tower, new home of the paper that Adolph S. Ochs had recently rescued from bankruptcy and turned into a model of accurate news coverage, had given its name to the corner at Broadway and Forty-second Street. On its completion in 1904 it was topped only by the thirty-two-story Park Row Building downtown; within nine years they would both be dwarfed by the sixty-story Woolworth building, built for $13,500,000 by the man who made his fortune in nickels and dimes.

More and more wealth was piling up in New York, fed by the continuing bull market on Wall Street. At the same time, antagonism toward the plutocrats and pressure for social reform were also gathering momentum. The ghastly Triangle Fire in 1911, when one hundred and forty-one garment workers died in a blazing sweatshop, would lead to the rewriting of New York's feudal labor code and to the rapid advancement of labor unions. Even among the very rich a certain awareness of these undercurrents could sometimes be detected. Huge and ostentatious dwellings were no longer in style. From about 1910 on, many of the showy Fifth Avenue mansions were deserted by their owners, some to be taken over by schools or charitable institutions, others simply torn down to make way for anonymous apartment houses where the rich could luxuriate less visibly (and where the loss of grandeur and wall space would render certain types of art objects obsolete). It was becoming increasingly fashionable to practice philanthropy on the grand scale. No one pursued good works more assiduously than the Metropolitan's trustee and secretary Robert de Forest, whose tireless efforts on behalf of slum housing, welfare, social work, and civic improvement generally had made him the city's best-known "Captain of Philanthropy."

At the Metropolitan, de Forest was equally determined to see improvements. A major reorganization was long overdue. For all his energy and dispatch, Cesnola had left what one newspaper critic called "the singular spectacle of a great museum inadequately catalogued, and without an adequate and expert staff." There were still only three curatorial departments —paintings, sculpture, and casts—and their curators detested one another. George H. Story, Fry's predecessor as curator of paintings, received a salary of $5,000 a year and was bitterly resented for that reason by John Alsop Paine, the curator of casts, who got only $4,000 although he had been at the museum longer. F. Edwin Elwell, the successor to Isaac Hall as curator of sculpture, received $3,200 a year and resented both his colleagues. Story used to complain to Cesnola about Paine's "idiotic whistling" during working hours, and on one or two occasions the two men nearly came to blows.

Art critics gibed continually at the Metropolitan's uncertain scholarship and cautious purchasing policies. So far as most European scholars were concerned the only *professional* art museum in America was the Museum of Fine Arts in Boston. The Boston Museum received no city funds at all, and so far it had had no Jacob S. Rogers, but its close ties with Harvard had helped to provide it with trustees and curators who were experts in their fields. Working with limited funds, they had purchased magnificently. In 1905, however, dissension over the plans for moving to a new building in the Fenway had caused Bostonian tempers to wax unseasonably warm. Edward Robinson, the director there since 1902, resigned rather suddenly that summer because he believed that his authority was being undermined. The Metropolitan trustees had seriously considered Robinson for their directorship, and they lost no time now in offering him the position of assistant director under Sir Purdon Clarke—a post that had not existed until then. Robinson accepted, and his appointment was announced in December.

While Sir Purdon radiated ineffectual goodwill, Robinson applied the principles and the professional standards he had learned even before coming to work at the Boston Museum of Fine Arts. One of the first Americans to receive a thorough grounding in classical archaeology, Robinson had studied abroad for several years after graduating from Harvard. He had worked in German museums and excavated in Greece. He spoke German, Italian, and French, and he entertained a very high opinion of the methods and manners of German scholarship. Even his looks verged on the Teutonic. He was tall and erect, with pale blue eyes and blond, almost white hair cut *en brosse*. Robinson believed in discipline. Most of the people who worked under him were so intimidated by his austere and glacial dignity that they missed his delicate sense of humor. Edith Wharton described Robinson in her autobiography as a delightful man who told amusing stories about the Metropolitan. One of the tales she remembered his telling with great flair had to do with a visit to the museum during the 1920s by the heir apparent of a Far Eastern country, who was making a tour of the United States. Robinson had spent two hours taking him and his entourage around the museum, going from one gallery to another and delivering a little lecture in each, which was then translated for the royal personage. During the whole of the tour, Mrs. Wharton relates, the visitor's face remained exquisitely and inscrutably immobile. "The Prince never asked a question, or glanced to right or left, and this slow and awful progress through the endless galleries was beginning to tell on Robinson's nerves when they halted before a fine piece of fifteenth century sculpture, a *Pietà*, or a Deposition, with a peculiarly moving figure of the dead Christ. Here His Imperial Highness opened his lips to ask, through his aide-de-camp, what the group represented, and Robinson hastened to explain: 'It is the figure of our dead God, after His enemies have crucified Him.' The Prince listened, stared, and then burst into loud and prolonged laughter. Peal after peal echoed uncannily through the startled galleries; then his features resumed their imperial rigidity and the melancholy procession moved on through new vistas of silence." *

Under Robinson's supervision as assistant director and from 1910 as director, the Metropolitan gradually built up a competent professional staff. The growth of the individual departments did not always proceed according to logic. Much thought had been given to the question of departmental organization—whether to follow the example of the South Kensington Museum and set up departments according to craft and material (ceramics, woodwork, metalwork, etc.), or whether to organize on art-historical lines, as the British Museum had done. Basically the British Museum system was the one followed, but with certain inconsistencies. The old Departments of Sculpture and Casts were abolished in 1905. The following year, a Department of Egyptian Art was set up on the British Museum model, and a Department of Metalwork was established, confusingly enough, along South Kensington lines. The Department of Decorative Arts took shape in 1907, mainly as a result of Pierpont Morgan's gift to the museum of the Hoentschel Collection of French eighteenth century furnishings and objets d'art; a huge, catch-all department, for many years it included everything from pre-Columbian stone figures to Turkish carpets and Chinese jades. The Department of Classical Art (subsequently changed to Greek and Roman Art) came into being officially in 1909, the Department of Arms and Armor in 1912, the Department of Far Eastern Art in 1915, the Department of Prints in 1916. In some cases—notably Arms and Armor —a department owed its creation to a single persuasive individual. A few of the early curators had professional museum training, but most of them did not. There was no college or university course that prepared students for the new and rather curious profession of museum curatorship. The curators were a remarkable and somewhat eccentric lot, and it took all of Robinson's disciplinary authority to keep them in check.

* Edith Wharton, *A Backward Glance*, D. Appleton-Century Co., 1934.

Robinson was not, however, the sole architect of the Metropolitan's re-organization. This honor belongs in equal part to Henry W. Kent, another Bostonian who vied with Robinson in icy formality and who was also, without a doubt, the greatest American museum man of his generation.

Like many men who did not go to college, Kent never ceased trying to make up for the deficiency. In his autobiography, somewhat dauntingly ti-tled *What I Am Pleased to Call My Education,* he explained that ill health throughout his childhood had denied him "the early training in school and college which I should have had." He spent his early years in Boston, briefly attended the Boston Latin School, and spent two years at the excel-lent and educationally progressive Norwich Free Academy in Norwich, Connecticut, but for the most part he was tutored privately at home. At eighteen he went to work in the Boston Public Library. The following year, he came to New York to take the first course ever given in "library economy"; the instructor was Melvil Dewey, head of the Columbia Univer-sity Library, inventor of the decimal system for classifying books, and the father of modern library science. Kent stayed on to work at the Columbia Library after finishing Dewey's course. In 1888 he was offered a dual posi-tion as librarian of the Peck Library at Norwich Free Academy, his old alma mater, and curator of the new Slater Memorial Museum there. The Slater Museum had been conceived as an integral part of the school and a visual counterpart to the library. It was a museum of casts and reproduc-tions (selected, incidentally, by Edward Robinson, who was then a curator of classical art at the Boston Museum), and its purpose was exclusively ed-ucational. Kent ran the museum and library for twelve years, during which his efficient management and his exhibition techniques came to the notice of a number of people in the museum field.

Edward Robinson had taken a leave of absence from the Boston Mu-seum in 1891 to act as purchasing agent for the Metropolitan's special com-mittee on casts. When the Metropolitan's greatly enlarged cast collection was ready for installation in the new north wing in 1894, Robinson recom-mended to the trustees that they hire Henry Kent to install it, and they did so. The results pleased everyone. De Forest, who was then chairman of the special committee on casts, was particularly impressed by Kent's precise, fastidious manner and fine attention to detail, and the two men remained on cordial terms from then on ("I owe everything to him," Kent would one day write of de Forest). A few years later Kent left Norwich to become the librarian of the Grolier Club in New York, among whose bibliophile members were several Metropolitan trustees. He took lodgings in a house on Washington Square, which by a jolly coincidence was just around the corner from the home of Mr. and Mrs. Robert de Forest. When de Forest became secretary to the board of trustees in 1905, he brought in Henry Kent as assistant secretary, at the frugal salary of $2,000 a year.

The lack of any coherent administrative system at the Metropolitan must have appalled a man of Kent's methodical temper. The only telephone was in the library, to which employees had to run when called. There was no information desk for visitors, and very little communication between members of the staff. Soon after his arrival Kent witnessed the lamentable spectacle of one curator inviting another to "come outside," and then, when the other declined combat, pursuing him through the galleries (Story and Paine, perhaps); Kent, who personally summoned a guard to quell the dispute, said he had never before known professional feelings to run so high. Officially, the function of the assistant secretary was to notify the trustees of meetings and to keep the minutes of their deliberations. Kent undertook to do a good deal more. He saw his job as one of providing a businesslike system of organization throughout the museum, and of acting as "the entrepreneur between the initiators of all action, the Trustees, and their employees."

Quietly and without fanfare, Kent initiated and set in motion the basic machinery of modern museum administration. His innovations were often simply applications of Melvil Dewey's library science to the museum environment. He set up a card catalog system for registering accessions, which previously had been recorded in huge bound volumes. The basic information about every work of art in the museum was recorded on one side of the card, and a photograph of the object was pasted to the reverse. A more detailed card catalogue was also started, with scholarly information supplied by the various curatorial departments, and clear procedures were established for loans and all other movements of art objects in and out of the building. Kent hired a photographer and had him set up shop in the basement, and in a short time the photo studio was turning out, in addition to prints for the registrar and the catalogue departments, a variety of enlargements, publicity photographs, and lantern slides for lectures. Kent's methods have endured with few changes to the present day. They proved so effective that they were gradually adopted in one form or another not only by the new museums that were springing up around the country (in 1905 there were forty-six galleries in the United States with art on view; by 1914 there were sixty), but also by most of the established older museums in this country and in Europe.

The Metropolitan Museum *Bulletin,* which started publication in November 1905 is usually cited as another of Kent's innovations, although the idea undoubtedly came from Robinson (who had established a similar journal for the Museum of Fine Arts in 1903). Kent undertook the editorial supervision of the *Bulletin,* which was intended to be "a ready means of communication between the officers and staff of the Metropolitan museum and its members." * It began as a quarterly, but there was so much to communicate that with the second issue it became a bimonthly and with the third, a monthly. Kent was also responsible for its typographical format. Having been for many years a close student and enthusiast of fine printing, he was able, very soon after he came to the Metropolitan, to persuade the trustees that a great museum's printing should be worthy at all times of its collections. With the trustees' approval Kent purchased a small handpress and set up a printshop in the basement, where all the museum's labels, letterheads, posters, invitations and announcements, business forms and other public documents were turned out under Kent's careful supervision and often to his own designs. The museum used outside printers for larger catalogues and for the *Bulletin,* but Kent saw to it that they were the best. Daniel B. Updike of the Merrymount Press in Boston, Carl P. Rollins of the Yale University Press, Bruce Rogers and a good many other leaders in the field of fine printing did work for the Metropolitan in their early days. Years later, when the Morgan Library held a special exhibition of Metropolitan Museum printed materials in 1938, several of these men took the occasion to stress their indebtedness to Kent. Asked at the time to discuss his own part in raising the level of museum printing generally, Kent re-

---

* The membership was increasing slowly, from 796 in 1880 to more than three thousand in 1910. Two new classes of membership were established in 1905—Sustaining Members who gave $25.00 and Fellowship Members who gave $100 or more—and receipts from this source, while never spectacular, helped to pay the rising costs of administration.

plied, with characteristic dryness, "There was a job to be done, nobody else was doing it, so I did it."

Kent performed countless dry but necessary jobs in this fashion, and very soon became the indispensable man at the museum. A year after he joined the staff he was made acting director during a period when Sir Purdon Clarke and Robinson were both away. There were no indications that Kent ever wanted to *be* the director, but as time went on it became increasingly clear that he considered his own position at least equivalent to the director's in authority. Librarians, Kent pointed out, were trained first of all as public servants. "Museum curators, museum directors, are not so trained," he said, "and few of them seem to have imbibed the notion of the importance of that relationship."

Education was a natural field for Kent's expanding operations. As a public servant, Kent studied the 1870 charter and decided, in spite of the ardent and ringing declarations of the founders, that the museum had actually done very little by way of furnishing "popular instruction." The promised exhibitions of industrial arts had never taken place. The Metropolitan's art school, established in 1880 as a sort of trade school in design for the "artist-artisan" element, had gradually evolved into elementary art classes similar (and inferior) to the classes at Cooper Union or the Art Students League; the trustees had abolished the school in 1894, declaring that their main educational effort in the future would be "to make the Museum itself intelligible and instructive." Since then, the educational effort had been limited to letting schoolteachers in free on pay days and sponsoring an occasional lecture. One of Kent's first actions was to arrange for a regular schedule of lectures at the museum on Saturdays and Sundays, "the former scholarly and the latter popular." A resolution had been adopted in 1905, providing that any New York public school teacher, upon application to the museum in advance, could bring her class in free at any time. A classroom was set aside for such visits in 1907, and Kent, who was appointed supervisor of museum instruction that same year, received the incoming school groups and instilled them with a properly reverential attitude. One sees him as the most elegant of schoolteachers, impeccably dressed in dark serge and a stiff white wing collar, his neat waxed moustache immobile as he enunciates the elevated message of art in cool, clipped Bostonese. Henry W. Kent, a lifelong bachelor, believed firmly in education, but, like some educators and most curators, he did not really believe in students.

A certain ambivalence about the idea of art education was characteristic of the period, as it is of our own. On the one hand, the trustees gave lip service to the museum's educational role in the community, mindful perhaps of Robert de Forest's observation that it was "good politics, as well as good policy," for an institution seeking city support to develop its relationship with the public schools. The museum's educational program did expand considerably during this period, along lines charted earlier by the Boston Museum. There was a gradual increase in the number of free and paid lectures, gallery talks by a salaried museum instructor (free to schoolchildren, twenty-five cents to others), the lending of lantern slides, and even a program for high school students that included sending out slides and other materials and offering special courses in art appreciation for public school teachers. The September issue of the *Bulletin* each year was devoted to educational work at the museum, and each September congratulations seemed to be in order.

By deciding to substitute for direct instruction in arts and crafts the educational goal of making its own collections "intelligible and instructive," though, the Metropolitan trustees had ventured upon uncertain and ambiguous terrain. Intelligible and instructive to whom, and at what level? There were different orders of intelligibility for the art scholar, the schoolchild, and the average adult visitor—*l'homme moyen sensuel*. A work of art could be interpreted in so many different ways—as an illustrated story or moral precept, for example, or as a lesson in fine craftsmanship, or even as a mystical aesthetic "experience" of the sort that connoisseurs loved to describe but could never quite define. What did an indefinable experience have to do with education at the public secondary school level? What did the average schoolchild experience, for that matter, as he filed through the endless galleries in a line of shuffling classmates? Neither Kent nor the trustees appeared to give much thought to such questions. Education, after all, was sufficient unto itself. It was the vivifying power, the genius of the Republic, the democratic ideal sanctioned by a half century of lyceum lectures and Chattauquas and public school building. Whatever was produced in the name of art education by a public museum must naturally be assumed to be good.

Unfortunately, for every schoolchild whose dormant aesthetic sensibilities were awakened by a visit to the Metropolitan, there were probably a dozen for whom the experience cemented a lifelong conviction that art was a wearisome bore. Few teachers suggested to their charges that a visit to the museum could be in the nature of a holiday. Art was a serious matter, and the goal was inspiration and uplift, not sensuous enjoyment. As though in recognition of this sober truth, the Metropolitan trustees decided in 1908 to amend their charter. In that section of the 1870 document which stated the museum's purpose as one of "encouraging and developing the study of the fine arts, and the application of arts to manufacture and practical life, of advancing the general knowledge of kindred subjects, and, to that end of furnishing popular instruction and recreation," the trustees voted to delete the last two words.

TEN

One of the marvels of the Boston Museum is its collection of Greek art. Although the Metropolitan's classical collections today are larger, the finest Greek vases and marbles in Boston are superior to anything in New York, or in any other American museum. Boston's supremacy in this field is the result of its ten-year head start over the Metropolitan, which did not begin seriously collecting Greek art until after Cesnola's death in 1904.

Up to that time the Metropolitan had felt no pressing need to do so. The museum had a good deal of "classical" material—the enormous Cesnola collection from Cyprus, Roman and Etruscan glass given by Henry Marquand, engraved gems, seals, and other small objects donated by C. W. King, Edward C. Moore, and others. There were also the plaster casts—architectural scale models of the Parthenon, the Pantheon, and the Hypostyle Hall at Karnak, copies of the *Discobolus* and other famous sculptures of antiquity. Cesnola, being Italian, had a natural interest in the arts of Rome. During his regime the museum acquired the magnificent series of Roman frescoes from a villa near Boscoreale, recovered almost intact after their burial for twenty centuries under the deadly volcanic ash from Vesuvius. In 1903, Cesnola had purchased and personally directed the reconstruction of an Etruscan *biga,* or chariot, found near Spoleto and dated between 700 and 600 B.C., which was considered one of the most important archaeological finds of the century. Cesnola seemed to think, though, that his Cypriote statues and artifacts made the acquisition of Greek works unnecessary; the museum already *had* a large collection of antique sculpture,

121

he reasoned, so why bother to buy more? During the years from 1892 to 1904, while the Museum of Fine Arts was quietly buying up the finest Greek works on the market, the Metropolitan did not even send a representative to the important European sales.

Boston's forehandedness was due in large part to Edward Perry Warren, a well-to-do Bostonian who lived in England. Warren had gone to Oxford, where he read classics and made friends with a bright and penniless young Englishman named John Marshall. Partly at Marshall's suggestion, he decided after graduating to devote his life and his inheritance to collecting Greek art. Marshall became his private secretary and confidential agent. Starting in 1894, the two men began systematic, large-scale operations in the classical art market, buying not only for Warren's own collection but also as semiofficial agents for the Boston Museum of Fine Arts, whose curator of Classical Antiquities at that time happened to be Edward Robinson.

They could hardly have picked a more auspicious moment. Many of the finest classical collections formed in Europe during the nineteenth century were being dispersed, which meant that for the first time in years there was a considerable quantity of classical material on the market. Marshall established himself in Rome, where he kept in close touch with the dealers and the scions of the great collecting families. Both Marshall and Warren attended all the Paris sales, where they consistently outbid the agents for the British Museum, the Berlin Museum, and the Louvre. Alexander Stuart Murray, the keeper of Greek and Roman Antiquities at the British Museum, complained that "There is nothing to be got nowadays, since Warren and Marshall are always on the spot first." In a market that was highly competitive and full of pitfalls—the danger of forgery being ever-present —Warren and Marshall became so dominant that competition almost ceased, and the Boston Museum acquired masterpiece after masterpiece. Harvard's great art scholar Charles Eliot Norton said that there never had been an American connoisseur of Warren's capacities. If Warren's life should by any chance be shortened, he said, the hopes of the Museum of Fine Arts "would die with him."

By 1906, Warren, Marshall, and Robinson had all transferred their allegiance to the Metropolitan. Personal factors contributed to the exodus, but the main problem was financial. When the Museum of Fine Arts decided in 1899 to move from Copley Square in downtown Boston to a new build-

ing in the Fenway, all available funds were commandeered for that purpose. Warren argued bitterly against the move. There would never again
be such an opportunity to acquire classical works of art, he said; the new
building could wait, the market that he and Marshall dominated would
not. Warren's brother Samuel D. Warren, who had become president of the
Museum of Fine Arts in 1902, was a strong backer of the Fenway move,
and relations between the two men became seriously strained. About 1904,
despite Robinson's and Warren's entreaties, the funds allotted to the purchase of classical art dried up entirely.

There is some cause for believing that Edward Warren influenced Robinson's decision to resign as director in Boston by promising to have him
appointed director of the Metropolitan, a plan that backfired when Morgan
hired Sir Caspar Purdon Clarke. Whatever the circumstances were, very
soon after Robinson moved to the Metropolitan as assistant director in
1905, John Marshall became the Metropolitan's salaried purchasing agent
for Greek and Roman art and Edward Perry Warren shifted his attentions
from Boston to New York. "I trust you will be interested to know," Sir Purdon Clark wrote to William Laffan in 1906, "that I have been able to transfer to the Metropolitan Museum the men and methods by which the collection of Greek and Roman antiquities in the Boston Museum of Fine Arts
have been so successfully built up since 1895."

The Classical Department at the Metropolitan did not come into being
officially until 1909, but from 1905 on, using the income from the Rogers
Fund, the museum was purchasing actively in this field. Robinson took on
the classical curatorship in addition to his duties as assistant director. In
1906 he engaged a young girl to catalogue a large collection of Greek vases
acquired that year, and liked her work so much that he asked her to stay
on permanently. Gisela A. M. Richter, the daughter of a well-known German historian, had studied archaeology at Cambridge and had also done
field work at the British School of Archaeology in Greece. She was visiting
America on her vacation when Robinson hired her, at five dollars a day, to
catalogue the vases, and before agreeing to stay on at the museum she had
to ask her parents' permission. Her parents agreed, on condition that she
be allowed three months off each summer to spend at home. Gisela Richter
soon became the assistant curator of Classical Art (the first woman on the
curatorial staff). She became full curator in 1925, when the title of the de-

partment was changed to Greek and Roman Art, and by the time she retired in 1948, after forty-two years' service, the department had made up
for a good deal of lost time.

Although the important Paris sales of Greek art were just about over by
the time Robinson and Marshall came to the Metropolitan, Marshall's
sharp eye and his great knowledge of the market paid rich dividends. Marshall received a purchase fund to use abroad as he saw fit. His annual consignment for the Metropolitan in 1907 numbered one hundred and twenty-
seven objects—eleven marbles, forty-five vases, twenty-seven bronzes,
thirty-one terracottas, and a miscellaneous assortment of gems, jewelry,
seals, and other works. The accession figures for the Classical Department
tell their own story—$45,000 in 1917, $94,000 in 1923, $185,000 in 1926. It
was a period when the trustees supposedly never met without buying a
Greek pot. Their purchases included such magnificent specimens as the Di-
pylon Vase, an eighth century B.C. krater that is one of the finest known examples of the early Geometric Style.

Marshall's purchases of Greek, Etruscan, and Roman bronzes established
the Metropolitan as a leader in this particular area, and he added greatly
to the museum's previous holdings in glass, gems, and other small objets
d'art. It was no failing on Marshall's part that he could not procure many
outstanding examples of Greek sculpture in marble. Ever since Lord Elgin
pried the pediment figures from the Parthenon and shipped them home to
England in 1803, Greek and Italian authorities had looked with increasing
disfavor upon the sending abroad of ancient monuments, and very few
Greek marbles left the country legally. Marshall did acquire a remarkable
piece in 1908, when the demolition of some old buildings at the corner of
the Via della Consolazione and the Via Montecaprino in Rome brought to
light the marble statue now known as the *Old Market Woman*, a superb
example of the Hellenistic Style and one of the Metropolitan's rare Greek
sculptures believed to be an original rather than a Roman copy. He bought
some extremely beautiful grave steles of the Classical Period, including the
lovely white marble relief of a young girl with two pigeons, carved about
450 B.C. on the island of Paros, and he put together a respectable showing
of Roman copies of early Greek works. Ironically, the most important
Greek sculptures in the museum came after Marshall's death in 1928: the
Archaic *Kouros*, the earliest Greek marble statue in the Metropolitan and

one of the earliest known sculptures in Greek art, which Gisela Richter purchased in 1932; the bronze *Sleeping Eros,* bought by Miss Richter in 1943, a piece that one leading Greek scholar considers to be not only an original bronze of the third century B.C. but "the most beautiful work of art representing a child preserved from antiquity"; and the marble *Aphrodite* acquired in 1952, a Roman copy of the same antique statue that served as model for the famous *Medici Venus* in Florence, but a copy of such exquisite quality that some scholars think it could be the original. The Metropolitan's *Aphrodite* has the further distinction of being the first naked woman ever to appear on the front page of *The New York Times,* which unblushingly carried a photograph of her when she was unveiled in 1952.

There were also, alas, a few items that did not turn out so well. Forgeries of classical sculpture have plagued the connoisseur since ancient times. In Rome during the Augustan Age, clever imitators traded on the Roman passion for Greek sculpture of the Classical Period and turned out dozens of works which they attributed successfully to Phidias, Praxiteles, Scopas, Myron, and other great names of the past. The classical revival of learning that contributed so significantly to the Renaissance in Italy also brought about a boom in the forgery market; even an acknowledged forgery, if its quality was sufficiently high, could be sold for as much as half the going price for an original. Michelangelo, at the age of twenty-two, carved a *Sleeping Eros* that probably resembled the one in the Metropolitan, gave it an artificial patina by burying it for several weeks, and then sent it off to a dealer who promptly sold it to Rafaello Riario, Cardinal of San Giorgio and a passionate collector, for two hundred ducats. The artist later boasted of his feat, which earned him, according to contemporary accounts, "the most outstanding fame." Not until our own time has a skillful forgery become worthless when exposed as such, but this has in no way deterred the forgers from practicing their trade and regularly discomfiting the experts. Along with virtually everyone else in the field, Marshall fell victim to forgers on several occasions.

Marshall's most spectacular purchase involved what were certainly the most colossal forgeries of all time. Between 1915 and 1921, he bought in Rome and shipped to the Metropolitan three huge terracotta sculptures that were identified at the time as Etruscan works of the sixth century B.C. The largest, a helmeted warrior brandishing a spear, stood eight feet high without its pedestal. There was also a somewhat smaller warrior figure, and a gigantic detached head. From the very beginning, questions arose about the authenticity and provenance of the three pieces, and as a result Marshall advised the museum not to publish or exhibit them right away. When Marshall died in 1928 he was still not sufficiently confident of the material to recommend its exhibition. Etruscan art has always been somewhat "problematical," as the archaeologists like to say; its origins are uncertain to begin with, and, because Etruscan artists worked in a mixed style that incorporated outside influences, it has always offered great opportunities to the forger. The Metropolitan finally resolved its own doubts in 1933, however, and put the statues prominently on display.

Almost immediately, the international art world began to buzz with rumors that the Metropolitan's Etruscans were not all they should be. An Italian art dealer told Miss Richter in 1936 that, according to Roman gossip, the statues had been made by a family named Riccardi in the town of Orvieto. Miss Richter made inquiries, found no evidence to support the rumors, and published, in 1937, a lengthy monograph on the warriors. Most American and foreign scholars accepted Miss Richter's conclusions that the statues were genuine. The importance and rarity of the find continued to excite speculation, though; if genuine, the statues upset a great deal of historical thinking about Etruscan art.

One European scholar who definitely did not accept Miss Richter's thinking was Massimo Pallottino, Professor of Etruscan and Italian Antiquities at the University of Rome, who published an article in 1937 branding as crude forgeries all three of the statues, which he referred to contemptuously as "mammozzi." Miss Richter, in her monograph, had drawn a stylistic comparison between the eight-foot "big warrior" and a small bronze statuette in the Berlin Museum; Pallottino charged that the statuette had actually served as the forger's model. Several other attacks appeared in print during the next few years. One Italian critic claimed (erroneously, as it turned out) that the clay in the statues contained ground-up glass from Peroni beer bottles. The American archaeologist Iris C. Love, who was then an undergraduate at Smith College, wrote and later published a paper on the Etruscan statues in which she contended, on stylistic grounds, that the big warrior and the colossal head were modern (the smaller warrior, according to Miss Love, was genuinely ancient). Many more scholars expressed their doubts verbally. On a visit to the Metropolitan in 1959, Italy's distinguished Professor Michelangelo Cagiani told the curator of Greek and Roman Art that he did not care to look at the Etruscan warriors, and added, "How can I, when I know the man who made them?"

An American art expert named Harold W. Parsons had often expressed his doubts about the Etruscan statues. Parsons lived in Rome and bought for the Cleveland and other museums, and it has been suggested that he may have harbored a rather keen desire to show up poor dead John Marshall, his old rival in many an art battle. Throughout the 1950s, semiretired and with a comfortable income, Parsons devoted himself to tracking down the mystery of the Etruscan warriors' provenance. In 1958 he wrote triumphantly to James J. Rorimer, who was then the director of the Metropolitan, saying that he had obtained and would soon produce "factual evidence" to prove that the statues were modern forgeries. Parsons' evidence did not actually appear until 1961, but when it did it showed that the persistent Roman gossip had been right after all.

In a legal deposition signed in the presence of Parsons and the American consul in Rome, a Roman taxi driver named Alfredo Adolfo Fioravanti swore that he had personally helped to make the Metropolitan's Etruscan statues, in collaboration with Riccardo Riccardi and his two cousins, in workshops in or near Orvieto between the years 1914 and 1919. The Riccardi, it seemed, were a family of distinguished forgers. Riccardo had learned the trade from his father (whose greatest triumph was a forged Etruscan *biga*, of all things, that he sold to the British Museum); the son had expanded the business by taking in his two cousins, Teodoro and Virgilio, and a friend of the family—Fioravanti. Both Teodoro and Virgilio had escaped service in the First World War because they had been judged to be *mezzo matto*, or not quite right in the head. They were sound enough to follow instructions, though, and they had helped Riccardo Riccardi and Fioravanti in the astonishingly successful and daring creation of a number of "Etruscan" works of art, including a very well known *Kore* in the Ny Carlsberg Glyptotek in Copenhagen. They worked entirely from photographs in poorly printed art books (Professor Pallottino's supposition that they had modeled the big warrior on a bronze in the Berlin Museum proved to be entirely correct), and the odd proportions of the Metropolitan's statues—the short legs and stocky build of the big warrior, for example, which had long troubled scholars—had been the result of cramped working quarters and a low ceiling. Ironically, the size of the statues had been one of the strongest arguments for their authenticity; the ancients often fired very large pieces of sculpture, but no modern kiln would accommodate a piece as large as these. Fioravanti's explanation was simplicity itself. The forgers had made each sculpture in sections, broken them, and fired the pieces separately. The statues had arrived at the Metropolitan in fragments, as excavated terracottas usually do, and the museum's restorers had performed the final stage in their creation.

Fioravanti was able to produce the tip of the thumb of one of the warriors, which fitted perfectly, and two samples of the black glaze used in the firing process. This in itself did not constitute proof of forgery—if the statues had indeed been ancient, the excavator might have kept back a few souvenirs. The Metropolitan, however, had been conducting scientific investigations of its own, and its findings tallied perfectly with Fioravanti's confession. Fioravanti volunteered the information that they had used manganese dioxide in their glaze; chemical and spectrographic analysis of the statues had already disclosed the presence of manganese dioxide, a coloring agent often used in modern ceramics but unknown in ancient times. Fioravanti also clarified several other technical points, and left no doubt in anybody's mind that he was speaking the truth. The Metropolitan announced to the press on February 14, 1961, that its Etruscan warriors were fakes, and, after a brief and no doubt painful period when they were left on view for the curious, the huge pieces were banished to the basement.

One of the many odd facts about art forgery is that in Italy, at least, the forger has little to worry about even if he is caught. The Italians have stringent laws to prevent the exportation of authentic treasures, but their secret admiration for anyone who can fool the authorities is reflected in the attitude of the courts, which usually accept the forger's plea that he did it to amuse himself. No action was taken against Fioravanti, who seemed immensely proud of his youthful achievements and quite delighted by the attention he received. As for Riccardi, who was clearly a master of his trade, there is no doubt that had he lived longer there would be a great many more dubious antiquities enshrined today in museums throughout the world. Riccardi's professional style commands admiration. When John Marshall went out to investigate the site near Orvieto where the statues

1872: Dodworth's Dancing Academy at 681 Fifth Avenue—The Metropolitan opened here.

1873: The Douglas Mansion on Fourteenth Street shortly before it became the museum's second home.

1880: The move to Central Park.

1888: First addition.

OVERLEAF: 1910: The palace in the park.

1910: Hunt's neoclassic facade with older buildings in rear.

1926: South Fifth Avenue wing.

1970: A new face for the second century. (Exterior and Interior)

OVERLEAF: The great hall in 1925 (in foreground, George
Grey Barnard's *Struggle of the Two Natures of Man*).

Exhibition style, *circa* 1900.   The Blumenthal patio, shown in Blumenthal's house.

The Hudson-Fulton Exhibition in 1909: rediscovering America's arts and crafts.

Morgan and friends in Egypt, Albert Lythgoe in foreground.

From the deck of his private dehabigeh, Morgan views the fellaheen.

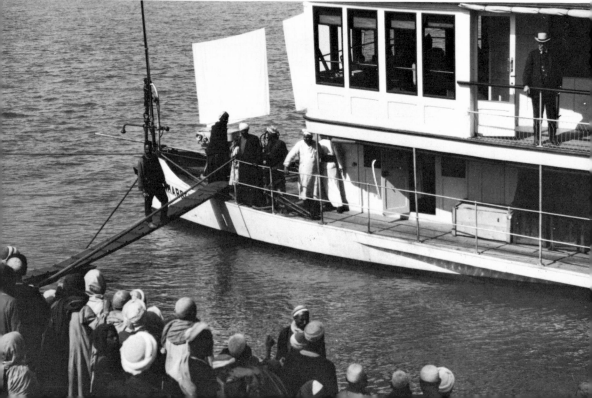

The prince of Wall Street in the saddle.

Deir el-Sahri: in search of Hatshepsut.

Charles Collens' preliminary sketches show the evolution of The Cloisters.

George Grey Barnard's original "Cloister Museum."

A recorded concert in the Cuxa Cloister.   OVERLEAF: The Cloisters, from the south.

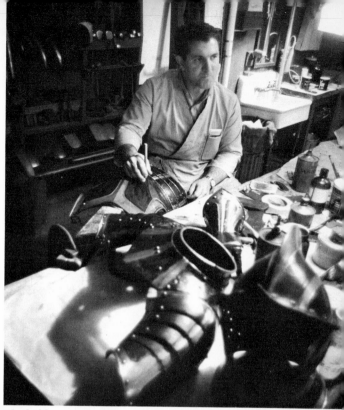

The hidden museum: Armorer Harvey Murton at work.

Restorations and repairs, *post* Cesnola.

had allegedly been found, he was stopped just short of his destination by a cordon of police. Marshall took this as a proof of authenticity, because in Italy the police were usually deployed to guard a newly discovered archaeological find. In this case, however, even the police were fakes— Riccardi had procured some uniforms and stationed a few of his friends there expressly for Marshall's benefit. Riccardo Riccardi died suddenly in 1919, as the result of a fall from a horse, and his *mezzo matto* cousins were not able to carry on the lucrative family business. Fioravanti drifted down to Rome and his taxicab. The forgery trade had meanwhile produced a new genius in Alceo Dossena.

Dossena, known as the "King of Forgers," came from a family of stone-cutters and practical artisans in Cremona. From early childhood he showed an extraordinary facility for working in marble, clay, bronze, and wood. Soon after the war his talent was discovered by a pair of shrewd art dealers in Rome, who set him to work carving sculptures in ancient, Renaissance, and medieval style. Dossena specialized in the early Renaissance masters. He became expert in reproducing the style of the Pisano brothers, Simone Martini, Vecchietta, Donatello, and Mino da Fiesole, but he took great pride in the fact that he never copied existing works of art. Dossena created original sculptures; if *others* attributed them to earlier masters, well, that was no concern of his. His wood carving of an *Annunciation* scene so convincingly evoked the style of Simone Martini that many Renaissance scholars reversed their previous assumption that Simone Martini had not worked as a sculptor. It was purchased for the Frick Collection. Several years later, when Frick's daughter was offered a tomb sculpture ascribed to Mino da Fiesole, one of her agents in checking on the piece happened quite by accident to come across Dossena in Rome. Dossena, whom the dealers had been careful to keep out of sight and hearing, was astounded and infuriated to learn that his sculpture, for which he had been paid 25,000 lire, was being sold to Miss Frick for six million lire. He eventually brought suit against the dealer, which precipitated a major scandal. Tremors of alarm seized private collectors and museum directors everywhere, for Dossena's production had been immense. Working in a large studio with several assistants, he had reportedly sold a million and a half dollars' worth of fake art in America alone.

The Metropolitan, as it turned out, had had a very narrow escape. Marshall bought in 1926 a small marble statuette of a maiden (*kore*) in the Greek Archaic Style, but while it was en route to New York he discovered evidence to make him think it might be a Dossena, and he cabled the Museum not to exhibit it. Gisela Richter put the piece on view three years later, labeled as a Dossena, in a special exhibition of fakes. A few months after Marshall bought the *kore*, a very well-known and highly respected European dealer offered Gisela Richter two life-size marble statues. After examining them for some time, Miss Richter came to the embarrassing conclusion that they were forgeries. Even more embarrassing, since the pieces had been vouched for by a prominent archaeologist and were still for sale, professional and legal considerations prevented her from mentioning the reasons for the Metropolitan's decision not to buy them. Even the useful word "problematical" was in this instance tabu. Another museum bought both sculptures, and a German scholar published a monograph calling them important original works. Shortly thereafter, Dossena cheerfully admitted in court that he had made both pieces "for fun." ("And I suppose he took the money for fun, too," Miss Richter observed.)

Like Han van Meegeren, who painted Vermeers and sold them not only to Hermann Goering but to a leading Dutch museum, Dossena was so good at his trade that one cannot help wondering why he did not become an original artist of his own time. His forgeries were of such high quality that some people continued to buy them even after the facts became known. The Victoria and Albert Museum (our old friend the South Kensington Museum, which changed its name upon moving into its present building in 1909), purchased three of his best pieces and exhibited them under his name. A few years later, unaccustomed to the life of fame and fortune that he had been leading since the scandal broke, Dossena drank himself to death.

Nowadays people often assume that technology is driving the art forger out of business. All a curator has to do, they think, is to take the object into the laboratory and subject it to infrared or X rays, or to chemical or spectrographic analysis, and its true nature will instantly stand revealed. Curators only wish it could be so. The trouble is, one does not begin to bombard an object with infrared rays until its authenticity has come into question, and even then the most sophisticated tests often produce inconclusive or debatable results. Most curators maintain that the only way to guard against forgeries is simply to look at originals over and over and over again, to train the eye by constant exposure so that when one comes upon a forgery it will look *different*, even though one cannot at first say why. Looking hard and often at originals is the basis of all curatorial training (Gisela Richter trained her hand as well, by taking evening classes in stone carving and pottery). What happens, then, if a universally acclaimed original, on which many trained eyes have looked long and hard, turns out to be a fake?

For nearly forty years the Metropolitan's Greek *Bronze Horse*, purchased by John Marshall in 1923, was accepted by virtually every classical scholar as one of the finest Greek bronzes in existence. Gisela Richter called it "without doubt artistically the most important single object in our classical collection." Writing in the Metropolitan Museum *Bulletin* in 1923, Miss Richter said that the lovely, fifteen-inch-high statuette of a walking horse "sums up, in a way, the beauty of Greek art . . . the composition is singularly rhythmical, and the modeling has just that combination of realism and stylization which gives Greek art of the first half of the fifth century its distinctive character." She compared it favorably to Verrocchio's *Colleone* monument and Donatello's *Gattamelata*, the two most famous equestrian statues of the Renaissance, and she suggested that it might conceivably have been made by Kalamis, the fifth century Greek sculptor known for his lifelike portrayals of animals. No one disagreed with Miss Richter. The horse appeared in almost every book on Greek art published after 1923. The Encyclopedia Brittanica gave it a full-page illustration, confidently dated it near 470 B.C., and said there was good reason to suppose it had been made by Kalamis. The horse was one of the most popular objects in the Metropolitan, judging from the thousands of plaster replicas of it that were sold by the museum's sales desk and by Brentano's bookstore, where the casts went for seventy-five dollars apiece.

It was not a curator who shot down the bronze horse. One morning in 1961, the museum's operating administrator, Joseph V. Noble, walking through the Greek galleries as he did twice a day on the way to his office, saw something that made him "do a double take," as he put it. Noble had passed by the Greek horse in its glass case a thousand times or more since he came to the museum in 1956, without noticing anything amiss. This particular morning, however, he happened to see for the first time a thin line running from the top of the horse's mane down to the tip of the nose. He stopped to examine it more closely. The line, he saw, also ran down the horse's spine, over the rump, and under the stomach. It suddenly occurred to Noble that this was a mold mark, of the kind that is left when a sculpture has been made by the process of sand-casting. Although Noble's job at the museum was administrative rather than curatorial, he also happened to be a collector of Greek and Roman antiquities and a recognized expert in the field of art forgeries. He was well aware that the sand-casting process had not been invented until the fourteenth century. The ancient Greek sculptors had employed the so-called "lost wax" process of bronze casting, in which a mold was built up around a wax model, then heated until the wax melted and ran out through a hole in the bottom; the molten bronze was then poured in, forming a sculpture with no seams.

Looking longer and harder, Noble saw other things. There was a small hole at the top of the horse's head, and another one lower down in the mane. The placement of the upper hole suggested that it was meant to hold a *meniscus,* or spike, which the Greeks used to put on their large statues to prevent birds from fouling them. It made no sense at all to have a *meniscus* on a small statuette—unless the statuette had been created by someone who did not know what the hole was used for originally. The other hole was obviously intended to hold a bridle, but it was far too low on the neck to be of any effective use—a mistake that any Greek artist of the fifth century would have been unlikely to make. Thoroughly shaken, Noble confided his suspicions to Dietrich von Bothmer, the curator of Greek and Roman Art. Von Bothmer happened to be going to Greece on museum business a few days later. While he was there he made a careful examination of the horses in the Olympia Museum and elsewhere, checking the placement of the *meniscus* and the bridle holes. The upshot was a letter from von Bothmer to Noble, requesting that the Greek *Bronze Horse* be removed from exhibition.

Nothing was said publicly about the museum's suspicions for six more years, during which the little horse was subjected to every known type of test. Noble, von Bothmer, and their colleagues were convinced that it was a forgery. The incontrovertible proof that they felt they needed was lacking, however, until 1967, when Noble heard that a company in New Jersey was using gamma rays to look for flaws in the hulls of atomic submarines (he discovered the company's name by seeing it on the side of a truck one day, while driving to the museum from his house in New Jersey). Gamma rays could penetrate through far greater thicknesses of metal than the X-ray equipment they had been using, and Noble decided to experiment with this new technique. The gamma ray shadowgraph showed the inside of the horse clearly. It showed the sand core, and the iron wire that had been used as a framework. "That was it," Noble said. Noble made the official announcement soon afterward, before an audience of eight hundred museum men, art experts, and connoisseurs attending one of four Metropolitan Museum seminars on art forgery. The little horse was brought out on the stage of the museum's Grace Rainey Rogers auditorium, and after a pause for dramatic effect, Noble looked down upon it kindly and said, "It's famous, but it's a fraud."

Some scholars refused to believe it. The technical evidence had been misinterpreted, they said. Dr. Carl Blümel, the retired director of the Berlin State Museum, argued publicly that the horse could perfectly well have been made *in sections*, cast by the lost-wax process, and then soldered together, thereby producing the line in question. The Greeks often did this, Blümel said, and the use of iron cores had also been mentioned by the ancients. Noble patiently refuted all arguments on technological grounds. In the meantime, however, something even more conclusive had happened. When the authenticity of a work of art is questioned, the object, if it is a fake, often just falls apart before the curatorial eye. The bronze horse, which had impressed two generations of classical experts as an ideal summation of Greek art, now began to look horribly wrong. The composition was no longer convincing. The eyes, instead of being round as they are in all Greek horse sculpture as well as in all living horses, were seen to be almond-shaped like those of Bambi the Deer—a sentimentalizing tendency that had appealed unconsciously to our own twentieth century taste. Amazingly enough, the most persuasive evidence of all came from a scientist at the American Museum of Natural History across the Park, Lewis S. Brown. Brown published a paper demonstrating that, until Eadweard Muybridge's serial photographs of animals and humans in motion appeared in 1887, *all* representations in art of moving horses and other four-legged animals had been anatomically incorrect—all, that is, except the Metropolitan's Greek *Bronze Horse*. He had been puzzled for years by this seeming exception to his findings, and he was greatly relieved to learn that the little horse had, in fact, been created subsequent to Muybridge's photographs.

At this writing the Metropolitan has not been able to trace the horse's provenance or to gain any information whatsoever about its anonymous and undeniably talented creator. The general feeling is that it was cast in Paris sometime during the 1920s, a fact that led Sir John Rothenstein, the former director of the Tate Gallery in London, to remark that the piece was really "a splendid example of French Postimpressionist sculpture." The Metropolitan's handling of the disclosure suggests, in any case, that a new attitude toward the tricky question of forgery may be in the making —something closer, perhaps, to the attitude that prevailed in Michelangelo's day. Far from demonstrating embarrassment or chagrin, the Metropolitan announced its forty-year-old error with an eye to maximum news impact, and happily reaped rich harvests of publicity as a result. The horse, Noble said proudly, was "one of the most important classical art forgeries ever discovered."

ELEVEN

Ever since Napoleon's Egyptian campaign in 1789, ancient Egypt had captivated the popular imagination. Two excavated mummies were among the main attractions of Peale's Museum in Philadelphia—Barnum later exhibited them with equal success. Egyptian architecture influenced any number of nineteenth century public buildings in America—notably the New York Halls of Justice, whose massive walls imitated Egyptian temple style but which the public, brought up on Sunday supplement Egyptology, christened "The Tombs." Obelisks sprouted in countless cemeteries, and the erection in 1881 of King Thutmose III's obelisk in Central Park was a national event. The seventy-one-foot obelisk, a gift from the Khedive to the United States, arrived in New York in the summer of 1880 and was hoisted into position the following February. The entire cost of the operation was paid by William H. Vanderbilt, who nevertheless failed to appear at the formal ceremony of presentation held at the nearby Metropolitan Museum.

Vanderbilt may very well have been in Egypt at the time. By the 1880s, a winter's tour of the Pyramids had become the height of fashion. Shepheard's Hotel in Cairo was entering upon its great days, and the firm of Thomas Cook & Son did a thriving business ferrying tourists up the Nile to Luxor in comfortable *dahabiyehs.* The era of amateur archaeology was nearly ended. Gone were the days when Giovanni Belzoni, the six-foot eight-inch former circus strongman who worked for the British Consul, could conduct his operations in the Valley of the Kings with the aid of a battering ram, crushing and demolishing more antiquities than he preserved.

135

Thefts and tomb robbings would continue, of course, as they had since the time of the Pharaohs, but thanks to the pioneering labors of William Matthew Flinders Petrie, the great Englishman who virtually invented modern scientific archaeology, professional excavators now studied and recorded the relationship of every ancient object to its environment, employed relatively accurate systems of dating and classification, and ex-cavated with such painstaking care that nothing, no shard or sliver of ancient material, was overlooked.

The Metropolitan in its early days had received a sizable number of Egyptian objects from various benefactors, and since 1895 the museum had made annual subscriptions to England's Egyptian Exploration Fund, in re-turn for which it received each year a group of the antiquities dug up by Flinders Petrie and others. In 1905, acting on a suggestion from his friend Laffan, Pierpont Morgan decided it was time for the Metropolitan to estab-lish its own Egyptian Department, and to equip and finance its own ar-chaeological expedition in Egypt.

The Egyptians were still granting concessions to foreign archaeologists under favorable terms—a fifty-fifty sharing of the excavated material—and French, British, German, Italian, and American archaeologists were all dig-ging there. The Harvard University-Boston Museum of Fine Arts expedi-tion under George Andrew Reisner, taking over in 1905 a concession form-erly held by the University of California, had been having great success at Giza, and within the next few years the Pennsylvania Museum, the Univer-sity Museum of Chicago, and the University of Michigan would all enter the field. It was estimated at the time—wrongly—that if the current rate of activity continued, all the potential excavation sites in Egypt would be ex-hausted within fifteen years. Morgan had decreed that the Metropolitan's Egyptian department should "rank permanently as the best in America," and because there was no time to lose he simply carried out another calm raid on the Boston Museum. When Laffan visited the Harvard-Boston dig in 1905 he had taken an immediate liking to Albert M. Lythgoe, Reisner's chief field man and the founder of the Egyptian Department at the Mu-seum of Fine Arts. Morgan met Lythgoe a few months later, approved of him, and tendered the usual attractive offer. In 1906, Lythgoe resigned from the Boston Museum and from Harvard, where he taught a course in Egyptology, to become the Metropolitan's first curator of Egyptian Art, and the following January the Metropolitan began excavations in Egypt that would continue with extraordinary success for the next thirty-five years.

The men who worked under Albert Lythgoe considered themselves singularly privileged. In a profession noted for eccentrics and rugged individualists, Lythgoe was a truly self-effacing man and an exceptionally kind one. "Although it was his energy and his ideals that inspired all of those who worked with him he always did everything possible to keep in the background and to give his collaborators the fullest opportunity to do their work," Herbert Winlock, Lythgoe's young assistant and eventual successor, wrote of him. "This unfailing generosity gained him the unquestioning loyalty of every one of his associates, and also, in the field, the devoted affection of his Arab workmen." Lythgoe built up a brilliant staff that included, besides Winlock, Arthur C. Mace, an Oxford scholar with eight seasons experience in the field; Ambrose Lansing, an American born in Egypt, who could speak Arabic like a native; the copyists Norman and Nina de Garis Davies and Charles Wilkinson, the draughtsman Lindsley Hall, the architect Walter Hauser, and the photographer Harry Burton, all of whom collaborated in planning and photographing the excavated tombs and copying the wall paintings found in them. Wilkinson went on in later years to found the Metropolitan's department of Ancient Near Eastern Art. Mace, Mrs. Davies, Wilkinson, and Burton were all English, and all got along splendidly together.

Lythgoe and his associates began in 1907 by excavating near the Pyramids of Lisht, about thirty-five miles south of Cairo. The following year they opened another dig at the Oasis of Kharga, deep in the Libyan desert, and in 1910 they established what soon became the Metropolitan expedition's main base of operations at Luxor, site of the ancient city of Thebes. Thebes had been the seat of the XI Dynasty kings who reunited Upper and Lower Egypt after more than a century of anarchy and civil conflict, and ushered in the period of Egyptian history known as the Middle Kingdom. It was a great era in Egyptian art, making up in delicacy and grace what it had lost of the Old Kingdom's majestic austerity, and the Metropolitan collection today is particularly rich in works of this period.

Archaeology, for the professional, is ninety-nine parts hard labor and frustration to every one part thrilling discovery. The staff of the Metropolitan expedition, however, led a pleasant life. Pierpont Morgan came out to Luxor soon after operations started there and decided that men who worked that hard should have something better than a tent to come back to in the evening. Morgan put up the money for a large, comfortable base headquarters. It was called Morgan House until someone realized that the great financier had merely advanced the money as a loan and then paid himself back out of museum funds; after that it was known as Metropolitan House. Modeled after a Coptic church, with thick walls to hold the nightly chill and keep it cool during the scorching midday, it had twelve bedrooms (single for bachelors, double for married couples), a high-ceilinged common room for dining, and a shady veranda overlooking, in front, the wide, fertile plain, and in back, the stark desert hills in which lay the great necropolis of ancient Thebes. To the north was the Valley of the Queens, while farther back, in hidden tombs cut into the rocky hills, lay the Valley of the Kings. It was here that Egypt's Director-General of Antiquities, Gaston Maspero, had found in 1881 the royal sarcophagi of Thutmose III, Seti I, and Rameses II, which he had taken down the river to Cairo while superstitious *fellaheen* lined the riverbank and cried out in anguish, mourning the departure of their god-kings' perturbed spirits.

Life at Metropolitan House was relaxed and civilized, unlike the atmosphere at the Oriental Institute of Chicago dig nearby where a sort of military discipline prevailed. There was bottled water for drinking and Nile water for bathing, carried up in goatskins by tiny donkeys and cooled by evaporation. Illness was rare. Now and then someone caught a mild case of influenza or dengue, and the expedition staff spent a good bit of time treating the *fellaheen* for what often turned out to be syphilis, but for the most part everyone stayed remarkably healthy. Lythgoe's native work force in the early days numbered between one hundred and one hundred and fifty diggers, who were paid five or six piasters a day. The long rhinoceros whips of the gang bosses used to distress the trustees who came out to visit, but Lythgoe reassured them by pointing out that the whips were rarely used, and then only to flick deftly at the trailing *djellaba* of a laggard. Every Tuesday was Arab market day, and nobody worked—they worked Sundays instead. For recreation there was reading, bridge or poker, letter writing, and in the days before the First World War, horseback riding in the desert.

The digging season lasted from October to June, when the heat grew too intense and the Americans went home. Each winter there were visits by trustees and other persons of consequence. Some, like Morgan, arrived and lived aboard their luxurious *dahabiyehs;* others stayed at Metropolitan House and required attention from the staff. King Albert and Queen Elizabeth of the Belgians came out once, after the First World War, and had lunch at Metropolitan House. All through the meal, young Herbert Winlock was itching to ask the Queen a question. During her recent American tour, it was said, the wife of New York's Mayor John F. Hylan had convulsed three continents by her jovial observation to the monarch, "Queen, you said a mouthful." Winlock was dying to know whether the story was true, but he could not get up the nerve to ask. He confided his curiosity after lunch to the Queen's equerry, who said he would inquire. A few days later Winlock received a note reading, "Her majesty does not recall the incident but says she heard so many incomprehensible things while she was in America that this was quite possibly one of them."

One of Lythgoe's many talents was that he got along beautifully with rich trustees. Morgan liked him without reservation. So did Edward S. Harkness, the Cleveland philanthropist whose father had once bailed John D. Rockefeller out of serious financial straits and reaped his reward in Standard Oil stock. Harkness' benefactions were limitless—it was estimated that he gave away one hundred million dollars in his lifetime to schools and colleges, hospitals, churches, and other causes. His wife and Lythgoe's wife were cousins and devoted friends, and it was largely as a result of his friendship with Lythgoe that Harkness became a Metropolitan trustee in 1912 and a benefactor on the grand scale. After Morgan's death in 1913 Harkness became the principal sponsor and support of the Egyptian Department, to whose expeditions alone he contributed over the years a total of $377,893. Actually Harkness knew next to nothing about Egyptology. When he came out to Luxor on his private *dahabiyeh* he was always rather at loose ends unless Lythgoe could be on hand to take him around (Mrs. Harkness, who preferred the Ritz in Paris to the *dahabiyeh,* rarely made the trip). Harkness simply liked Lythgoe and wanted to help him, and his help took spectacular forms. In 1913, when the Egyptian government offered to sell the Metropolitan a complete, recently unearthed mastaba-tomb of an Old Kingdom dignitary named Peri-nebi, Harkness quietly put up the funds necessary for its purchase, shipment, and installation. His other gifts to the department included an important part of the Three Princesses jewelry, and the collection of precious objects assembled by the Earl of Carnarvon—the finest collection of Egyptian antiquities ever assembled by a private individual. Clearly the right sort of friend for a curator to have.

The Egyptian Department grew very rapidly. There was barely time each summer to assimilate, catalogue, and place on exhibition the vast amount of material from the museum's excavations—tomb sculptures, wall paintings and reliefs, jewelry, pottery, Greco-Roman and early Christian objects from the Oasis of Kharga and a new small dig at Wadi Natrun, scarabs, seals, papyri, and hundreds of other objects. The income from the Rogers Fund kept the expedition running smoothly, along with timely contributions from Harkness, Henry Walters, and several other trustees. When the museum had moved up from Fourteenth Street to Central Park in 1880, the Egyptian collection could be carried in one small envelope; in 1911, it filled ten new galleries in the recently extended north wing on Fifth Avenue. The trustees repeatedly authorized large expenditures for the purchase of Egyptian antiquities of periods not covered by the museum's own excavations, as a result of which the collection developed as a comprehensive survey of the entire, thirty-century sweep of Egypt's ancient civilization. Occasional grumblings were heard from other departments, but Lythgoe had Morgan's full support and nothing more was needed.

In the field, Lythgoe's young protégé Herbert Winlock was proving to be an exceptionally gifted archaeologist. Winlock came from a family of scientists. His grandfather had been director of the Harvard Observatory. His father, William Crawford Winlock, was for many years the assistant secretary of the Smithsonian Institution in Washington, D.C. When he was growing up Winlock often visited his father at the Smithsonian, and each time he went he would stop to look at the Egyptian mummies lined up in a corridor. They fascinated him, and for a while he spent all his free time carving miniature mummy cases out of wood from his father's empty cigar boxes. He even found a practical use for them. Having chanced to dig up a dead cat in the back yard, and being somewhat disgusted by its state of decomposition, Winlock began a series of experiments in home mummification. His subjects were mice, which he would embalm with the aid of various spices filched from the kitchen shelf (the cook was puzzled), wrapping them carefully in layers and layers of muslin before interring them in a series of perfectly carved and painted nesting coffins. The family worried for a time that he would become an undertaker, but Winlock's interests were scientific, not mortuary. A selection of his best mummy cases, presumably empty, was once exhibited at the Smithsonian.

Winlock entered the Class of 1906 at Harvard, where he acquired the nickname "Hebe" and a reputation for conviviality. He made a lot of friends, wrote bad puns for *The Lampoon,* and worked as little as possible until his senior year, when he did so well in Lythgoe's Egyptology course that Lythgoe brought him along to the Metropolitan as his assistant. No one ever loved the profession of archaeology more than Winlock. A man of action if ever there was one, he took to field work with enormous gusto and great resourcefulness, evolving techniques that nobody had thought of and getting along famously with the Arab workers. He liked and admired the *fellaheen* and never tired of telling stories about his dealings with them. One of his favorites had to do with the birth of his second child. Winlock's wife had gone home for the accouchement, and the telegram announcing the event had not specified whether it was a boy or a girl. One of the Arabs sadly assured Winlock that of course it must be a girl—"If it had been a boy, she would have said so."

During the First World War Winlock enlisted in the field artillery and served with distinction, rising to the rank of major. As soon as possible after the armistice he was back in Egypt, cranking up the Metropolitan's partially suspended operations, hiring diggers, planning new excavations. He liked to wear his military leggings and campaign hat, which seemed to give him added authority. Friends often described him as looking like a Roman proconsul, with his shaggy brows, rugged bone structure, and balding head. He was not tall, but his boundless energy, his direct, no-nonsense approach to every job, and his keen mind which cut straight to the marrow of archaeological problems made people look up to him. Like Lythgoe, he was generous to others and very well liked; unlike Lythgoe, he was not deaf to the demands of his own career. After 1919, with Lythgoe's encouragement, Winlock gradually took over the effective management of the Egyptian expedition.

Full-scale operations had resumed at Luxor in the fall of 1919. The following spring, Winlock made one of his most spectacular finds. He and his crew had spent eight unproductive weeks digging, and frustration was running high. Over in the nearby cliffs was a large, rock-cut tomb that Winlock had had his eye on for some time. It was a gloomy place, full of bats and snakes, and it had been excavated before by others, but the excavators had not mapped it and Winlock thought they might possibly have overlooked something. He decided to risk a fortnight's work there. On the evening of March 17, toward sunset, the expedition photographer, Harry Burton, went to dismiss the workmen who were digging out the tomb and found them all in a state of intense excitement. In clearing out the debris of fallen stone chips at one end of the chamber, a workman had noticed that small fragments kept sliding past his hoe to disappear into a crack between the rock floor and the tomb wall. The head workman came over and they both began scraping away the debris with their hands; the chips kept sliding into the crack. Could there be another, undiscovered chamber underneath? Burton arrived at this point. He struck several matches in the dark corner of the tomb, then scribbled a note on a scrap of paper and sent one of the boys running down with it to Metropolitan House. Winlock and the others had just come in from their day's work when the note arrived. Tired and somewhat sceptical, they gathered up flashlights and made their way back up the cliff. The sun had set by the time they reached the tomb. Winlock lay on the ground, held his flashlight to the crack, and beheld "one of the most startling sights it is ever a digger's luck to see." As he later described it:

> The beam of light shot into a little world of four thousand years ago, and I was gazing down into the midst of a myriad of brilliantly painted little men going this way and that. A tall slender girl gazed across at me perfectly composed; a gang of little men with sticks in their upraised hands drove spotted oxen; rowers tugged at their oars on a fleet of boats, while one ship seemed foundering right in front of me with its bow balanced precariously in the air. And all of this busy going and coming was in uncanny silence, as though the distance back over the forty centuries I looked across was too great for even an echo to reach my ears.

What they had stumbled on was an untouched cache of tomb figures made for the great noble Meketre, a Chancellor and Steward of the Royal Palace in the reign of King Mentuhotep II, who reigned about 2050 B.C. It was the custom of such dignitaries to provide for a pleasant afterlife of the soul by ordering these little spirit-models, which would continue throughout eternity to perform the services that the deceased had enjoyed during his lifetime. The models usually were placed in the tomb itself, and not many of them survived the depredations of centuries of grave robbers. Meketre, for some reason, had caused his models to be placed in a secret room adjoining the tomb, and as a result they had survived virtually intact. It was the largest and most complete series of tomb figures ever found, offering a remarkably detailed picture of daily life in ancient Egypt. Almost every activity of a large country estate is represented by the little wooden figures, crudely carved but full of sharply observed life. Clerks count cattle of different breeds; herdsmen tend their flocks; oxen are fed, slaughtered, butchered, seasoned, and prepared for the table; bakers tend their ovens; brewers blend the ingredients of a mash; women spin and weave yarn to make cloth; carpenters ply their adzes on rough timbers and saw them into planks; boatmen steer and row a variety of river craft while servants prepare food and drink for the nobleman's refreshment on board; and—a scene never before come upon—shapely walled gardens for the dead soul's delectation, with copper pools capable of holding water and little trees with each leaf carved and pegged in place and plump fruit growing from the branches. Although the Cairo Museum retained several of the models, the Metropolitan's share makes one of the most delightful and revealing exhibits to be found in any collection.

The 1920s decade was a great period of Egyptian archaeology, highlighted in the public's mind by the opening in 1923 of the tomb of Tutankhamen. For six years, a private expedition financed by Lord Carnarvon and directed by the English archaeologist Howard Carter had been looking for the tomb of this XVIII Dynasty monarch. Tutankhamen was a successor to the heretic King Akhenaten, who broke with Egypt's priest-ridden theology, moved the capital from Thebes to Tell el Amarna, and threw the country into chaos as a result. His son Tutankhamen, bowing to the powerful priests, had restored Egypt's old gods and moved the royal court back to Thebes, and a number of archaeological clues pointed to the location of his tomb somewhere in the Valley of the Kings. Curiously enough, the Metropolitan had received in 1909, as a gift from the American millionaire archaeologist Theodore M. Davis who had made several important finds in the area (and who had transferred his support from the Boston Museum to the Metropolitan when Lythgoe came there in 1906), a cache of embalming materials that were later identified with the last rites of Tutankhamen. The Davis cache would have led directly to the tomb had it been interpreted correctly. As it happened, Carnarvon and Carter had just about given up hope in 1922, and they had agreed that the current season would be their last in the Valley of the Kings. On November 4, just five days after the start of Carter's operations, one of his workmen discovered a concealed stairway underneath the previously excavated tomb of Rameses VI. It led to an intact, sealed doorway. Carter opened a small hole in the door and, looking in, saw the incredible, heart-stopping fulfillment to every archaeologist's dream, an unransacked royal tomb full of "strange animals, statues and gold—everywhere the glint of gold."

The find made headlines in almost every newspaper in the world, and provided Sunday supplement copy for years to come. It also created a great many new headaches for archaeologists. Carter's rather small force of excavators could not possibly cope with the enormous job of planning and clearing the tomb and classifying its contents (the work took ten years in all). Lythgoe promptly and generously came to his rescue, assigning four of the Metropolitan expedition's most valued members—Arthur Mace, Harry Burton, Walter Hauser, and Lindsley Hall—to work for Carter for as long as he needed them. Winlock kept the Metropolitan's own excavations going on a reduced scale, and the following season, when Carter got into difficulties with the Egyptian authorities, it was Winlock who more or less saved the day.

Howard Carter, for all his brilliance, had a very low boiling point. Several years before, he had personally arrested two slightly drunken French diplomats who were causing a disturbance in a tomb he was excavating. Since the French still maintained considerable influence in Egypt—the Director-General of the Egyptian Antiquities Service was by tradition a Frenchman—it was strongly suggested that Carter make a formal apology to the French Ambassador. He refused, and lost his job as a result. When Lord Carnarvon hired him he was eking out a thin living by painting and selling watercolors of Egyptian birds and cadging occasional meals from the commissary of a friendly expedition. He hit it off splendidly with Carnarvon, a great sportsman and automobile racer who came out to Egypt to recuperate from a near-fatal auto smash and promptly fell in love with archaeology.

The opening of Tutankhamen's tomb—the only intact Pharaonic tomb discovered in modern times—and the subsequent worldwide publicity had greatly added to nationalistic sentiment in Egypt, where many elements were clamoring for full independence from foreign (mainly British) control. The Egyptians were eager to change the fifty-fifty *partage* understanding with foreign archaeologists. Carter's irascible temper boiled over once again during negotiations, and the Egyptian government angrily revoked his digging concession, seized possession of the Tutankhamen tomb, and barred Carter from the premises. A lawsuit followed, but when Carter's lawyer insulted the Egyptians by saying that their government had acted "like a bandit" the proceedings were broken off indefinitely. Carter gave Winlock a power of attorney to represent him in any future dealings with the Egyptians (Winlock assured him that "you can't sneeze without my permission, and I doubt if you can spit"), and sorrowfully left the country. He might never have been allowed to return if there had not been a complete change of government that fall, following the assassination of the Sirdar. Prompted tactfully by Winlock, the new regime quietly gave Carter permission to come back and continue his work in the tomb, which Winlock had watched over carefully in his absence.

The Egyptians did manage to rescind the fifty-fifty agreement soon after the opening of Tutankhamen's tomb. The new law on excavations was purposely vague with regard to the excavator's share, leaving it more or less up to the discretion of the Egyptian authorities, and this served to cut down the number of foreign expeditions working in Egypt. The Metropolitan was too heavily engaged to think of withdrawing. Winlock had up to six hundred diggers and basket boys working for him by this time, and in spite of the new law he managed to send a decent proportion of his excavated material back to New York. He used to work himself into impressive rages for the benefit of Pierre Lacau, Maspero's successor as Director-General of the Egyptian Antiquities Service, pointing out to him that the Metropolitan trustees (august beings akin to Old Kingdom deities) would not vote the funds for next year's expedition unless enough first-rate offerings were sacrificed to the museum. As a result the department grew steadily larger, filling more and more galleries and overflowing into four huge storerooms. It had become a virtual museum-within-a-museum, with its own repair shop, its own restorers, and an annual budget exceeded only by that of the Paintings Department. When Lythgoe retired in 1929, conferring the double crown of the department and the expedition on Winlock, the Metropolitan's Egyptian collection was without a doubt the most comprehensive to be found in America.

Toward the end of the twenties decade, Winlock brought off a brilliant coup that demonstrated once again his persistence and his archaeological sixth sense. One of the major landmarks in the ancient Theban necropolis was the Temple of Queen Hatshepsut, built about 1500 B.C. in the great bay of the desert cliffs known as Deir el Bahri. A number of previous expeditions had excavated in the temple, but no one had done much about the long avenue, or causeway, leading up to it from the Nile valley. Such causeways were known to have been lined with statuary in the days of Queen Hatshepsut. Lythgoe and Winlock decided in 1923 to excavate on the north side of the causeway, and almost immediately they started to find fragments of stone statues that had been deliberately smashed. There were hundreds of these fragments, some mere chips of stone, others large blocks weighing as much as a ton. The arduous task of piecing them together continued for several years; the historical piecing-together took less time.

Queen Hatshepsut had been a scandalously unconventional ruler. The daughter of King Thutmose I, she had married her half-brother, who became King Thutmose II. When he died in 1504 B.C., his infant son by one of the royal concubines became the new divine king whom we know as Thutmose III (the same one memorialized by the Central Park obelisk), Hatshepsut became regent pending the boy's maturity. The taste of power whetted loftier ambitions. Shattering all tradition, Hatshepsut had herself declared Pharaoh in her own right. For more than twenty years she reigned over Upper and Lower Egypt, providing an energetic and for the most part benevolent administration and carrying out an ambitious building program. Her principal adviser, confidant, and no doubt intimate companion was her chief steward, Senmut. Hatshepsut and Senmut built the great temple at Deir el Bahri and filled it with statues of herself in various guises—as a sphinx, as the god Osiris with a ceremonial beard tied to her chin, and as the young princess she had been at age twenty, when, as Hatshepsut herself avowed, "to look upon her was more beautiful than anything; her splendor and her form were divine; she was a maiden, beautiful and blooming." (Chivalrous Winlock saw no reason to doubt the description, observing that Hatshepsut "was probably as good a judge of her own charms as any of her sisters have been since mirrors were invented.") She died mysteriously in 1479 B.C. The manner and circumstances of her death are unknown, but the records do show that immediately following this event King Thutmose III, now fully mature, ordered every trace and image of his stepmother destroyed. All the statues of Hatshepsut were hacked to pieces and thrown over the side of the great causeway, where they gradually disappeared under sand and debris.

Not all the fragments had remained where they fell. Egyptian stonemasons from the time of Thutmose III onward had apparently rummaged in the stone pile beside Hatshepsut's causeway, carrying away likely pieces to use on other building sites, and Winlock's diggers found fragments as much as half a mile from the temple. Others, as it turned out, had traveled a great deal farther.

By 1928, several complete statues of Hatshepsut had been reconstructed. There was one exceptionally beautiful granite head of the Queen, though, for which no fragment of a body had ever been found; conversely, the Metropolitan staff had put together six smashed sphinxes for which no heads had turned up. That summer, while going over some old German archaeological records in the Metropolitan library, Winlock found a document that set him to thinking. The Prussian archaeologist Lepsius, who had dug in the Valley of the Kings from 1843 to 1845, had purchased from the local Greek consul a seated statue of Queen Hatshepsut, unfortunately headless, and a granite sphinx's head wearing the Pharaonic crown. Both pieces were in the Berlin Museum. Winlock procured photographs of the Berlin statues and studied them carefully. The following fall, on his way out to Egypt for the winter season, Winlock made a side trip to Berlin. In his baggage were plaster casts of the Metropolitan's bodiless head and of a fragmentary female nose that he thought might belong to the Berlin Museum's sphinx head. The cast of the Metropolitan's head fitted the Berlin Museum's seated torso precisely. Winlock and the director of the Berlin Museum next inspected the Berlin sphinx head. "If you will allow me?" Winlock said, pushing hard with his thumb against the sphinx's nose. The nose broke off, being a plaster restoration; Winlock clapped on the cast of the Metropolitan nose, which fitted perfectly. An amicable bargaining session ensued, the upshot of which was that both museums kept their Hatshepsut heads and exchanged torsos, to the benefit of more complete Hatshepsuts and untold legions of New York schoolchildren who pass by the reconstituted image of this estimable lady on their way through the great hall of the Metropolitan. Those who lightly stroke her knee, it is said, will thereafter be exempt from the temptations of politics.

TWELVE

When Bashford Dean was a young zoology instructor at Columbia, his students used to wait in awe for the moment when he would go to the blackboard, take a piece of colored chalk in either hand, and draw—swiftly and simultaneously with both hands—the exact outline of some complex natural specimen. In those days Dean's interests lay mainly in the armored fishes of the Devonian period. His brilliant work in this field led him to the stimulating theory "that the arthrodires and their allies were neither peculiarly specialized dipnoans as held by Eastman and others, nor modified crossopterygians as suggested by Tate Regan, but . . . a wholly independent class of chordates." For anyone as ambidextrous as Dean, it was no problem at all to jump from arthrodires and chordates at Columbia to arms and armor at the Metropolitan Museum.

The transition even had a sort of formal logic, there being many similarities and parallels between the evolution of armor on fishes and on men. Dean had been fascinated by human armor since his childhood. One day his mother had taken him on a visit to the house of Carlton Gates in Yonkers, where the boy's eyes lighted on a medieval jousting helmet; he asked and was allowed to hold it in his hands, and at that moment a collector was born (years later, at the executors' sale of the Gates estate, Dean tried to buy the same helmet but was outbid by an older and wealthier fancier). At the age of seven he could draw rousing pictures of knights in combat. At age ten he made his first serious purchase, buying two daggers at the sale of the Cogniat collection in 1877. He would later devote the same tireless energy to tracking down pieces of armor that in his younger, scientific days he devoted to the search for elusive embryonic and fossil fishes; for Dean, the study of armor became, as one friend described it, "almost a branch of zoology." He was the only man who ever held curatorial posts at both the Metropolitan and the American Museum of Natural History.

Dean came from a well-to-do family of impeccably Old New York lineage. His paternal great-great-grandfather, John Dean, had been a captain in the Revolutionary Army, and had taken part in the capture of the unfortunate Major André. Members of the Dean family had been living in the vicinity of Riverdale, on the heights just north of Manhattan, since the seventeenth century. Bashford Dean greatly embellished the family tree in 1893 by his marriage to Alice Dyckman, whose family farm at the northern tip of Manhattan Island had been there since Colonial Days. Alice looked like a Franz Hals portrait and had an independent income, which helped no end when Dean started collecting. They lived in Riverdale in a large house called Wave Hill, which overlooked the Hudson River; among its previous tenants were Mark Twain and Theodore Roosevelt. The house was owned by George W. Perkins, one of J. P. Morgan's banking partners, who leased it to the Deans for life at a nominal rental. Today it is an historic landmark, owned by New York City and open to the public.

A short, squarish man with a jutting chin and a direct way of looking at people, Dean was phenomenally intelligent. He spoke seven languages fluently, including Chinese, which he used to practice with his laundryman. His research on armored fishes had taken him on extended travels to Alaska, Europe, Scandinavia, and Russia. In 1900 he went to spend several months at the Marine Biological Laboratory of the Imperial University in Tokyo, primarily to study the Japanese frilled shark. Dean rapidly mastered Japanese and was soon being received by the leading Japanese families. The Emperor presented him with a silver bowl. A great *daimyo* invited him to his country estate for the annual festival of his ancestors—Dean later claimed that he actually heard the ancestral voices. In several of the houses he visited, Dean saw magnificent samurai armor and weapons—sword blades tempered so finely that a lustrous wavy band (call the *yakiba*) played along the cutting edge, bows longer than any made in Europe, body armor composed of several thousand lacquered iron or leather scales laced together in bands. To his amazement, he learned that Japanese armor had been used ceremonially within the last thirty-five years, and that some of the great armorers were still living. It was at this point that Dean began seriously to study and collect armor. Within three years he had formed the finest collection of Japanese armor outside Japan, which he loaned to the Metropolitan for an exhibition in 1903.

The Metropolitan trustees had always been receptive to armor. The Cogniat collection, from which Dean bought his two daggers, had been shown at the museum in a loan exhibition in 1875, and in 1896 the trustees had gratefully accepted one hundred and sixty-six pieces of armor collected by the late John S. Ellis and presented by his widow. The Gothic Revival, which reached its peak in England midway through the nineteenth century, had infected many of America's new money barons with a craving for armor. In their gloomy mansions the gleaming battle harnesses, halberds, and broadswords served much the same function as the large and elegant English portraits that were becoming such a fad—they provided a sense of history, a link with a nobler epoch untainted by railroads, oil shares, or retail commerce. Pierpont Morgan never acquired much armor because he wanted only top pieces, few of which were available by the time he started to collect. The single piece he did buy, a parade helmet made for the French king Francis I by Philip Negroli, the "Michelangelo of armorers," is probably the finest single object in the Metropolitan's armor collection.

Among the other trustees the most enthusiastic armor collector was Rutherfurd Stuyvesant, who had acquired a comfortable fortune by the simple expedient of reversing his name. Born Alan Stuyvesant Rutherfurd, he became Alan Rutherfurd Stuyvesant at the request of his great-uncle, Peter G. Stuyvesant, a wealthy merchant with no heirs and a direct descendant of the peg-legged early governor of Nieuw Amsterdam. As a result of this transformation Rutherfurd Stuyvesant inherited his great-uncle's fortune and became a notable sportsman, world traveler, and collector. He was also, in 1870, the youngest member of the Metropolitan's first board of trustees. Stuyvesant had been collecting armor since the 1860s, attending all the important European sales and gradually turning his family home in New Jersey, "Tranquillity," into a medieval arsenal. He and Joseph Choate were the only two members of the original board of founding trustees to continue on into the Morgan era. By this time Stuyvesant was spending half of each year in Paris, and it was there, in 1904, that he snared the Duc de Dino's important armor collection for the Metropolitan.

The Duc de Dino was a great aristocrat, a descendant of the ancient Talleyrand-Perigord family in France. He was also a dedicated bon vivant, a womanizer, and a collector of armor—three rather costly hobbies whose demands often exceeded his means. When J. P. Morgan learned through a friend that Dino, being unusually short of cash, planned to sell his armor at auction, he cabled the news to Stuyvesant in Paris; Stuyvesant went around immediately to call on the Duke and offered to buy his collection outright, thus saving him the trouble of an auction. After a moment's thought the Duke said he would take $240,000 for it. Stuyvesant wrote out a check on the spot. He did not mention that there were not sufficient funds in *his* account at the Crédit Lyonnais at that moment to cover the check, and, fearful that any delay might cause the Duke to change his mind, Stuyvesant cabled Morgan in New York. The message arrived at three o'clock in the morning. Morgan, who was then vice-president, immediately called a meeting of Metropolitan trustees in his library. He informed them that their colleague Stuyvesant had bought the Dino armor collection in Paris, that he knew nothing more about it, but that they could not let down a fellow trustee. The inevitable shakedown ensued, with Morgan going around the table announcing how much each man would contribute (they were reimbursed later out of the Rogers Fund). The full amount reached the Crédit Lyonnaise in time to cover Stuyvesant's check. Dino tried to hold out for more money, but Stuyvesant kept him to his word and the entire collection arrived at the Metropolitan in 1904.

Cesnola was still director then. He knew very little about armor and seems to have cared even less, for he sent the Dino cases down to the basement without bothering to unpack them. Stuyvesant was furious when he came back to New York and found them there. Morgan asked Stuyvesant if he knew of anyone who could catalogue and install the Dino armor, and Stuyvesant suggested that they get Bashford Dean. Actually, Cesnola knew and rather liked Dean, who had helped him install the Ellis armor in 1896 and had also loaned his Japanese armor to the Museum in 1903. As soon as Dean opened the first few cases of Dino armor, he realized that it was an exceptionally fine collection. There were a number of historical pieces, such as the battle harnesses of Philip II of Spain and Frederick of Saxony, the sword cane of Don Juan of Austria, and the magnificent silver and gilt-bronze ceremonial parade helmet of Louis XIV. Dean told Morgan that he had made a great purchase at a bargain price, which delighted the financier. Morgan, in fact, was so impressed by the dynamic Columbia professor that he had him write a new catalogue for the museum's entire armor collection.

Dean's scientific career was in full swing at this time. Having served as co-founder (with Henry Fairfield Osborn) of the Department of Zoology at Columbia, he and Osborn had gone on to found a department of vertebrate palaeontology at the American Museum of Natural History, where Dean accepted an additional appointment as curator of the Department of Reptiles and Fishes. He resigned his Columbia professorship in 1906, when Morgan suggested that he become honorary curator of Arms and Armor at the Metropolitan—honorary meaning unsalaried. After this, arms and armor gradually took precedence over science. Although Dean continued to write and publish extensively in both fields—his three-volume magnum opus, the *Bibliography of Fishes,* won him the Eliot Medal of the National Academy of Sciences in 1923—most of his prodigious energy over the next twenty years went toward building the Metropolitan's collection of arms and armor, which today ranks among the first five in the world.

It might perhaps be asked what business a collection of arms and armor has in a museum of art. The Boston Museum, for once, had not stolen a march on the Metropolitan in this field; it has no armor to this day. Most of the great European armor collections are housed in separate museums of their own—the Waffensammlung in Vienna, the Armeria Real in Madrid, the Royal Armor Gallery in Dresden, the Musée de l'Armée in Paris, and the Tower of London. Part of the reason for New York's inclusion of armor among the fine arts was undoubtedly that Morgan, Stuyvesant, and a few other trustees liked it and wanted it there—and it can certainly be argued that the sheer sculptural artistry of much fifteenth and sixteenth century armor amply qualifies it for inclusion. It is highly doubtful, however, whether the Metropolitan's collection would have grown so large or so comprehensive had it not been for the unique personalities and passions of two men, whose relationship was a classic example of the strange, precarious, and highly complex game that is so often played out between curator and collector. One of these men was Dean. The other was William H. Riggs, an elderly American living abroad, and the greatest private collector of arms and armor of his time.

"He needs much who would become a successful collector," Dean once wrote. "He should begin early; he should be devoted and persistent; he must have at hand the necessary time and means; he must feel that he has a mission to accomplish; he should have what people call 'good luck'; and, most of all, perhaps, he must be born with a 'seeing eye' to fit him to pick and choose." According to Dean, William Riggs possessed every one of these qualities in full measure. He was born in Washington, D.C., in 1837, the son of the prominent banker Elisha Riggs, who was the J. P. Morgan of his day. Riggs had an adventurous youth. He went out west with one of the Benton-Beale expeditions, enjoyed several brushes with hostile Indians, and was once saved from drowning in the Arkansas River by Kit Carson, Colonel Beale's principal guide. The youth of fifteen returned from this trip with a large collection of Indian artifacts, costumes, and other ethnological material, which subsequently perished in a warehouse fire.

When Elisha Riggs died in 1853, his son decided to go abroad for a technical education that would equip him to take over the family mining interests in the Alleghenies. He entered the Sillig Academy in Vevey, Switzerland, an exclusive boarding school for the sons of rich men. One of his classmates there was J. Pierpont Morgan. Riggs and Morgan had been born within three weeks of each other, and at Vevey they became close friends. Unlike Morgan, though, Riggs never did return home to enter business. While he was at the Sillig Academy he started collecting Swiss swords and daggers, and within the year this hobby developed into an insatiable and lifelong passion.

At the Technische Hochschule in Dresden, where he went after Vevey to take engineering courses, he neglected his studies and spent hours and days in the galleries of the royal armory, whose director befriended him and gave him valuable advice. Riggs spent almost all his time between 1856 and 1860 traveling about Europe in search of armor. He met all the important collectors and dealers. He even got to know the local antiquaries in small towns throughout Germany and France. Riggs had the means, the time, the "seeing eye," and the persistence to track down every clue. At a dinner party in Vienna, he learned from a curator at the Munich Museum that some very rare helmets were to be sold the next day from the ancient arsenal of Mayence; Riggs took the night train, turned up at the arsenal before it opened, and was on his way home with the helmets before the Berlin and Paris dealers arrived. In Florence he made a sensational strike, securing the collection of the Marquis Panciatichi Ximènes whose wish to dispose of his arms is said to have lasted only twenty-four hours—just long enough for Riggs to pack the armor into baskets and carry it away. There was a good deal of armor changing hands during this period. Suits that had been rusting away in the attics of old castles for centuries were being brought out, cleaned, and sold to the new-rich bourgeois collectors whose love of the Gothic sometimes induced them to buy the entire castle as well. Duplicates from some of the great royal collections were being sold, the proceeds going to buy finer pieces. Among the most active competitors were Napoleon III, the Kings of Belgium and Italy, and the Czar of Russia, but time after time it was Riggs who took the top prizes. He traveled ceaselessly, ransacking palazzos in Venice, Genoa, and Milan (where he acquired two works by the Milanese master Negroli that had once been promised to the Italian government), haunting the old armor towns of Augsberg and Munich. He devoted a year to combing southern Spain. Spanish grandees embarrassed him by presenting as gifts magnificent pieces of armor passed down through many generations. Riggs crisscrossed Spain on horseback, his acquisitions following on a train of pack mules. He was once detained for several days by a notorious bandit named José Maria, who took a great liking to him and, instead of robbing him, made Riggs a present of an old dagger. He journeyed to the Middle East, was sunstruck at Sinai, and nearly died of fever near Jerusalem.

Riggs had established his base in Paris, in a large house in the Rue d'Aumale, which soon became a gathering place for scholars, connoisseurs, and artists. Viollet-le-Duc, the architect who was the leading exponent of the Gothic Revival in France, spent a great deal of time there. So did the amateurs Victor Gay, Baron de Ressman, and Sir Richard Wallace, and the painters Gustave Doré, Fortuny, and Gérôme. Adelina Patti sometimes sang for his guests, accompanied on the piano by Franz Liszt, in a little theater at one end of the long gallery.

During the Franco-Prussian War in 1870 Riggs bought an even larger house at 13, Rue Murillo, near the Parc Monceau. He rearranged the whole top floor as an armor gallery. The room was eighty feet long by about fifty wide; it was never heated in winter for fear of condensation forming and rusting the armor, and it was never quite large enough for the collection. Although Riggs constantly weeded his collection, selling or exchanging pieces for better examples, the armor kept piling up in closets and overflowing to the basement. As the years went on, Riggs became more and more engrossed in the collection, forever cleaning, repairing, and rearranging it with the help of his armorer and assistants, until eventually, as sometimes happens, the collection came to dominate the man. The old days of brilliant dinner parties and buying trips were forgotten. He had been known to go as long as fifty days without leaving the house. A lifelong bachelor—he once said that he could never marry because a woman might interfere with his lifework—he became, in his later years, a sort of recluse, an eccentric old gentleman like his friend and teacher Père Carrand, the Lyons archivist who used to wear a lace jabot and antique shoe buckles and who lived almost entirely in the past.

In the back of his mind, Riggs had always harbored the idea that the collection would eventually serve, as he put it, "to instruct and please the art-loving people" of his own country. This generous incentive did not escape the notice of the Metropolitan's founding trustees. As early as 1872, John Taylor Johnston wrote a letter to Riggs in Paris, reminding him of their shipboard conversation "on our passage to New York from Brest" four years previously, in the course of which Riggs had spoken vaguely of giving his armor to New York City; Johnston wanted to give notice that the Metropolitan Museum was now in business, and that a better final resting place for the Riggs armor could not be found. Although Riggs had made only two brief visits to his homeland since he left it in 1853, the Metropolitan went so far as to elect him a trustee and a vice-president in 1870—he resigned in 1874, with thanks. The prospects, however, remained for many years discouraging. Riggs apparently doubted the Metropolitan's ability to survive without government support, and he talked more and more about leaving his armor collection to the Smithsonian Institution in Washington. "I fear the Washington people will get it," Marquand wrote Cesnola in 1890, after visiting Riggs in Paris. "They promise him everything." But the Washington people did not promise quite enough to suit Riggs. The government wanted him to endow the collection with a sum sufficient to main-

tain it permanently, and the space arrangements proposed by the Smithsonian were not to his liking. In 1893 Marquand heard that "Mr. Riggs has
fallen out with Washington." In 1899, Rutherfurd Stuyvesant called on
Riggs in Paris and reported back that the tide was turning in the Metropolitan's favor. Marquand was overjoyed. "The gift of Mr. Riggs would be
the crowning achievement of the Metropolitan Museum," he said. "I will
do all I can to promote it." But a month later Frederick Rhinelander was
cautioning Cesnola not to be too hopeful—Riggs "is uncertain in his intentions and we can only hope that his present state of mind will be confirmed."

The game of cat-and-mouse is one that collectors enjoy far more than
museum men. The psychology of play varies, but the basic structure remains the same—the mouse, a formidable opponent and a master escape
artist, prolongs by every means his refusal to be pinned down, because
once that happens the game is over. Riggs kept the Metropolitan Museum
guessing for more than forty years, and he might never have been pinned
down at all if it had not been for Bashford Dean.

Dean entered the picture in 1904, when he went with Rutherfurd Stuyvesant for his first visit to the house at 13, Rue Murillo. Afterward he set
down in his neat, small script a few impressions of William Riggs: "He was
a man of sixty, clearly a scholar and a great personage—slightly built,
shoulders stooping, nose aquiline, hands and feet surprisingly small, eyes
clear and very bright. His face lighted up when he talked and he had
charm of manner. . . . One could never forget his resonant voice which
slurred no syllable, nor hurried, nor failed to choose a word which precisely 'fitted.'" Riggs spoke English when he had to, but after all these
years he was more at home in French.

Dean also saw the collection, and found that it far exceeded all reports.
"There are historical pieces out of number," he wrote back excitedly to
acting director Edward Robinson, "authentic—such as part of an armor of
Henry VIII, a half suit of Alva, of the Grand Constable, of Henry II, Francis I, several of the Duke of Hohenaschau—sword of Max[imilian] II, Karl
V, Henry IV . . . he has something like 100 suits, several *thousand* swords,
300 casques . . . The pieces have all been selected with great care and the
collection is probably ten times, surely five times, the size of the Dino
collection."

Riggs took to Dean immediately. A few weeks later, the election of Riggs's old schoolmate Pierpont Morgan as president of the Metropolitan put to rest any remaining doubts in his mind about the museum's permanency. Now the game began in earnest. When Dean became honorary curator of Arms and Armor at the Metropolitan in 1906, Morgan made it clear that he wanted him to devote his principal efforts to securing the Riggs collection.

Riggs and Dean corresponded regularly for several years, and saw one another frequently whenever Dean came to Europe. The older man accepted Dean as a pupil and friend; the museum, for its part, did everything it could to encourage the relationship. In a long, rambling letter written late in 1907, Riggs told Dean that he had been "strongly touched" by the news that the Metropolitan's trustees had "done me the great honor of naming me an honorary member for life," and also noted that the time was approaching when he must see his native land again and "make a definite decision about the disposition of my collections." There were, however, "certain complications" regarding his affairs in Europe, which might delay both the trip and the decision. The main complication seemed to be a hotel property that Riggs owned in Luchon, a small thermal spa in the Pyrenees. The hotel had been losing money, and he was trying very hard to get rid of it.

Three months later, Dean wrote to say that "Mr. Morgan is planning to set aside a magnificent gallery in the new wing of the Museum for the armor collection." The museum was expanding in all directions, having retained the firm of McKim, Mead and White to push the Fifth Avenue wing farther north, build a new library, and construct a large wing for decorative arts behind and parallel to the north Fifth Avenue wing. It was clearly indicated to Riggs that he could have his pick of the new galleries.

Bashford Dean spent that summer in Europe, "continuing my training in arms and armor," as he put it, and casting Riggs in the flattering role of master teacher. He wrote back "hopeful news" to Edward Robinson at the Metropolitan—"the most hopeful I have had." Nothing was definite, however, and Dean warned that Riggs *is now so elderly and so sensitive that I hope and pray that whatever happens no whisper of it will be published —or it may cause him to alter matters.*" Dean's letter went on to report that he had found the man to put the Metropolitan's own armor collection in shape. This was Daniel Tachaux, who came over to work for the museum in 1910. Tachaux had been trained by Ludwig Klein, the official armorer to Napoleon III. He owned a complete armorer's *outillage*—iron forming stakes set into huge wooden blocks, heavy cutting shears, chisels and hammers of all kinds for beating and patinating and embossing and planishing, some of them dating back to the sixteenth century. The Metropolitan later bought the entire collection, which is still being used by the present armorer, Harvey Murton, in the museum's basement armory. Tachaux not only repaired what needed repairing, but also filled out many incomplete harnesses with plates and elements of his own making, and the mounted knights in the great armor hall today owe much to his skill. At first, though, the museum paid only a quarter of Tachaux's salary and received only a quarter of his time—Stuyvesant, Clarence Mackay, and Dean made up the remainder, in return for Tachaux's work on their private collections.

Dean's "hopeful news" was premature. The following February, a cautious letter from Robinson to Riggs showed that the museum was as much in the dark as ever. "The rumor has reached me—based, I must say, upon nothing more serious than gossip—that your wonderful collection of armor might sometime find a permanent home here," Robinson wrote. In view of the museum's building projects, he added, it would be most helpful to know whether there were any truth to the rumor. On the other hand, "if the report which has reached me is without foundation, or my suggestion appears as an intrusion, take no further notice of the matter. If in due course I receive no reply from you I shall understand."

There was no reply. But when Dean went to Paris in June 1910, Riggs himself brought up the subject. As Dean wrote excitedly to Morgan, *"He said he particularly wished to see you at this time as he thought he was now ready to make the formal gift to you."* Robinson, "exhilarated by the extraordinarily good news," began planning to put the Riggs armor on exhibition the following spring. Unfortunately, the meeting with Morgan never took place and the gift-making decision was not made. Robinson (who had by this time succeeded Purdon Clarke as director) wrote to Morgan that summer about the "Riggs situation." "Knowing now something of Mr. Riggs' temperament," he said, "I can see the gulf that always intervenes, and probably always will intervene, between his intending to do a thing and actually doing it." Robinson added that it would be a serious problem if they continued to make preparations for housing the Riggs armor in Wing H, which was nearing completion, and then did not get the armor.

Little by little, though, Riggs's language grew more specific. In the fall of 1911 he told Robinson that he hoped to see Morgan in Paris next spring, when he would "submit to his judgement my desires as to the definite removal of my armour and art collections to 'New York Metropolitan Museum' for their future safe-keeping." (Note the careful avoidance, however, of words like "donate" and "gift.") Riggs said he had now definitely decided against giving his collection to the Smithsonian, the main reason being that he was sure "Mr. Morgan *will perfectly agree with me as to all I may submit to his approval.*" Absolute secrecy was essential, he added, because if the French government learned that he was planning to export his treasures it might intervene; premature publicity would endanger the gift.

Matters suddenly came to a head in the spring of 1912. Morgan and Riggs met in Paris, and Riggs said that he had decided to give his entire collection to the Metropolitan. Morgan's gratitude did not prevent him from having his lawyer draw up a codicil to Riggs's will, making the gift legally binding. But when Morgan left for London a few days later the codicil had not been signed. Riggs told Dean, who was staying at his house, that he could not sign it until October—"and by that time," as Dean anxiously wrote to Metropolitan Vice-President Robert de Forest, "his indecision might have become even more acute." According to Dean, Riggs had aged considerably in the last year; he seemed physically feeble, and showed a marked disinclination to decide *anything*. Dean managed to maneuver him into signing the codicil. The next day, though, when Dean brought up the delicate question of packing the armor and shipping it to New York, Riggs dropped a singular bombshell. He could not possibly think of shipping the armor, he said, while his hotel property in Luchon was still so heavily on his mind.

A deadly foreboding assailed Dean. There was no telling what might happen unless some definite action confirmed the gift. Riggs changed his mind several times a day, and he could always revoke the codicil. Feeling powerless, Dean rushed across the Channel to London to get Morgan's advice. He described Morgan's awesome reaction in a letter to Henry Kent at the museum: " 'So Mr. Riggs can't pack his collection and catalogue it be-

cause his mind is upset by troubles with his hotel property at Luchon?'
He took his cigar in his fingers, and his eyes blazed. 'How much would it
cost to buy the property at once?' 'Five to six hundred thousand francs,' I
said. 'Well, buy it—I'll take it and lose a couple of hundred thousand
francs. Not a bad investment, if the Museum gets a collection worth three
millions of dollars!' " Dean came away marveling at the Jovian audacity of
Il Magnifico, and wondering whether he would be able to pull it off. He
abjured Kent to "pray for me that my feet may not stumble in this tortuous
job of mine."

The Grand Hotel de Luchon et du Casino, the somewhat ramshackle
subject of these deliberations, was a sprawling wooden structure with six
floors and one hundred and thirty rooms, and taking it off Riggs's hands
proved to be no easy matter. Riggs had apparently been inveigled into
buying it years before by a rather mysterious Mme. Vestri—long departed
from the scene—and as Dean pithily observed to Kent, "He has so long
been bothered with it that he couldn't get along without it." He was unwilling to sell it at a loss, for that would reflect upon what he considered
his own excellent business judgment. Under the previous manager, the hotel
had consistently lost money. That June, Riggs had just about decided to sign
a long lease with another tenant, who he hoped would prove a more efficient
hotelkeeper. Dean knew that once the lease was signed Riggs would devote most of his time keeping an eye on the place, supervising inventories
and books and making suggestions, and that as a result there would be no
chance of getting the armor until he died, if then. The negotiations
dragged on. Toward the end of the month, in a moment of irritation, Riggs
said he was so "tourmenté" by the "damned hotel" that he would gladly
sell it for a mere four hundred thousand francs. It was the moment Dean
had been waiting for. He immediately made his offer to buy the hotel himself at that figure. The astonished collector agreed, and then a few seconds
later tried to retract, "but," as Dean reported, "I held him to his word."
Riggs thought Dean was buying it for the Metropolitan; he was not supposed to know of Morgan's role in the transaction.

The worst of it, so far as Dean was concerned, was that he was now
stuck with running an unsalable hotel. He spent the summer of 1912 as a
"miserable hotelier." The prospective new tenant backed off at the last moment, and Dean had to rehire the former manager and let him run the

place for one third of the proceeds. A few guests arrived. Dean sent "brief, exact, and frequent reports" to Morgan, and complained that Morgan "hasn't even sent me a line" in return. He was decidedly startled to learn that Morgan was planning "to charge up the wretched old hotel to the account of the Museum"; as Lythgoe had learned in the case of the Egyptian expedition's headquarters at Luxor, what at first appeared to be Morgan gifts had an odd way of turning into Morgan loans. In point of fact neither Morgan nor the museum owned the hotel as yet. The museum (through Dean) had promised to buy it from Riggs for 400,000 francs; half that sum had been advanced to him on account, and the Metropolitan had assumed all the carrying charges on the property. But Riggs remained the legal owner until the museum should arrange for its sale to a third party. The whole situation was hideously complicated. It was, Dean said, "the most difficult and involved [problem] of any I've had to do with."

After convincing himself that the hotel was at least running smoothly, Dean went back to Paris and began with Riggs the enormous job of cataloguing the collection. Riggs was cheerful, talkative, and full of stories about every piece of armor. The "travaux forcés," as he called it, continued through the fall and winter, during which Dean also kept up his vain attempts to find a buyer for the hotel. Recognition of his Herculean efforts had come in the form of a full curatorship of the new Department of Arms and Armor, established in the fall of 1912—up to then, armor had been considered part of the Decorative Arts department.

Morgan's death in the spring of 1913 came as a stunning shock to everyone. Riggs was shaken by the news, but instead of undermining his resolve, as Dean feared it might, the event had the opposite effect. Morgan had given a splendid example of leaving his house in order, Riggs told Dean, and he himself must hasten to do the same. Riggs began at once to prepare for a trip to America—his first since 1868. He wanted to see the space that the Metropolitan had set aside for his armor. "It seems clear that as he *must* see the hall before shipping his collection, the sooner he sails the better," Dean wrote to Robinson. Riggs ordered his new clothes and linens for the American trip and sent his steamer trunk out to be repaired. The Luchon hotel remained unsold, which worried Dean. "The only cheerful side," Dean wrote Robinson, "is that Mr. Riggs appreciates what is being done for him and will, if the strain is physiologically possible, send his collection over next fall."

Riggs and Dean sailed at last on May 3, 1913, aboard *La France*. They reached New York on the ninth, and Dean immediately carried his friend off to Wave Hill in Riverdale. The museum had not made any definitive space commitments for the Riggs armor—the prospects having remained so unsettled—and in lieu of anything more impressive it was decided to show him two large galleries at the far end of Wing H, the new northward extension of the Fifth Avenue wing; these two galleries had previously been promised to the Egyptian Department, whose staff never forgave Dean and *his* staff for the theft. Riggs was evidently delighted with the space. On the evening of May 12, at any rate, after a dinner at Edward Robinson's house on Irving Place, he announced to the officers and members of the executive committee that he was presenting his collection of arms and armor to the Metropolitan. The gift, Riggs said, was attributable mainly to his admiration for the late J. P. Morgan, and it was being made without conditions or restrictions. In fact, Riggs did not even want it to be shown by itself; he wanted it merged with the museum's other armor in chronological arrangement, "so that the Museum's exhibit of arms and armor should illustrate in an unbroken series all the stages of the armorer's art." It seemed, all in all, a handsome conclusion to a forty-year wait.

Riggs signed the formal deed of gift in the living room of Wave Hill on June 5, in the presence of Robert de Forest (the Metropolitan's new president), Edward Robinson, Bashford Dean, and several of the trustees. He was promptly elected a Benefactor and a trustee for life, and asked to sit for his portrait at the museum's expense. Two weeks later he sailed back to France.

The museum had hoped to show the Riggs collection that fall, but packing and shipping it took much longer than Dean expected. There were endless delays, caused by "the difficulty I have to get Mr. Riggs to give up the objects. . . . I realize, better perhaps than anyone, what it means to him to part with his treasures, each of which he loves more perhaps than anyone will ever love the *whole collection!*" In the end he held back a few treasures to which his attachment was deepest. All these eventually joined the rest, for Riggs continued to make gifts to the museum until his death in

1924; during the war, he even managed to acquire for the museum what many other collectors considered the finest suit of armor in existence—the etched and gilded parade armor of Francois I's master of artillery, Galiot de Genouilhac—contributing $5,000 toward its purchase price of $80,000 from his old friend the Duchesse d'Uzès. A new codicil to his will ceded to the Metropolitan whatever it wanted from his Paris house. Public announcement of the gift was made finally in February, 1914—once the armor had left France and entered the museum—and the new armor galleries were opened to the public a year later. De Forest congratulated Dean for his "great work" in securing at long last the collection that placed the Metropolitan among the foremost armor galleries in the world. Certainly, de Forest said, "it would not have been there except for you. It represents on your part a monumental display of perseverance, patience, tact and judgement."

Much to Dean's disgust, the Metropolitan remained in the hotel business for five more years. The French government leased the "wretched old hotel" in Luchon during the First World War, as a home for convalescent soldiers. After the war, Riggs's sentimental feeling for the place prevented the museum from selling it at a sacrifice figure. As de Forest pointed out, Riggs's goodwill was worth much more than the hotel had cost originally, and there was no point in angering him. The hotel was finally sold in 1920, at the drastically sacrificial figure of 150,000 francs, to a pair of gentlemen who had no previous experience in hotelkeeping. One of them, François Gays, had been employed for many years as a personal valet; the other, Monsieur Marchat, as an armorer. Their former employer, who arranged the sale and put up the necessary funds himself, was William H. Riggs.

THIRTEEN

Henry James, that connoisseur of intimations, had proved to be an accurate prophet. There was money in the air, all right, and an astonishing amount of it was being converted into works of art. During the eight years of Pierpont Morgan's presidency, the Metropolitan's acquisitions piled up so fast that not even a doubling of the available gallery space could begin to accommodate them.

Annual consignments from Lythgoe's Egyptian expeditions made up a large part of what Edward Robinson termed "the rapid and bewildering increase in our collections," but the other departments of the museum were growing almost as rapidly, through gifts and purchases. Several large money bequests had fattened the purchase funds. John Stewart Kennedy, de Forest's ally in the losing battle to oust Cesnola, died in 1909 and left the museum an unconditional bequest of stock worth $2,600,000. In 1912 the museum received more than $900,000 in purchase and operating funds from the will of the publisher Joseph Pulitzer, and another totally unexpected windfall from a ten-dollar-a-year member whom no one on the board had ever met. The donor was Francis L. Leland, a New York banker who modestly informed Morgan and de Forest that he wanted to do something for the museum and handed over an envelope containing twelve hundred shares of stock in the New York County Bank, of which he was the president. At the time the stock was valued at $900 per share, which would have made the gift worth more than a million dollars; unfortunately, Leland specified that the stock could not be sold, and it became virtually worthless when the bank failed during the Depression.

Robinson's efforts to build a professional staff received every encouragement from Morgan. The Classical and Egyptian departments were staffed,
as we have seen, with the somewhat unwilling assistance of the Boston
Museum of Fine Arts. The Department of Decorative Arts was formed in
1907, principally to accommodate the Hoentschel collection that Morgan
had bought in Paris the year before, at a price reportedly exceeding a million dollars. Georges Hoentschel, a French architect and designer, had
amassed two separate collections in his large house on the Boulevard Flan-
drin. One section was devoted to the decorative arts of the French eighteenth century, with examples of the great ébénistes and master craftsmen
and a vast quantity of *boiserie,* ormolu, and porcelain. The other section
was Gothic—sculpture, choir stalls, columns from churches, mantels, several splendid tapestries, and the finest set of early Limoges enamels and
ivories in existence. Morgan placed the Gothic section on loan to the museum (the first important medieval objects to be shown there) and presented the eighteenth century collection as a gift, expressing his desire
"that it should be made the nucleus of a great collection of decorative art."
On Morgan's initiative, a new wing had been designed specifically for the
Hoentschel collection by the fashionable firm of McKim, Mead and White;
it ran parallel to and behind the north Fifth Avenue wing, and was completed in 1909. Meanwhile, the Department of Decorative Arts was taking
concrete form under the guidance of its European first curator, William R.
Valentiner.

Valentiner came highly recommended. He had worked previously as an
assistant to Wilhelm Bode, the director-general of the Kaiser Friedrich Museum in Berlin. Bode enjoyed enormous authority and never hesitated to
use it to get what he wanted. When a wealthy collector once protested that
he did not like a painting that Bode wanted him to buy, Bode replied
firmly, "That is not the question. The museum needs it; we cannot let it go,
and we cannot afford to buy it. Meanwhile, you might just as well have it
and you'll probably learn to like it." Valentiner had learned his trade
under Bode, who described him to Robinson as "the most gifted and best
equipped young student of art that I have ever had in the museum," and
added that, while he hated losing him, he was pleased that Valentiner
should find occupation in the museum "where works of art are now coming

together more than anywhere else"—an impressive tribute from an active rival. Valentiner was already known at this time as an authority on Rembrandt and the early Dutch and Flemish schools (Bode called him "certainly superior to R. Fry" in this field). His work with Bode had given him a thorough grounding in other fields of art, though, and he soon proved to have a good eye and a quick mastery of styles and periods. This was fortunate, for the Metropolitan's Decorative Arts Department took in everything in the museum that did not fall under Paintings, Greek and Roman Art, or Egyptian Antiquities. The old Departments of Sculpture and Casts had been abolished in 1905. Valentiner's domain, which ranged from Assyrian bas-reliefs and Islamic plates to the group of Rodin sculptures donated in 1910 by the New York banker and tobacco magnate Thomas Fortune Ryan, comprised more than a third of the objects in the museum.

Like some giant amoeba, the Department of Decorative Arts would from time to time divide and give birth to a new curatorial entity—Far Eastern Art in 1915, Near Eastern Art in 1932, and Medieval Art, "Renaissance and Modern Art," and the American Wing in 1933. The first curator of Far Eastern Art was Sigisbert Chrétien Bosch-Reitz, a well-connected Dutch scholar whose brother was chamberlain to Queen Wilhelmina of Holland. Bosch-Reitz took over in 1915 a large and heterogeneous collection of Asian objects that had been accumulating since 1879, the year that several trustees and other subscribers banded together to buy a group of thirteen hundred Chinese ceramics selected by Samuel P. Avery. Other gifts followed—Japanese pottery and porcelain from Charles Stewart Smith; more than a thousand Ch'ing dynasty decorative jades from Heber R. Bishop; a magnificent Han dynasty bronze vase presented in 1887 by the Chinese diplomat Chang Yen Hoon, who had the misfortune, a few years later, to incur the displeasure of the Dowager Empress—objecting to his "too liberal views," she had him beheaded. Boston, as usual, had established a comfortable lead in the Oriental field. The Department of Asiatic Art of the Museum of Fine Arts had been in existence since 1890, and its Japanese curator, Okakura Kakuzo, had laid the foundations of a collection that has not yet been surpassed in this hemisphere. Bosch-Reitz bought shrewdly and well, however, and organized his department on an efficient and professional footing. He was known around the museum as "Old

Dutch Cleanser," because of his passion for neat and orderly arrangements —a trait that was not shared by his more colorful successor, Alan Priest, of whom we shall hear more later on.

Paintings at the Metropolitan were the responsibility of Bryson Burroughs, who came in 1906 as Roger Fry's assistant, took over as full curator in 1909, and served continuously until 1934—twenty-eight years in all. Burroughs was himself a painter. Although his personal taste was classical—he admired Ingres above all other artists, and his own work resembled that of his teacher Puvis de Chavannes—Burroughs' sensibilities were broad enough to appreciate a great deal of what was being done in modern art. He worked hard to bring in Renoir's *Madame Charpentier and Her Children,* which Roger Fry recommended in 1907; he cleverly brought it up for decision at a time when the older trustees on the purchasing committee were out of town, and won approval from the younger and more daring spirits—a stratagem that nearly brought about his dismissal. In 1913 he struck an even more intrepid blow for modern art by recommending the purchase of a Cézanne from the notorious Armory Show in New York. Compared to Matisse's *Blue Nude* or Duchamp's *Nude Descending a Staircase,* Cézanne's gentle landscape *La Colline des Pauvres,* painted in 1890, may have seemed more palatable to the trustees than it would have under different circumstances, but it held no appeal whatsoever for Robert de Forest and several other trustees. Although de Forest voted against it, a narrow majority of the purchasing committee went along with Burroughs' argument that "It would be a popular purchase . . . and would make valuable friends for the museum," and the painting thus became the first Cézanne to enter a public collection in America.

Modern art, however, intruded only slightly upon the trustees' deliberations. Even the Barbizon school had fallen from grace by this time, largely deserted by American collectors who were buying under the influence of the flamboyant Joseph Duveen. Duveen had decided about 1910 that modern pictures were cutting into the capital funds that he planned to tap. He advised his clients not to buy any, and offered instead, at increasingly ethereal prices, eighteenth century English portraits by Gainsborough, Romney, and Lawrence, Dutch masterpieces by Rembrandt and Hals, and Italian paintings of the early and high Renaissance. "You can get all the pictures you want at fifty thousand dollars apiece," Duveen told his millionaire clients. "That's easy. But to get pictures at a quarter of a million apiece—that wants doing." Although Morgan was not a particular client of Duveen's, preferring to buy from Jacques Seligmann and one or two other dealers, he thought in similar terms, and it is not surprising to find that the Metropolitan Museum during his presidency purchased accordingly. Veronese's opulent *Mars and Venus United by Love,* purchased at Christie's in London for the bargain price of £8,000, arrived in 1910, as did Tintoretto's *Doge Alvise Mocenigo Presented to the Redeemer* and Rubens' great *Wolf and Fox Hunt.* (Duveen had trouble persuading his clients to buy Rubens, whom he himself admired tremendously; Duveen clients did not care for Rubens' fat ladies, but they were sometimes willing to purchase and present them to museums.) The next year, the Metropolitan bought its first Botticelli, the *Three Miracles of Saint Zenobius,* and also an *Epiphany* from Giotto's workshop and a *Meditation on the Passion* labeled Mantegna but believed even then to have been painted by Carpaccio (in 1945, under examination by infrared light, the Carpaccio signature showed up clearly beneath the fraudulent "Andreas Mantinea," nailing the matter down once and for all). Several of the major gaps that Roger Fry pointed out in 1906 had been closed by 1913. A great many more were filled later that year by the will of Benjamin Altman, the New York department store merchant whose collection was the only one of the era that could hold its own beside Morgan's.

Altman was the son of Bavarian Jews who came to America about 1853 and settled on the Lower East Side of Manhattan. When his father died Altman left school and went to work in a succession of small dry goods stores, where he gradually accumulated enough capital to open his own shop on Third Avenue near Tenth Street. In 1870, the year the Metropolitan was founded, Altman moved his dry goods business to Sixth Avenue and began expanding into other areas of merchandising. By the time he moved again in 1906 to the store's present location on Fifth Avenue at Thirty-fourth Street, B. Altman & Co. was one of the city's largest and most prosperous department stores. Altman himself, who probably made more money than Morgan, attained none of Morgan's prominence in the public eye. He never married, had few friends and no social life. Aside from business, the only thing he seems to have cared about was his art collection.

He began collecting about the turn of the century, starting with Chinese porcelains which he bought from Henry Duveen, Joseph's uncle. Uncle Henry won his confidence so securely that when Altman went on to other branches of art he usually followed the genial dealer's advice. Altman's tastes developed rapidly, though, and while other New York millionaires were buying Barbizon landscapes and portraits of cattle, Altman bought Rembrandt. According to Wilhelm Bode, Altman's collection, while considerably smaller and less varied than Morgan's, was "decidedly superior to it in quality, especially in the picture section."

It is interesting to compare Altman and Morgan as collectors. Both wanted top quality and only top quality in whatever they bought. Their purchasing methods, however, were diametrically different. Morgan bought lavishly and made his decisions with awe-inspiring speed—his raids upon the private collections of Europe were carried out, as an editorial in *The Burlington Magazine* put it soon after his death, "with the rapid decisive energy of a great general." If Altman liked an object, he would often go home and read books on the subject and consult various other opinions, expert and lay, before deciding to buy it. "His method of proceeding was the despair of dealers," the critic Gustav Kobbe wrote of him in 1914. "When they thought a picture almost as good as sold to him there would be hesitation, delay, and often what seemed like vacillation . . . . Where it took Mr. Morgan barely five minutes to conclude a purchase of a painting for $750,000, Mr. Altman might have taken weeks and even months for reflection and then have decided not to buy." When Altman did decide to buy, the price never stopped him. Although he lived a fairly frugal existence and traveled, as Joseph Duveen once remarked, "like a Cook's tourist," he almost always accepted the value placed upon an object by a dealer he trusted. With Morgan, contrary to popular myth, there were numerous occasions when he declined a purchase with the curt explanation, "Price too high."

Both of them got most of what they wanted, but their collecting goals were not the same. Although Morgan's eye for the quality of a piece was as fully developed as Altman's, his feeling for works of art was basically romantic and historical rather than aesthetic—what he responded to in an object was mainly its importance in the evolution of culture. Altman cared very little about historical associations. He wanted aesthetic quality in its most exquisite and perfect form. His four hundred and twenty-nine Chinese porcelains were the choicest of their kind, from the complete series of large Ming vases to the delicate *clair de lune* pieces that were considered the most beautiful in existence. His fifty paintings showed the same rarefied discrimination at work. After a brief flirtation with Barbizon pictures, Altman soon progressed to Rembrandt; he acquired more Rembrandts than any other American collector, and nearly all of the highest quality (Altman just missed getting Rembrandt's *Aristotle Contemplating the Bust of Homer*, which Duveen sold to Mrs. Collis P. Huntington instead). He was one of the first Americans to buy Holbein, whose haunting portrait of Margaret Wyatt, sister of the Elizabethan poet Thomas Wyatt, entered his collection in 1912. He owned four superb Memling portraits, a great Dürer, two Velasquez portraits, Vermeer's lovely *Girl Asleep,* and a group of Italian primitives that rivaled those of the Philadelphia collector John Johnson, who specialized in this school.

Neither Altman nor Morgan showed any particular interest in the eighteenth and nineteenth century English portraits that were so much in demand among their contemporaries. Morgan, to be sure, had bought the famous Gainsborough *Duchess of Devonshire,* but for sentimental rather than aesthetic reasons—the painting had been stolen from Agnew's London gallery in 1876 a few hours after Morgan's father had purchased it as a present for his son; when Morland Agnew finally ransomed the picture back in 1901, in a three-way negotiation in a Chicago hotel suite with a Pinkerton man acting as go-between, Morgan unhesitatingly claimed it— for $150,000. He seems to have felt no pressing need for aristocratic English lords and ladies on his walls, however, and it is highly unlikely that either he or Altman would have considered paying $850,000, as Henry E. Huntington did in 1921, for Gainsborough's treacly *Blue Boy.* Henry Huntington was the nephew of the railroad buccaneer Collis P. Huntington, who was once described to a jury by Joseph H. Choate, the attorney for his opponent in a lawsuit, as a "man who owns money, houses, many railroads, many banks, many newspapers, many judges, many legislatures." When Collis died in 1900, Henry promptly married his late uncle's seventy-year-old widow Arabella, thus doubling the size of his fortune. Morgan did not think much of that move, either.

Like Morgan, Altman occasionally fell victim to overenthusiastic attributions. The *Portrait of a Man* that he bought as a Giorgione is now believed to have been painted by Titian—a loss not in quality but in rarity, Giorgione having died at the age of thirty-three while his friend Titian lived and painted until he was ninety-nine. A Filippino Lippi in Altman's collection has been downgraded to Workshop of Filippino Lippi, and two of his Rembrandts, *Portrait of the Artist's Son Titus* and *Old Woman Cutting Her Nails,* are no longer listed as Rembrandts by the Metropolitan. One of the most famous objects in the collection, the gold and enamel Rospigliosi Cup that was sold to Altman as the work of the sixteenth century Florentine Benvenuto Cellini, is certainly not by Cellini, although whoever made it was clearly a master goldsmith. Altman's mistakes were those of attribution, not of artistic quality, and the vast majority of his paintings, porcelains, bronzes, enamels, tapestries, rugs, antiquities and other works of art testify to the keenness of his eye and the success of his methods.

Naturally enough, the Metropolitan had been keeping *its* keen eye on the Altman collection for some time. Few people had actually seen it, for Altman, who was mortally afraid of publicity, did not allow strangers into his house and disliked lending his treasures. When the Metropolitan organized a major loan exhibition of Dutch paintings in connection with the Hudson-Fulton celebration in 1909, Altman refused at first to lend anything to it. The Hudson-Fulton Exhibition was part of the statewide observance of the tercentenary of Henry Hudson's exploration of the Hudson River in 1609 and the centenary of the first use of steam navigation on the river by Robert Fulton. The Metropolitan mounted two important exhibitions in this connection—a show of American paintings and "industrial arts" from 1625 to 1825, and an exhibition of Dutch paintings of Hudson's time.* New York collectors had made a specialty of Dutch paintings, and the exhibition included a total of one hundred and forty-nine pictures, among them thirty-seven Rembrandts, twenty Franz Halses, and six Vermeers. Altman's refusal to lend his pictures caused the trustees much distress. When one of them ventured to ask the reason, Altman said that he was just living up to his reputation as the meanest man in New York. In the end, though, he relented and let the museum borrow six paintings—

* This was stretching a point historically, since the high period of Dutch art, from 1625 to 1670, came considerably after Hudson's death.

three Rembrandts, one Hals, a Ruisdael, and the Vermeer—which were listed under "Addenda" in the catalogue.

A few months before the Hudson-Fulton exhibition in 1909, Edward Robinson had cautiously sounded out Altman with regard to the disposition of his collection. As Robinson afterward reported to Morgan, Altman said he had considered leaving it to the Metropolitan, but that he was deterred by the museum's new policy of not accepting conditional or restrictive bequests. Altman felt very strongly that his collection belonged together as a unit. After explaining the reasons behind the museum's new policy, Robinson managed to suggest that in the case of a collection so magnificent as Altman's, an exception could perhaps be made.

The merchant was pleased by Robinson's tactful comments, but he wanted official confirmation from the Metropolitan's president. He also insisted that the matter remain strictly confidential—he did not want Morgan's friend Laffan or even Sir Purdon Clarke to know about it. Robinson wrote to Morgan, who was in Egypt at the time. On March 1, Morgan cabled Robinson from Cairo: "Letter received. My desire is great to meet his views and I will do whatever I can to accomplish it if requirements not too minute." Altman thought this a very satisfactory response. He told Robinson he would think the matter over and have his lawyer draw up a new will accordingly. By a happy chance, his lawyer was Joseph H. Choate, the Metropolitan's most venerable trustee in point of service.

Two months later, Altman and Choate were still wrestling with the pertinent clauses in the will. "Even now he is unwilling to commit himself definitely," Robinson wrote to de Forest, "as he says there are two or three other possibilities with regard to the disposal of his collections which he wishes to consider." One such possibility was the founding of an "Altman Museum of Art," a course that would later be followed by the industrialist Henry Clay Frick. Altman was also determined to provide for the future employment of Theodore Y. Hobby, a young man who had started his career as a ribbon clerk at B. Altman & Co., and risen to the position of Altman's confidential secretary and private curator.

Altman finally signed the new will in June. The museum had agreed to all his requests. It would "provide and permanently maintain . . . one suitable room of sufficient size to contain all my paintings, statuary, rock crystals, Limoges enamels, and one other suitable room to contain my Chinese porcelains, said rooms to be adjoining and opening into each other." There were to be no other works of art in either room. The paintings would be hung "in a single line, and not one above the other." The museum, moreover, would honor Altman's wish that it employ Theodore Hobby as permanent keeper of the Altman Collection. (Altman left a fund of $150,000 to pay the salaries of Hobby and Arthur J. Boston, another personal secretary for whose future he wished to provide.) If any of these conditions were broken, or if the museum should change its mind about them at any time, the entire collection was to go to an Altman Museum of Art for which contingency funds had been set aside.

The bequest remained a secret until Altman's death in 1913. The trustees then accepted it formally, conditions and all, with emotions akin to jubilation. Robinson described the collection, which numbered nearly a thousand objects and was valued at $15,000,000, as "without question the most splendid gift that a citizen has ever made to the people of the city of New York," while John W. Alexander, a Metropolitan trustee and the president of the National Academy of Design, said flatly that it would put the Metropolitan "in the forefront of the world's treasure houses, with the Louvre and Madrid." Theodore Hobby arrived with the collection in the spring of 1914 and stayed until 1954, seeing to it that the departed owner's wishes were carried out. Although the terms of the bequest have been interpreted rather ingeniously since 1913 (the two adjoining rooms giving way to a somewhat meandering procession of Altman pieces through several galleries), by and large the Altman gift has remained a monument to one man's taste and a living proof that flexibility, where museums are concerned, is sometimes the better part of principle.

For years it was more or less assumed that the Morgan collection, which was in proportion to the Altman as the ocean to an inland sea, would also come to rest eventually at the Metropolitan. No one, however, had quite dared to put the matter to Morgan directly.

Ever since his semiretirement from business in 1907, Morgan had devoted the greater part of his time to art affairs. He clearly relished being president of the Metropolitan. Robert de Forest told how, at one of the formal receptions for members held each year in the great hall of the museum, he and the other trustees were shocked to see in the line a young woman, the wife of a museum attendant "who knew no better," who was dressed informally and carrying a baby. Morgan "shook hands with her as graciously as he did with the lady in full evening dress who preceded her," de Forest reported admiringly, "and as she passed by said to me, 'Quick, get that baby's name, so that I can make him a life member of the museum.'" Morgan not only put up the $1,000 to make the infant (a girl, as it happened) a life member, but also set aside $5,000 more so that she could study art in Europe when she grew up. Unfortunately, she developed chronic eye trouble and never used the scholarship.

Morgan himself spent more than half the year abroad, looking at works of art and frequently buying them. He moved grandly from place to place —London, Paris, Aix-les-Bains, Monte Carlo, Rome, Venice—accompanied by a retinue of servants, art experts, relatives, and usually a charming female companion, all of whom helped to insulate him from the army of dealers and impoverished aristocrats and confidence men who laid siege to his hotel wherever he went. Everyone, it seemed, had something for his eyes alone. Morgan said wryly that the most expensive words in any language were *"unique au monde,"* but he never wearied of looking. In Egypt he traveled up the Nile in his private *dahabiyeh,* the *Khargeh,* built to his own specifications and navigated by his own crew. His audiences with the Pope in Rome were in the nature of summit meetings between temporal and spiritual powers. The German Kaiser dined with Morgan on board the *Corsair,* his ocean-going yacht; Queen Alexandra came to tea at his London house; museum directors throughout Europe lived in hope of his summons.

Morgan's biographer Frederick Lewis Allen describes him in these last years as "a somewhat bulky gentleman, six feet tall, seating himself in an armchair in a European hotel suite, and pulling toward him a card table on which is a silver box containing two packs of cards" for his favorite game of solitaire. One could as well picture him in the West Room of the marble library on East Thirty-sixth Street in New York: red brocade walls bearing the Chigi coat of arms; paintings by Perugino, Raphael, and Botticelli; on one side table the marble head of Saint John the Baptist by Desiderio da Settignano, on another the gorgon-crested helmet hammered out of cold steel by Philip Negroli of Milan, the Michelangelo of armorers—

Morgan himself seated behind his great square desk discussing the latest book sale catalogues with his librarian, the slim, green-eyed, waspish, and fiercely loyal Belle da Costa Green. One of the most remarkable facets of this extraordinary man was the way his personality stamped and dominated even such a setting as this. "Every smallest ornament or richest picture had the hallmark of his individuality," Morgan's friend Bishop Lawrence said of him. "However rich the trappings, they took their proper place, merely as trappings of the man. It was this that made his manner of life seem princely."

Nowhere did Morgan's life appear more princely than at Prince's Gate, his large double house overlooking Hyde Park in London. Morgan had inherited the house from his father, and it was here, for reasons that were mainly financial, that the bulk of his art purchases had accumulated. Some European countries made it difficult to export works of art from their shores; the United States, by levying a stiff duty on all imported artworks, had made it even more difficult to bring them in. The U.S. duty on art at this time was at least twenty percent of the declared value, and in some cases more than that—Jacques Seligmann noted that on a total bill of $30,000 paid to his firm by an American client in 1906, $7,000 had gone for customs duty. For Morgan, whose collections immediately after his death were valued at $60,000,000, the duty would have been prohibitive. Morgan had placed a number of his finest treasures on loan to the Victoria and Albert and other museums, and the directors of these institutions were not without hopes. In 1909, however, two events altered the outlook considerably. The United States Congress passed the Payne-Aldrich tariff bill, which disappointed American tariff reformers by maintaining a high level of protectionism, but which specifically abolished the import duty on works of art that were more than one hundred years old. The enactment in England soon afterward of greatly increased death duties gave Morgan a further incentive. Toward the end of 1911, he set in motion the vast process of packing and shipping his collections to America.

He did so in typically magisterial style. Morgan paid the transatlantic fares of a special agent for the United States Treasury Department and a customs inspector of the Port of New York, both of whom came to London and spent a full year there, at Morgan's expense, examining each case as it was packed in a locked storeroom of the Victoria and Albert, under the supervision of Jacques Seligmann, and then affixing their official seals to the cases so that they would not have to be opened again upon arrival in New York. There were three hundred and fifty-one cases in all, not including the books and manuscripts. The packing and shipping went on continuously from February 1912 until January 1913 (shipment number five was scheduled to leave on the S.S. *Titanic* on April 12, 1912, but it was not ready on time). As each case arrived, it was taken directly to a basement storeroom at the Metropolitan. The Metropolitan's assumptions, however, were soon to be rudely shattered.

Early in 1912, when the first of Morgan's shipments had arrived and newspaper editors were taking it for granted that they were coming to the Metropolitan for good, Robert de Forest placed a note of clarification in the museum *Bulletin*. It was true that Mr. Morgan's art collections were being transferred to New York, the vice-president said, but "of Mr. Morgan's further intentions we have no knowledge." It would be a "pleasant dream" if he should decide to place them permanently with the Metropolitan—"Nor would it be out of line with Mr. Morgan's never-failing public spirit if this dream should come true." But it could only come true if the museum had space in which to show the collections, and, as de Forest pointedly noted, "it has no such space now."

De Forest was touching on an extremely delicate situation. Under the Metropolitan's charter, all construction funds were to come from the city. The city had recently financed the building of the Fifth Avenue facade and its two northern extensions, the second of which was opened in time to receive the Riggs armor in 1914. It had also paid for the construction of the Decorative Arts wing, which opened in 1910. The museum's collections were growing so rapidly, though, that more gallery space was urgently required, and as early as 1909 the trustees had approved McKim, Mead and White's plans for two new wings (later designated J and K) that would extend south from the main entrance on Fifth Avenue. The city authorities had so far failed to appropriate the necessary funds for these two south wings, and de Forest had this failure in mind when he noted, early in 1912, that the museum had no space to house the Morgan collection.

In municipal quarters, however, the idea seemed to have taken root that if Pierpont Morgan wished to immortalize his name by leaving his art collections to New York, he could very well afford to pay for their accommodation. The matter hung fire all through the spring and summer, while Morgan packing cases piled up in the Metropolitan's basement. Morgan had become increasingly annoyed by what he considered the city's parsimonious attitude. He was even more annoyed by the suggestion, hinted at rather broadly in de Forest's *Bulletin* note, that if the city appropriated the funds for Wings J and K the Metropolitan would get the Morgan collections. On his return from Europe that fall, Morgan summoned Edward Robinson, the director, to the West Room on Thirty-sixth Street. Robinson's subsequent memorandum of their meeting indicates that it was not a happy occasion:

> Friday, November 29, 1912. Mr. Morgan sent for me to come to his Library, and told me that he wished it distinctly understood by the City authorities and whoever else ought to know of it, that he had no intention of giving or bequeathing his collections to the Metropolitan Museum. He said that the value of these collections at the present time was about fifty million dollars, and he regarded this as much too large an asset to take out of his estate in case it might ever be needed. He wished me to confer with Mr. de Forest as soon as possible, report to him what I had been told, and decide with him what was the best method of making this known to those concerned. He said further that he did not wish the City to grant the money asked for this year upon the understanding that it was to be devoted to the permanent housing of his collections, and then learn afterward that the collections were not to become the property of the Museum. His understanding was that this money was asked for in accordance with the Enabling Act which Mayor McClellan had secured from the Legislature in Albany, and was for the general purposes of the Museum. At the time when the application was made, he added, he had not agreed to send his collections to this country, and it could have been upon no such understanding that the money was asked for.
>
> This is the first intimation Mr. Morgan has ever made to me of his ultimate intentions with regard to his collections.

A month later, Morgan's mood had darkened considerably. He himself had been summoned to Washington, to testify before the Pujo Committee which was investigating alleged abuses of power by the "money trust." Morgan had acquitted himself with effectiveness and dignity, scoring something of a personal triumph before the hostile committee, but the strain of the experience had left him exhausted and irritable. Robinson called upon him once again at the library. This time he was able to tell Morgan that the museum had received assurances from the Board of Estimate that it would shortly approve the new building funds. Morgan replied "with some vehemence" that no matter what they decided, "nothing whatever was to be done with any of his things for an indefinite time." Morgan had previously wanted to have the cases containing his miniatures opened so that the fragile miniatures could be kept under observation. Now, however, he emphasized that nothing was to be removed from any of the cases, with the exception of the paintings which he had agreed to let the museum hang for a temporary exhibition in 1913. Robinson hazarded a remark on the possible dangers of allowing furniture, textiles, and other materials to remain for a long time in packing cases, which "might contain moths or other destructive agents," but Morgan was adamant. Nothing was to be unpacked, under any circumstances. In view of Morgan's dire mood, Robinson thought it wise not to press the point.

On January 7, 1913, Morgan sailed for Egypt. He was seventy-five, tired, and ill. He traveled up the Nile in the *Khargeh* with his daughter, Louisa Satterlee, but the desert air did not lift his spirits, and his health continued to deteriorate. They decided to return to New York. During a stopover in Rome, Morgan's condition grew much worse. He rallied sufficiently to attend church on Easter Sunday, but on the evening of March 30 he slipped into a coma. Louisa Satterlee and her husband, who had been summoned from New York, sat by his bedside throughout the night, listening to his murmured words and phrases, many of which seemed to refer to his childhood in Hartford and at school in Vevey. The last words they heard him say were, "I've got to go up the hill." He died a few minutes before noon on March 31.

To the world at large it came as a shock to learn than Morgan's wealth was so much smaller than had been imagined. His estate in 1913 was estimated, excluding the art collections, at $68,000,000—considerably less than those of his contemporaries Frick, Harriman, George F. Baker, or Andrew W. Mellon, and not even in the same league with Andrew Carnegie or John D. Rockefeller, Sr. (who was reported to have said, on seeing the published figures of Morgan's estate, "And to think he wasn't even a rich man!"). What no one had realized was that Morgan habitually spent almost everything he earned. During the last two decades of his life the vast bulk of his earnings had gone into his art collections, which were valued separately, after his death, at approximately $60,000,000. It is doubtful whether any collector of recent times has ever devoted such a large proportion of his estate—nearly fifty percent in this case—to works of art. It suddenly became evident to a number of people, including the trustees of the Metropolitan Museum, that Morgan had meant what he said to Robinson in 1912 about his art collections. He could not *afford* to give away such a large asset—not, at least, until the inheritance taxes and other demands upon his estate had been settled in full.

Morgan left his art collections to his son. He did so, however, with the clear understanding that John Pierpont Morgan, Jr., would carry out his father's express "desire and intention," as affirmed in the will, "to make some suitable disposition of them or of such portions of them . . . which would render them permanently available for the instruction and pleasure of the American people."

The Morgan paintings had been exhibited at the museum in 1913. In 1914, the younger Morgan authorized the trustees to exhibit the collection in its entirety. It filled the whole second floor of the newly opened northernmost Fifth Avenue wing, and drew thousands of visitors (total attendance that year reached 913,230, a record not surpassed until 1920). As it turned out, this was the first and last time that the Morgan collection was ever seen as a whole. The demands on the estate had turned out to be more serious than anticipated. As a result, many of the finest works of art in the collection were sold—too precipitately, some people felt. Duveen and his rivals snapped up the Chinese porcelains, the tapestries, the miniatures and many other objects large and small, and sold them at greatly increased prices to their millionaire clients. Frick paid $1,200,000 for the five panels painted by Jean Honoré Fragonard for the Comtesse du Barry, which Morgan had bought in 1899 for $310,000. The designation "ex-Morgan collection" had become a seal of quality and extreme desirability, and collectors bought "Morgan" pieces in the same sense that they purchased "Medici" paintings—the name carried a magic all its own.

In the end, although the greatest collection of modern times was widely dispersed, approximately forty percent of Morgan's treasures came to rest permanently at the Metropolitan. Acting "in pursuance of my father's wishes," J. P. Morgan, Jr., gave the Raphael *Colonna Altarpiece* in 1916, together with the entire medieval section of the Hoentschel Collection (previously on loan) and the great sixteenth century sculpture groups of the *Entombment* and the *Pietà* from the Château de Biron in southern France. One year later, he gave most of what remained of the Morgan collections. The 1917 gift comprised somewhere between six thousand and eight thousand objects in all—paintings, sculpture, ancient glass and pottery, Egyptian material, alabaster reliefs from the Assyrian palace of King Ashur-nasirpal II at Nimrud, silver plates from Cyprus, Merovingian and Carolingian gold, medieval champlevé enamels, Byzantine ivories, Gothic woodcarvings, Renaissance works of all kinds, furniture, jewelry, reliquaries—magnificent objects from virtually every center and period of Western art from 3000 B.C. up to the recent past. The vast assemblage was exhibited in the Decorative Arts wing (renamed the Pierpont Morgan Wing in 1918), where it was supposed to be kept together as a unit for the next fifty years. In 1943, however, J. P. Morgan, Jr., canceled even this restriction and gave his consent for the Morgan collection to be distributed throughout the museum. Today, more than half a century later, most of it remains on permanent display.

The world that Pierpont Morgan knew and inhabited so largely did not long survive his death. Europe, drifting toward the mass suicide of world war, would no longer control the political and economic fate of half the globe; America, the new industrial giant, would no longer be allowed to pursue its own destiny in relative isolation from the burdens and frustrations of world power. It was the artists, as usual, who sensed most directly what was happening around them. In the watershed year 1913—when American and European art collectors broke all records by the volume of their buying and the prices that they paid for eighteenth century English portraits, Renaissance paintings and other seemingly gilt-edged securities —men like Picasso and Kandinsky were creating a new art that reflected graphically the impending cataclysm and upheaval. It would be some time, of course, before the new art could be seen in the Metropolitan Museum. Although the Morgan era died in 1913, the influence of Morgan continued as a dynamic force for many years to come, during which the museum sometimes seemed to consider itself a bulwark against the curse of modernism. And yet, in a sense, it was Morgan himself who had helped to under-write the immense popular success of art in our time.

A parallel has often been drawn between Morgan and Lorenzo de' Medici. As the Metropolitan director Francis Henry Taylor wrote in 1957, "both men looked upon money as a source of maximum power and infallibility—never as an end in itself. And both induced in their contemporaries a new attitude towards the significance of works of art." It was this new attitude that could perhaps be seen as Morgan's most far-reaching legacy. Morgan was not by any means the first prominent American businessman to collect art. Johnston, Marquand, Belmont, Vanderbilt, Altman, Havemeyer and others had preceded him in this field, which he entered only when he was past sixty. No one, however, had made the purchase of art seem so noteworthy or so exciting an occupation. Morgan detested publicity and sought to avoid it, but newspaper reporters clustered about him wherever he went; everything he did seemed to fascinate the public, and no other event during the year 1913 received so much space in the world press as his death. Each time Morgan scored one of his spectacular coups in the art market—snapping up this or that famous collection, buying a painting, endowing a museum—the newspapers reported the event in detail. The shipping of his collections from London to New York was headline news throughout the country. There is no telling what effect all this had on the average American, for whom fine art and its appreciation had always been something slightly suspect, tinged with European snobbery, and probably best left to the ladies. When a man who had been so outstandingly successful in business turned virtually all his energy and attention to works of art, and did so with the intensely dramatic authority that characterized all Morgan's actions, the effect on other businessmen and plain citizens across the nation was profound and lasting. A great many people, reading of Morgan's collecting triumphs, decided that works of art must be important.

When Francis Leland handed over his surprising gift of New York County Bank stock to the Metropolitan in 1912, he told Edward Robinson, rather shyly, that he had long admired the Metropolitan and that he thought "the bringing of the Morgan collections to America the greatest event that had ever happened to any country."

"And," said Robinson, "I did not disagree with him."

PART III
CURATORS
AND
COLLECTORS

FOURTEEN

In New York, cultural power rests with the lawyers. Businessmen and bankers may predominate on the boards of universities and concert societies, the opera and the museums, but the men who shape and control these institutions are usually lawyers, whose counsel in cultural as in tax matters has for their wealthy clients the force of holy writ.

There were six lawyers among the Metropolitan's founders and incorporators. One of them, Joseph H. Choate, set the organizational pattern for the museum—writing the charter and the constitution, negotiating with Boss Tweed and his successors in the city government, establishing the "partnership" of municipal and private support. Choate was still on the board in 1913, the last remaining link with the founders. The trustees were so deeply under the spell of the late J. P. Morgan at the time that they offered the presidency first to his son, J. Pierpont Morgan, Jr., who modestly declined the honor, but their next choice was Choate, and when Choate also declined they made him honorary president anyway. Choate would remain active at the museum until he died, attending every meeting of the board, tendering sage and witty advice but refusing to vote on any issue that involved questions of art scholarship—such matters, he had always maintained, should be decided by the professional staff. He missed the museum's fiftieth anniversary by less than three years, dying suddenly of heart failure on the evening of May 4, 1917, after an exhausting day of banquets and speeches in honor of the British and French war envoys who were on a fund-raising visit to New York. The Metropolitan trustees, meanwhile, had elected another lawyer, Robert Weeks de Forest, as the museum's fifth president.

Nearly twenty years had gone by since de Forest led the radical "impressionist" faction of trustees in the bitter battle to oust Cesnola. In the interim he had become the city's unrivaled "Captain of Philanthropy," the most public-spirited New Yorker of his generation. There was scarcely a charitable activity in which he failed to take some leading part. De Forest had been the principal founder in 1898 of what is now the Columbia University School of Social Work—it was formerly the New York School for Social Work, and before that the "School of Philanthropy for Young Ladies." He labored tirelessly for slum clearance, better housing, and more efficient and honest city government, and it was said that he could have had the Fusion nomination for mayor in 1908—an opportunity he sidestepped because of his patrician distaste for politics and politicians. In this respect de Forest differed markedly from his colleague Elihu Root, a fellow lawyer and Metropolitan trustee. As a young legal apprentice, Root had been assigned by his firm to assist in the defense of Boss Tweed at his trial in 1873. He rose from this early misfortune to become the most prominent corporation lawyer of his day, and went on from there into politics, serving as Secretary of War in President McKinley's cabinet, as Secretary of State under Teddy Roosevelt, and as a United States Senator from New York. Root won the Nobel Peace Prize in 1912 for his diplomacy in the Far East, and he would reach even greater heights of esteem as the chief consulting architect of the World Court in The Hague. Born in the small upstate New York town of Clinton, Root moved progressively into larger and grander spheres until the scope of his influence was truly international. De Forest's ambitions, however, were restricted almost entirely to the city of his birth.

No one could outpoint Robert de Forest as a scion of Old New York. He was a direct descendant of Jesse de Forest, the leader of a band of seventeenth century French Huguenots who fled religious persecution on the Continent and offered their services as colonists first to the English Virginia Company, which found them unsuitable, and then to the Dutch West India Company. Impatient with the delays in colonial assignment, Jesse ventured off on his own to South America and died there; in 1624, however, his followers boarded the Dutch West India Company ship *New Netherland* and sailed for the northern colonies, where they helped to found the settlement of Nieuw Amsterdam. Sixteen de Forests fought in the American Revolution (presumably for the right side), and the family had long been prominent in the affairs of New York. Robert, who studied abroad for several years, once toyed with the idea of being an artist—a course that would later be followed by his younger brother Lockwood. After graduating from Yale in 1870 and from Columbia Law School in 1872, however, he entered the family law firm of Weeks and de Forest and settled down to the cultivation of well-to-do clients. One of these clients happened to be John Taylor Johnston, the Metropolitan's first president and the owner of the Central Railroad of New Jersey. Young de Forest was soon listed as the Central's general attorney, and he would eventually become one of its vice-presidents. In the meanwhile, he had solidified the connection by marrying Johnston's daughter Emily, and moving into the comfortable house at Seven Washington Square where his wife had been born. The house was a wedding present from the elder Johnstons. Its furniture had been made to order for Emily's grandfather by an immigrant Scottish cabinetmaker named Duncan Phyfe, whose workshop on Fulton Street had even furnished the mattresses and pillows. Some of their furniture is now on view in the Metropolitan, where Duncan Phyfe has a room to himself.

The de Forests had announced their engagement on the day the Metropolitan was founded in 1870, and de Forest liked to say that he had been associated with its "worries and pleasures" ever since. Elected to the board in 1889, he had devoted himself mainly to the museum's legal and financial problems. The successful negotiation for the Rogers bequest was largely his doing (with assistance from Elihu Root). De Forest and Choate were instrumental, moreover, in getting Congress to approve a clause in the 1909 Payne-Aldrich bill that abolished the duty on imported works of art more than a hundred years old (a few years later, the New York lawyer-collector John Quinn would argue successfully for repeal of the duty on modern art as well). De Forest got along smoothly with Pierpont Morgan, who intrusted to him most of the administrative responsibilities of the museum. In fact, de Forest maintained in later years, from 1904 on he himself had been largely responsible for all decisions "relating to scope and policy" at the Metropolitan, a claim that Morgan, Laffan, and a few other departed trustees might have thought surprising.

In his thinking about the museum de Forest was closer to the ideals of the founders than Morgan had been. He took very seriously the words of the original charter, which listed among the museum's primary goals "the application of arts to manufacture and practical life" and the furnishing of "popular instruction," and, being a Captain of Philanthropy, he was determined to see that these goals were not overlooked in the fever of acquisition that marked the Morgan years. By 1913, thanks to Henry Kent's programs for schoolteachers and their classes and the institution of gallery talks, de Forest felt satisfied that the museum had made at least a start on the educational obligations it had neglected in its earlier years. He was so satisfied with Kent, in fact, that he prevailed upon his fellow trustees to elect Kent secretary to the board in his place, when he became president in 1913. "Popular instruction" continued to descend upon legions of school-children, with debatable results. Both acquisition and education were severely curtailed, however, by the outbreak of the war in Europe.

Metropolitan curators fought on both sides in the First World War. William Valentiner, the curator of Decorative Arts, returned to his homeland soon after war was declared and enlisted as a private in the German army, where he served with distinction and was decorated for bravery.° Arthur C. Mace, assistant curator in the Egyptian Department and the man in charge of the dig in Lisht, left to join the British Army. Herbert Winlock and a number of the younger staff members served with the American Expeditionary Force, while Bashford Dean, at the age of fifty, wangled a commission as major in the Ordnance Department. Dean went overseas in 1917 to study the helmets used by Allied soldiers, then came back and designed a better one that incorporated some of the finer points of the Galiot de Genouilhac casque. Dean's helmet did not find favor with the brass in Washington—they opted instead for the shallow, round hat worn by the British Tommy. Twenty years later, though, the GIs in the Second World War used a helmet based on Dean's design, and the U.S. Air Force outfitted bomber pilots and aerial gunners with a modified version of the plated

° Valentiner came back to the U.S. in 1921 to catalogue the Widener Collection. He became director of the Detroit Institute of Art, and later moved to the Los Angeles County Museum where he had a great influence on West Coast collectors.

body armor that Dean had designed and published in his 1920 book, *Helmets and Body Armor in Modern Warfare.*

The tremendous increase in the museum's collections during the Morgan era had sent operating costs soaring—from $200,000 in 1904 to $400,000 in 1914. Paid attendance and membership fell off sharply during the war, and so did the city's appropriations; the city, which had paid sixty-eight percent of the museum's maintenance costs in 1910, was paying only twenty-eight percent of them by 1919. The result was a severe financial pinch. Although staff salaries were cut, and work on the new south wing abandoned, the annual deficit rose alarmingly. Most of the income from bequests could be used only for buying works of art. What was really needed, de Forest said, was a large general endowment that was not restricted to art purchases, a fund in the neighborhood of $5,000,000, whose income could be applied wherever it was needed. But where, in wartime, was the museum to get five million unrestricted dollars?

Several major bequests did come in during the war years. Theodore M. Davis, the copper magnate who financed his own archaeological digs in the Valley of the Kings, died in 1915 and left the Metropolitan his entire collection, which included more than eleven hundred Egyptian objects and several noteworthy paintings. In 1916 the publisher Harris Brisbane Dick bequeathed the bulk of an estate valued at $1,000,000 as a purchase fund, and the following year the museum fell heir to approximately $3,000,000 in securities from Isaac Dudley Fletcher, a director of coal companies, traction firms, and banks, together with the large Fletcher art collection which included Rembrandt's *Head of Christ*, a good Rubens, and an embarrassing number of mediocre pictures. In announcing the Fletcher bequest in 1917, de Forest made a statement clarifying the museum's policy on conditional or restrictive gifts. Recognizing "the desire of donors for some lasting recognition of their gifts," he said, the Metropolitan would label each object with the donor's name, group together those objects that naturally belonged together, identify the donor in its catalogues and handbooks, and exhibit the entire collection together, if the donor wished, *for a limited time*—in the case of Fletcher's collection, for one year. But, de Forest concluded, the museum "cannot wisely prevent the proper arrangement of its growing collections as an integral whole by accepting gifts conditioned on perpetual segregation." In other words, no more Altman-type guarantees.

The firmer policy did not seem to drive away prospective donors. William K. Vanderbilt, whose vast marble château at the corner of Fifth Avenue and Fifty-second Street was stocked with good, bad, and appalling art objects of all kinds, bequeathed to the museum in 1920 a small but superb group of paintings (among them Rembrandt's *Noble Slav* and François Boucher's deliciously erotic *Toilet of Venus*), and two pieces of French eighteenth century furniture that are still the finest in the museum—a black lacquer and gilt-bronze secretary and a matching commode, made for Marie Antoinette about 1785 by the celebrated *ébéniste* Jean Henri Riesener. A year later Michael Dreicer, the Fifth Avenue jeweler who made pearls fashionable in wealthy society (it had formerly been thought bad luck to wear them), left the museum his collection of paintings and medieval and Renaissance decorative arts, with the understanding that they would be kept together for twenty-five years; as it turned out they remained together only half that time, for in 1933 the museum returned fifteen paintings and twenty-one other objects to Dreicer's widow, in exchange for her permission to disperse the rest. (Today the Paintings Department wishes the trustees had been less hasty; several of the pictures returned to Mrs. Dreicer are now in the National Gallery.)

The Metropolitan actually declined a huge collection of nineteenth century paintings, rugs, tapestries, bronzes, and majolica offered in 1925 by Senator William A. Clark, because of the Senator's condition that it be kept permanently together and on display. Clark's collection went to the Corcoran instead. The Metropolitan's eighteenth and nineteenth century galleries were greatly strengthened, meanwhile, by nearly two hundred paintings from the collection of Collis P. Huntington, the California railroad baron. In spite of his rough business tactics, Huntington had been one of the first American millionaires to take an interest in art. He went in enthusiastically for aristocratic portraits by Raeburn, Romney, Gainsborough, and Lawrence (Lawrence's ever-popular portrait of *The Calmady Children* was his), but he also owned Vermeer's *Lady With a Lute* and two Rembrandts—*Flora,* and a portrait of *Hendrickje Stoffels.* When he died in 1900, Huntington left his collection to the Metropolitan with the provision that his wife Arabella and their son Archer (born before their marriage and adopted by Huntington after it) would retain the use of it during their lifetime. Arabella—the remarkable lady who sought solace after Huntington's death by marrying his nephew, and who was primarily responsible for the art collecting of Collis, Henry, and Archer Huntington—continued to add to the collection after 1900; as previously noted, Duveen sold her Rembrandt's *Aristotle Contemplating the Bust of Homer*. She died in 1924. The following year, Archer M. Huntington relinquished his life interest in the collection and turned over most of the paintings to the Metropolitan, with no restrictions at all. Archer considered giving the world-famous *Aristotle*, along with the other two Rembrandts and the Vermeer, but then decided to hold on to it for a while longer.

So much generosity might simply have driven the Metropolitan deeper into debt, had not new sources of operating funds opened up as well. Periodically, it seemed, some unknown friend of the museum would give financial proof of his affection, astounding the trustees and enraging his relatives. Jacob Rogers had done so in 1903, Frederick C. Hewitt in 1908, Francis Leland in 1912. One day in 1917, Edward Robinson's eye happened to fall on a minuscule paid notice in a New York newspaper stating that John Hoge of Zanesville, Ohio, had left some money in equal shares to the Metropolitan Museum and to the Actors' Fund in New York. He mentioned it to de Forest, who had never heard of Hoge. The Actors' Fund was equally in the dark. Robinson wrote to the Hoge executors in Zanesville, but received no reply, so the museum sent a man out to investigate. He learned that under Ohio law, if a bequest was advertised in the legatee's home town, and the legatee did not show up to claim it, the bequest was automatically void. In view of the size of the Hoge bequest, a number of Zanesville citizens had obviously been hoping that neither legatee would show up.

John Hoge, it appeared, had made a fortune in New York City real estate before he retired to Zanesville. His bequest to the Metropolitan (unconditional and unrestricted as to use) was a piece of real estate at the corner of Fifth Avenue and Forty-first Street, directly across from the New York Public Library, and its assessed value in 1917 was just under $1,-000,000. A nephew of Hoge contested the will, and claimed at the hearing that his uncle had been failing mentally when he wrote the codicil favoring the Metropolitan. Hoge's loyal stenographer jumped up at this point and indignantly told the court that on the day of his death her employer had made a spectacular killing on the stock market. The Metropolitan eventually won its case on appeal, and sold the property to Rogers Peet and Company for more than $1,000,000.

Speaking at the Metropolitan's half century anniversary exercises in the spring of 1920, President de Forest said that the number of gifts received from many parts of the country—the largest of all coming from Jacob S. Rogers of Paterson, New Jersey, and the fifth largest from John Hoge of Zanesville, Ohio—proved that the Metropolitan was truly a national and not just a New York institution. What had been true in the past, however, would not apply in the future. By 1920 there were ninety-two American museums devoted to the fine arts, more than twice as many as there had been in 1904. Every major city in the country had its palace of art, most of them inspired by or modeled after the Metropolitan or the Boston museums, and all of them competing, to a certain extent, for available millionaires and their collections. In the future the Metropolitan would have few important benefactors whose primary association was not with New York. The museum's influence might be national, but its support, from now on, would come almost exclusively from New York money.

Money, fortunately, is New York's forte. The big bull market on Wall Street was beginning about this time to drown wartime austerity in a haze of speculative euphoria. Spurred by the phenomenal growth of the automobile industry, the postwar boom was in full swing by 1924. During the next three years the number of Americans who paid taxes on incomes of more than a million dollars would rise from seventy-five to two hundred and eighty-three, and a large proportion of these would be New Yorkers. With Coolidge in the White House, business had become the national religion; the businessman, an object of deep suspicion as recently as the time of J. P. Morgan, was well on his way to becoming, in Stuart Chase's phrase, "the dictator of our destinies . . . the final authority on the conduct of American society." To the immense gratification of lawyers de Forest and Root, more and more New York businessmen seemed to be looking with increasing favor upon the Metropolitan Museum. Unrestricted million-dollar gifts from Morgan's old banking friend George F. Baker in 1922 and from John D. Rockefeller, Jr., in 1924 swelled the general endowment and helped to erase the annual deficit; they also engendered other donations. The museum was wealthier than ever, solidly conservative in outlook and appearance, and shimmering with social prestige. To associate oneself with such an enterprise, to have one's name carved imperishably upon a marble slab in the great hall—two tablets of benefactors had been unveiled by Elihu Root at the fiftieth anniversary exercises—this was recompense indeed for the careworn and status-hungry businessman.

Some such notion may have been in the mind of the millionaire publisher Frank A. Munsey when he made out his new will in 1921, although it had always been difficult, if not impossible, to fathom Munsey's reasons for doing anything. It pleased Munsey to think of himself as a newspaperman. Actually, he had made his money as a real estate manipulator and a remarkably successful plunger in the stock market. Munsey was at one time the largest stockholder in U.S. Steel, which he bought heavily at a little more than $20.00 a share and kept until it had crossed $200. He bought and sold real estate in Manhattan, Long Island, and New England; he owned a highly profitable grocery chain, The Mohican Stores; and over the years he had gained control of a number of New York's leading newspapers. He made money on everything but his newspapers. As a result he killed them one by one—the *Globe*, the *Mail*, and the *Herald*—becoming in the process the most hated man in the history of American journalism.

Most newspapermen who had worked for Munsey remembered him afterward with contempt and rage. Munsey seemed to enjoy firing reporters and editors. He fired them for a variety of reasons all his own—because they had gray hair, because they were too young, or too fat, or left-handed. When he decided to kill the venerable *New York Herald* by merging it with the *Tribune*, he did not bother to inform the *Herald*'s managing editor, Charles Lincoln, until he handed him the announcement of the paper's demise to be set in type for the forthcoming (and final) issue—then, as an afterthought, he told Lincoln that he wanted him to stay on and manage the *Tribune*. Lincoln declined, saying he regretted every moment he had served under Munsey. William Allen White wrote that Munsey had "contributed to the journalism of his day the talent of a meat packer, the morals of a money changer and the manners of an undertaker." Impassioned diatribes of this kind missed the point, according to the historian Allen Nevins. Munsey, Nevins wrote, was "an astonishing personality who failed to find his true place." He was "a master of money-making who, with disastrous consequences to himself and journalism, tried to be a master of the world of print." Nevins pointed out that in the days following the *Herald*'s

closing Munsey honored money claims that many on his staff thought unjust, and that when he fired a man arbitrarily he was quite capable of giving him a year's salary outright, and then rehiring him when the year was
up. No one denied that he was a difficult man, and even Nevins conceded
that "those about him in his last years often felt as though they were dealing with a powerful, untrained, erratic child." He never married, had no
close relatives and few friends, and divided his time between a six-
hundred-acre estate in Manhasset, a gigantic house in the Adirondacks,
and his suite at the Ritz. He had moved to the Ritz from Sherry's, which
tried hard at one time to lure him back. Munsey's rebuff was typical. "The
Ritz," he explained, "always gives me plenty of butter."

Whether or not Munsey had ever visited the Metropolitan Museum was
an open question. He had been an annual member since 1916, but art was
not one of his interests. Munsey's biographer, George Britt, reported that
Munsey had once looked into the museum's financial arrangements and
been favorably impressed, and other acquaintances pointed out that his
friend and legal counsel David B. Simpson was an art lover. Whatever the
cause, his decision was characteristically casual. According to Britt, Munsey sat down in 1921 to write a new will. After dictating a number of bequests accounting for less than one sixth of his fortune, he fell silent. The
lawyer asked whom he wished to name as the residuary legatee. "What's
that?" Munsey asked. The lawyer explained. "Oh," Munsey said. "Well,
give it to the Metropolitan Museum." When Munsey died four years later
and the bequest was announced, no one could have been more surprised
than the Metropolitan trustees.

Although Munsey's estate was rumored at the time to be as high as
$40,000,000, the Metropolitan's share came down in the end, after several
years of negotiation, the sale of the Mohican Stores and various parcels of
real estate from Park Row to the Adirondacks, to approximately $10,-
000,000. It was the largest money gift ever made to the Metropolitan or
any other museum, and it made the Metropolitan the wealthiest institution
of its kind in the world. Best of all, from the museum's point of view, it
came without strings or restrictions of any kind. De Forest continued afterwards to argue for larger city appropriations and annual contributions
from the trustees, but for some time to come his arguments would sound
somewhat less compelling.

FIFTEEN

The notion that the Metropolitan should collect and exhibit Early American arts and crafts really originated in the fastidious mind of Henry W. Kent. It would never have occurred to the founders. Johnston, Prime, Marquand, and others of their generation probably had dozens of Colonial antiques tucked away in attics or out-of-the-way corners (the de Forests, as we have seen, had a house full of Duncan Phyfe), but no one thought of these as Early American—they were just grandmother's old things. As a New Englander of genteel but not quite elite caste, however, Kent felt a profound reverence for ancestors not his own. He had developed an interest in Colonial furniture and silver while serving as librarian at the Norwich Free Academy, where he had also come into contact with some of the pioneer collectors in this field. At a time when the collecting emphasis at the Metropolitan was overwhelmingly Europe-oriented, Kent found his golden opportunity to strike a blow for Early Americanism.

The occasion was the Hudson-Fulton celebration in 1909. Virtually every New York museum and civic group was planning some special event to commemorate Henry Hudson or Robert Fulton, or both. There would be a nine-day regatta on the Hudson River and a great parade down Broadway. A replica of Hudson's *Half Moon* would sail upriver to Albany. Wright and Curtis would span the river by airplane, and make the first flight over Manhattan. The Metropolitan was getting together a major exhibition of Dutch paintings—the most resplendent show ever mounted in America, the art critic Royal Cortissoz called it. Kent's proposal that the museum also put on an exhibition of American "industrial arts" from 1625 to 1825, together with American paintings of Fulton's time, sounded rather peculiar to some of the trustees, but it received a favorable hearing from the secretary, Robert de Forest, who also happened to be Chairman of the Committee on Art Exhibits of the Hudson-Fulton Celebration Commission. De Forest did the necessary persuading. "It being the first time such an exhibition has been made," he told the Commission, "it is hoped that a new emphasis may be given to the importance of our early workmen."

De Forest's statement was slightly inaccurate, for a large display of Colonial furniture, pottery, textiles and other so-called applied or industrial arts had been one of the features of the Philadelphia Centennial Exhibition in 1876. Although the emphasis then was historical and patriotic, rather than aesthetic, the Centennial had been responsible for a minor boom in Colonial "reproduction" furniture during the latter part of the nineteenth century, a period that had also seen the beginnings of serious collecting in the field of Americana.

The first collectors were all New Englanders, most of whom knew or came to know each other. Irving P. Lyon, a doctor in Hartford, started his collection the year after the Philadelphia Centennial, and in 1891 he published the first authoritative book on the subject, *Colonial Furniture in New England*. A Hartford cabinetmaker named Albert Hosmer began collecting soon after Lyon, concentrating mostly on early furniture from the Connecticut Valley. Charles L. Pendleton, of Providence, and Albert Hastings Pitkin, another Hartford resident, entered the lists before the turn of the century. By far the most important collector, though, as well as the most important lender to the Hudson-Fulton exhibition in 1909, was a well-to-do Boston lawyer named H. Eugene Bolles. Bolles used to spend his summer vacations hunting for old furniture. He would comb the countryside in his horse-drawn buggy, stopping at farmhouses and asking to see the oldest pieces of furniture. The farmers thought him touched, which did not deter them from selling to him. Bolles always tried to find out as much as he could about each piece, asking all sorts of questions about the family and where the furniture had come from, and as a result he became quite an expert on styles, woods, and methods of the early craftsmen. He also knew and compared notes with Lyon and Hosmer in Hartford. A few years before the Hudson-Fulton exhibition, Bolles and his cousin George S. Palmer, who lived in Norwich and had also become an ardent collector, bought out Lyon and Hosmer. They divided the combined collections according to period, Bolles taking the early pieces (mostly pine and oak) made during the era from the sailing of the *Mayflower* through the end of the seventeenth century, while Palmer took the more elegant eighteenth century furniture and silver. A large part of both the Bolles and the Palmer collections came down in 1909 to the Metropolitan, where it formed the core of the exhibition of early American "industrial arts."

De Forest had said that the exhibition itself was to be looked upon as an experiment, an opportunity "to test out the question whether American domestic art was worthy of a place in an art museum." A good many of his colleagues had their doubts on that score, not the least of whom was Edward Robinson, the acting director. Robinson felt that American furniture and applied arts were not in the same class with the decorative arts of Egypt, Greece, and Western Europe. He showed a distinct lack of enthusiasm for the whole venture, much to Henry Kent's annoyance, although he did unbend enough to concede, in a *Bulletin* note on the exhibition, that the early American craftsmen had shown a good sense of line and proportion and that "their work is never vulgar." The public settled the question by flocking in great numbers to see the show, which they gave every appearance of enjoying far more than the display of Rembrandts and Halses in the paintings galleries.

While the Hudson-Fulton exhibition was still in progress, Bolles told Henry Kent that he might be willing to sell his entire collection. Kent lost no time in passing this news on to de Forest. The collection, which numbered approximately six hundred objects in all, was valued at more than $100,000, and de Forest knew just where to go for the money. Three years before, the Wall Street speculator and railroad investor Russell Sage had died and left his widow a fortune estimated at $70,000,000 or more. Inspired perhaps by a desire to mitigate her late husband's rather unsavory reputation as a financial manipulator and a former close associate of Jay Gould, Margaret Olivia Sage was doing her best to give away the money. She donated millions to education and millions more to the advancement of science and religion. The Sage Foundation "for the improvement of social and living conditions in the United States" had been set up in 1907 with the help of Mrs. Sage's legal adviser—Robert de Forest. The eighty-

one-year-old widow, a former schoolteacher, had never before shown any
burning interest in Americana, but she had greatly enjoyed the Hudson-
Fulton show at the Metropolitan. After a few agreeable conversations with
her legal adviser, she purchased the Bolles collection in 1909 and presented it immediately to the museum, which until that moment had not
owned a single stick of American furniture.

The question now was how best to install it. Although the Hudson-Fulton exhibition had been a huge popular success, everyone agreed that
much of the effect had been lost by showing the early chairs, beds, utensils,
and other small objects lined up against the wall in large, high-ceilinged
galleries where they looked, as Elihu Root said, "like fishes out of water."
Such objects were much better seen in the intimate surroundings for which
they had been designed. The solution, obviously, was period rooms.

The period room was a relatively new idea in museum development. It
had originated in Europe, where a number of museum administrators during the latter part of the nineteenth century had started to think along
strictly national, rather than international, lines. The Swiss National Museum in Zurich initiated the new technique in 1898, when it opened sixty-
two small rooms constructed and arranged to show the chronological development of Swiss arts and crafts from the sixteenth to the eighteenth
centuries. German museums in Munich, Lubeck, and Hesse-Darmstadt
made similar arrangements, and several Scandinavian museums experimented with complete houses reconstructed in outdoor parks. The movement soon spread to America, taking root first in New England. As soon as
Kent learned that Bolles wanted to sell his collection, in fact, he had invited de Forest, Mrs. de Forest, and R. T. Haines Halsey, a collector of
early Americana who would later become a Metropolitan trustee, to ac-
company him on a motor trip to Salem, Massachusetts, where he took them
around the newly installed period rooms at the Essex Institute, a local historical society and museum.

The Metropolitan itself had acquired two European period rooms in
1906—a seventeenth century wood-paneled chamber from the Swiss alpine
village of Flims, and a lushly baroque bedroom from the Palazzo Sagredo
in Venice. Over the next twelve years, the museum managed to track down
and purchase American interiors from almost every section of the Eastern
seaboard. Its efforts were not always appreciated. The Society for the Pres-

ervation of New England Antiquities became thoroughly aroused when the Metropolitan purchased the Wentworth-Gardner house in Portsmouth, New Hampshire—one of the most beautiful of Wallace Nutting's chain of restored Colonial houses; the Society's president practically accused the museum of vandalism. The Boston *Herald* chimed in with a sarcastic editorial suggesting that no doubt New Yorkers were suffering acutely from a lack of Colonial beauty. In the end, the museum decided not to remove the house, but simply the paneling and furniture from one of its upstairs bedrooms. Outside New England, though, there was little opposition.

The principal scout, scholar, and benefactor during this period was Richard Townley Haines Halsey, who became a trustee in 1914 and was immediately named chairman of the committee on American Decorative Arts. There was no curator at first. American materials other than paintings fell under the jurisdiction of the Department of Decorative Arts, and it was not until 1918 that the museum hired Charles O. Cornelius, a young expert on New York furniture, to look after them. Halsey did most of the acquiring and installing. A successful stockbroker on Wall Street, he had started collecting in and around New York at about the same time that Bolles began in Boston. From 1914 on he collected primarily for the Metropolitan. He negotiated the purchase of George S. Palmer's eighteenth century collection in 1918, getting it for the incredibly low price of $30,000. Halsey sold his seat on the Stock Exchange in 1923 and from then until his death in 1941 he devoted most of his time to the museum.

Although American arts and crafts remained for many years part of the Decorative Arts Department, the collection really gained its independence in 1922, the year Robert and Emily de Forest announced their plan to finance the construction of a new building designed specifically for it. Emily Johnston de Forest had become an avid collector of early American furniture, with which she furnished her large country house at Cold Spring Harbor. She sometimes took Henry Kent and other members of the Metropolitan staff with her on buying trips up the Hudson Valley and into New England, and she liked to say that her French chauffeur, Barbier, was so well trained that he would stop automatically whenever he saw a sign reading "Antiques." The de Forests' gift made it unnecessary to apply to the city for funds to build the new American Wing.

Kent drew up the first rough plans, based on the idea of a loft building in which the various period rooms would dictate the placement of the windows. This created all sorts of architectural problems—architects like to have windows go where *they* want them—and the museum's regular architectural firm of McKim, Mead and White refused the assignment. De Forest next offered the commission to his friend Grosvenor Atterbury, who accepted. Atterbury loved Colonial architecture and had done the restoration of New York's City Hall and Connecticut Hall in New Haven. The main thing, as he saw it, was "to restore to all the old works of art . . . such a background and an atmosphere that, recognizing their old homes and each other, they will settle down contentedly . . . and be tempted, themselves, to tell their own stories." While construction was in progress, de Forest learned that the Assay Office at 15 Wall Street, a fine old neoclassical building erected in 1822 to house the United States Branch Bank, was about to be torn down. De Forest arranged to purchase the Tuckahoe marble facade and have it transported to the museum, where it was set up facing a small enclosed courtyard planted as an Early American garden, with boxwood and shrubs and a paving of millstones from Connecticut.

Halsey and Cornelius supervised the installation of the period rooms. The plan called for a chronological layout showing the development of native arts and crafts from the mid-seventeenth century to about 1820, which was as far as the museum originally intended to trace them.* The earliest rooms were on the third floor—a parlor from the Hart House in Ipswich, a copy of the "Old Ship" Meetinghouse from Hingham, and other seventeenth century interiors fitted out with objects from the Bolles collection. Descending, the visitor passed through increasingly elegant surroundings as the Colonies gave way to the rooms of the Federal Period and the later Republic, culminating in the beautiful ballroom from Gadsby's Tavern, eight miles from Mount Vernon, where George Washington had celebrated his last birthday ball in 1798. A magnificent Georgian entry hall from the Van Rensselaer manor house in Albany was added on later, in 1931, as was the Verplanck drawing room. Halsey negotiated the delicate compromise that enabled the museum to accept the Verplanck family furniture, its only example of a fine Colonial interior from New York. The Verplanck heirs' insistence that their furniture be housed permanently in a room bearing the family name had run afoul of the museum's policy forbidding "frozen"

* Today the collection embraces all periods including the contemporary one.

gifts; Halsey came up with the deft compromise of a museum pledge to return the furniture whenever it found itself unable or unwilling to meet this condition, thus proving once again that the best museum policies are made to be bent.

The official opening of the American Wing on November 10, 1924, provided the trustees with another of those well-loved occasions for congratulatory speechmaking. De Forest gave a dinner for the board at the University Club, where they dined on Supreme of Chicken Tosca and listened contentedly to lengthy addresses by their host (who referred charmingly to his "insignificant gift"), and by Henry Kent, Grosvenor Atterbury, R. T. Haines Halsey, and the Honorable Elihu Root. De Forest said that he and his wife would be satisfied "if we have helped to rescue the modest art of our forefathers from undeserved oblivion." They had wanted to see whether American domestic craftsmanship was not a chapter, "or at least a paragraph," in the history of art. It was now up to the public to decide, de Forest said. "We await, with interest, the verdict."

In its review of the American Wing the next day, *The New York Times* (which had long since ceased to be the museum's most hostile critic) called it "from a certain point of view the most significant piece of good fortune which has ever befallen the Metropolitan Museum of Art." A significant number of visitors seemed to share this view, and ever since it opened the Wing has proved immensely popular. It has also come in for its share of criticism. Period room installations have always been controversial in museum circles. Frank Jewett Mather, Jr., the greatly respected Princeton art scholar, objected to the "antiquarian sentimentality" that sought to make works of art feel "at home" in museums by trying to reproduce their original surroundings. Why stop at reconstructing a Renaissance chapel to house an altarpiece? Mather scathingly inquired. "Why not introduce a priest, waxen or in the flesh? Why not hold a Mass, oral or phonographic?" Elaborately false period installations were fine in romantic opera, Mather said, but not in the museum; the inescapable fact about works of art in museums was that they *were* homeless, and the curator's job was not to pretend otherwise but to bring out their *museum* values. Other critics complained that the period rooms were inflexible, that they could not be altered or added to without great difficulty and expense, and that important works of art tended to become lost in the general "atmosphere" of the period. Security was another problem. Edward Robinson had argued that the American Wing installations would require a guard in every room. Halsey disagreed, and to back his contention he personally loaned all the three hundred-odd loose small objects in the original installation, and was pleased to report after six months that with one guard patrolling several rooms, nothing had been lost. Over the years, however, there has been a good deal of petty pilferage in the American Wing. The guards who work there call it the "Five and Ten," because of the great number of small and removable items on display. Children sometimes cannot resist pocketing souvenirs. Others, adults included, fall under a compulsion to sink down upon seventeenth century daybeds or to finger and otherwise test the quality of fragile homespun fabrics. The temptations are greater at the Metropolitan than at some other museums because most of its period rooms can be entered; the velvet rope across the door is rarely used, except when there is a shortage of guards or an especially large crowd of visitors—situations that recur, it must be noted, with increasing frequency. The problems and drawbacks are all accepted in the sacred name of education, although it has occasionally been suggested that the educational viewpoint of the American Wing is a rather narrow one. Schoolchildren can learn a good deal about their relatively well-to-do forefathers—the country gentleman, the merchant, the plantation owner—but a visit to the Wing will provide no insights into the domestic life of the tenant farmer or the Negro slave.

Even its critics concede, however, that the American Wing has been phenomenally influential. The Metropolitan was the first major museum to initiate systematic, large-scale collections in the field of American decorative arts. There are today more than two thousand so-called historic house museums in the United States, all of them dedicated to the same general principles as the American Wing and most of them founded since 1924. Colonial Williamsburg, founded in 1926 by John D. Rockefeller, Jr., and opened to the public in 1932; the New England restorations of Deerfield and Sturbridge villages; and Henry F. du Pont's Winterthur Museum of Early American Arts in Delaware all owe something to the earlier ideas and efforts of de Forest, Kent, and Halsey. The American Wing did not invent the modern fascination with our forefathers—a development that suggests to some social thinkers a certain faltering of national self-confidence and élan—but it certainly contributed heavily to the popular taste for "Early American," as well as helping to stimulate scholarly interest in the field.

The discovery that historical relics had value has resulted in some rather strange offers to the museum. A lady in Florida once offered the chair that Betsy Ross sat in when she made the American flag. Another woman sent in a photograph of the iron that Betsy had used to *press* the flag. Both these items were declined, as was the offer from a Texas widow to donate the pickled body of her late husband, whom she claimed had been "the handsomest man in Deaf Smith County." Perhaps the strangest phenomenon of all, however, has been the duration and intensity of the vogue for Early Americana. Until quite recently the only "period" furniture that had ever retained a high market value beyond its own period was the incredibly luxurious *ébénisterie* of the French eighteenth century master craftsmen; today, however, the prices commanded by our Puritan ancestors' crude and functional pine furniture equal and sometimes even exceed those paid for French ebony, gilt-bronze, and marquetry pieces. Rarity is an important factor, of course, there being so little authentic made-in-America furniture (our wealthier ancestors preferred to import their chairs from Europe). The demand is so great that reproductions of Colonial pieces sell for stimulating prices in all the best department stores, while low-priced copies can be found almost anywhere—even, astonishingly enough, in Paris.

For a time in the 1950s the fad showed signs of slackening. Few authentic pieces remained to be bought. Reproductions of cobblers' benches no longer blocked the access to every suburban sofa, and the hinterlands of New England and Bucks County saw fewer young matrons intent on acquiring the "honest" little slat-back, with just a trace of the original paint on one leg, that was guaranteed to bring on spinal fusion if sat upon for more than ten minutes. Then the Kennedys moved into the White House, and Early American stock went up about forty points.

The redecoration of the White House with American art and antiques led to at least one encounter between the Metropolitan and Jacqueline Kennedy, whose zeal in seeking out suitable material had attracted national attention. The curator of the American Wing at that time was James Biddle, an extremely well-connected member of the Philadelphia Biddles and a personal friend of the Kennedys. Early in 1962, Biddle received a letter from John Russell Hunter regarding the Forbes Plateau—a large and elaborate piece of nineteenth century silverware made to display flowers or fruit on a dining table—which had been on loan from the Hunter family to the Metropolitan for the last forty years. Hunter said that he was thinking of presenting the plateau to the "refurbishment" of the White House. Biddle wrote back in considerable dismay. The plateau, he said, was a central feature of the Phyfe room in the American Wing. It was a unique piece, one of only two such plateaus bearing the mark of an American maker (in this case the Connecticut silversmith John W. Forbes), and its loss would come as a great blow to the museum. Besides, Biddle added, the White House already had a beautiful French silver-gilt plateau purchased by President Monroe. Further communications were exchanged, which served to increase Biddle's sense of foreboding. In March, Biddle made a last-ditch plea. Choosing his phrases with curatorial subtlety, Biddle told Hunter that he must decide for himself whether he would prefer "to aid in the decoration of the White House or in the enrichment of the largest public collection of art in the country."

Biddle left soon afterward on a trip to the Far East. When he got back the Forbes Plateau was gone. He found on his desk at the museum a letter from Mrs. Kennedy informing him that she was planning a hundred-gun salute on the White House lawn to celebrate the first time anyone had managed to get anything away from the Metropolitan. In his reply Biddle said that the pleasure of reading her note and learning of its effect on the trustees was partial compensation for the loss. The museum replaced the Forbes Plateau with what Biddle called "a plated English cousin of inferior degree." History, at least, had been served.

SIXTEEN

Ever since 1880 the Metropolitan had been expanding in all directions. New wings had sprouted on the average of one every ten years, and the amount of gallery space had been quadrupled. With the completion of the American Wing in 1924, this stately and inexorable expansion came to a halt. No new addition to the museum would be built for the next twenty-five years. A time of consolidation and slowed growth was at hand, a time for curatorial entrenchments and long, quiet afternoons. For those who craved surcease from the Jazz Age, the Metropolitan had become an ideal refuge.

Overcrowded galleries were never a problem, although the number of visitors rose steadily. Annual attendance passed the million mark for the first time in 1921, making the Metropolitan second only to the Louvre in this respect. The twenty-five cent admission charge on Mondays and Fridays deterred many art lovers, although members, schoolchildren, and teachers were admitted free at all times. The only occasions when the museum seemed really crowded were the free concerts on Saturday evenings, which had been started as a wartime experiment in 1918. An orchestra of fifty or more musicians chosen from various symphonic groups would assemble on the balcony of the main hall, and play, under the direction of the well-known concertmaster David Mannes, selections that ranged from light classics to complete symphonies of the romantic sort. There were some misgivings at first about the size of the concert audiences—one concert in 1922 drew ten thousand people—but Edward Robinson was pleased to report at the close of the fourth season that "there has been no symptom of disorder, no case has been jostled by the crowds about it, and not an object in the Museum has been injured." New Yorkers, it seemed, were becoming reasonably civilized.

The general layout of the museum collections had not changed appreciably since the opening of the Morgan (Decorative Arts) Wing in 1910. As you entered the museum from Fifth Avenue, Egyptian Art lay to the right of the great hall, in eleven large galleries, and beyond that was Arms and Armor. To the left of the entrance one found Classical Antiquities, extending back to a Roman sculpture court at the south end of the museum.* If you walked straight ahead, past the staircase, you came to the original brick building, Wing A, which had been for many years the Hall of Casts —architectural casts of the Parthenon and the Hypostyle Hall of Karnak and the Cathedral of Notre Dame, sculptural casts of the *Dying Gaul,* the *Gattemelata* and the *Colleoni* equestrian monuments, and nearly all of Michelangelo's more famous statues. Casts were going out of favor and their days at the museum were numbered, but for the moment there was nothing to replace them. The splendors of the Morgan Wing stretched away to the north, followed by the American Wing's more homely delights.

The majority of visitors did not come to see these things. They came to see the paintings. "Where is the art?" they asked, and any attendant would direct them immediately to the paintings galleries on the second floor. Bryson Burroughs' attempt to arrange the paintings in chronological and stylistic order were greatly hampered by the problem of restrictive bequests. Although the trustees had turned down Senator Clark's collection in 1925 because of the conditions he imposed, the Hearn, Wolfe, Altman, and Dreicer pictures still had to be kept together, and Burroughs hung them in the galleries to the left of the staircase. Unrestricted paintings were to the right, arranged according to schools. A few of the major gaps that Roger Fry had noted in 1907 were still waiting to be filled, although after 1929, the memorable year of the Havemeyer bequest, this could no longer be said.

---

* The south Fifth Avenue wing (Wing K) had been started in 1914 and the exterior completed before the city's appropriation ran out. Wartime cutbacks and the city's failure to provide new funds prevented completion of the interior gallery space and the Roman Court until 1926.

Henry Osborne Havemeyer, who made his millions as head of the American Sugar Refining Company, was a large, overbearing, and sometimes ill-mannered businessman, whose connection with the Metropolitan went all the way back to 1888. Learning in that year that the museum wanted but could not afford to buy a Gilbert Stuart portrait of Washington—the so-called *Carroll Washington*—Havemeyer bought it himself and presented it to the trustees. Although his benefactions continued, he was not elected to the board. "Havemeyer is a hard man to *get along with!*" Marquand wrote to Cesnola in 1891. "Though very knowing—I fear he won't do." The federal authorities also had their doubts about Havemeyer. An investigation of the Sugar Trust in 1907 resulted in a federal suit against Havemeyer's firm, which was accused of systematically underweighing its imported sugar and withholding the duties accordingly; a judgment was obtained, and the firm was obliged to pay the government more than $2,-000,000.

In art matters Havemeyer followed the lead of his second wife, Louisine, whom he adored and pampered (he had previously been married to her aunt). Louisine had been initiated into art by the American painter Mary Cassatt, a childhood friend from Philadelphia. Miss Cassatt lived in Paris and knew all the Impressionists—her long liaison with Degas will no doubt serve someday as the vehicle for a heavy-footed Broadway musical —and through her Louisine Havemeyer came into intimate contact with the contemporary painting that was causing such outrage among conservative French critics. By 1889 she had converted her husband, whose initial tastes ran to murky landscapes and cow pictures, to an appreciation of Courbet. Manet came next, and then Degas. The Havemeyers' New York town house at One East Sixtieth[66th] Street began to fill up with brilliant examples of the most advanced painting, which they purchased in Paris under Mary Cassatt's watchful eye. Louisine even managed now and then to get around her husband's moral objection to nudes—like Andrew Mellon and several other collectors, he did not care for naked ladies and gentlemen on his walls, particularly when they had a contemporary look. Louisine persuaded him to buy the great Courbet *Woman with a Parrot*, but only on condition that it be placed on immediate loan to the Metropolitan; the sensuality of the subject, a lushly painted nude lying on a bed, her hair cascading about her while she plays with a green parrot, was not the sort of thing he wanted his growing daughters to see every day. Mrs. Havemeyer also yearned for Manet's famous *Olympia,* the painting that shocked the French Academy and that is now one of the highlights of the Jeu de Paume, but here the sugar baron drew the line.

The Havemeyers' collecting passion spilled over into many other fields of art. They bought Chinese porcelains and Persian lusterware, Venetian glass, Japanese tea jars, Ming bronzes, Renaissance and Oriental sculpture, rare manuscripts, and, starting about 1900, they began to hunt for Old Master paintings. They acquired several superb Rembrandts, but in the Italian school they fared less well. Without Mary Cassatt to guide them, they soon fell into the hands of a shady Italian dealer who introduced them to decayed and dubious aristocrats, took them off on arduous journeys into the Tuscan hills, and once even had them pose as wine merchants so that they might gain access to a private villa containing an alleged Old Master. Louisine thrilled to the adventure of it all. In her memoirs she recorded the delightful surprise of finding, in the course of a trip by third-class railway carriage in Italy, that "The Poor are good-natured and kindhearted, and their pleasant chatter, where it did not rise to the confusion of a din, was not disagreeable." (The experience may even have influenced her to buy Daumier's *Third Class Carriage* in 1913.) They acquired in this manner a number of pictures attributed to Raphael, Titian, and Tintoretto, but only two of them turned out to be authentic—the Bronzino *Portrait of a Young Man* and Veronese's *Boy with a Greyhound,* both of which are now in the Metropolitan.

From Italy they went on to Spain and their greatest collecting triumphs. Steered once again by Miss Cassatt, the Havemeyers fell in love with El Greco, whose work was almost unknown to American collectors at that time. Throughout most of the nineteenth century, in fact, his early paintings had often been attributed to Titian or Tintoretto, and his later, more disturbing works had fetched little or nothing on the London market. The Havemeyers really made the modern market for El Greco, and to a lesser degree for Goya as well. They bought El Greco's breathtaking *View of Toledo,* his sole landscape and one of the most hallucinating pictures ever painted; the powerful El Greco portrait of *Cardinal Don Fernando Niño de Guevara* (whose black-rimmed spectacles bothered Havemeyer at first); and a magnificent *Ascension of the Virgin,* which had been sold in 1853 for ten guineas—Havemeyer paid $17,000 for it, and offered to give it to the Metropolitan, which turned the picture down because it had just bought an El Greco *Adoration of the Shepherds* on the recommendation of Roger Fry. Their Goyas, if anything, were even more splendid. They bought five, among them the unforgettable *Majas on a Balcony*, a scintillating portrait of the Duke of Wellington, and the strange, visionary *City on a Rock*, which some art scholars now consider the work of an artist named Eugenio Lucas.

Havemeyer missed very few of the pictures he wanted, because he was willing to pay whatever they cost and to make up his mind immediately. Louisine, who had so expertly channeled and directed his taste, continued to add to the collection after his death in 1907. (She also took an active part in the movement for women's suffrage. At the age of 64, to the intense dismay of her family, she was arrested in Washington, D.C., along with a group of suffragettes who had burned Woodrow Wilson in effigy; she spent the night in jail, and later toured the country on the movement's "Prison Special" train.) In her will she left everything to her three children, but shortly before her own death in 1929 she added three codicils. The first provided for one hundred and thirteen works of art to go to the Metropolitan. The second added twenty-nine more paintings to this gift, and the third authorized Horace Havemeyer, her son and executor, to give the museum any works of art not mentioned in the will that he chose to give. Horace and his sisters were more than generous. Not only did they give a total of 1,972 works of art to the museum, but they consulted the curators in each department to make sure that the museum received only what it wanted. The sole conditions were that each object be labeled as belonging to "The H. O. Havemeyer Collection," and that they be for "permanent exhibition." The museum was free to arrange and place them however it wished.

Although the Havemeyer gift enhanced almost every department of the museum, it was the painting and the print departments that profited most handsomely. The Havemeyer Manets and Degases and Courbets were so fine that all three of these artists—who had been very weakly represented before—could thereafter be seen better in the Metropolitan than anywhere else. Their Spanish paintings compared favorably with anything outside the Prado. Their six Rembrandts, five Cézannes, and two Poussins, their

Hugo van der Goes and their Ingres were all of absolutely top quality, and their gift of one hundred and eighty-two prints—from Dürer and Rembrandt down to Cézanne—was by far the most important that had been made to the Print Department up to that time. Each painting and print, moreover, seemed to have a quality that made it representative of their own individual taste and perception. Havemeyer pictures do not have the rich, bravura look of Morgan or Altman pictures—their appeal is subtler, and in some ways more penetrating. It was probably the most personal collection ever presented to the museum, and yet it fitted almost miraculously the pressing needs of half a dozen different departments, and transformed the paintings collection from a rather spotty survey of Western European art into a remarkably balanced treasure-house, one that could for the first time truly hold its own in comparison with the great galleries of Europe.

A gradual tendency to reduce the number of paintings on exhibition could be noted at the museum during the nineteen twenties. Pictures no longer mounted one on top of another almost to the ceiling in old-style installations, against walls uniformly covered in red billiard cloth. Henry Kent's Education Department worked diligently, moreover, to aid the bewildered visitor. Free gallery talks were given every Saturday and Sunday afternoon, for those who had the foresight to apply in advance, and the staff of five "museum instructors" was kept busy during weekdays as well. If a group, or even a single visitor desired a guided tour, they could go to the information desk in the main hall, say what part of the museum they wanted to visit, and ask for a guide; the instructor who specialized in that area would then come running. The problem of single gentlemen requesting repeated assistance from young female instructors was dealt with firmly, but grateful visitors who insisted on tipping sometimes caused embarrassment. One instructor who tactfully declined a tip from a Florida businessman received from him, a week later, a crate of slightly overripe avocados. Another delighted client insisted on taking the entire teaching staff to Beatrice Lillie's current play on Broadway.

In addition to gallery talks and lectures, the educational staff continued to encourage visits by school classes and even started sending out lantern slides to public school teachers to use in preparation for a visit. "Story hours" for children, complete with lantern slides and a storyteller in costume, preceded the adult lectures on Sunday afternoons. The museum library welcomed visitors as well as staff members, and sought to answer all questions courteously and quickly. Founded in 1880 and presided over from 1905 to 1941 by a distinguished Briton named William Clifford, the library had grown up with the museum, supported liberally by the Rogers Fund. Clifford often said that good manners made for greater efficiency, and some visitors used to come in with questions mainly for the pleasure of receiving his answers. When someone wanted a book, Clifford would summon the porter by drumming with two fingers on the edge of his desk—the sound brought the porter instantly but never seemed to disturb the readers.

The museum spelled out its educational "credo" from time to time in the *Bulletin*. The major premise was that every human being had been born with a potential love of beauty, and that the Metropolitan's task was to educate and refine that innate sense through exposure and explanation. There was less talk than there used to be about refining public taste and improving the quality of craftsmanship in the "industrial arts." Art no longer had to "pay" for its keep. Ideal beauty was in the ascendant, although seldom defined. One should know it when one saw it, that was the point, and how better to do this than to study its hushed but indubitable presence in the museum? For more advanced acolytes of the beautiful, the museum initiated in 1923 a series of lectures for students of New York University's Department of Fine Arts. *The New York Times* acclaimed this step, stating that the Metropolitan, together with the American Museum of Natural History across the Park, "has become one of the city's greatest educational forces."

As secretary and administrative czar of everything but the curatorial departments, Henry Kent held sway over a vast domain. Education, publications, registration and cataloguing, the photographic studio, the library, the Department of Industrial Relations, and the Extension Division all fell under his supervision, which was ever-vigilant. Down in the basement, unseen and unsuspected by the average visitor, a subterranean complex of shops and services had grown up over the years. The printshop, Kent's particular delight, made all the museum's labels, posters, invitations, pamphlets, forms and blanks, and even printed up stationery for the staff. All the display cases, cabinets, mounts, and other such necessities were made on the premises by a force of carpenters that at one time numbered sixty men. An army of masons, machinists, painters, engineers, electricians, roofers, and riggers worked to keep the museum operating smoothly, while a staff of one hundred and thirty attendants (guards) kept its eye on the public. No serious thefts or attempted thefts had ever been reported. The museum took no chances, though, and every attendant was required to take pistol practice in the basement two or three times a year. The first annual pistol-shooting competition was held in 1929, before an interested group of museum attendants, staff members, trustees, and representatives of the New York City Police Department. Robinson presented a silver cup to the winning team and a bronze medal to the losers, and said the event had shown "a gratifying spirit of esprit de corps among the men who protect the property of the Museum."

Needless to say there was no union of maintenance workers or guards. The shop foremen, supervisors, and heads of departments took their orders from Kent, who had the reputation of being scrupulously just but somewhat inhuman. "Why should I thank a man for a good job if he's paid for it?" Kent once inquired. A smallish man with a long, thin head, white hair, pince-nez, and a little waxed moustache, Kent sat in his inner office behind a very large desk and made things come out even. The outer office was populated by a tribe of blindingly efficient, unmarried, and utterly devoted young ladies, all ready on the instant to perform Kent's bidding. Few of Kent's "willing slaves," as one of their number described them, had had more than a high school education. Kent trained them, and in time the senior trainees went out from the secretary's office to rule over the outposts of Kent's museum empire. The tribal queen was Winifred Howe, who had charge of museum publications. Miss Howe had beeen a pupil at the Norwich Free School when Kent was librarian there, and her worship of the master shone through the pages of her dogged, two-volume history of the Metropolitan.° Her rather elaborate speaking voice led the younger girls to refer to her (behind her back, of course) as "Winnie the Coo." Kent's own accent became increasingly British as he grew older. This seemed to make him, if anything, more aloof and disdainful in his contacts with subordinates. It had a powerful effect on the attendant who stood guard outside

° A History of the Metropolitan Museum of Art, 1905–1941, Vol. II, by Winifred E. Howe, published for the Metropolitan Museum of Art by Columbia University Press, New York, 1946.

the door to the secretary's office; over the years he developed an accent that was almost indistinguishable from Kent's. Not many people liked Kent, but most of the staff were willing to concede that the Metropolitan's preeminence owed much to his organizational and administrative skills.

As the largest and richest art museum of the Western hemisphere, the Metropolitan was also a natural target for much of the criticism aimed at art museums in general. Public museums had never lacked critics, but the spirit of irreverence that characterized the 1920s decade produced any number of new slings and arrows. Some of the sniping was directed at the social prestige and conservatism of the Metropolitan's board of trustees—often said to be the most exclusive club in New York. In an article on the Metropolitan entitled "Some Impertinent Questions," the critic Murdock Pemberton concluded his list by inquiring, "What is the next little picture you are going to buy?" and "Are you convinced that the painter of it is a gentleman?" American artists complained regularly and predictably that there was not enough American art in the museum, and that the income from the Hearn Fund was being allowed to pile up unspent. Much more disturbing, from the museum's point of view, were the attacks on the museum's effectiveness as an educator. The men who ran the Metropolitan had always laid great emphasis on the educational side of things, and every annual report since 1870 had pointed with pride to steps taken to instruct and uplift the populace. Lately, however, influential voices had raised some rather searching questions about museum education in general.

John Cotton Dana, the director of the Newark Museum, proclaimed that "No other public institutions give so little in return for the money spent on them as museums." Dana contended that instead of teaching or encouraging public taste, most art museums still directed their main attention to the "cultured few," and fostered a snobbish cult of the "museum piece, which . . . must be rare, expensive because desired by the wealthy, and of toothsome age." The Newark Museum under Dana had experimented with all sorts of revolutionary new techniques, sending paintings and objects out on loan throughout the community and putting on striking exhibitions of objects that were in no sense "museum pieces." Dana's idea, which sounds strikingly contemporary today, was to put art into daily life. He felt that it should be possible for a museum to exhibit a cheap glass of water in such a way that viewers could look at it with fresh eyes and see in it the beauties

of line and mass and reflected color. "Art is not in a museum save in relatively unimportant quantity," Dana argued. "Art is where it is seen and not
merely where self-constituted experts have placed it."

Other writers on art questioned whether "education" as such belonged in
a museum at all. "The museums and galleries terrify us," the British critic
Clive Bell wrote. "We are crushed by the tacit assurance frowned from
every corner that these treasures are displayed for study and improvement,
by no means to provoke emotions." Benjamin Ives Gilman, the greatly respected secretary of the Boston Museum of Fine Arts from 1904 to 1924,
also questioned the pedagogical emphasis. The purpose of an art museum
was aesthetic, not dogmatic, Gilman said. The trouble with comprehen-
siveness was that it tended to make the museum a place where, as one critic
phrased it, "every separate object kills every other, and all of them together, the visitor." Art could exist only in relation to life, and perhaps the
true function of museums was to make people more intensely aware of
their own existence. The goal was not culture or knowledge, but joy.

Not many Metropolitan trustees were swayed by this sort of talk. The
trustees, after all, had expunged the word "recreation" from their charter in
1909, and their successors were not likely to embrace joy as the ultimate
goal now. Another attack that they could not very well ignore, though,
since it was directed specifically against the Metropolitan, was Frank Jewett Mather, Jr.'s, charge of "jumboism." Mather, the co-founder with Allan
Marquand (Henry Gurdon Marquand's son) of the Fine Arts Department
at Princeton, made his criticism in an article called "Smaller and Better
Museums" which appeared in the *Atlantic Monthly* in 1929. American Museums were growing too large, he said, and in doing so they were defeating
their own purpose. The Metropolitan, having long ago accepted the quanti-
tative ideal, best exemplified the trend and its drawbacks, which Mather
identified as confusion and fatigue for the ordinary visitor and administrative chaos for the staff. "The Metropolitan Museum is conducting more activities than can possibly be conducted properly under one roof and under
one administration," Mather stated. In London, Paris, Berlin and other European capitals, separate museums were devoted to painting and sculpture,
decorative arts, national art, arms and armor, and Oriental art; by attempting to incorporate this impossibly broad range of art objects in one museum, Mather charged, the Metropolitan failed to do justice to any of them.

Mather urged decentralization. He argued that the Metropolitan and its sister institutions in Boston, Chicago, and other big cities should establish branch museums specializing in one category or another, thereby leading to greater interest and pleasure for the public and more efficient administration generally.

The Metropolitan's president took Mather's criticism seriously, and set out to answer it in detail. De Forest reviewed the original premises on which the Metropolitan had been founded, and recalled the statement of another and earlier Princeton professor, George F. Comfort, who had said in 1869 that the museum "should be based on the idea of a more or less complete collection of objects illustrating the history of art from the earliest beginnings to the present time." The purpose of "a more or less complete collection" was education in art for the mass public. Once that premise was accepted—as it had been by the founders—a large and comprehensive museum had become necessary.

De Forest conceded that the Metropolitan's collections could become too large. It would be worthwhile, he said, to consider dividing the present space into exhibition galleries for the general public and study collections for the serious student—an experiment that had already been made by a number of science museums, by the Victoria and Albert in London, and by the Boston Museum of Fine Arts in 1909, when it moved into its new building; the so-called "Boston Plan" of dual arrangement had never worked too successfully in Boston because both the general and the study galleries were easily accessible to the public and a good many people never did learn the difference. Some limitation on the amount of material on public display was necessary, though, and de Forest said that the Metropolitan's acquisition policies in the future should be altered accordingly. "From now on," he wrote, "I think our purchases should be limited to objects of definite importance, needed for permanent exhibition." Better examples could always be substituted for lesser works in the museum collections, and the lesser works could perhaps serve as the nucleus for various branch museums throughout the city. Even more care should be exercised, moreover, in the acceptance of gifts that did not fit a major need of the museum.

On the issue of decentralization, though, de Forest held his ground. The applied or decorative arts, Oriental art, American arts and crafts were as necessary to the Metropolitan's purpose as the fine arts of painting and sculpture. "We are perfectly conscious of the charm of a small museum," de Forest told his audience at the sixtieth anniversary ceremonies in 1930. Like the Japanese custom of showing a single picture or a single flower in isolation, the segregation of art into particular categories might afford greater aesthetic pleasure. "But such a limited sphere is not ours," de Forest concluded. "While the aesthetic value may be greater, the educational value would be less. The needs of students would not be met. The inspiration which our Museum gives to schools and colleges, not only in art but in history and in the development of civilization, would be lacking." Dana and Gilman notwithstanding, de Forest never doubted for a moment that the Metropolitan was fulfilling its educational goals.

Although de Forest probably spoke for the majority of the trustees and the staff, he also spoke for the older generation, a generation that still remembered the founders and whose dominance at the museum was coming to a close. Several of the trustees were past eighty, although in the president's case one would scarcely have guessed it. Small and dapper, with sparkling blue eyes and a white beard that made some people think of Santa Claus, de Forest still tramped the Adirondack mountains of his summer home in Keene Valley, and defeated thirty-pound salmon on annual fishing trips to the Cascapedia River in Canada. He was getting deaf, though, and friends thought it sad that on his eightieth birthday in 1928, when he was enthroned as "Abou ben Adhem," sultan of philanthropy, at a celebration attended by more than two hundred and fifty friends and admirers, he could barely hear the glowing tributes paid to him. While de Forest sat smiling upon his throne, *The Times* reported the next day, a caravan of three "Arabs" brought in a magic carpet containing the symbols of his long career of public service—"a casket with the jewels of charity and kindness, a spray of blossoms representing the flowering of art, a toy house signifying improvement of housing conditions and a metropolitan map showing the development of the Regional Plan of New York." Birthday greetings from many of the city's famous citizens were read, after which "an angel appeared, who wrote in a golden book Mr. de Forest's name and title, 'Abou ben Adhem.' " All those present added their own names, and a group of school children closed the program with a dance "as two little negro boys in red turbans entered with a huge birthday cake bearing eighty candles."

Edward Robinson's seventieth birthday came round a few months later. The staff assembled in their new basement lunchroom for tea and birthday cake, which had been baked in the shape of a Greek temple and was handed around by two female members of the Classical Department staff wearing modern Greek costumes. Afterward, everyone adjourned to the main hall of the museum where the attendants stood at attention, drawn up in ranks that formed the figure seventy. Tall and graceful, with snowy hair and transparent skin that reminded a newspaper interviewer of "the sculptured busts that decorate the vast halls of the museum," Robinson received their salute. He had been director for twenty years. His frosty formal dignity still intimidated the younger curators and assistants, but the older staff members genuinely admired and respected him, and it was nearly impossible to think of the museum without his austere figure at the helm.

Less than three years later, the entire staff gathered to mourn the deaths of Robinson, de Forest, and three trustees of long standing—Edward D. Adams, George F. Baker, and Charles W. Gould. A new era seemed to be at hand. As sometimes happens on these occasions, though, the portents were slightly premature.

SEVENTEEN

William Sloane Coffin, the new president of the Metropolitan, had a great deal in common with his predecessor. Like Robert de Forest, Coffin was a lifelong New Yorker, an active proponent of slum clearance and social welfare, and a connoisseur of Early American furniture—an interest that he carried over into the family business, which was the furniture store W. and J. Sloane. On the Metropolitan board since 1924, he had become its first vice-president in 1930 when Elihu Root stepped down from that post for reasons of age and health. Coffin was a quiet, modest businessman who had never been as prominent in civic affairs as his older brother Henry Sloane Coffin, the president of Union Theological Seminary. His main interest lay in the museum's educational program. Coffin wanted to establish branch museums in all the boroughs of the city. During his brief term as president, the Metropolitan's teaching staff went outside the museum for the first time to lecture to public high school students—an age group that subsequent museum administrators have wooed periodically ever since, each time believing that they were the first to do so. Coffin died in 1933, after only two years as president and before he had time to develop his educational ideas. He was succeeded by George Blumenthal, whose election came as a huge surprise to a number of people.

Blumenthal, a retired investment banker and an art collector, was the first and at that time still the only Jewish trustee of the Metropolitan. Some of his colleagues occasionally gave thought to this slightly embarrassing situation. "About a quarter of the people of the city are Jews and a large proportion of the art treasures of the city are in Jewish hands," William Church Osborn, one of the oldest and most active trustees, had pointed out in a 1928 letter to de Forest. Both Osborn and de Forest agreed that the Metropolitan ought to give greater recognition to Jewish prominence in the city's cultural affairs—de Forest said it had been his own earnest solicitation on this point that had been responsible for Blumenthal's election to the board in 1909, "with Mr. Morgan's approval." When Coffin died, the trustees' choice to succeed him was William Church Osborn. Osborn was Old New York, socially prominent, wealthy, and Protestant—the very model of a Metropolitan trustee—but he was also heavily involved in politics and civic affairs, and felt he could not take on the added responsibility. He was probably instrumental, however, in the decision to offer the presidency to Blumenthal.

There were good and sound reasons for the choice. George Blumenthal was an extremely astute financier. Born in Frankfurt-am-Main in 1858, he had come to America at the age of twenty-four to work in the New York office of Lazard Frères, an investment house whose main headquarters were in Paris. He had shown such brilliance and flair that he became a senior partner while still in his thirties, and was soon afterward in charge of the New York firm. During the financial panic of 1896, when J. P. Morgan formed a syndicate of leading bankers to stop the outflow of gold, Blumenthal was one of the two men he turned to—the other was Jacob H. Schiff. Since his retirement from Lazard in 1925 Blumenthal had devoted much time to the financial affairs of the Metropolitan and of Mount Sinai Hospital, where he had been president of the board since 1911. William Sloane Coffin said that credit for the Metropolitan's excellent financial condition during his presidency belonged entirely to Blumenthal, who was then chairman of the financial committee. Blumenthal had established his own personal fund for the museum in 1928, when he made a gift of $1,000,000 with the stipulation that the income be added to the principal until both he and his wife had died; he controlled and invested the fund himself, and managed to increase it substantially during the Depression. He had made a number of other gifts to the museum, including, in 1923, the sum of $2,-000 for a station wagon ("Not a Rolls-Royce!" he had warned) to carry members of the Egyptian Expedition back and forth from Metropolitan

House to the Valley of the Kings, a journey that formerly took forty minutes each way by donkey.

Blumenthal vastly admired the elder J. P. Morgan, and his own art collection in some ways reflected Morgan's. The main impetus to his collecting, however, had been a domestic tragedy. George and Florence Blumenthal lost their only child in 1909 (the same year that Blumenthal came on the Metropolitan board), and in an effort to create new interests for his stricken wife, Blumenthal took her to Europe and encouraged her to study art history. They met Bernard Berenson, who encouraged her further. Mrs. Blumenthal knew Berenson's principal sponsor and disciple, Mrs. Jack Gardner, and had been greatly impressed by the Italianate palace that this redoubtable lady had created for herself on the Boston fens. On their return from Europe the Blumenthals bought land at the corner of Park Avenue and Seventieth Street and began to build a large town house comparable in many ways to Mrs. Gardner's Fenway Court. The central architectural element of the house was an enclosed, two-story patio from a Spanish castle built about 1515 near the southeastern coastal town of Velez Blanco; its magnificent stone carvings and noble proportions made a fitting environment for the medieval and Renaissance treasures that they had begun to collect on a large and lavish scale.

A curious story about Mrs. Blumenthal was told by Alfred H. Barr, Jr., the director of collections for the Museum of Modern Art, in his book on Matisse.* One day in 1910, when a show of Matisse drawings was on view at Alfred Stieglitz's avant-garde "291" gallery in New York, Mrs. Blumenthal came in, asked the price of the drawings (twenty dollars apiece, she was told), and picked out three of them. Stieglitz, who had strong proprietory feelings about his artist friends, was reluctant to sell them to her—he knew that the Blumenthals were buying mostly Gothic and Renaissance art, and he did not like the idea of Matisse drawings in such a setting. "When she explained that she intended to give them to the Metropolitan Museum," Barr related, "Stieglitz was dumbfounded. 'What, the Metropolitan Museum of Art! Why, they'll never accept them.' Mrs. Blumenthal drew herself up proudly. 'The Museum will take what I offer it,' she said." Barr added that the museum did take and even hang all three drawings,

* Alfred Barr, Jr., *Matisse: His Art and His Public,* Museum of Modern Art, New York, 1951.

which were in all probability the first works by Matisse to enter a public museum anywhere. There is no record of the Blumenthals ever having purchased another example of twentieth century art.

When the Park Avenue house was finally completed in 1920, after delays caused by the war, Florence Blumenthal settled into it, according to the dealer Jacques Seligmann, "like a fairy-tale princess." In the evening, Seligmann said, "she often wore Renaissance velvet gowns, in dark jewel-like colors which not only enhanced her beauty but gave her an air of having been born to this superb environment where every work of art seemed timelessly at home." Her husband, who adored her, never seemed to fit in quite so well. A small, froggy man with a thick German-Jewish accent, he had a disconcerting habit of ushering guests into the elevator on the ground floor and then dashing up the stairs to let them out when they reached the drawing room level. Florence's absorbing interest in art collecting literally saved her life. But it was George Blumenthal who became the connoisseur.

Collectors respond to works of art for a variety of reasons, most of which have little to do with aesthetic value. Only a very few love art objects for their own sake, and, of those few, the majority respond to them mainly through the visual sense. There exists, however, a tiny minority whose feeling for works of art is tactile rather than visual—who collect, as it were, with their fingertips. George Blumenthal was a collector of this rare type. He did not much care for paintings, and sometimes said that he got little pleasure from things he could not touch. What he loved best were small, exquisitely carved objects—ivories and enamels, bronzes, medieval and Renaissance jewels and wood carvings. William Ivins, the Metropolitan's first curator of prints, told of a meeting of the purchasing committee at which Blumenthal initially opposed the acquisition of some prehistoric flint instruments; the discussion veered to other matters, Blumenthal's sensitive fingers began to play over the chipped surface of a flint knife, and by the time the committee took up again the question of their purchase Blumenthal was enthusiastically in favor of it. He was not interested in the scholarly side of art. "Where the scholar labors to know about objects, the connoisseur trains himself through all his senses to know objects," Ivins wrote in a catalogue note on the Blumenthal collection, and he added that of the two kinds of knowledge, "not only is connoisseurship much the rarer but it is the more profound." Blumenthal's collection gave the clearest evidence of this quality. No president of the Metropolitan before or since has been so knowing a connoisseur.

At the time he became president, though, Blumenthal's interest in art was at a low ebb. He and his wife had spent most of the year 1930 in France, which was for many years a second home to them. They owned a large house in Paris, filled with French eighteenth century furniture, and a country place on the Riviera near Grasse. Over the years they had donated a pavilion for the Hôpital des Enfants Malades in Paris, given eight million francs for scholarships at the Louvre, and established a foundation to assist young French artists and writers, and the grateful French government had elected them both to the Legion of Honor. Their many French friends helped to celebrate Blumenthal's seventy-first birthday at their Paris house in 1930. Sojourning on the Riviera that spring, Blumenthal set a new record at the Nice Casino by winning more than $90,000 in less than half an hour—somewhat superfluous in his case, but cheering none the less. A year later, Florence Blumenthal died and her husband's world collapsed in pieces. He lost all interest in art collecting. The Paris house and all its contents were put up for auction in 1932 (the furniture and art objects brought $440,000, in the depth of the Depression). Some of Blumenthal's friends feared he might never recover from the loss of his adored Florence, but then, in 1934, the Metropolitan trustees named him to succeed the late William Sloane Coffin, and the wily old financier entered a new and active phase of his career.

There is still disagreement in some quarters over Blumenthal's financial stewardship of the Metropolitan. Part of the problem was that Blumenthal, who had always been decidedly autocratic and secretive in his business affairs, never really let the other trustees have much to say about financial matters. He would bring a single copy of the annual financial report to the board meeting, and announce that his colleagues were welcome to examine it if they so desired; the general impression was that he would be much happier if they did not. This rather disturbed his fellow trustees. Finally one of them, Ogden Mills, threatened to resign unless Blumenthal agreed to have copies of the statement made for each of them, which he did reluctantly from then on. Blumenthal retained his chairmanship of the financial committee when he became president, and handled most of the museum's investments himself. His investments during the Depression were ultraconservative—in striking contrast to his aggressive, sometimes risky manipulations up until 1925 at Lazard Frères where his partners had sometimes wished he would devote more time to investment banking and less time to the stock market. The Crash in 1929 permanently altered most men's investment thinking, however, and Blumenthal had become an arch conservative in financial matters, as well as a bitter opponent of the New Deal. "I know you do not wish to put your country into bankruptcy," he wrote to Franklin D. Roosevelt in a much-publicized 1933 letter, "but if that was your purpose you certainly could not adopt more efficient measures than those resorted to for several months." He advised an immediate halt to present New Deal policies and a return to sound money and the laws of supply and demand—only thus, he warned, could "chaos and ruin" be avoided.

While it could be said that Blumenthal's handling of the museum's endowment funds was defensive rather than brilliant and that the income from investments declined severely during these years, it must also be conceded that his cautious policies kept the Metropolitan afloat throughout the Depression, when a number of other public institutions were going under. Operating expenses were cut to the bone, and purchases were strictly limited—as de Forest had recommended in 1930. Some great treasures were lost to the museum during this period, including a *Pietà* sculpture attributed to Michelangelo, the so-called *Palestrina Pietà* now in the Accademia Museum in Florence, and the Henry Oppenheimer collection of drawings, undoubtedly the finest private collection in existence at that time. Blumenthal himself blocked the Oppenheimer purchase. William Ivins had learned that it was going to be put up for auction, and he felt that if the museum made an offer for the whole collection before the sale it might very well get it. Blumenthal at first agreed. He knew and appreciated drawings; in 1935, when a great album of Goya drawings suddenly appeared at auction in Paris, Blumenthal, knowing that his fellow trustees would not act swiftly enough, bought the entire album himself and then sold it to the museum for what he had paid. The president had some very odd quirks, though, and when he learned that the Henry Oppenheimer who owned the drawings was the same Henry Oppenheimer who had once been involved in a banking dispute with the Blumenthal family in Frankfurt, he flatly refused to let Ivins have anything to do with him. The collection was dispersed at auction. Several years later, the Metropolitan bought from Duveen, for a very high price, a Fouquet metalpoint that had been one of Oppenheimer's principal treasures.

Everyone's favorite story about Blumenthal had to do with a marble sculpture group by Giovanni Bologna, the most famous Florentine sculptor after Michelangelo, which the Metropolitan had a chance to buy in 1940. It was the only marble sculpture by Bologna outside Florence, and Preston Remington, the curator, had a complete and dazzling rundown on its history. It had been commissioned about 1568 by Francesco de' Medici, the Grand Duke of Tuscany, for the Casino Mediceo in Florence. A successor, the Grand Duke Ferdinand, had sent it in 1601 as a gift to the Duke of Lerma, prime minister to the Spanish King Philip III, who placed it in his gardens at Valladolid; when Lerma fell from power in 1621 it passed into the collection of Philip IV, who presented it in 1623 to Charles I of England (then the Prince of Wales), who was visiting the Spanish court; Charles I in turn gave it to the Duke of Buckingham, and at some point during the next century it passed into the possession of King George III, that misguided monarch, who gave it in 1778 or thereabouts to Thomas Worsley, the Surveyor-General of His Majesty's Board of Works, whose descendants now wished to sell it. Remington reeled off these illustrious names with pride, certain of the impression he was making on the trustees of the purchasing committee. Blumenthal alone seemed unimpressed. When Remington had finished, the president sniffed and said, dryly, "They all seemed to want to get rid of it, didn't they?" The Metropolitan did not buy the sculpture, which is now one of the treasures of the Victoria and Albert Museum.

Although Henry Kent complained in 1933 of the trustees' "very general intention not to buy anything," the museum actually made some notable purchases during the Depression. Not counting gifts or bequests, the Paintings Department acquired in the years from 1931 to 1939 such major works as David's *The Death of Socrates*, Raphael's *The Agony in the Garden* (a predella panel for the *Colonna Madonna* given earlier by J. P. Morgan), Fra Filippo Lippi's *Saint Lawrence Enthroned*, Ingres' *Odalisque en Grisaille*, Fragonard's *Portrait of a Lady With a Dog*, Titian's *Venus and the Lute Player*, Tintoretto's *The Finding of Moses*, and two towering masterpieces that had previously hung in the Hermitage in Leningrad—Watteau's *Mezzetin* and Van Eyck's *The Crucifixion; The Last Judgment* diptych. The Greek and Roman Department also did well, bagging several excellent sculptures including an original Greek marble *Kouros* in the Archaic style, dating from the end of the seventh century B.C. and believed to be one of the earliest surviving sculptures in Greek art. Important purchases of armor, Far Eastern art, and drawings (the Goya album) were also recorded; in addition several new departments were formed and began active buying.

Over the years the museum had accumulated a considerable quantity of Near Eastern material. The American collectors of Morgan's era and earlier tended to collect in all sorts of fields, and as a result a great deal of the Oriental and Islamic material that appeared on the market in Paris, London, and Vienna during those years came to America. Naturally a lot of it ended up at the Metropolitan—glass and pottery from Edward C. Moore in 1891, manuscripts, paintings, metalwork, ceramics, rugs, and other objects from Isaac D. Fletcher, V. Everit Macy, George D. Pratt, J. P. Morgan, and H. O. Havemeyer. In 1930 John D. Rockefeller, Jr., purchased in England and gave to the Metropolitan the huge *Winged Bull* and *Winged Lion* from the palace of Ashur-nasirpal II at Nimrud, which had been excavated in the first half of the nineteenth century by the great English archaeologist Sir Henry Layard. The Metropolitan began its own excavations in the Near East soon afterward, first at Ctesiphon, near Baghdad, and later at Nishapur in northeastern Iran. Interest in the arts of Mesopotamia and the later Near Eastern civilizations was growing rapidly, and in 1932 all this material was taken away from Joseph Breck's sprawling Decorative Arts Department and grouped together in a new Department of Near Eastern Art under Maurice Dimand, a knowledgeable scholar who immediately began systematic purchases to round out the collection. A year later, the Decorative Arts Department split into three separate components—Renaissance and Modern Art, under Preston Remington; the American Wing, under Joseph Downs; and Medieval Art, under James J. Rorimer.

A basic change was taking place within the museum—so gradually that few people were aware of it. As the Metropolitan's curatorial departments became more specialized and more independent professionally, the power and influence of the trustees subtly waned. There were no visible lesions of authority—the trustees still set the policy and voted on all important purchases, although they were increasingly inclined to approve whatever works of art the curators and the director recommended; what had changed was their general feeling about the museum. For nearly half a century the trustees had tended to think and even speak of it as "our museum," just as they had looked upon the museum staff as "their" employees. Such habits of mind were tacitly supported by men like Henry Kent, who saw himself as the "entrepreneur" between the trustees, exalted beings whose word was law, and the staff, mere underlings whose expertise was a commodity to be used as the board saw fit. To a certain extent Edward Robinson had shared and reflected Kent's point of view. Blumenthal, however, was sharp enough to understand that the trustees' (and the president's) duty was to have the museum run but not to run it. "I am not planning any new departures," he told a *New York Times* interviewer after his assumption of the presidency. In contrast to de Forest, Blumenthal made no attempt to chart courses of action or to initiate new programs and policies. What he did do was to place increasing confidence and responsibility in the professional staff, the people who should and did run the museum, from the director on down.

The new director, Herbert Winlock, appeared ideally equipped to take on this larger responsibility. His election, however, had been almost as much of a surprise as Blumenthal's. The man everyone had expected to get the job was Joseph Breck, who had succeeded William Valentiner as curator of Decorative Arts. Breck had come to work for the museum in 1909 as Valentiner's assistant. He had resigned in 1914 to become director of the new Minneapolis Institute of Arts, but then, when Valentiner himself resigned to go home and fight in the German army during the First World War, Robinson persuaded Breck to return in a dual capacity as curator of decorative arts and assistant director of the Metropolitan. Breck was an able, hard-working, and rather tactless man who never quite managed to become an art scholar. Students at Princeton's Department of Fine Arts, then the principal training ground for future art scholars and art historians, used to regale each other with blunders culled from labels in the Metropolitan's decorative arts galleries. This in itself would not necessarily have prejudiced the trustees against Breck, but the truth was that nobody really liked him. Among the staff he was known as "The Prussian," in reference to his cold and rather petulant sense of discipline. Everyone was resigned to Breck's being named director after Robinson's death in 1931, and Breck fully expected it, but by this time the trustees were convinced that he would not do. They did want the new director to come from within the museum, though, and as Coffin wrote to Osborn, "the only man on our staff who is entirely competent for the task and has no enemies, to the best of my knowledge and belief, is Herbert Winlock." It cost Winlock much soul-searching to accept the post, for he loved the life of a field archaeologist and hated leaving it for a desk in New York. On the other hand, the Depression and Egypt's emergent national passions were rapidly bringing to an end the great days of foreign digging there, and the frustrations of fieldwork were mounting. Winlock took office as the new director early in 1932. Breck swallowed his disappointment, and two years later dropped dead of a heart attack, at the age of forty-eight, while on a summer walking tour in Switzerland.

Winlock's brisk and engaging personality seemed guaranteed to shake up a somewhat somnolent museum. Where Robinson had been aloof and unapproachable, Winlock was informal, friendly, and utterly unpedantic. On his first day as director, so the story went, he found two memos on his desk. The first informed him that several cartons of toilet paper were missing from the storeroom. The second noted that pigeons were making a mess of the American Wing's courtyard. "Well," Winlock said, "at least we know the pigeons didn't steal the paper." Winlock even managed to persuade Jimmy Walker, New York's popular but sadly incautious Mayor (he would be driven from office later that same year) to come to a board meeting in his capacity as an ex-officio Metropolitan trustee. Walker had never come before. His political cronies, fearing a trap of some insidious kind, tried hard to dissuade him from venturing into the lair of the fine arts, but jaunty Jimmy went and impressed the trustees no end with his intelligent and perfectly sober questions.

Winlock remained curator of the Egyptian Department for several years after becoming director, and some of his colleagues complained that his consuming interest in archaeology kept him from paying sufficient attention to their needs. It is true that he was an archaeologist first and last. He never pretended to any special knowledge outside his field, he detested modern art, and the art of flattering and soothing wealthy benefactors eluded him entirely. After his first stroke in 1937, from which he never fully recovered, friends said it had been a tragic mistake for him to give up field work for administration. He had always been at his best and happiest on a dig. In *Who's Who* he used to list his home as "New York and Luxor, Upper Egypt," and in the staff dining room or at the Century Club downtown he would inevitably steer the conversation around to Egypt, the *fellaheen,* the desert, and the ancient tombs.

But those who had counted on Winlock to wake up the Metropolitan were disappointed. Although the professional staff continued to extend its hard-won gains in influence and prestige, the pattern of life in the great museum went on much as it had for decades, oblivious to the profound and accelerating changes taking place in the world outside.

EIGHTEEN

Sir Caspar Purdon Clarke's only recorded witticism came in reply to a New York reporter who had asked him what made a good museum curator. "A guess, a bluff, and no one to contradict you," Sir Caspar said, with a slight twitch of his walrus moustache. One could scarcely blame him for sidestepping the question. Even today, museum people find it hard to define the curatorial role, while most laymen have only the haziest notion of what a museum curator does.

According to the Oxford English Dictionary, the word curator originally referred to someone appointed "as guardian of a minor, lunatic, etc." or to "one who has a cure of souls." When it began to be applied to paid custodians of private collections in the seventeenth century, the word kept the overtones of its earlier meaning. The museum curator, or "keeper," as he was more often called in England, guarded the objects under his care and also repaired (cured) them when they suffered damage or decay—a function now delegated to the professional restorer. Stated in its simplest terms, the modern curator's job is to take care of the works of art in his department, to display them in a manner best suited to bring out their aesthetic and educational importance, and to advise the trustees regarding new purchases in his field. In practice, though, the curatorial function teems with complexities and contradictions.

A curator must be an expert in his field, but what sort of expert? Should his knowledge be of the encyclopedic and scholarly sort, or should it be the sensory knowledge of the connoisseur? Both are necessary, although most curators are far too busy running their departments and keeping abreast of the art market to have time for serious scholarship. The curator is often compared to the university professor, but the two jobs are not at all alike. University art scholars regard curators as people who are up to their ears in social and administrative obligations, to the exclusion of their serious work. Curators regard art scholars as people who know all the books and theories but who work primarily from photographs, and as a result never really look at what they are talking about.

The social implications are even more tangled. The curator is essentially a servant. He serves the public, to whom the material must be made as attractive and as understandable as possible; he also serves the trustees, who usually lack expert knowledge and must therefore be "sold" on the beauty and importance of certain works of art. The service role can sometimes be galling. Metropolitan curators for many years were not permitted to sit down when they appeared before the trustees of the purchasing committee —they would come in, speak their piece, and leave. It was also the custom for trustees' wives, once a year, to donate evening gowns and other articles from their wardrobe to the wives of curators, the transaction being carried out through the director's wife as intermediary. Curators today have far more cachet, but their position is still socially anomalous. What's more, they now have to spend a great part of their time cultivating wealthy collectors, a species whose motives, whims, and egos are notoriously unpredictable. With prices in the art market as high as they are today, the curator can no longer simply recommend objects and hope that the trustees will provide the funds; when something surpassingly important comes on the market he very often must go out and raise the money himself, usually from collectors who have reason to trust his judgment. The successful curator is one who can sense and act upon the subtle nuances that influence collectors, nuances that often have very little to do with the intrinsic beauty or value of works of art. He must be a diplomat, a psychologist, and a *very* good listener. Tact is his watchword; patience, infinitely extended, his rationale. He is not terribly well paid. On the other hand, he often spends his vacations in Europe.

By the time Herbert Winlock took over as director in 1932, at least three curatorial departments had achieved a lordly semi-independent status within the Metropolitan. Their curators had all been with the museum for fifteen years or longer. Utterly dissimilar as they were in most respects, they had in common the fact that each had come with no previous museum experience or training. They were amateurs in the old sense—men whose knowledge proceeded from a deep love of what they were doing—but they contributed more than they knew to the evolution of the curatorial profession, and they set styles that would greatly influence their successors.

Bryson Burroughs, curator of paintings, who first appeared on the scene in 1906 as Roger Fry's assistant, was a tall, lean, muscular Ohioan with a gaunt face and warm eyes. He had actually been born just outside Boston, but his family moved to Cincinnati when he was a baby. Burroughs' youthful ambition was to be a champion bicycle racer. He won the state championship one year, but soon afterward he fell in love with painting and entered the Cincinnati Art School. Several years of study at the Art Students' League in New York, and at the École des Beaux Arts and the Académie Julian in Paris, were followed by several more years as a poorly paid artist struggling to support a growing family—he had married a fellow art student named Edith Woodman, two of whose sculptures are now owned by the Metropolitan. Burroughs won several medals in art exhibitions, and even achieved a certain notoriety in 1905 when a painting of his five small children wading in a New Hampshire brook drew the ire of Anthony Comstock, the self-appointed guardian of public morals; Comstock objected to the nudity of the minor Burroughses, and ordered the painting removed from the window of a gallery on Madison Avenue. When it became clear that the life of art could not provide for his family, Burroughs turned to museum work as an agreeable compromise. Roger Fry described his assistant as "one of the most charming creatures I've ever met, a young and unsuccessful but quite good artist . . . a man who has never bothered about anything but just gone his own way—with no money and no reputation but with peace in his heart." He was a great comfort in what Fry called "this weltering waste of the American people."

Burroughs came to the museum with the understanding that he would work there only in the afternoons—his mornings were to be kept free for his own painting. Even after he became a full curator in 1909 he continued for the next twenty-five years to paint each morning, arriving at the museum about noon and doing whatever had to be done in the few hours before he made his regular late afternoon appearance at the Century Club downtown. Although he rarely exhibited his work, the Metropolitan, the Corcoran, the Art Institute of Chicago, and a number of other museums bought his paintings, and the Century gave him a retrospective exhibition in 1933. Burroughs' pictures are rather puzzling today. Painted in the pale, cool tonality of Puvis de Chavannes, the artist who most influenced him as a student in Paris, they have a fey, cartoon-like quality that is hard to reconcile with the dedication that he gave to them. Their subject matter is often a classical myth in a modern setting—Ariadne perched on a Long Island sand dune, or Saint Ursula in a flapper dress, embarking from a pier with a steamer trunk marked "U." They could almost, but not quite, be covers for *The New Yorker*. Winlock, who scorned modern art, greatly admired Burroughs' paintings and owned several of them. "No picture of his lacks some sly, unexpected little dig at the conventional," Winlock once remarked. Although Burroughs' own taste in art remained strictly classical, his humor and gaiety of mind seem to have kept him from succumbing to the dogmatic ideals that so often afflict classicists.

His mind, to a remarkable degree, remained open to forms of art that many of his contemporaries refused to see at all. Burroughs took a considerable risk in 1913 when he recommended Cézanne's *La Colline des Pauvres*—the first Cézanne to enter a public collection. Far from neglecting American art, as has sometimes been charged, he did his best to spend the income from the Hearn Fund for American paintings that most of the Europe-oriented trustees despised, and his memorial exhibitions of Thomas Eakins, Albert Pinkham Ryder, Winslow Homer, and other native artists did much to secure their reputations. Ignoring fads and fluctuations in taste, Burroughs purchased shrewdly and well for a quarter of a century, buying not necessarily what he liked but what he knew the museum should have. In his gentle, relaxed way he was probably the finest paintings curator of his time, although few people realized this until later.

Burroughs' greatest coup came in 1919, when he acquired Pieter Bruegel's painting *The Harvesters*, a world masterpiece of towering importance (it is often said to be the first true landscape in Western art), for the incredibly small sum of $3,370.79. The painting was offered to the museum in 1917 by Paul Jean Cels, a young Belgian artist and collector, who had bought it from the French collector Jacques Doucet. Cels's asking price was $10,000, and a number of potential buyers had already turned it down because they thought it a copy of a lost original. The original, together with four others in the same series of paintings by Bruegel depicting the seasons or the months of the year (there may have been twelve in all, although only five are definitely known), had hung for many years in the Belvedere gallery in Vienna, from which it was taken in 1809 by Napoleon's conquering troops as booty for the Louvre. After Napoleon's final defeat in 1815 the Louvre returned another painting in the same series, *The Dark Day*, to the Belvedere, but *The Harvesters* vanished from sight. Long and intensive study convinced Burroughs that Cels's picture was not a copy at all, but the lost original. By this time Cels had died in Australia. The purchase was negotiated with his heirs through the Belgian consul in New York, Pierre Mali, who happened, oddly enough, to be Robert W. de Forest's brother-in-law. Subsequent study and analysis confirmed Burroughs' identification, and Dr. Ernst H. Buschbeck, the former Director of the Kunsthistoriches Museum in Vienna, has even identified the frame—all five pictures in the series were similarly mounted when they hung in the Belvedere in 1809, Buschbeck stated, but only *The Harvesters* still hangs in its original frame.

Burroughs also bought drawings—there being until 1960 no separate Drawings Department. Carrying on where Roger Fry left off, he acquired a number of Old Master drawings including two fine Leonardos, and in 1924 he bought a red-chalk study of the *Libyan Sibyl* by Michelangelo, one of the most important of all Michelangelo's drawings and at that time the only work by that master in America. The drawing was brought to Burroughs' attention by his friend John Singer Sargent. Sargent had received a letter from the widow of the Spanish collector Aureliano de Bereute saying that she wished to sell some works of art, including the *Libyan Sibyl*, and asking his help in finding an American buyer. Today, such electrifying information would bring curators, directors, and probably a clutch of trustees across any intervening ocean by the next jet plane. The art world was more leisurely in 1924, though, and Burroughs did not even get a letter off to the Señora for three months. In it, he said that he planned to visit Madrid that summer, and hoped to see the drawing then. He did so, and bought not only the Michelangelo *Sibyl* but also an El Greco portrait head, paying for both the sum of $35,374.24. Edward Robinson thought the price "absurdly high." Today, the drawing alone would bring well over a million dollars.

The bequest of Michael Friedsam in 1931, added to the legacies of Marquand, Altman, and Havemeyer, helped to round out the department's survey of European painting. Friedsam had been Benjamin Altman's closest business associate (he became president of the store when Altman died in 1913), and he believed, firmly but mistakenly, that his own collection of paintings and decorative arts was far superior to Altman's. He left it to the Metropolitan with strict instructions that it was to "be kept together and separate and apart by itself," just as Altman's had been, but a special committee of the trustees persuaded his executors to interpret the terms of the bequest so liberally that this restriction miraculously disappeared. In accepting the collection, the trustees referred to Friedsam's "well-known and practically expressed interest in education," which somehow made it possible for "the influence of the collection . . . [to] to be promoted in the widest degree without the hampering conditions usually associated with restricted gifts." Friedsam's Italian, Flemish, and German paintings, his prints, Chinese porcelains, tapestries, medieval and Renaissance sculptures, and other works of art were distributed throughout the museum, and although there is still one small gallery devoted exclusively to his pictures, no one would ever know it. Few episodes have demonstrated so clearly the value of having lawyers on the board.

Although the Metropolitan's painting collection was and still is weak in Italian painting of the early and high Renaissance, by 1931 it had grown very strong in the art of Flanders, the Netherlands, and Spain, and thanks to the Havemeyers it brought the visitor right up to the golden sunburst of French Impressionism. Bryson Burroughs greatly regretted the loss of an *Odalisque à l'Esclave* by Ingres, his favorite artist, which the trustees turned down because they thought it indecent—it is now in the Walters Art Gallery in Baltimore. When another Ingres *Odalisque* was coming up for sale in Paris, it was agreed that Mrs. George Blumenthal, who was living there at the time, would bid on it for the Metropolitan; she did not raise her voice, however, and the painting went to the Louvre. Burroughs ventured to ask Blumenthal if he knew of any reason why his wife had not bid as planned. "Mrs. Blumenthal don't need no reason," the president replied. Perhaps she thought it indecent. Not until four years after Burroughs' death did the museum finally get its Ingres *Odalisque en Grisaille,* a rather questionable picture whose loosely drawn left leg, ending in a foot with only four toes, leads some critics to wonder whether Ingres painted it.

In spite of occasional frustrations, though, Burroughs could look back on a career of remarkable achievements. In 1933, when the Metropolitan bought Hubert van Eyck's great *Crucifixion and Last Judgment* diptych, Burroughs told William Ivins that he felt he had accomplished what he had set out to do. He had wanted when he came to the Metropolitan in 1906 to secure some modern paintings not then in fashion, and also by some magic to procure examples of Old Masters whose work was so rare and so strongly held that even to think of acquisition had seemed fruitless. This he had done. The Metropolitan's collection of paintings, which in 1906 could scarcely compare with that of even a third-rate provincial museum in Europe, now held its own with all but the Louvre and one or two others. Burroughs died later that year. He had retained to the last the gaiety and warmth that his friend Ivins said was "inseparable from any true understanding of the world—which for him was a delightful place full of lovely things, flowers, babies, young boys and girls, and old ladies and gentlemen, filled with hope and dream, and perpetual interest and charm."

From its inception in 1912 the Arms and Armor Department had been a sort of museum-within-a-museum. It had its own armorer and its own repair shop in the basement. Bashford Dean, the curator from 1912 to 1927, was a wealthy man who dealt with trustees and benefactors on their own level. He made it a point each year to spend the equivalent of his annual salary in gifts to the department. If the trustees failed to approve funds for the objects he recommended, Dean would go out and raise the money from his collector friends—men like Clarence H. Mackay, George D. Pratt, and Henry Walters, who was forming a museum of his own in Baltimore but who could seldom refuse a request from Dean. One of Dean's favorite maneuvers, when an important collection of armor came on the market, was to borrow the funds to buy it himself, then put it up for auction and use the profits he could count on in advance to buy in the best pieces. Dean was named a Benefactor in 1924, his own gifts to the museum having by that time exceeded the value of $50,000. He was recognized as one of the world's leading authorities on arms and armor, and not even the Metropolitan's director was in a position to give him instructions. In 1926 his department undertook its own archaeological expedition, a search for armor from the Crusades under the ancient fortress of Montfort in Palestine; financed entirely by Mackay, Stephen H. P. Pell, Archer M. Huntington, and Dean himself, it was exhilarating but unproductive. Dean used to buy armor for several of the major collectors, as well as for the Metropolitan and for himself. He even bought some pieces for William Randolph Hearst, but the two men eventually had a falling out over an armor collection in Paris, which Hearst acquired after Dean thought he had bought it. As a result of that dispute, Hearst never gave anything to the Metropolitan, which had once entertained vague hopes for his gigantic and motley collections.

When the Riggs armor finally came to the Metropolitan in 1913, Dean needed an assistant to help catalogue and install it. A distant relative of Dean's, a high school teacher in Long Island City, suggested to her brightest pupil that he apply for the job. Stephen V. Grancsay came over one Saturday in 1914, was interviewed by Dean, and started work as soon as school was out. He stayed for forty-eight years, becoming curator when Dean was made a trustee in 1927. Grancsay took his cue from Dean. Although he had no fortune of his own, his expert knowledge of collections and collectors often enabled him to go outside regular museum channels to get what he wanted. In 1927 Dean sent him to Poland, to see if he could track down a very rare breastplate that went with a backplate that Dean had just discovered in London. Dean felt sure that the backplate had come originally from the Radziwill collection. Grancsay traveled to Warsaw and from there to Nieswicz, where Prince Radziwill had his ancestral estate eight miles from the Russian border. The prince refused at first to receive him. Patience and tact soon won out, however, aided by Grancsay's volunteering to clean and restore the Radziwill arms and armor collection which was rusting away under broken bottles and debris left by German and Russian troops during the First World War. He marshaled twenty youths from the town and worked for three weeks, at the end of which the prince was so delighted that he presented Grancsay with three cases of armor as recompense. The Metropolitan thus acquired several very rare chain mail face defenses and brayettes (a sort of medieval athletic supporter), an extraordinary horse frontal for what must have been a stupendously large horse, and a number of other treasures—but not the breastplate. Grancsay

found that on his way home, in the Musée de l'Armée in Paris, where it
had been ever since Napoleon confiscated it from the Radziwill estate more
than a century before.

Although the great era of the Arms and Armor Department was coming
to an end by this time, important pieces continued to be acquired throughout the Depression. Dean had hoped to establish his own armor collection,
for which he had built a Gothic hall adjoining his house in Riverdale, as a
branch of the Metropolitan. This proved impractical, but when Dean died
in 1928 his bequest of $205,000 to the museum, to which were added
money gifts from several of his friends, enabled the Metropolitan to acquire nearly all the most important works from his collection. His place on
the board of trustees was taken by Clarence H. Mackay, who had what
was then acknowledged to be the finest collection of armor in private
hands. Mackay's father had been a pick and shovel miner who struck it
rich in Nevada's Comstock Lode. Mackay had enlarged the fortune and become a controlling investor in various utilities and telegraph companies.
An ardent sportsman and music lover, he also collected Italian paintings
and sculpture, and was said to keep a daily tribute of one perfect flower in
front of his favorite Bronzino bust. When his assets were virtually wiped
out by the 1929 crash, Mackay was forced to sell a number of works of art.
The Metropolitan bought a Raphael predella panel (*The Agony in the
Garden*) and Mantegna's *Adoration of the Shepherds* from him in 1932,
and also the embossed and gilded armor of the Earl of Pembroke (which
Dean had tried to get for the museum in 1921), and the magnificent har-
ness of the Earl of Cumberland—the best-preserved Elizabethan armor in
existence, made for the most distinguished English knight of his time.

When Mackay died in 1938, Blumenthal asked Grancsay's advice as to
how the museum might help dispose of his remaining armor. Grancsay was
indignant. He knew the collection intimately, had bought many of the best
pieces himself, and felt very strongly, as he told Blumenthal, that the museum's duty was not to help *disperse* the collection but to buy it. His ora-
tion drew a reprimand. The trustees did not feel like spending any more
money just then, not even for Mackay's two magical Sassettas which eventually crossed the Atlantic once more and came to rest in the National Gallery in London. Grancsay mortgaged his own modest securities and bought
as much of the Mackay armor as he could afford, some of which he later

sold to the museum at cost. He still owns a good many other pieces, which the Metropolitan may get eventually. And then again, as retired but still very hale Stephen Grancsay sometimes intimates, it may not.

Prints did not gain entrance to the Metropolitan until nearly fifty years after it was founded. Cesnola saw no reason to collect them. The early trustees must have agreed with him, for they turned down the important print collection of their colleague Samuel P. Avery, who gave it to the New York Public Library instead. The Boston Museum of Fine Arts established its Print Department in 1887, but in New York, where a few wealthy bankers bought prints the way they bought first editions—as a pleasant lunchtime hobby—the notion that woodcuts, etchings, engravings, or lithographs could be considered in the same breath with the fine arts did not gain ground until much later. In 1916, the publisher Harris Brisbane Dick died and left his collection of prints to the museum, together with an estate worth approximately $1,000,000. A group of New York print collectors had for some time been urging the museum to start a Print Department; now the step could no longer be delayed. But who would organize and run it?

The trustees' first thought was to offer the job to Paul Joseph Sachs, the Harvard scholar who had played a leading part in the development of the Fogg Museum in Cambridge. Sachs declined, but recommended in his turn a man who he said would make an "ideal curator," a New York lawyer named William Mills Ivins, Jr. Although Ivins had no museum experience and no professional qualifications, de Forest and his fellow trustees thought highly enough of Sachs's judgment to take a chance. Ivins was appointed curator of the newly created Department of Prints in December 1916 at an annual salary of $5,000, and one of the notable museum careers in America was launched.

Ivins had found his true vocation early but had not acted on it. As a precocious Harvard student majoring in economics, he had discovered and been fascinated by Dürer's prints in the Fogg Museum. Later, at the University of Munich, he spent far less time on economics than he did studying German sixteenth century prints in the print room. A visit to Paris at this time was made memorable by his discovery in a Left Bank print shop of an album of Goya's *Disasters of War*, which he bought for sixty francs. He collected as assiduously as he could afford to from then on, but soon after returning from his European studies he decided to follow in his father's and brother's footsteps by taking a law degree at Columbia and entering the New York law firm of Cravath and Henderson, where he spent the next ten years preparing corporate mortgages. By 1916, he had come to the conclusion that he was "far more interested in prints than in the possession of them." The Metropolitan's offer meant a substantial drop in salary, but he accepted it without hesitation.

At his first meeting with the trustees, Ivins outlined the plan he would follow for the next thirty years. Although his principal efforts would go toward acquiring prints that were valuable as works of art, the print collection of a museum, he said, "cannot be formed solely upon Yes or No answers to the question: Is it a work of art? Rather it must be, like the library of a professor of literature, composed of a corpus of prints in themselves distinctly works of art, filled out and illustrated by many prints which have only a technical historical importance." Ivins understood more clearly than most of his contemporaries the tremendous impact that prints had had on the history of the world. His writings on this subject anticipate a great deal of what has been said more recently by Marshall McLuhan and other social theorists—the main difference being that Ivins always wrote clearly and intelligibly. Beginning with the invention of the woodcut in the fifteenth century, he maintained, the various techniques of making exactly repeatable pictorial statements had changed the way men looked at the world, and had been largely responsible, together with the companion invention of movable type, for the rapid diffusion of knowledge that made possible the growth of modern science and technology. Prints were far more important as visual documents than as works of art; nevertheless, many great artists had made prints, and Ivins would do his best to see that they were represented in the Metropolitan by the best possible impressions. He made an exception, however, in the case of the greatest printmaker of all—Rembrandt. A number of New York collectors owned Rembrandt etchings and engravings; Ivins counted on these coming eventually to the museum, as indeed they did, from George Coe Graves, Mrs. H. O. Havemeyer, Felix M. Warburg and several others.

Ivins knew all the New York print collectors personally, and from the beginning of his work at the museum he could count on outside help when he needed it from men like Felix Warburg and Mortimer L. Schiff. His great problem at first was the lack of ready cash; relatively inexpensive prints appearing on the market would be snapped up by others before he could get his purchase recommendation approved by the trustees. Ivins found a novel solution. He purchased a number of first-rate prints himself, and put them, anonymously, in a loan exhibition at the Metropolitan. Just before the show opened he took his most obstructive trustee around it. The trustee noted print after print that had been loaned anonymously, and asked who the lender was. Ivins told him. "Why didn't you buy these for the museum?" the trustee demanded. Ivins explained that without ready funds this was impossible. The result was that the Print Department soon afterward received an annual curatorial budget for the purchase of items costing less than $1,000—and for which no authorization from the trustees was required. Most of the other departments received similar funds. The system was abolished by Blumenthal during the thirties, much to Ivins' annoyance, but it has since been reinstated.

Ivins built the Print Department just as he had said he would, learning very rapidly what he had to learn and forgetting nothing. His knowledge was virtually encyclopedic, his eye unerring, his scholarship the most acute of any Metropolitan curator before or since. It is largely to his credit that today the Metropolitan's print collection, though it cannot compare in size with those of London, Paris, and Vienna and may perhaps be smaller than that of the Museum of Fine Arts in Boston, is without question the most comprehensive collection to be found in this hemisphere. It includes fine examples of nearly every kind of printed picture, from Dürer engravings to trade cards, and it is used constantly by every department of the museum as well as by outside students, writers, designers, and countless others. Having amply justified the trustees' risk in hiring him, Ivins went on to become one of the most respected men in the entire museum profession. Unfortunately, he was also the most difficult and abrasive character who ever worked at the museum.

A tall, long-faced man with a beaked nose and a penetrating stare, he was known behind his back as "Poison Ivins," or sometimes "Ivins the Terrible." His tongue was so sharp, his intellect so quick, and his legal training so thorough that he won every argument and left his victims fuming with helpless resentment. In the director's lunchroom, a restaurant in the basement to which the male curators were invited each day for lunch (female curators were not admitted for years; they had their own cafeteria), Ivins made every conversation an intellectual battle of wits. A large Webster's dictionary on a stand was kept near the head of the long table, to be consulted during the semantic disputes that regularly arose. Time after time Ivins would go to the dictionary, read out in a rasping voice the definition that proved his point, and return to the table where he had just made a new enemy. Ivins had a cruel streak that led him to probe for people's weak points and watch them squirm. He also had an abstract passion for the truth, which made him magisterially contemptuous of what he considered the glib nonsense talked about art and the circular reasoning indulged in by some of his colleagues.

Ivins' favorite target was Gisela Richter, the curator of Greek and Roman Art. They took an instant dislike to one another, which never abated during their more than twenty years of joint service to the museum. Some people felt that the frequent attacks on Greek art that ran through Ivins' published writings were really veiled attacks on Miss Richter, whose own books on Greek sculpture were and still are considered definitive in the field. Ivins found Greek art static. He disliked its "abstract lack of personality, the composite group-photograph quality" of the celebrated marbles. "Lovely as the Venus of Melos may be," he wrote, "she is the final epitome of all the dumbness of all the Dumb Doras—utterly devoid of thought, emotion, and expression." He also thought it surprising that classical scholars could speak with such assurance of original statues that were known only by Roman copies of uncertain provenance, or write so vibrantly of the glories of Greek painting, "when no Greek painting of any importance has survived (leaving out vase painting)." To one acquainted at first hand, as Ivins was, with the difficulties of dating and attribution that arose in the study of even such fully documented artists as Rembrandt and Daumier, the certainty with which Miss Richter and her fellow scholars dated and attributed ancient statuary seemed "little less than astounding." Classical art, he concluded, was "a field of learning in which circularity of reasoning, explicit as well as implicit, is recognized as a legitimate procedure." Miss Richter had no gift for counterinvective; she did her best to ignore Ivins' barbs, but they hurt and shocked her nonetheless.

Kent was another Ivins *bête noir*. At first the two men got along rather well, having a common interest in printing and printed books, but the relationship soon soured. Ivins took to saying that all Kent really cared about in a book was that it be a clean copy with nice margins. They used to quarrel so bitterly in the museum that those within earshot would be sure that one or the other would have to resign, but the next morning they would both be back to pick up the argument where they had left it the day before. Ivins thought Kent a frightful snob. He ridiculed Kent's ultra-British manner of speaking, and his custom of taking younger members of the curatorial staff to the opera. He had great sport with a letter of introduction that Kent had written for one of the young ladies on his staff, who was going abroad to study museum methods in Europe. "Miss Scherer," Kent had written, "will visit London, Vienna, and Berlin as well [as Paris], and . . . will occupy herself with the process of reproduction in those cities." Kent and Ivins had a brief rapprochement in the late thirties, which ended one day when they were returning together from lunch. Emerging first from the taxi with an armload of books and papers, Ivins stumbled and fell to the curb in front of the museum, breaking his eyeglasses and bruising himself severely in a number of places. According to the assistant secretary of the museum at that time, Ivins later claimed that Kent had *pushed* him. They barely spoke to each other after that.

In the end, Ivins' sharp tongue cost him the directorship. He had served as assistant director of the museum since 1933, and when Herbert Winlock suffered a stroke in 1937, while descending the stairs of the museum, Ivins took over as acting director. Winlock retired in 1939, too ill to continue as head of the museum. Ivins had every reason to expect that he would be named director, but by this time the trustees had decided that he had neither the administrative ability nor the tact necessary for the job—several key members of the staff, in fact, had indicated that they would resign rather than serve under Ivins. It was the story of Breck all over again, except that in Ivins' case the fall was from a greater height, and the tragic flaw more clearly self-imposed.

In some ways Ivins might have made a superb director. He saw the museum as a whole, and he brimmed with ideas for shaking the place up and bringing it to life. Ivins' penchant for overturning applecarts was in fact the real reason for his continuing quarrel with Henry Kent, who lived for the applecart. Although he wrote with a quill pen that he kept in a glass of shot and sharpened with a penknife, Ivins' ideas seem as fresh and stimulating today as they did twenty years ago, and most of his books are still in print. It was Ivins who suggested the idea for the hugely successful "Life in America" exhibition in 1939—the first time that genre paintings had been used in this way to provide a visual historical narrative. Appointed counselor to the board of trustees in 1940, in addition to his other duties, Ivins argued strongly against further expansion of the museum—the space problems could all be solved, he said, by getting rid of duplicates and the surplus accumulation of many years, and by putting all but the most important works of art into study-storage. Ivins also spoke out for contemporary art, saying that the museum should buy and exhibit it "whether or not it is liked by the trustees and officials, and whether or not they believed it will continue to be of interest in the future."

Behind Ivins' intellectual brilliance was a curious and touching modesty in the face of works of art. "The trouble with art in this country is that people don't look at it," he once told a lecture audience—"they go to a shop and buy a book and read about it. . . . Art needs no explanation—it only needs looking at." In his *Bulletin* articles he kept his own incisive comments to the minimum and devoted most of the space to reproducing prints, preferring as he said to "let the artists speak for themselves." Ivins had a marvelous gift for bringing any subject into clear focus and making the reader see it with fresh eyes. He never did learn tact or patience, though, and the major curatorial rewards escaped him.

His last years were very sad. He retired to Woodbury, Connecticut, in 1945, where two years later his wife died and left him bitterly alone. He had quarreled with most of his friends. The books he was finally free to write did not get written; his visits to the Metropolitan were few and brief. Something of what he felt can be deduced from an address he made in 1944 to the Association of Art Museum Directors in Chicago. Ivins had not been invited to attend the meeting, an oversight that he took as a personal affront (he had attended several previous sessions when he was assistant or acting director of the Metropolitan). In an effort to remedy the situation, the sponsors had asked him to deliver the principal address. He refused at first, but later changed his mind. His subject was the importance of an art museum library; his main theme, however, was the failure of the museum movement in America.

"To a great extent," Ivins told the assembled museum directors, "our museums have been dominated by men who have been so busy with their wangling and their pedantry that they have had no time to waste on basic ideas." He described most museum staffs as "a frighteningly woolly-minded and illiterate group," whose poverty of mind showed most unmistakably in their catalogues and explanatory labels. "What conceivable bearing on art and culture have the facts that an object once belonged to the Duke of Dufflebury, that it was shown at the Sanitary Fair, that it was in such and such auctions, and that Doctors Kleinwitz and Rondedecuir disagree as to the year in which it was made?" Ivins scornfully inquired. "Such stuff as this is neither scholarship nor learning, it is mere bookkeeping, and it is awfully dull and stupid and entirely aside from all cultural issues . . . the public yawns at us and goes to a movie or a baseball game. And the public is right." The only facts of any importance that the public should know about a work of art, Ivins said, were those describing the intellectual and imaginative background that had produced it—and this sort of information the museums made no attempt to provide.

"If I have seemed to speak bitterly," Ivins concluded, "it is because of the sickening realization of my own failure in that critical and never ending search for understanding which is the only excuse for a job in a museum."

NINETEEN

Germain Bazin, the director of the Louvre, has described The Cloisters as "the crowning achievement of American museology." Curators here and abroad often speak of the Metropolitan's medieval branch in Fort Tryon Park as the most perfect museum of the twentieth century, the ideal environment for great works of art. The creation of this paragon among museums is also, perhaps, the supreme example of curatorial genius working in exquisite harmony with vast wealth.

The story begins not with the curator, though, but with George Grey Barnard, an American sculptor of great energy and some talent. The son of a Presbyterian minister, Barnard spent a good part of his Iowa childhood stuffing birds and small animals, a hobby that led to his first job as a taxidermist for the Iowa Academy of Sciences. In 1882 he enrolled in the Art Institute of Chicago, determined to become a sculptor. The following year, having sold a portrait bust for three hundred dollars, he gathered up his modest savings and went to Paris, where he entered the Académie des Beaux Arts and lived for the next ten years on the edge of poverty, subsisting mostly on rice and spending whatever money he could scrape up for marble and other materials. Like his near-contemporary Rodin, Barnard rejected the smooth and lifeless ideals of the French academic sculptors of that day. His professional debut at the 1894 Salon du Champ de Mars, where he showed eight sculptures, caused something of a sensation. The largest work, an eight-foot marble group that he later called *Struggle of the Two Natures in Man*—its two naturalistically modeled nude figures symbolized spiritual man breaking free of his earthly nature—was bought by Alfred Corning Clark, the founder of the Singer Sewing Machine Company. Clark presented it to the Metropolitan, where it stood for many years at the foot of the grand staircase. It is now in storage.

His reputation established, Barnard returned to New York and taught for several years at the Art Students' League. A few sculpture commissions came his way, but, like Bryson Burroughs, he found it very difficult to support a wife and child on his earnings as an artist, and he was seriously considering giving it all up when his friend William Clifford, the librarian at the Metropolitan, persuaded him to apply for the important commission then being tendered for sculptural decoration of the new Pennsylvania State Capitol in Harrisburg. Barnard got the commission. He signed a contract to deliver two complex sculptural groups comprising thirty-three heroic-sized figures—it was the largest single order ever given to an American sculptor up to that time—and took his wife and daughter back to France. They settled in the village of Moret-sur-Loing, near Fontainebleau, where Barnard threw himself enthusiastically into the project.

It soon became evident that he had seriously underestimated his costs. Barnard's fee for the Harrisburg commission barely covered the price of the marble needed to fulfill it, and because he preferred to do all his own stonecutting rather than entrust any of it to assistants, the time needed to finish the work was much greater than he had anticipated. When his contract money ran out in 1906, the work was still less than half done. A new contract was negotiated, but just at this critical juncture the exposure of graft and corruption in the planning of the Pennsylvania State Capitol threw his sponsors into confusion, and all state funds were cut off.

Dire necessity disclosed that George Grey Barnard, like his large sculpture in the Metropolitan, had more than one side to his nature. For several months previous he had managed to supplement his fast-shrinking capital by buying and selling what he called "antiques"—fragments of medieval stonework that he picked up from local farmers, whose forebears had been in the habit for centuries of patching and repairing their houses, barns, and hencoops with stonework from ruined churches. Barnard paid the local citizenry one franc for a stone figure with pointed (Gothic) toes, and half a franc if the toes were blunt, indicating a later period. He was able to sell these finds to dealers in Paris at a gratifying profit. The money thus earned "comes 1000 times easier than by my own sculpture," he wrote his parents, and by the time his contract funds dried up he had decided that it might be possible to finance the completion of the Harrisburg commission by this means. He began traveling extensively, combing Dijon and the Vosges region and eventually working his way south into Languedoc and the eastern Pyrenees, regions rich in medieval remains. In the fall of 1906 he suspended work on his own sculpture entirely, and devoted the next half year to what he called "peddling antiques."

A great storyteller for whom modesty was no impediment, Barnard loved to describe his treasure hunting in adventurous detail. He claimed that he had found his limestone relief of the *Miracle of Saint Hubert and the Stag* embedded in the enclosure of a pigpen, and that the magnificent thirteenth century tomb figure of Jean d'Alluye was being used, face downward, as a bridge over a stream. He pictured himself a roving and romantic figure, bicycling across French fields and spotting Gothic masterworks in the mire. The truth was that he bought much of his material from dealers and sold it to other dealers, showing in the process such an old-fashioned Yankee horse-trader's talent that he invariably came out on top. Barnard, a short, rugged man who liked to think he resembled Lincoln, was more than a match for the wiliest Paris dealers. He also had a trained sculptor's eye for superior stone carving, and a ripening passion for Gothic and Romanesque art that helped him track down the finest examples.

Toward the end of 1906, Barnard conceived the more ambitious scheme of buying architectural elements from medieval cloisters. The great monastic orders had established abbeys all over Europe during the Middle Ages —the Benedictine order alone, at the height of its power and influence in the twelfth century, controlled more than three hundred monasteries in France, Italy, Germany, and Spain. Gradually deserted as monasticism declined, pillaged and burned during centuries of war and revolution, dismembered by generations of farmers, some of the ruined monasteries still preserved relatively intact their central cloister, the open court with a covered and arcaded passageway along the sides, where most of the monks' activities other than worship had taken place. It was here that medieval architecture, which found its highest expression in the cathedrals, showed its more intimate and personal aspect. In a few intensive weeks of "hunting cloisters" in southern France, Barnard managed to acquire sizable portions of four Romanesque and Gothic monasteries—Saint-Michel-de-Cuxa, Saint-Guilhem-le-Desert, Bonnefont-en-Comminges, and Trie. Saint-Michel-de-Cuxa had been for several centuries the most important Benedictine abbey of the entire region. Founded in 878 and finally deserted toward the end of the eighteenth century, its reddish-grey stones were spread all over the neighborhood when Barnard arrived. Ten of Cuxa's graceful Romanesque arches had been used to embellish a public bathhouse in the village of Prades, and it was the fashion for the local citizens to have at least one column from the abbey in their garden. Although he failed to get the bathhouse arches, Barnard managed to acquire some forty-eight columns and fifty-six arches from the Cuxa cloister, together with the carved architectural base on which the columns had rested. No private buyer or dealer was likely to take such a volume of stonework off his hands; Barnard, however, was counting on the Metropolitan Museum.

Roger Fry, who was at that time the Metropolitan's European buying agent, had seen fragments from the Cuxa cloister and indicated serious interest. In a letter to Sir Caspar Purdon Clarke, Barnard said that the reassembled cloister would be "a poem to Americans who never can or will see Europe." Both Clarke and Fry were to arrive soon to inspect the prize. Barnard's hopes soared for a sale that would solve at one blow all his financial problems—he was asking $100,000 for the cloister. Somewhere along the line, however, J. P. Morgan and his confrères must have decided that cloisters did not fit into their current plans. Clarke and Fry never arrived. Although he eventually lowered his price for the Cuxa material to $50,000, Barnard could find no buyers for that or any other cloister. Bitterly blaming Fry, he stored the massive accumulation of architectural elements in his Moret studio and went back to "peddling stones from house to house in Paris."

That fall a group of New York businessmen took over Barnard's tangled financial affairs. They secured additional financing for the Harrisburg commission, and put Barnard on a personal allowance to cover expenses. He was thus able to resume work on the project, which he finished in 1910 and exhibited at the Paris Salon to great acclaim. Several important commissions followed, including the monumental statue of Lincoln in Cincinnati that is considered his finest work. Barnard could not stop buying medieval stonework, however, and in 1911 he began to talk of establishing a public museum in New York, a museum where young American artists could learn from the master stone carvers of the Middle Ages how to use a chisel, and where the "spirit of Gothic" could once more cast its spell. His fortunes had improved sufficiently for him to consider financing such an ambitious project himself. As it turned out, though, a somewhat belated outbreak of French national pride nearly undid all his labors.

Barnard had reopened negotiations in 1913 with the owner of the Prades bathhouse, Mme. Baladud de Saint-Jean, for the twelve arches from Cuxa. The lady agreed this time to sell them, and the stones were in the process of being numbered and crated when an official of the French Administration of Fine Arts appeared on the scene with an order forbidding their sale. Barnard found himself in the middle of an international *cause célèbre*, and the target of violent attacks in the French press. He stood his ground for three weeks, but then, realizing that in France as in America one cannot fight *L'Hôtel de Ville,* he announced grandly that he was making a gift of the disputed Cuxa material to the people of France. While the papers that had vilified him were busy praising his noble gesture, Barnard made haste to ship all the rest of his cloisters material out of the country. The Prades incident had stirred up a number of administrative beehives in Paris, and the French Senate was moving to tighten up the old laws governing the classification and preservation of *"monuments historiques."* On the last day of 1913 the Senate passed a new, much more stringent law, which would have prevented Barnard from shipping out another stone. He had managed to anticipate it by two days. His entire collection was safely in or en route to its new destination, an unfinished brick building that Barnard was putting up next to his studio on Fort Washington Avenue, in one of the less Gothic sections of Washington Heights.

Barnard's "cloister museum" opened to the public just before Christmas the following year. A relatively simple structure laid out in the form of a church, it contained elements from the four cloisters and a great many individual works of medieval sculpture presented in ways that Barnard felt appropriate to the "spirit of Gothic." It was well publicized—Barnard saw to that—and the reactions to it were generally enthusiastic. Henry W. Kent, having become a great proponent of period room installations for American decorative arts, thoroughly approved of Barnard's period museum and recommended many of Barnard's display techniques to the designers of the new Cleveland Museum for which he had been asked to be a consultant. Arthur Kingsley Porter, whose novels had helped to stir interest in the Middle Ages, told Barnard that he found it "the most beautiful museum I have ever seen." Another visitor who came away favorably impressed was John D. Rockefeller, Jr. The straitlaced only son of the world's richest man was introduced to Barnard by Welles Bosworth, the architect of the three-thousand-acre Rockefeller country estate in Pocantico Hills, New York. From Barnard's point of view the meeting could hardly have been more propitious: Rockefeller purchased Barnard's own sculpture of *Adam and Eve* for Pocantico Hills, and also some one hundred objects of medieval art from the Barnard collection. The meeting was to be even more propitious for the Metropolitan Museum of Art.

"I can think of nothing so unpleasant," John D. Rockefeller, Jr., once said, "as a life devoted to pleasure." Few rich men have ever felt so keenly the burdens of great wealth, or worked so hard to discharge its responsibilities. Frederick T. Gates, his father's senior partner in the Standard Oil colossus, had been the first to realize the implications of the enormous fortune that he saw rolling up "like an avalanche." Gates had warned the old man that he must distribute it faster than it grew, adding, "If you do not it will crush you and your children and your children's children." The junior Rockefeller, whose strict Baptist upbringing left him with little inclination for pleasure in any case, devoted his entire adult life to the unending struggle to distribute the avalanche.

As a boy, Rockefeller was religious, obedient, conscientious, and painfully shy. He chose Brown over Yale because he thought he might have a better chance to conquer his social problem at the smaller college, and in fact he made great progress in that direction, becoming president of his class and manager of the football team and even developing a modest aptitude for ballroom dancing—a skill that necessitated his first and only rebellion against his mother's Baptist scruples. In later life he managed to go on calling a few of his college friends by their first names, but he could never do so with anyone else. ("I don't see how you do it," he once confessed to MacKenzie King and Raymond Fosdick, his biographer, at his summer home in Seal Harbor; "I wish I could, but I just wasn't built that way.") One of the upperclassmen at Brown urged him to try being "a shade more reckless, or careless as to whether or not you reach perfection within five years, and see if you don't find more happiness." But happiness was not one of Rockefeller's primary goals. He wanted to do right in the eyes of his God, his father, and his own conscience, three taskmasters that for him were probably indistinguishable.

These days the puritan conscience is in disfavor. It served and guided the younger Rockefeller through a remarkably productive life, nevertheless, and it did not prevent him from growing and changing with the times. Starting out with the inherited views of an economic royalist, he came around to a firm belief in the rights of organized labor. He progressed from narrow Baptist sectarianism to leadership of the movement for a united church. A lifelong teetotaler, he was at first a strong supporter of Prohibition; when he became convinced that the experiment was a failure and that its evils far outweighed its benefits, he published an open letter whose calm and cogent arguments gave considerable impetus to the movement for Repeal. Rockefeller never gave money to any enterprise unless he believed that it would somehow serve the public good. Wealth to him was a sacred trust; his own life a form of stewardship. In his younger years he seemed perennially anxious and troubled, weighed down by the millions that threatened always to crush him. As he grew older he relaxed a little, and sometimes even gave indications that he enjoyed his life. He was a gentle, kind, and thoughtful man, with an iron streak down the middle.

The bright spot in Rockefeller's life was his marriage. Abby Aldrich Rockefeller, the daughter of Senator Nelson Aldrich of Rhode Island, was an effervescent and lively girl with a taste for art. When they moved soon after their marriage in 1901 into their new house on West Fifty-fourth Street, Abby improved the walls with Italian primitives from Duveen's. From Duccio and Piero della Francesca she went on to Goya and Chardin, and then eventually into modern art, becoming, with Lillie P. Bliss and Mrs. Cornelius J. Sullivan, one of the founders of the Museum of Modern Art in 1929. Although her husband would eventually give $5,000,000 to Abby's Modern Museum, plus the land on which it was built, he never really cared for pictures and modern art frankly embarrassed him. He found in modern paintings nothing more than "a desire for self-expression, as if the artist were saying, 'I'm free, bound by no form, and art is what flows out of me.'"

Like many an American millionaire, though, Rockefeller's indulgence of his wife's artistic tastes led to the development of his own. What he responded to in art was craftsmanship, painstaking attention to detail, and perfection of form—all of which he found in the Chinese porcelains that he began to collect in 1913. Porcelains had the formal purity, the cool impersonal perfection that he never found in paintings, and he soon became uncharacteristically passionate about owning them. When Duveen offered him first choice of the J. P. Morgan porcelains in 1915, Rockefeller picked out a million dollars' worth, and then had to go to his father for financial help. His letter justifying the purchase is revealing and touching:

> . . . I have never squandered money on horses, yachts, automobiles or other foolish extravagances. A fondness for these porcelains is my only hobby—the only thing on which I have cared to spend money. I have found their study a great recreation and diversion, and I have become very fond of them. This hobby, while a costly one, is quiet and unostentatious and not sensational. . . . Is it unwise for me to gratify a desire for beautiful things, which will be a constant joy to my friends and to my children as they grow to appreciate them, as well as to myself, when it is done in so quiet and unostentatious a manner?

Evidently he convinced his father, who gave him the money.

Duveen, always a subtle student of character among the rich, also managed to interest Rockefeller in Persian carpets of the Polonaise variety—woven with gold and silver threads for the royal families of Poland. Carpets led on to tapestries. Rockefeller bought from Duveen a set of ten eighteenth century tapestries from the Gobelins workshop, the so-called *Months of Lucas* series made originally for the son of Louis XIV and Madame de Montespan. Not long afterward, he learned from Welles Bosworth that a French dealer was in New York with a truly extraordinary tapestry series called *The Hunt of the Unicorn*. The most magnificent Gothic tapestries in existence, they were also among the best preserved—in spite of having been used for a period during the French Revolution to keep potatoes from freezing in a damp cellar. Since the early years of the nineteenth century they had hung in the château of the de la Rochefoucauld family at Vertéuil. In 1920, the story went, Count Gabriel de la Rochefoucauld decided that he wanted to install a golf course. He was told that it would cost him a million dollars. The Count got his golf course, and Rockefeller got the Unicorn Tapestries.

The Metropolitan could scarcely fail to notice such a collector. Rockefeller, who in 1919 had bought from the New York dealer Kelekian a huge Assyrian winged bull and a winged lion from the palace of Ashur-nasirapal II and presented them, together with two ancient Near Eastern relief sculptures, to the Metropolitan, was elected to the board of trustees in the spring of 1921. He declined the election, explaining that it was against his policy to serve on any directorates other than his own philanthropic ones. Ever since his first visit to George Grey Barnard's cloister museum, though, Rockefeller's interest in medieval art and architecture had been growing stronger. The art of the Middle Ages appealed to him for many reasons. Like his Chinese porcelains, it was marked by superb craftsmanship. It was basically anonymous, expressing not the individual artisan but the spirit of the age. And the profoundly religious spirit of Gothic and Romanesque sculpture went straight to Rockefeller's Baptist soul. When Barnard offered in 1925 to sell his cloister museum to the Metropolitan for $700,000, Rockefeller, who just the year before had made a substantial contribution to the Metropolitan's endowment for general operations, saw in this a new opportunity to advance the public good. He quietly turned over to the museum shares of stock worth slightly more than a million dollars, and the following spring Barnard's museum, its exhibits rearranged and enlarged by some forty works of art from Rockefeller's own collection, reopened as a branch of the Metropolitan.

Rockefeller had always found George Grey Barnard a trifle overwhelming. The sculptor's personality was anything but quiet and unostentatious, and Rockefeller never quite knew what to say when Barnard started to talk about his triumphs, or to relate how Auguste Rodin, on first seeing the *Struggle of the Two Natures in Man,* had wept openly because he realized (according to Barnard) that he would never create anything so fine. Rockefeller declined to buy any of the medieval material that Barnard subsequently gathered together as a means of financing his *Rainbow Arch,* a gigantic new sculptural project; Barnard sold much of this second collection to the Philadelphia Museum, but did not live to carry out the *Rainbow Arch.* With Barnard more or less out of the picture in 1926, though, Rockefeller began to take an active part in planning for the future of his gift.

By 1927, Rockefeller and the Metropolitan had come to feel that the Fort Washington Avenue site was inadequate. The neighborhood was changing, with new apartment buildings crowding in on all sides. It so happened that Rockefeller himself owned fifty-six acres of wooded land not far to the north, overlooking the Hudson. He had bought it in 1916 and offered it to New York City as a public park; the city had refused the gift because of the landscaping expenses involved. Now Rockefeller renewed his offer, saying he would pay for the landscaping himself, but requesting that four acres at the north end of the tract be set aside for a new museum building of medieval art. In 1930, Mayor James J. Walker's administration accepted the gift of what is now Fort Tryon Park, and The Cloisters found its future home.

Charles Collens, the architect who designed the Riverside Church in New York, had been working for some time on a clay model of the proposed new medieval museum. The concept had already gone through several metamorphoses. Rockefeller originally wanted it to be modeled after Kenilworth Castle in England—he loved English history, and had often visited the famous old ruin celebrated by Sir Walter Scott. Collens' early sketches carried a strong suggestion of battlements and keeps, but in time Rockefeller had decided that such a setting would not be appropriate for works of art that were for the most part religiously inspired. After a trip to Spain and southern France, where he studied the old churches and monasteries in the region of Saint-Michel-de-Cuxa, Collens set to work on a model that incorporated the general shape and structure of a medieval monastery without attempting to imitate any one building in particular.

He consulted regularly with Rockefeller and with Joseph Breck, the Metropolitan's assistant director and curator of Decorative Arts, who had a great deal to do with the early designing and planning. Rockefeller did not care overly for Breck. He was becoming more and more favorably impressed, however, with Breck's young associate curator, a recent Harvard graduate named James J. Rorimer. Rorimer, for his part, took in a great deal more than the plans and sketches for The Cloisters. Following the latest curatorial methods, he was making a careful and detailed study of John D. Rockefeller, Jr., learning how his mind worked and how best to influence its thinking.

Rorimer belonged to a new generation of curators—the generation trained by Paul Joseph Sachs. As art museums proliferated throughout the country, the lack of qualified curatorial talent had become increasingly acute. Princeton and a few other universities had departments of fine arts, but their graduates tended to become art historians or teachers rather than curators. Starting in 1923, though, Harvard instituted a graduate course designed specifically to train future museum curators. The students met once a week in Paul Sachs's book-lined living room at Shady Hill (the former home of Harvard's first professor of art history, Charles Eliot Norton), where they absorbed the most intimate secrets of the professional art world. Sachs was a remarkable teacher. A small, rotund, exquisitely groomed connoisseur who had quit banking as soon as he made enough money to indulge his passion for art, he talked very little about art history and a great deal about dealers, collectors, trustees, and how to get along with them. He took his students on occasional trips to New York and other cities, where they met dealers and saw private collections. He gave them all sorts of practical advice—"You'll be on your feet a lot, so get in the habit of moving from one foot to the other," he would say, demonstrating elegantly—and he always managed to talk about a painting as though it were the most exalted manifestation of the human spirit. "What he really did was teach you how to make the right sort of noises in front of pictures," one of his former students said. Sachs communicated more than his own enthusiasm, though, and his students—men like Alfred H. Barr, Jr., Philip Johnson, Preston Remington, and James Rorimer—went out to staff and eventually, in many cases, to direct the country's leading museums.

Rorimer had come directly to the Metropolitan from Harvard in 1927, at the age of twenty-two, beginning as an assistant in the Decorative Arts Department. He brought with him an extensive body of practical knowledge that he had acquired long before he ever left home to enter Harvard. His father, Louis Rorimer, was Cleveland's leading interior designer. The firm of Rorimer and Brooks Studios employed a large staff of trained craftsmen who could make just about anything a client required—replicas of sixteenth century tapestries, fancy woodwork of all kinds, marble sculpture, as well as the more sedate interiors of all the Statler hotels then sprouting up around the country—and Louis Rorimer saw to it that his son grew up knowing how to bevel an edge and dress marble and match colors. James and his younger sister also accompanied their parents on frequent trips to

Europe, where their father would point out in fascinating detail the aesthetic and architectural marvels of earlier centuries, and train the children's eyes to see what most tourists would miss. Somewhat later, as a student at Harvard, Rorimer would travel through Spain with Walter Cooke, a wealthy collector and founder of the Fine Art Institute at New York University; Cooke was a great authority on Spanish art and architecture, and from him Rorimer acquired a knowledge and a love of the Romanesque style that was to be of great use to him later on. The truth of the matter was that neither Collens nor Breck had as sure a grasp of the historical and architectural requirements of Romanesque and Gothic architecture as Rorimer did.

Rockefeller noted this fact, and in the spring of 1929, when both Robinson, the director, and Breck, the assistant director, were away on vacation, he suggested to Rorimer that he go up to the future parkland and see if he couldn't string some lines that would show just where the various walls, ramparts, and approaches would fit into the four-acre site of The Cloisters. Rorimer did considerably better than that. With the help of Rockefeller's caretaker, who happened to be a brother of the movie actor Leo Carillo and who knew how they did things in Hollywood, he made a detailed, full-scale mock-up of the proposed building in wood and burlap, to the height of the first floor. Both Rorimer and Carillo prayed that it wouldn't rain before Rockefeller came up to see their handiwork. It didn't, and Rockefeller was elated. "Isn't it wonderful to have money enough to project a scheme in such a grandiose way?" he said, standing happily on a wooden rampart. The whole job had cost twelve hundred dollars—a good bit more than the string layout that Rockefeller had had in mind, and therefore something of a risk. Rorimer understood Rockefeller's eagerness to see something *built*, though, after months of working with sketches and clay models; he knew when to take risks, but he also knew just how far he could go.

The stock market crash that September threw a pall of uncertainty over The Cloisters project. Rockefeller did not lose interest in it, and he was gratified the next year when the city decided to accept his offer of land. No one had any idea how much money he was prepared to spend on the project, though, and there were indications that he sometimes had doubts about the necessity for financing a medieval museum in a period of severe economic and social distress. Breck complicated matters further by making frequent changes and additions to the plans. This situation came to a boil in the spring of 1933. "Since Mr. Breck apparently regards the plans as still merely in process of development," Rockefeller wrote to Collens' partner, "would it not be wise and in the interest of economy to discontinue any further work on the final working drawings and full size details until Mr. Breck advises me that he has completed his study and is through making changes?" Breck dutifully signed a resolution drawn up by the trustees stating that no further changes would be made in the plans, and went off to Europe, leaving everything in Rorimer's hands until he returned. He died a month later, while walking in Switzerland. His vast Decorative Arts empire was broken up into a Department of Medieval Art, the curiously titled Department of Renaissance and Modern Art, and the American Wing. The man named as curator of the new Medieval Department, which included The Cloisters, was twenty-nine-year-old James Rorimer.

Now began the most delicate and subtle phase of the whole affair. Rorimer had studied his man thoroughly. He knew that Rockefeller wanted to be personally involved with every detail of the planning and construction. He knew that there were to be no more changes in the plans. And yet Rorimer was deeply dissatisfied with certain aspects of the designs worked out by Collens and Breck. He proceeded, therefore, to work from *within* the proposed building.

George Blumenthal, whose wife had just died, was preparing to sell his house in Paris. Rorimer persuaded him to dismantle the music room so that four fifteenth century windows and a twelfth century doorway could go to The Cloisters (Blumenthal agreed on condition that the transportation costs come out of The Cloisters' budget), along with several other medieval works of art; the gift effectively got rid of four Collens windows and a Collens doorway that Rorimer disliked. Little by little Rorimer managed to acquire other architectural bits and pieces—old window frames, columns, even a complete refectory room—out of the modest purchase fund that Rockefeller had set up. He took great pains to keep Rockefeller informed of every development. Gradually, without ever suggesting a change in the plans, he managed to transform the museum in accordance with his own vision of what it should look like.

This vision was taking concrete form meanwhile in the basement of the

Metropolitan, where a group of W.P.A. craftsmen had been put to work by Rorimer on an elaborate wooden scale model of The Cloisters. No detail was overlooked in this model. Each doorway, window, and column was exactly where it would be in the museum. Tiny pedestals supported minuscule plaster replicas of the sculptures that would be there, each one lit by concealed illumination. Collens was eager for Rockefeller to see the model, but Rorimer insisted that they wait until it was perfected. At last the job was done to his satisfaction. Rorimer arranged for Rockefeller and Collens to come in the next morning at nine o'clock, before the museum opened. No one else was present in the basement room that morning when Rockefeller first saw the model. He walked around it slowly, leaned down to peer through a Romanesque portal towards a perfect replica of the Moutiers-Saint-Jean doorway that he had given to the museum, and drew in his breath. "Mr. Rorimer," he said, in obvious amazement, "is this the way The Cloisters are going to look?" Rorimer's reply is legendary. "No, Mr. Rockefeller," he said quietly. "This is the way they could look if you wished them to."

Not long after this artful performance, Rockefeller set aside securities worth $2,500,000 to pay the entire cost of constructing and maintaining the new Cloisters, and all uncertainty about the project vanished. Nor did his gifts stop there by any means. The great Catalan tombs of the Counts of Urgel, the Spanish frescoes from the monastery of San Pedro de Arlanza, the Pontaut Chapter House, the famous Chalice of Antioch, the thirteenth century Virgin from the choir screen of Strasbourg Cathedral, the glorious Mérode altarpiece—these and approximately ninety percent of all the other works of art now on display at The Cloisters came either as outright gifts or through purchase funds that he supplied. Rockefeller made it absolutely clear, moreover, that the museum was free at any time to sell or trade any objects he had given it if by doing so the quality or the balance of the collection could be improved. Furthermore, as Rockefeller wrote to him in 1936, Rorimer was never to "feel under the slightest embarrassment in giving me your frank opinion of any object belonging to me which I may submit for the consideration of the museum as a possible gift to it."

Rorimer took him at his word. Only once did he come close to overstepping the bounds of propriety. Studying The Cloisters' plans one day, Rockefeller noticed that one of the rooms had been designated as a "Tapestry Hall." He asked what tapestries Rorimer planned to place there. "I was thinking," Rorimer said, "of something like the Unicorn Tapestries." According to Rockefeller's biographer, the millionaire uttered a shocked "What?", and nothing more was said. The tapestries covered the walls of a room in Rockefeller's house—a room that had become his favorite retreat. All the same, he presented them to the Metropolitan in 1937, and they were in place for the opening of the new Cloisters the following year.

There is no doubt that the personal relationship between Rockefeller and Rorimer played a major part in the creation of The Cloisters. No curator has ever studied his benefactor more assiduously, or made so few mistakes in dealing with him. Rorimer never asked Rockefeller for money; moreover, when they had agreed on a project or a purchase, and there was a surplus afterward, Rorimer invariably made certain that it was paid back in dollars and cents. Like so many rich men Rockefeller had a streak of parsimony in his nature, and a mortal hatred of waste. On one of the countless mornings that Rorimer stopped by at the Rockefeller house for breakfast, to discuss Cloisters matters before the working day began, Rockefeller handed him a letter that he had intended to mail—it did not surprise Rorimer to see that the stamp had been steamed off the envelope. Rorimer countered his patron's qualms about spending so much money for art in the midst of the Depression by reminding him of all the men he was employing on The Cloisters construction. He understood and respected Rockefeller's extreme secretiveness where money was concerned, his reluctance to have dealers and other interested parties know about his plans and expenditures. Rorimer was secretive himself, and loved nothing better than to surround his activities with an aura of mystery.

The two men also shared a totally absorbing interest in their joint vision of what The Cloisters could be, an interest that was not unlike the artist's passion for his own evolving masterpiece. Rockefeller came nearly every day to the building site, trudging through the mud and taking measurements with the foot rule that he always carried in his back pocket. For Rorimer, the project became an obsession. He dropped out of what had been a fairly active bachelor's social life in New York, and turned down so many dinner invitations that one Christmas his friends gave him a recording of their voices repeating endlessly, "The Cloisters . . . The Cloisters . . . The Cloisters . . ." His unceasing labors made Rockefeller respect him all the more. Years later, when Mrs. Rorimer was discussing with Rockefeller how hard her husband worked, Rockefeller said that he had been brought up to believe that a man's work came first and his children second —leaving Katherine Rorimer to wonder where on that list he would put his wife. Whatever other qualities entered into their relationship— ambition, for example, or the mutual sympathy between two extremely shy men who were never altogether at ease in social gatherings—the main bond was that they trusted one another completely. Rockefeller had exceptionally high standards for the people he worked with, and Rorimer fulfilled every one of them.

When the new Cloisters opened to the public in the spring of 1938, their reward was complete. Praise and nothing but praise resounded on all sides. George Grey Barnard, who had died just the year before, would have been profoundly touched by some of the letters from ordinary visitors who wrote to say how delighted and in some cases how moved they had been by the atmosphere and the "spell" of the place—which seemed not so much a museum as a living evocation of the Middle Ages. The details—the warm gray of the Connecticut stone chosen because it resembled the stone found in southern France, the central tower that echoed the ancient tower of Saint-Michel-de-Cuxa, the slight, deliberate irregularities of proportion that simulated medieval hand craftsmanship, the planting in the gardens, the superb placement and lighting of the works of art—all Rorimer's tireless attention to quality and authenticity added up to a remarkably unified effect, and one that most people found entrancing.

No one was more entranced than Rockefeller. He came again and again, informally, once arriving by an oversight on a Monday when the building was closed and going away again without a word to anyone—just as he had done years before in France when he went out to see the restorations to Versailles that he had financed, and, arriving too late in the day for admission, meekly turned around and went back to Paris. But neither Versailles nor Fontainebleau nor the Cathedral of Rheims—all of which Rockefeller had paid to have restored during the 1920s because the French government could not afford the work—nor even the restoration of Colonial Williamsburg, on which he spent more than sixty million dollars, ever gave him more satisfaction than he drew from The Cloisters. In his last years he would still come in all weathers to Fort Tryon Park and stand on the ramparts high above the Hudson—looking across the river to the wooded cliffs that he had bought and presented to the Palisades Interstate Park Commission so as to preserve unspoiled the view from The Cloisters —and then he would go down through the Cuxa Cloister to his favorite room and sit looking for a long time at the Unicorn Tapestries. "I hope you take as much pleasure and satisfaction in The Cloisters, so largely your own creation, as I do," he wrote to Rorimer in 1951. "Both inside and out it seems to me as nearly perfect as a building and collection of this kind could be."

A year later he did his best to insure that perfection's permanence. Rockefeller had spoken several times of increasing his endowment of The Cloisters. The sum he had in mind had been the subject of much speculation at the museum, with estimates ranging up to five million dollars. It turned out to be twice that. Early in 1952, Rockefeller transferred securities with a market value of ten million dollars to the trustees of the Metropolitan. There were no strings of any kind. The deed of gift stated that the fund was "available for use in the broadest way for any purpose for the enrichment and development, structurally or otherwise, of The Cloisters." It was, the Metropolitan's president said, "a superb and perfect document."

James Rorimer's father had also taken a great interest in the evolution of The Cloisters. He came many times to the site, offered a number of helpful suggestions, and eventually donated the furniture for the curator's office in the tower—made to his son's order by Rorimer and Brooks Studios in Cleveland. At the formal dedication in 1938, Louis Rorimer said to one of the Metropolitan curators present that it was in some ways a pity that all this had come to his son so early, for nothing else in his life could ever match the satisfaction of being given the materials to create a masterpiece. The curator did not argue the point. But it was clear to a good many people even then that James Rorimer would not be content with a single masterpiece, and that his ambitions were already fixed on a loftier goal. At the age of thirty-three, though, Rorimer could afford to wait.

PART IV
THE MASSES
ARRIVE

TWENTY

The Metropolitan was showing its age. Immensely rich, swathed in dignity and neoclassic grandeur—Hyatt Mayor, Ivins' successor as curator of prints, once described it as the only building in New York that was impressive horizontally—the dowager empress of American museums had nevertheless fallen into disrepair and disrepute. No major addition or improvement had been undertaken for seventeen years, and the physical plant was showing signs of deterioration. The older buildings lacked adequate ventilation or hot water; in the director's office, one washed one's hands with water heated over an electric burner. Steam radiators made the galleries bone-dry in winter, and there was no way to control the summer humidity. During heavy storms, buckets were set out to catch the drip from leaking skylights. Throughout the museum stretched gallery after gallery whose exhibits were badly presented, badly labeled, and badly lit.

Attendance had been declining for a decade. Membership had fallen off even more sharply, and so had the city's annual appropriations—from $501,495 in 1930 to $369,592 in 1939—although the museum's operating costs, which now included the cost of running The Cloisters, continued inexorably to rise. Some of the decline could be attributed to the Depression, but not all of it. The fact was that some three hundred new art museums had been established in the United States between the two World Wars, the most recent being the huge National Gallery in Washington, D.C., founded in 1939 with a grant from Andrew Mellon and opened to the public in 1941. For the first time art museums outnumbered museums of science and natural history in this country, and they were being supported enthusiastically, for the most part, by the local citizens. Some of the new museums looked to the Metropolitan or the Boston Museum of Fine Arts for inspiration and guidance, but many others took their cue from places like the Art Institute of Chicago, which was showing a lively awareness of the modern world, or the extremely active Museum of Modern Art in New York where Alfred H. Barr, Jr.'s, brilliant exhibitions and catalogues were preparing the way for a new generation's acceptance of the most advanced trends in art. The Museum of Modern Art had been born, in a sense, as a result of the Metropolitan's negligence; if the older museum had not disdained to notice modern art, there would have been no need for it.

The Metropolitan trustees, whose average age in 1939 was sixty, were not unaware of the rising tide of criticism being directed against what several of them still referred to as "our" museum. Blumenthal, William Church Osborn, Elihu Root, Jr. (the son of the statesman), Myron C. Taylor, and others of the more active board members had been stung by the complaints, and most of all by the charges that the Metropolitan was ignoring its educational responsibilities. Ignoring education! For seventy years each incoming administration had proclaimed its renewed dedication to the cause of "popular instruction" in the fine arts. Education was the *fons et origo,* the rationale for public and private support. And yet, the critics now said that the moneyed upper classes were the only ones being served and that the Metropolitan was "unduly apathetic" in its educational program. Something had to be done. Poor Winlock, cut down by failing health, had not been able to conquer age and inertia. A strong hand at the helm was essential. Taking a deep breath, the trustees passed over Ivins the Terrible and reached out to Worcester, Massachusetts, for the most mercurial, the youngest, and in some says the least likely new director in the Metropolitan's history.

Francis Henry Taylor sometimes told people that he had become a medievalist by accident, while teaching English to French schoolchildren at the Lycée in Chartres. This was in the twenties. Every Friday, Taylor said, he would go up to Paris, spend a bibulous weekend on the town, and take the last train back to Chartres on Sunday night. Arriving in the small hours somewhat the worse for wear, he would go into the Cathedral to sober up

—it was cool in there, and blissfully quiet. After several of these recupera-
tive visits, he started to look around at the stone carvings, the architecture,
the great rose window . . . It was the sort of story that his more pedantic
detractors took very seriously.

Long before Chartres, Taylor had planned to become a doctor. His
father, William Johnson Taylor, was an eminent orthopedic surgeon in
Philadelphia, for many years the president of its College of Physicians. His
mother's family, the Newbolds, belonged to the upper strata of aristocratic
Philadelphia society. Taylor was born in 1903, the youngest of five children, a premature baby who suffered chronically from a tendency to over-
weight. He had a strict, rather religious (High Episcopal) upbringing, went
to church schools in Philadelphia and then to Kent, and would have gone
on to Harvard if family tradition had not dictated that he enter the University of Pennsylvania. Taylor infuriated his teachers, being a brilliant student who never worked very hard. Later on he used to say that he had
been "educated above my brains," but nobody took *that* seriously. He was
once suspended from college for refusing to engage in any form of physical
exercise, which he detested; that summer in France, where he often spent
vacations with his family, he took fencing lessons and managed to win
reinstatement in the fall. Taylor hated being fat, and dieted strenuously
but ineffectually at intervals. When he entered college he thought he
would not have to suffer any more schoolboy gibes about his girth, but
within a week, he said, everyone was calling him "satchel-ass." He compensated for his physical burdens by developing a verbal adroitness that
made people think twice about making fun of him to his face, and one
gathers that many of his classmates and even some teachers were afraid of
his tongue.

Taylor adored France. He had been brought up by a French nurse, had
learned to speak French before English, and continued to speak it fluently
and idiomatically all his life. He had, in fact, a great flair for languages.
When his difficulties with chemistry at college put an end to any thoughts
of following in his father's footsteps as a doctor—his chemistry professor
said he would let Taylor pass the freshman course on condition that he
promise never to take another—he decided he would become a language
teacher instead. The Lycée in Chartres was his first job. Taylor found it
somewhat less enticing than his weekends in Paris, and he quit after a year

to enter the Sorbonne. It was Henri Foçillon, the Sorbonne's great art historian, who got him seriously interested in medieval art. Taylor was Foçillon's first American pupil, and the two men remained close friends until Foçillon's death in 1947.

After a year at the Sorbonne, Taylor came home and entered graduate school at Princeton. He left without getting his doctoral degree because in 1927 he was offered a job as assistant curator at the Philadelphia Museum of Art, where a great transition was pending. The Philadelphia Museum, established during the Centennial in 1876, was preparing to move into its new building in Fairmont Park. Taylor and Henri Marceau, another young assistant curator, had their offices in the huge, virtually empty new building, while Fiske Kimball, the director, still had his in the old Memorial Hall on the Centennial grounds. Kimball was a dynamic museum man, highly irascible and profane at times but willing to give his assistants a great deal of independence. The Medieval Department was Taylor's responsibility. He bought most of the objects—many from the second collection of George Grey Barnard—and installed them so successfully that there have been few changes made since he left. Taylor also edited the museum's bulletin and other publications, served as first curator of the new Rodin Museum that had been established by Jules E. Mastbaum under the Philadelphia Museum's supervision, and did much to enliven the city's somewhat staid social gatherings. Because he was old Philadelphia himself, he could get away with things that would have consigned an outsider to instant oblivion. Marceau recalls vividly the evening that Taylor arrived, very late, at a *bal masque,* wearing a clerical surplice and spouting an unbroken stream of profanity in French—"only Francis could have done it," Marceau said. Gregarious and witty, a surprisingly nimble dancer in spite of his two hundred pound bulk, Taylor also proved to be more of a diplomat than Fiske Kimball, who was forever getting into rows with people and losing legacies. He was married to a striking and intelligent girl, the former Pamela Coyne of Boston and Bryn Mawr ("Now I can't be Pope," Taylor had quipped to friends after the wedding in 1928), and a comfortable Philadelphia career seemed to be assured.

Even to a native Philadelphian, though, the city's cultural climate left something to be desired. The trustees of the museum, with few exceptions, were ultraconservative or apathetic. There was a chronic shortage of operating funds. The Depression had more or less wiped out the purchase funds, moreover, and vast stretches of the Fairmont Park building would remain vacant for decades. After four years, Taylor grew restless. He applied for and won a Guggenheim fellowship for study and travel. Before he had a chance to use it, though, he was offered the directorship of the Worcester Museum.

Worcester was then and still is one of the best small museums in the country. Founded in 1896 through the efforts of Stephen Salisbury III, a wealthy local hardware merchant who donated the land for the original museum and left it nearly $3,000,000 in his will, it had been something of a pioneer in popular art education and had the longest continuous record of museum work with schoolchildren. A major expansion of the building had taken place in 1921, and another one was in progress. The Worcester trustees wanted a young and energetic director, but they had not quite realized that Taylor was only twenty-seven when they hired him—at his first meeting with the board, they asked him not to give his age to the press. Thomas Hovey Gage, the treasurer and later the president of the museum, took the new director aside after the meeting. "Taylor," he said, "you are very young. I'm old enough to be your father. We can get along on anything except one point."

"What's that?" Taylor asked.

"Don't ever tell me anything is a unique opportunity," Gage replied. "I've been a member of this board for forty years and I've never known a year in which there was not a unique opportunity." The two men got along splendidly from then on.

Taylor came in brimming with ideas. He wanted to make the museum a community center for the whole area, and one of the first things he did was to buy a motion picture projector and invite the public to evening showings of documentaries, travelogues, and foreign films like *The Grand Illusion* which could not be seen then in any commercial theaters. Taylor started a program of concerts in the museum, often managing to engage first-rate performers traveling between Boston and New York. He also put new life into the educational program. School visits increased tenfold during his tenure. The perennial problem of how to reach high school students occupied a Taylor-inspired joint conference of the Worcester Museum and the Child Study Association of America, held at Fieldston School in 1932, and many of its recommendations were later put into practice at Worcester. With a grant from the Carnegie Corporation, Taylor set up a regional program of art education for public and private schools throughout New England; the program included courses for university credit, study sheets, record collections, and circulating exhibitions keyed to high school courses —Life in Ancient Egypt, Shakespeare's England, the French Revolution. Taylor saw to it that they went to all the top New England preparatory schools, figuring that today's graduates of Exeter, Andover, Groton, and St. Paul's should be tomorrow's benefactors of Worcester and other museums.

In his buying for the museum Taylor followed a basic plan. He wanted to build a "teaching collection" of the highest quality, and to him this meant a comprehensive survey of world art. Worcester had fine early American paintings and a scattering of excellent material in other fields. Taylor sought to fill the gaps. He bought well, acquiring Egyptian and Greek antiquities, Chinese paintings and sculpture, medieval and Renaissance works, Persian miniatures, and a number of important European paintings including Piero di Cosimo's *The Discovery of Honey*, Quentin Massys' *Rest on the Flight to Egypt*, and a fine François Clouet that was thought then to be a portrait of Diane de Poitiers (a great favorite of Taylor's) but is now believed to be of someone else. Another Taylor innovation was to put books in every gallery—basic art books dealing with the period on exhibit, articles about specific works, anything to encourage the reader to look at art more intelligently. He also set up study rooms for each department of the museum, where any visitor could go and read books and periodicals and even handle certain objects under the watchful eye of a junior curator.

Many of the museum's most important acquisitions during this period came from the excavations at Antioch that were sponsored jointly by Worcester, Princeton, the Louvre, the Baltimore and later the Fogg museums. Taylor went out to the Antioch dig for a few weeks one season, and suffered miserably. Some archaeologists claim that his many verbal assaults upon their profession (Taylor once described the attributes of a true archaeologist as "jealousy, infallibility, coupled with a sense of persecution and a madness for his own subject") date from his discomforts and ineptitudes in the field on that occasion. Life on a dig, for a man of Taylor's gourmet tastes and gourmand physique, may indeed have been disheartening, but this did not prevent Taylor from getting what he wanted from Antioch for the Worcester Museum.

Taylor's exhibitions at Worcester soon attracted national attention. Temporary special exhibitions were a museum rarity in those days, but Taylor saw in them a means of getting people into the museum who had never come before. The first important exhibition of his regime, "Seventeenth Century Painting in New England," was built around Worcester's extraordinary portraits of John Freake and his family, painted by an unknown American artist. Two years later he put on a show called "Art and the Machine Age," which prophetically called attention to the "latent and accidental beauty in fine machinery" (Worcester had long been a center of the machine tool industry), and a big loan exhibition of "Rembrandt and His Circle" that was arranged jointly with the Art Institute of Chicago. The latter included *Aristotle Contemplating the Bust of Homer,* which was then owned by Duveen and would later be acquired by the Metropolitan for a record-breaking figure. Next, in 1937, came "The Dark Ages," the first major exhibition in America of early Christian and pagan art of this period, a dazzling show of which Taylor was particularly proud. In it was the silver and parcel-gilt Antioch Chalice, the earliest Christian chalice known, which a number of romantically inclined scholars had suggested might be the Holy Grail itself. Taylor did not *say* it was the Holy Grail (scholars now date it fourth or fifth century A.D.). On the other hand, he did not discourage newspaper stories headlined "Holy Grail Exhibited . . . Under Constant Guard," and as a result hordes of people flocked in to see it.°

Taylor's exhibitions sent Worcester's attendance soaring. They also attracted the notice of a great many museum people in other parts of the country, many of whom felt that Taylor was developing an entirely new approach to the public. Exhibitions like "The Dark Ages" and "Ways of Seeing" (an experiment in visual perceptions that Taylor got the Broadway

---

° The chalice was acquired in 1950 by the Metropolitan. It is exhibited at The Cloisters, where on the early morning of Easter Sunday, 1964, it suddenly levitated. Or so it seemed to the terrified guards. Thomas Pelham Miller, the curatorial assistant, solved the miracle by discovering that the plexiglass sheet on which the chalice rested had buckled slightly, putting the chalice off center and activating the electric alarm.

stage designer Lee Simonson to put together for him in 1939) were educational without being in the least condescending. Visitors who had never gone to museums for enjoyment often found afterward, much to their surprise, that they had enjoyed themselves immensely. After seeing Taylor's installation of Flemish paintings in 1939 (an exhibition sponsored jointly by Worcester, the Philadelphia Museum and the John G. Johnson Collection), many visitors wrote to say that it had been like a religious experience for them. The word "museum," which used to fall so leadenly on the ears of adolescents and adults alike, seemed to be taking on in Worcester a new and more agreeable tonality.

In several lively articles published by the *Atlantic* and other magazines, Taylor laid waste the forests of museological deadwood and brandished the torch of reform. It was time, he said, for American art museums to put into action the democratic and educational ideals that they had so long and so mellifluously preached. It was time for them to stop high-hatting the public in the name of scholarship. "The public . . . have had their bellyfull of prestige and pink Tennessee marble," Taylor wrote in 1939, in obvious reference to the National Gallery. Arguing that anachronistic palaces of art copied from European models were not what the American people wanted or needed, Taylor concluded with customary brio: "We in the art museums of America have reached a point where we must make a choice of becoming either temples of learning and understanding . . . or of remaining merely hanging gardens for the perpetuation of the Babylonian pleasures of aestheticism and the secret sins of private archaeology."

The trumpet calls of Taylor's rhetoric resounded and reverberated throughout the museum world, and apparently penetrated to the board room at the Metropolitan, whose trustees were still struggling with the knotty problem of how to replace their ailing director, Herbert Winlock. Taylor's name had actually come into their deliberations as early as 1937, when R. T. H. Halsey, the American Wing's guiding spirit, had mentioned him in a letter as "somewhat of a rough diamond" but of all contemporary museum men "the only one who approaches Winlock's class." William Church Osborn and a number of other trustees did not see it quite that way at the time. What the Metropolitan needed, they thought, was not a rough diamond but an older and thoroughly respected scholar. They approached Charles Rufus Morey at Princeton, and also G. Harold Edgell, the greatly admired director of the Boston Museum of Fine Arts. Both men declined, and Morey in turn recommended Harvard's Paul Joseph Sachs. "Paul Sachs Highly Recommended to Us," Osborn cabled Blumenthal, who was in Paris. Blumenthal squashed that idea. Even if Sachs were qualified on other grounds (which Blumenthal doubted), it would be extremely unwise, he thought, to consider him on account of the positions already held at the museum by Harry B. Wehle, the (Jewish) curator of paintings, James J. Rorimer, the (Jewish) curator of medieval art, and by Blumenthal himself—a rather intriguing insight into the delicacy of Blumenthal's own role as a Jew among Wasps.

A number of other men were under consideration as well. There was Walter Milliken of the Cleveland Museum, and Russell Plimpton, director of the Minneapolis Institute of Arts—both of whom had previously worked at the Metropolitan. There was Fiske Kimball, difficult as everyone knew he could be at times. There was also Horace Jayne, an outstanding Orientalist who had worked with Taylor and Marceau at the Philadelphia Museum and gone on to become director of the Pennsylvania University Museum. Osborn saw them all. The longer the trustees deliberated, though, the more youth and energy seemed to take precedence over age and experience. Paul Sachs himself urged the election of Francis Taylor. He and Taylor had met in Paris during the 1920s, and it is a measure of both men that Sachs, when asked for his opinion, recommended Taylor over any of his own former pupils. The trustees were also aware that during Taylor's ten years at Worcester the attendance there had jumped from forty-seven thousand to one hundred and forty-seven thousand a year.

Eventually the list narrowed down to two men, Taylor and Horace Jayne. In the fall of 1939, by a stroke of administrative confusion that defies unraveling, the directorship of the Metropolitan was offered to both men simultaneously!

Blumenthal nearly exploded when he heard about it. Taylor had been his choice, but somehow there had been a misunderstanding and Osborn had offered the post to Jayne. Taylor was told to settle the matter with Jayne one way or another. The two men were old and very close friends— each had been an usher at the other's wedding—and they came to an amicable agreement. Taylor would be the director, and Jayne would assume the newly created post of vice-director. By combining their talents, they hoped to bring greater leverage to the task of rejuvenating the Metropolitan.

TWENTY-ONE

The new order at the Metropolitan, which was exciting and frustrating in about equal measure, reflected the new director's highly complex personal style. Francis Taylor's ponderous bulk, his jet black, piercing eyes and imperious profile—he liked to think he looked like François I—his facility in languages, his energy and flamboyance and vesuvian flow of ideas all made him seem an imposing and for some of the staff a rather frightening figure. He was totally unpredictable. He could be warm and impulsively generous, but he lost his temper easily, flying into sudden tantrums and saying dreadful things to people, then calling them up later to apologize. Extremely sensitive to criticism—"Francis can dish it out but he can't take it," his wife once said—he had nevertheless the social ease and assurance of someone brought up among the first families of Philadelphia. Whereas Cesnola, Purdon Clarke, Robinson, and Winlock had all shown a certain deference to the trustees, it never occurred to Taylor that he was in any way less than their equal. He was the first director to be elected a full member of the board (Cesnola, as secretary, had been a trustee ex-officio), and he exercised more real power at the museum than anyone since the elder J. P. Morgan.

Two events marked the transition to Taylor's era. The turnstiles disappeared from the main entrance, ending seventy years of pay days (Mondays and Fridays) and establishing free admission every day of the week. Nothing could have expressed better Taylor's primary goal of getting the people into the museum. The other and less happy event concerned Henry W. Kent.

After thirty-five years' service to the Metropolitan, twenty-seven of them as secretary, Kent had become the symbol of the old order. His empire extended into every administrative nook and cranny, and, while he never seemed to want to be the director, it was quite clear that he expected the director to follow his advice. The Department of Education, which Taylor intended to reorganize thoroughly, fell under Kent's jurisdiction. So did the library, the registration and catalogue departments, all museum publications including the monthly *Bulletin*, the photo studio, the maintenance departments, the woodworking and metalworking shops in the basement, the Extension Division, the Department of Industrial Relations, and even the museum restaurant, whose management Kent supervised down to such details as the identifying labels for each wax-paper-wrapped sandwich (for years Hyatt Mayor kept pinned over his desk a sheet of blue paper bearing, in Kent's precisely hand-lettered Bodoni capitals, the word "H A M.") No one had contributed more to the Metropolitan or to the American museum movement than Henry Kent, but everyone knew that the time had come for him to step down—the question was when and how. It happened within a few weeks of Taylor's arrival in 1940. As part of the general reorganization of administrative responsibilities, Taylor had engaged Laurence S. Harrison, a former engineer and an executive of International Business Machines, to be the Metropolitan's business administrator in charge of all routine operations. Harrison was something of an efficiency expert, and his first project was to investigate each department, report on its methods, and recommend improvements. When he got around to the secretary's office, Kent told him that he wanted a copy of his report. Harrison said he had instructions to report only to the director. Kent insisted, and upon Harrison's continued refusal, went to take the matter up in person with Taylor. He emerged from Taylor's office looking very grim. A few days later, he resigned.

As secretary emeritus, Kent maintained some contact with the trustees, offered advice when asked, collected awards and citations from many museums and typographical societies, and masked with icy reserve whatever feelings he may have had on the subject of his abrupt retirement. He died in 1948, of a heart attack, alone in his room at the Nichewaug Inn in Petersham, Massachusetts, where he had gone every summer for the last thirty-three years of his life.

Taylor's youth and his commitment to change made friction with some of the older staff members inevitable. It was not at all like Worcester, where his small staff had worked together on major projects and paid scant attention to departmental lines. The curatorial departments at the Metropolitan had built up, over the years, a good deal of jealously guarded independence. The museum in those days was like a series of fortified and frequently warring hill towns, with each curator in full control of his staff of assistants, secretaries, clerks, technicians, and maintenance men, none of whom could be used for work in other departments without the curator's approval. On Harrison's recommendation many of the shops and services in the basement, including Kent's beloved printshop, were done away with —it was more efficient and less costly to have the work contracted for outside. Taylor wanted to bring the remaining carpenters, electricians, and other skilled workmen together under one noncuratorial authority, and he wanted the curatorial people to cooperate more closely with one another. Harrison, who tried to bring this about and who also sought to introduce time clocks, daily work reports, and other controls that had proved successful at IBM, bore the brunt of heavy opposition from the staff. Finding himself blocked at nearly every turn, he devoted more and more of his time to experiments in lighting; as a result of his efforts, the Metropolitan today has the best but also the most fiendishly complicated system of gallery lighting of any major museum. In addition to resisting Harrison, the curators flatly refused in several cases to deal with Horace Jayne, the vice-director in charge of curatorial administration. They had always dealt with the director, and they intended to go on doing so.

Ivins, whose bitterness at being passed over for the directorship had made his tongue more adder-like than ever, naturally presented the thorniest problem. Ironically, his ideas about the museum were very close to Taylor's. Both of them had realized that advanced technology was going to create a great deal more leisure time for a great many people, and both believed that museum education could no longer content itself with telling people what they should like and why. Taylor shared Ivins' contempt for the pretentious twaddle of much art scholarship, and, like Ivins, he wanted to develop an approach to the layman that would inform without condescending to him. Although they did not agree on everything—Ivins opposed the physical expansion of the museum, for example, believing that space problems could be solved by putting duplicate or secondary material away in study collections and leaving only the most important works on permanent display—they agreed on the basic assumption of what the Metropolitan must be in the future: not a static repository of treasures, but a dynamic educational force in American society, or, as Taylor put it, "a free and informal liberal arts college, a college without entrance requirements in which each individual may learn according to his capacity."

Relations between Taylor and Ivins reached a breaking point in 1946, after an unpleasant incident in the director's dining room. This had become a scintillating place under Taylor, with lively conversation on all sorts of nonmuseum topics replacing the rather solemn discussions of previous years. Taylor had opened the lunchroom to ladies of the staff, which enlivened things further but which also led to the rupture with Ivins. One day at lunch, Taylor told a story that Ivins considered utterly unfit for the delicate ears of two female staff lecturers, who happened to be present. He rebuked Taylor publicly and angrily for telling it. Taylor turned white, rose from the table, and stalked out of the room. Ivins retired very soon after this.

A certain degree of friction also existed from the start between Taylor and Rorimer. Two years younger than Taylor, Rorimer had established himself so solidly in the confidence of John D. Rockefeller, Jr., that Rockefeller would deal only with him on Cloisters matters. When Taylor approved the installation of a small display of arms and armor at The Cloisters in 1940, against Rorimer's wishes, word came back that Rockefeller was offended and the exhibition was promptly removed. Taylor subsequently wrote a letter to Rockefeller asking for an opportunity to discuss with him "certain aspects of The Cloisters from a management angle." Rockefeller replied coolly that he had no "relation to the Museum or The Cloisters other than that of any other contributor," and that it would be inappropriate for him to discuss such matters. Giving way to one of his rages, Taylor once petrified an assistant curator in the Medieval Department by pounding his desk and yelling, "I hate Rockefeller, I hate Rorimer, and I hate The Cloisters!"

Another source of irritation was Alan Priest, the undisputed *enfant terrible* of the museum. Priest had taken over the Department of Far Eastern Art in 1928, when S. C. Bosch-Reitz, its first curator, resigned and went back to Europe. Priest was only a graduate student at Harvard at the time, but he had been out to China on two expeditions with Langdon Warner, the Fogg Museum's great Orientalist, and he came highly recommended by Paul Sachs. Short, sandy-haired, and eccentrically dressed—in winter he affected a long cape that reached to his ankles—he had always done just as he pleased at the museum, buying shrewdly in the areas that interested him, such as Chinese sculpture and costumes, and hardly at all in those that did not. The sort of scholarly pretentiousness that so irritated Ivins and Taylor merely amused Priest. His delightful articles in the *Bulletin*, with their chatty asides and exclamations ("Heavens!" "Wonderful!"), reminded readers that with Oriental art it was often impossible to arrive at definite attributions or dates, and Priest was not above presenting his own conclusions as "interesting and harmless opinions, probably not far from the truth," or saying, of a T'ang dynasty crown, that "if this did not belong to at least an imperial great aunt, it ought to have." Priest's casual manner tended to rile his superiors. Winlock found his letters from China one year "merely anecdotal," and replied to them so testily that Priest, who had been addressing him as "Hebe my dear," changed back to "Dear Mr. Winlock." An inveterate practical joker, Priest once sent word to the immigration authorities that a notorious narcotics smuggler was on board an incoming ship, and gave a description that exactly fitted Henry Kent. He later gloated that Kent, who was on the ship, had been searched from head to toe.

By the time Taylor became director, Priest considered himself impregnable. A lifelong bachelor, he was the darling of several wealthy ladies who doted on his eccentricities and were deliciously shocked by his behavior. "Now, Alan, don't do anything outrageous," they would plead, whereupon Priest would dutifully think up some new outrage—once he appeared at his hostess's box at the opera with his hair cut very short and curled into tiny Buddha ringlets. Priest used to brag that his friendships with Mrs. John D. Rockefeller, Jr., Mrs. Otto Kahn, Mrs. Alice Longworth, Mrs. Murray Crane and several others gave him such power at the museum that he could have a swimming pool built in the main hall if he chose. Try as he might, Taylor could not get him to mend his ways or even to come to work on time. Priest liked to sleep until noon, drift in at about two in the afternoon, and then work until late at night. His staff covered up for him shamelessly whenever Taylor called, and Taylor complained that he ran his department from his bed. Arriving late at a meeting of the purchasing committee of the trustees one afternoon, Priest saw Taylor glaring at him from the head of the table; he glared right back, walked straight through the room to a small lavatory at the other end, and holding the door open with his foot flushed the toilet twice before returning.

Taylor fulminated against Priest, saying that he was *"ni enfant, ni terrible,"* but he also recognized his brilliance. It was generally agreed that Priest's installations were the best in the building. He had a marvelous eye and a theatrical flair, when it came to exhibitions, that Taylor greatly admired. Taylor, moreover, could never stay mad at anyone very long. Priest's antics amused him, and he fluctuated between wanting to fire him and deciding that he was a genius and therefore irreplaceable.

One of Taylor's most unpopular acts was to establish age limits for retirement—sixty-five for men, sixty for women. No staff member had ever been obliged to leave the museum because of age before—William Clifford, the librarian, who was in his nineties, still came to work every morning and spent the day dozing at his desk—and the new ruling infuriated not only the older gentlemen on the staff but most of the ladies, who deeply resented what appeared to be discrimination against their sex (a few years later all Metropolitan employees came under Social Security regulations and the sixty-five age limit became mandatory for both sexes). Taylor, however, was determined to demolish the idea of the museum as a sanctuary for the favored few, and especially for those who worked there. He hated the dilettante approach to museum work, the feeling that it was a pleasant job for someone with a small private income and a distaste for pushy, mercantile life. He was often very rough on curators like Alan Priest and Preston Remington, the elegant curator of the amazingly titled Department of Renaissance and Modern Art. For many of the younger members of the staff, though, Taylor's arrival came like a breath of fresh air in a closed room.

Everyone worked much harder and longer, and there was a great sense of movement and excitement and productive confusion. Taylor seemed to take a personal interest in each member of the staff. He knew all the guards by name, asked after their families, and always found ways to help out those who were having personal problems, even if it meant dipping into the director's contingency fund or his own pocket. No director had ever taken much notice of the lower echelons before, and they loved him for it and worked twice as hard on his account. Taylor also got along rather well—in the beginning—with the trustees. He understood business-men without being in the least awed by them; the businessmen, for their part, felt entirely at home with Taylor. They enjoyed his jokes and off-color stories—a bit too rough at times, maybe, but then what a grand fellow he was, none of your arty preciousness about Francis, was there? Taylor liked Blumenthal, and could imitate his German-Jewish accent to perfection. Blumenthal was famous for his dry remarks. When the trustees were discussing one day whether or not it would be proper to open a special exhibition on Easter Sunday, Blumenthal was overheard to mutter, "What would they be doing, laying eggs, maybe?" Taylor also enjoyed telling of the time when Blumenthal was asked to give a reference for a servant who had once worked in his house. Blumenthal and his second wife, the former Mrs. Ann Payne Clews whom he had married in 1935, were in the habit of illuminating their Spanish patio entirely by candlelight. After thinking for a moment, Blumenthal said, "Oh, yes, he was my second candleman." He later amended this to "my third candleman—otherwise I would have remembered his name." At museum receptions Blumenthal, William Church Osborn, and Taylor would stand together in the middle of the main hall to receive the guests. The sight of them—Blumenthal short and wiry, Osborn tall and patrician, and Taylor looking like a cross between François I and the actor Sidney Greenstreet—made an arresting tableau.

In the spring of 1941, Blumenthal lay dying in his house on Park Avenue. One or more members of the Metropolitan curatorial staff were on hand at all times, in case the old financier might want to discuss some matter involving the museum or his bequest to it, but most of the time he lay in a coma in his upstairs bedroom, saying nothing at all. Once, when Taylor was in the room, Blumenthal roused momentarily—just long enough to sit up in bed and say, "You don't know anything! Nobody knows anything!" Another time, he opened one eye and said to the curator of paintings, Harry Wehle, "You won't get the Joos van Ghent!" He was only teasing. In the end, the Metropolitan received the great *Adoration of the Magi* by this very rare master, together with all the other pre-1700 works of art in Blumenthal's collection. Blumenthal had originally intended to bequeath his house, with all its furnishings and works of art, to be kept intact as a branch of the Metropolitan. His experience as president and trustee had convinced him that the difficulties this involved would be too great, however, and so he gave orders that the house was to be dismantled and sold for the benefit of the museum, which could retain the Velez Blanco patio and any other architectural elements it wanted to incorporate into its own building plans. Aside from a request that the collection be shown together for a few months after his death, there were no restrictions whatsoever.

The Second World War affected the Metropolitan far more profoundly than the First. Many of Taylor's new projects had to be curtailed, all plans for building construction and rehabilitation were shelved, and thirty-five members of the staff went into service. Rorimer joined the army as a private, rising eventually to captain and playing an important role in the special unit of the Seventh Army that tracked down, salvaged, and repatriated many of the great art treasures looted by the Nazis. Alan Priest, in an access of patriotic zeal, spent a lot of money getting his teeth put in order and was furious when the army rejected him. Horace Jayne was sent by the State Department on a secret mission to China, and became the first nonmilitary American to get into Peking after the war. The problem of keeping an adequate staff during the war years would have been acute, had not all of the most valuable works of art left the museum as well.

The danger of air raids weighed heavily on the minds of many New Yorkers in 1941. Field Marshall Hermann Goering had ordered the German aircraft industry to produce planes capable of carrying five-ton bombs to New York, so as to "stop somewhat the mouths of arrogant people over there." An air raid alarm (happily false) sent two hundred and eighty fighter planes into the air from Mitchell Field that December. German U-boats were sinking Allied ships off the coast of Virginia, the Statue of Liberty had been blacked out, and sightseers were barred from the top of the Woolworth Building. Taylor and William Church Osborn, who had succeeded Blumenthal as president, considered several courses of action. For a time they talked of storing the most valuable works of art in the empty tunnel under the museum. The tunnel ran directly beneath the Fifth Avenue galleries, and until recently had contained four forty-eight-inch water mains from the Central Park Reservoir. The trustees, fearing leakage, had been pleading for years with the city to take them out, and the city had finally done so in 1939, leaving a cavern twenty-six feet wide, ten feet high, and four city blocks long. The floor was not paved, though, and in wet weather it was a sea of mud. Murray Pease, the expert conservator-restorer whom Taylor had hired away from the Fogg Museum, advised against putting works of art down there. The trustees also looked into an abandoned mine up the Hudson—an expedient that had been followed in England by the National Gallery. Early in 1942, however, it was announced that the Metropolitan had hidden its major treasures away in a country house "a hundred miles inland."

The house was Whitemarsh Hall, a hundred-and-fifty-room mansion twelve miles northwest of downtown Philadelphia. It had been built in the 1920s by Edward T. Stotesbury, a partner in the Philadelphia banking firm of Drexel and Company (J. P. Morgan's Philadelphia associate). Set in a private, three-hundred-acre park and decorated largely by Duveen, the house had seen many lavish parties before Stotesbury's fortune evaporated in the Depression. Stotesbury had died in 1938 and his executors had been trying ever since to sell the place. For the Metropolitan, which leased the premises for two years, it seemed a perfect citadel: constructed of fireproof steel and concrete, with air conditioning and humidity control throughout, its own electrical system and water supply, and the natural security of a fenced park. Of course it *was* rather close to Philadelphia, but then who would want to bomb Philadelphia?

The great exodus began in February 1942. Working mostly at night, packing each object in special cases designed by Murray Pease, the staff moved ninety van-loads within the next few weeks. Fifteen thousand works of art made the trip—French furniture, medieval ivories and Renaissance bronzes, Chinese porcelain, Egyptian mummies, Persian rugs, Gothic tapestries, and five hundred paintings. They spent the next two years in seclusion, watched over by a small staff from the Metropolitan and visited once a month by the curators. The American Philosophical Society, the Brooklyn Museum, Cooper Union, and a number of private collectors also arranged to store their treasures in Whitemarsh Hall, leading Hardinge Scholle, the director of the Museum of the City of New York, to refer to the house as a *"monument hystérique."*

Having stripped the museum of its main attractions, Taylor had the problem of filling up the empty gallery space. He attacked it with gusto, and so successfully that attendance at the museum rose substantially in 1943, reached an all-time high the following year, and has been going up ever since. One obvious method was to put on special exhibitions. Taylor mounted eleven of these in 1942, ranging from "The Art of Rembrandt" to a show of "Advertising Art" and one of "Cartoons," and including the very popular "Artists for Victory" show of American paintings selected by a jury of American artists. Taylor also dusted off and reinstalled a large number of the old plaster casts that had been put away in 1938, when the Hall of Casts (the original Wing A of the museum) was converted into the principal Arms and Armor gallery. Casts rather embarrassed the trustees, who in 1938 had appointed a special committee with power to lend or dispose of them whenever possible, but Taylor saw them as the great drawing academy of Western art. He once considered installing them in the attic, around the skylight domes of the main hall—an oddly shaped area then being used as the museum's photo studio. These plans never materialized, and today the Metropolitan's casts of the great sculptures of antiquity and the Renaissance gather dust in a city-owned warehouse underneath the Riverside Drive viaduct at 158th Street.

Even before the exodus to Whitemarsh, Taylor had cleared out five galleries to make room for what he called the Junior Museum. No special facilities had ever been set aside for the school groups that came in ever-increasing numbers to the Metropolitan. The children had no place to hang their coats, eat lunch, or receive any sort of orientation, and Taylor thought this led to more confusion than was necessary. His original installation consisted of a small auditorium, a gallery fitted with tables and benches that served as a lunch-and-study room, and rather rudimentary coat rooms and toilet facilities. Taylor hired a first-class teacher, Louise Condit, to run a program designed to interest children and prepare them for what they would see in the main museum. The results were so successful that a much larger Junior Museum was included in the postwar building plans, and many other museums around the country soon adopted similar facilities and programs.

Wartime austerity also brought to light an almost forgotten resource, the Crosby Brown collection of musical instruments. The nucleus of this collection had been given in 1889 by the wife of John Crosby Brown, an early trustee who served as treasurer of the museum and who was also a partner in the investment banking firm of Brown Brothers. With the help of missionaries and Brown Brothers agents in various parts of the world, Mrs. Brown and her son, William Adams Brown, a Professor of Dogmatics at Union Theological Seminary (and known accordingly to his students as "Doggy" or "Billy Dog" Brown), had built it up to be the finest and most complete collection of musical instruments in existence—more than three thousand examples, from prehistoric bone flutes to rare eighteenth century pianofortes to modern saxophones, covering the history and development of music throughout the world. For forty years the collection had been of no more interest to the Metropolitan trustees than the lowly plaster casts. When William Sloane Coffin became president in 1931 he had suggested giving it to the Juilliard School of Music. Winlock and the board of trustees had formally agreed soon afterward to place the instruments on extended loan to the New York Public Library, which was then planning to establish a Musical Center for books, records, and other materials on musical history. William Adams Brown strongly favored the transfer, mainly because the instruments had been so badly neglected by the Metropolitan. According to Curt Sachs, a German ethnomusicologist who had been chosen to head the new Musical Center, if left without care much longer "the instruments are condemned to death." When the Musical Center fell through for financial reasons, Doggy Brown urged the Metropolitan to hire Curt Sachs as curator and restorer. His request was turned down—Sachs had made some rather critical remarks about the Metropolitan on the radio, and neither Taylor nor the trustees wanted anything to do with him. The world's greatest collection of musical instruments continued to molder away in the museum until 1941, when Emanuel Winternitz arrived in the nick of time to rescue them.

Winternitz had been a well-known lawyer in Vienna before the war, and also, like most Viennese, an accomplished amateur musician. His parents had known Brahms, his mother played the piano beautifully, and Winternitz himself lectured on music and performed in chamber groups. He happened to be out of the country at the time of the Anschluss in 1938. Unwisely, he returned. It was a terrible time, with Jewish arrests and suicides taking place every day. A seventy-two-year-old lady whom Winternitz knew slightly was arrested for burying silver in her garden—Jews were supposed to turn in their silver to the Nazi authorities. She was taken to the Hotel Metropol where beatings and torture were the routine methods of interrogation, and her daughter frantically begged Winternitz for help. As it happened, Winternitz knew somebody who knew somebody else, who knew a third party, who in turn knew a Nazi official, and in the immemorial Viennese way he managed eventually to get the old lady released. Meanwhile, he had been trying in vain at every foreign consulate to get a visa for himself, and had been warned not to sleep at home. Out of the blue, the old lady he had helped received a visit from an English friend, who had come to see her daughter in a Vienna hospital. The Viennese asked the intrepid Englishwoman whether she couldn't do something for "that nice Mr. Winternitz," and to Winternitz's astonishment he was summoned the next day to the British Embassy and presented with a valid visa.

Although his passport was not entirely in order, he decided to take a chance and booked a berth on the overnight train to Switzerland. The man in the berth above him was a Nazi officer. Winternitz lay awake all night. The train stopped at dawn and two officials—an Austrian and a Nazi— knocked at the door of their compartment. They looked briefly at Winternitz's passport, handed it back, passed on. There was still the customs inspection to get through. The Nazi officer was not in the compartment when the inspector came. The inspector, a young Austrian with a Tyrolean accent, peered into Winternitz's valise, which contained a pair of shoes, an extra shirt, and a few toilet articles, and then he pointed to the luggage rack where Winternitz had placed several cigar boxes. The cigar boxes contained Leica negatives of Palladian villas and churches, photographs that Winternitz himself had taken, over many years, on holiday trips in Italy; he hoped to use them for lectures, and they were the only personal possessions aside from his few items of clothing that he had dared to bring out. The inspector shook his head angrily—no photographs. It seemed that journalists had been smuggling out photographs that were embarrassing to the Nazi authorities—pictures of people being taken away by soldiers and of Jews being forced to scrub the streets with their hands. Winternitz tried to explain that his negatives were nothing like that, but the inspector would not listen. He ordered him off the train.

At this point Winternitz suddenly lost his temper. Always before he had managed to keep his head and say the right things, but now he began to shout. He told the customs inspector that in the First World War he had enlisted at the age of seventeen and served three years in the Alpine troops —he spoke the Tyroler dialect to prove it; he said that he had been decorated, had served the fatherland as well as anyone, but now they had taken everything from him, had even denied him the right to earn a living, and all he wanted was to leave the country and start over somewhere else. Perhaps these would help him make a new life, look—a church, a palace, nothing dangerous about that, was there? *Look at them!* The inspector, startled and no doubt amazed to hear his own dialect spoken, glanced at a few negatives and retreated in confusion. A few minutes later he was back. Winternitz felt sure he had brought a Nazi official to arrest him. The inspector opened the compartment door a crack. "Good luck in your new life," he whispered, and passed on down the corridor. The train started to move. Winternitz saw the Swiss flag approaching the window, and then it passed and he was in Switzerland.

The Palladian villas served him well. Winternitz lectured many times in Switzerland and in England on the evolution of the Palladian style. Eventually he made his way to the United States, where he was befriended by Paul Sachs (no relation, incidentally, to the ethnomusicologist Curt Sachs) and through him invited to give a lecture at the Fogg Museum. This led to other invitations, including one from Francis Taylor at Worcester. Taylor and Winternitz took to each other right away. Winternitz returned to Worcester several times, and spent many pleasant hours in the Taylors' house improving his English. He had taught himself English mainly by reading comic strips, fitting together the words and the pictures, and his vocabulary at the time was full of expressions like "Take that!" and "Oh, my gosh!" He used to write out his lectures in German, translate them, and then memorize the translation, but his *gemütlich* warmth and charm were so winning that his audiences never suspected. After the first Worcester lecture Taylor advised him to go into politics. Startled, Winternitz asked why. "Inside of four minutes you had that audience in the palm of your hand," Taylor told him. "You belong in politics."

When Taylor moved down to the Metropolitan in 1940 he invited Winternitz to give several lectures there. Winternitz had heard about the

Crosby Brown collection. He went to see it one day, before a lecture, and was appalled by its condition. The smaller instruments, he said, were mounted "like herrings" in huge glass cases, their fragile woods exposed to full sunlight from shadeless windows. Some of the old lutes looked "like cow skulls in paintings by Georgia O'Keeffe." A rare Chinese drum had been cut in half so it would fit into the case, hot air registers blew directly on the legs of keyboard instruments, and in the storeroom a pigeon had built its nest in an eighteenth century harpsichord. Winternitz begged Taylor to put him in charge of the collection. Taylor refused—the trustees still hoped to get rid of it somehow. But then the war came, fifteen thousand works of art migrated to Whitemarsh Hall, and Taylor asked Winternitz what he should do about the musical instruments. Winternitz advised against sending them to Whitemarsh; the change of climate and humidity, he said, would surely finish them off. At this point Taylor gave in and asked Winternitz to take charge of the collection. Winternitz had just been offered a permanent teaching post in the philosophy department at Vanderbilt University, but the lure of the dying instruments was too strong. He joined the Metropolitan in 1942 as "keeper" of the Crosby Brown collection, the trustees having decreed that no new departments could be created during the war.

In remarkably short order he was able to repair and restore the great majority of the instruments. With the stringed instruments this was often simply a matter of tuning, to restore the natural tension on which their structure was based. Winternitz was also rumored to take certain instruments to bed with him at night, on the theory that natural body heat was the best anodyne. The famous Cristofori piano—made in 1720 in Padua by Bartolommeo Cristofori, the inventor of the pianoforte—required a good deal more effort to put into playing condition, but playing condition for every instrument was Winternitz's goal; as a musician, he felt that the instruments could not survive if they were never played. This idea led quite naturally to the famous series of concerts of "Music Forgotten and Remembered." Winternitz arranged four concerts at the Metropolitan in 1942, all of unknown pieces by Renaissance and baroque composers, played upon the old instruments for which they had originally been written. The performers included Paul Hindemith, Wanda Landowska, George Szell, Adolf Busch, Mieczyslaw Horszowski—many of them old friends of Winternitz who, like him, had taken refuge in America—and the audience at first was composed primarily of professional musicians and their students. The concerts soon became immensely popular. A great many New Yorkers joined the Metropolitan in order to hear them—they were free to members—and membership rose sharply for the first time in nine years. The postwar revival of interest in baroque and pre-baroque music has been attributed largely to Winternitz's concerts, which continued all through the war and drew ever larger and more enthusiastic audiences to the museum.

The changes that Francis Taylor had set in motion during the darkest days of the war gathered momentum as the tide of battle turned in Europe and the Pacific. By 1944 the threat of German air raids had receded sufficiently for the art treasures to be recalled. Fifteen thousand objects returned without a single one being damaged. Princess Juliana of the Netherlands and twelve thousand others attended the spring opening of the redecorated paintings galleries, which featured a loan exhibition of Dutch paintings, those perennial New York favorites. It was the harbinger of the great series of postwar loan shows which, more than any other single factor, established Francis Taylor as the leading museum director of the day.

The international loan shows were really a by-product of the war. European museums had sent many of their greatest treasures into hiding. Hitler's art-looting squads had stolen thousands of paintings and objects of art, whose return necessitated months and sometimes years of searching. Many of the museum buildings in Europe had suffered heavy damage, and most of them needed thorough renovation before they could once again display their possessions properly. In the interim, museum directors who had formerly resisted lending major works were often quite willing to let them travel. Largely through Taylor's initiative, and with active assistance from the State Department, some of the greatest treasures of European museums traveled to the United States soon after the war and were seen at the National Gallery, the Metropolitan, and usually one or more other museums.

The first such exhibition, in 1947, was a show of English paintings by Hogarth, Constable, and Turner. It was followed that fall by an exhibition of two hundred French tapestries from European museums and church collections, an incredibly rich gathering that included twenty-four panels from the *Apocalypse* tapestries of Angers and the entire *Lady With the*

Unicorn series from the Cluny Museum, which made a fascinating comparison with the Unicorn Tapestries at The Cloisters (Rorimer compared
them, and concluded firmly that "rabbit for rabbit, dog for dog, the [Clois-
ters] . . . tapestries are definitely more alive, more brilliantly conceived
and executed.") The next year saw "Paintings from the Berlin Museums" at
the Metropolitan, and the year after that Taylor presented a monumental
survey of Van Gogh. In 1949 came the brilliant display of "Art Treasures
from the Vienna Collections," for which he and the new curator of paintings, Theodore Rousseau, had negotiated patiently for two years.

Each of these shows received wide publicity and drew record-breaking
crowds. Attendance at the main museum passed the two million mark in
1950—more than double the 1940 figure. Young people were flocking to the
Metropolitan, and not just in school groups, either. The sense of excitement
and innovation that was Taylor's trademark had spread throughout the
museum, and it seemed to bring out the best efforts of even the prickliest
curators. For many people the most memorable exhibition of this whole period was not one of Taylor's, but Alan Priest's 1945 show of "Costumes
from the Forbidden City." The largest and most gorgeous collection of
Chinese court robes ever assembled, it had as the *pièce de résistance* a
room that Priest, at his most theatrical, had chosen to present as a tomb.
The costumes in it had actually been found in the tomb of a son of the Emperor Ch'ien Lung (ruled 1737–1796). The prince had been buried with all
his concubines, who had dutifully lain down to die and then quietly
seeped out through their royal garments, leaving them more or less intact
but with stains that over the ensuing two hundred years had turned a marvelous golden-bronze color. Priest had the room painted the same shade of
golden bronze, with streaks of suppurating green showing through here and
there. Mannequins in various postures simulated the concubines. From a
medical supply house Priest had rented a human skeleton which he
painted gold, and arranged as though reclining on a couch in the robe of
the Emperor's son. The skeleton had one weirdly effective glass eye. Priest
first tried putting a glass ball in both eye sockets, but decided this made it
look too much like a Japanese scholar, so he used only one. Taylor's high
church sensibilities were offended, and he ordered the skeleton removed
from the show; Priest took it out, but kept it in hiding and replaced it just

before the opening, and the sensation was so great that Taylor said nothing further.

There was no doubt about it, the exhibitions of the Taylor era were attracting a great many people who would never willingly have set foot in an art museum before the war. A mass public for art was in the process of being born in America, for a variety of reasons some of which are still not fully understood. The trend showed up in rising attendance at most of the country's art museums, and it would soon be reflected and given added impetus by popular magazines such as *Life*, which began about 1947 to devote more and more space to "news" about the fine arts. Increased leisure, widening educational horizons—the college degree was fast becoming as essential as the high school diploma had been—the ability to travel, the acceleration of social change, relief after five years of war and anxiety over the new mushroom-shaped cloud that overshadowed the future—these and many other factors contributed to a great hunger for visual and sensory stimulation of all kinds. People flocked into museums without knowing exactly what it was they were looking for, and the Metropolitan, under Francis Taylor, did its best to make them feel, not necessarily at home, but as though they belonged there.

The education program went into high gear. Taylor merged the old Department of Educational Work, the Department of Museum Extension, and the Department of Industrial Relations into a single new Department of Education and Museum Extension, first under Richard F. Bach and later under Sterling Callisen. He initiated a series of lectures at the museum in connection with New York University, and set up an ambitious program of traveling exhibitions to the city's public high and junior high schools. The Junior Museum expanded its activities and started putting on its own special exhibitions, such as the highly successful "E Pluribus Unum" show in 1949 which combined paintings, prints, photos, costumes, furniture, motion pictures, slides, and recordings to help children visualize the persons, places, objects, and customs of the period from 1783 to 1800, when the United States was emerging as an independent nation. "E Pluribus Unum" was organized jointly by the Junior Museum and the American Wing, which was also being made more appealing to schoolchildren by its new "keeper," Lydia Powel. Joseph Downs, the Wing's scholarly first curator, had resigned in 1940 to take over Henry F. du Pont's Winterthur Museum. To replace him Taylor appointed Lydia Bond Powel, a member of the museum's educational staff whom he had known as a child in Philadelphia. Taylor gave her the English-sounding title of "keeper" because she lacked the necessary museum qualifications to be a curator. Under her care the American Wing became a brighter and more cheerful place. Lydia Powel was also the enunciator of Powel's Law, which she formulated after observing Taylor's rather unsuccessful efforts to raise money. Under Powel's Law, "The rich prefer to give to the rich."

The costumes that Lydia Powel and Louise Condit used for "E Pluribus Unum" came from the former Museum of Costume Art, which the Metropolitan absorbed in 1946. This organization had been founded ten years before by Irene Lewisohn, Aline Bernstein, Lee Simonson, and others interested in costume history and design, and its merger with the Metropolitan was welcomed by everyone except the staff of the Egyptian Department, which had to give up some of its gallery space as a result. The Costume Institute, as it was called after the marriage, came with a sizable dowry and has supported itself ever since on the proceeds of its annual "Party of the Year," an October ball held at the Metropolitan and attended, at $100 a ticket, by all the notables of the garment industry. With more than sixteen thousand costumes dating from 1690 to the present, plus a library of books on costumes and costume design, it is widely used by professional designers of all kinds and is today the only department of the museum that specifically carries out that section of the 1870 charter providing for "the application of arts to manufacture and practical life."

Dozens of other projects large and small poured from Taylor's office and kept the museum in a state of constant turmoil. Architectural plans for postwar construction and renovation were nearing completion. A major fund-raising campaign on the occasion of the Metropolitan's seventy-fifth birthday in 1945 had set out to raise $7,500,000, most of which was earmarked for expansion. Negotiations were in progress for a merger with the Whitney Museum of American Art, which was planning to move from Eighth Street into new quarters adjoining the Metropolitan. A complete reorganization of the Metropolitan's curatorial departments was also under discussion. Taylor wanted to get rid of the haphazard groupings that had evolved over the years, with some materials classified geographically (Far

Eastern Art), others historically (Greek and Roman Art), and still others according to function (Arms and Armor). His plan was to reestablish curatorial responsibilities under five main divisions: 1) American Art, including paintings, sculpture, and decorative arts; 2) the Ancient Arts of the Mediterranean Basin, including Egyptian, Greek, Roman, and Near Eastern; 3) Oriental Arts, including Chinese, Japanese, Indian, and Islamic; 4) Graphic Arts, including paintings, drawings, and prints; and 5) Western European Decorative Arts.

Needless to say there was resistance to many of Taylor's projects. Some people felt that he had too many ideas, that with Taylor everything came in lightning flashes and that by the time someone got around to acting on a project Taylor himself might very well have lost interest in it. ("At least you can't accuse me of consistency," Taylor used to say). Others—the trustees in particular—were beginning to worry that Taylor had not the slightest interest in knowing where all the money was to come from. He never could hold on to money, spent his director's contingency fund within the first six weeks of the year (often on hospital bills for an employee's wife or some such act of goodwill), and detested dealing with the city officials of the Board of Estimate. Money, however, was definitely becoming a problem. The seventy-fifth anniversary campaign turned out to be a stunning failure, with only $1,000,000 raised by the end of 1946. Wealthy New Yorkers at this period seemed willing to support hospitals, schools, and charities, but not cultural institutions. Taylor, moreover, had done little to cooperate with the professional fund raisers or with the campaign chairman, IBM president and Metropolitan trustee Thomas J. Watson. In a crowded elevator in the IBM building one day, when a girl operator gave a sudden squeal, Taylor enriched everyone's day by remarking loudly, "I'm delighted to see that some things around here are still being done by hand." He was doing little to enrich the Metropolitan's endowment, however, and for the first time in many years there was an annual deficit.

Any number of storm signals were flying in 1947, when William Church Osborn stepped down as president of the museum. Osborn had been an interim president. He had accepted the post because his fellow trustees had insisted, and in his six years as president he had helped greatly to smooth the transition into Taylor's new era. Osborn was one of those rare men, according to his subsequent obituary in *The Times*, "who without haste or

bustle and with apparent ease do well many and important things, and
have time enough to think and never forget the art of courtesy." He had
served forty-three years on the Metropolitan board, and he could see that a
younger man was needed. A time of troubles lay ahead. For Taylor, who
had always enjoyed a good row and who savored the spice of controversy,
the next few years would afford many lively diversions.

TWENTY-TWO

One of the strongest arguments for the founding of the Metropolitan had been the need to do something for American artists. An American painter of the 1860s had to go to Europe to see great paintings. The founders believed that the presence of edifying examples at home would greatly encourage the development of native artists, just as the presence of glassware and metalwork would provide our rude artisans with models "to imitate and excel."

American painters of that era no doubt appreciated the thought, but they tended to point out that it would be more encouraging if the museum simply bought their pictures and forgot about the Europeans. This attitude greatly irritated Cesnola, who complained that the New York artists "considered our Museum to have been established for their own pecuniary benefit," and who lost no opportunity to avoid buying their work. A few paintings by Thomas Eakins, Eastman Johnson, Asher B. Durand, and other contemporaries found their way into the collection in those years—often as gifts from the artist—but William Blodgett's purchase in 1871 of one hundred and seventy-four "Old Masters" had placed the emphasis on European art and there, by and large, it had remained.

The Hearn Fund, established in 1906 by the retail department store merchant George A. Hearn's gift of $125,000, which he increased to $250,000 five years later, stilled for a time the complaints of the New York artists. By then even J. P. Morgan had conceded that the Metropolitan should do more about American art, and the trustees, ingenuously enough, had published a list of American artists whose works were particularly desired. Hearn, a trustee since 1903, took full charge of the Hearn Fund and did most of the buying with it until his death in 1913. He bought rather well, acquiring a number of fine Winslow Homers, and he also made full use of the clause in his gift that enabled the museum to sell or trade paintings it had bought with the fund for what it considered better examples. Soon after Hearn's death, though, Robert de Forest and his fellow trustees managed to get the terms of the Hearn Fund reinterpreted. Hearn had said that the income should be used to buy paintings by "living" American artists. Rather cleverly, de Forest suggested that this could be construed to mean works by artists *living at the time of the gift* in 1906. With the concurrence of the trustee law committee, the terms of the fund were so construed for some time afterward—which meant that the Metropolitan purchased paintings by John Singer Sargent and other safely established members of the older generation, and ignored the younger artists.

A good many art critics and other rote thinkers of the day thoroughly approved of this policy. The "ash-can" realism of Robert Henri, John Sloan, Everett Shinn, and other young insurgents who made up the group known as "The Eight" seemed a deliberate affront to good taste, and the 1913 Armory Show had been altogether unforgivable. Hideous and unspeakable tendencies had been let loose upon the land—blue nudes and nudes that descended staircases, wild beasts and other Parisian monstrosities had invaded the genteel uplands of painting and sculpture, turning them (it was never explained quite how) into dangerous breeding grounds of Bolshevism and gross sexuality. How much better to ignore such tendencies, which would surely disappear soon enough in any case. The Metropolitan continued to buy the American paintings approved by the ultraconservative Society of American Artists, but it bought fewer and fewer of them, and the unspent income from the Hearn Fund—approximately $10,000 a year—accumulated steadily.

As the odious tendencies grew stronger and began to gain acceptance in some quarters, though, criticism of the Metropolitan's policy on American art began to build up again. "So far as one can judge from the Hearn collection, American art might have ceased in 1913," the New York architect Charles Downing Lay wrote in a 1927 letter to the *Herald Tribune*. Lay charged that a huge surplus had accumulated in the Hearn Fund. De

Forest, in his reply, conceded that there was a surplus of $90,000 in the fund, and promised that the situation would shortly improve. It did. A few months later, the Metropolitan spent the entire $90,000 on one picture—Sargent's *Portrait of the Wyndham Sisters.*

Ignored by the Metropolitan, the Society of American Artists, and the National Academy of Design, the younger artists banded together to put on their own exhibitions. One of their most active supporters was Gertrude Vanderbilt Whitney, the heiress who had spurned the uptown life of established wealth and social position in favor of the downtown life of art—in her case, sculpture. Gertrude Whitney moved to Greenwich Village in 1907, and her studio at 19 Macdougal Alley became a meeting place for The Eight and other liberal spirits. In 1914 she bought an old house at 8 West Eighth Street and turned it into the Whitney Studio Club, a place where nonacademic artists, who were denied entrance to the big official exhibitions, could show their work. During the First World War the club began holding annual members' exhibitions on the principle of "no prizes, no juries." The membership grew rapidly, from twenty or so to more than two hundred, and soon represented nearly every current in American art.

By the late twenties, Gertrude Whitney and her friend Juliana Force, who ran the club, felt that their battle was essentially won. A more open spirit governed the New York art world, dealers were selling more and more American pictures, and a few daring critics had conceded that American art did exist after all. Mrs. Whitney's policy of purchasing from the annual members' exhibitions had resulted in a permanent collection of about six hundred works—probably the largest collection of American art anywhere. Rather surprisingly, in view of all the recent criticism in vanguard circles of Hearn Fund buying, Gertrude Whitney decided in 1929 to give her collection to the Metropolitan. Juliana Force journeyed uptown to call upon Edward Robinson, who was still director then. She was prepared to offer not only the entire Whitney collection, but also an endowment sufficient to build a new wing to house it. She never got around to mentioning the endowment, however, because Robinson flatly refused to consider accepting the collection.

Angry and indignant, Juliana Force and Gertrude Whitney decided within the next few hours to establish their own museum. Thus the Metropolitan, which had been at least indirectly responsible for the founding of the Museum of Modern Art in 1929, became directly responsible for the establishment in 1930 of the Whitney Museum of American Art. The new museum opened to the public in 1931, in a series of remodeled buildings on West Eighth Street. The annual, open exhibitions continued, the collection grew larger and larger, and the Whitney became the focus for all new and nonacademic trends in American art. In time, even the haughty uptown Metropolitan was obliged to take notice of the Village upstart.

Bryson Burroughs looked kindly upon it. Burroughs was sometimes blamed, quite unfairly, for the Metropolitan's lack of enthusiasm for American art, but the fact of the matter was that he had to deal with it as a sort of sideline to the main business of acquiring European paintings—there being no separate curator or Department of American Art—and after Hearn died Burroughs got no help at all from the trustees. For a time he hoped that the Metropolitan would eventually get Chester Dale's large collection of French and American nineteenth and twentieth century art. He discussed the subject with Dale in the 1920s, and the former stockbroker gave him reason to think that his pictures might fill the modern gap in the same way that the Havemeyer Impressionists had filled an earlier one. The problem was that Dale wanted his pictures kept together as a unit, with no others included among them; it was the familiar condition that the trustees had accepted in the case of Benjamin Altman and would subsequently accept in the case of Jules Bache—both of whom collected Old Masters—but they would not accept it to accommodate Dale's moderns. The Metropolitan did make Dale a trustee in 1952. By then Dale was also a trustee of the Chicago Art Institute, the Philadelphia Museum, and the Museum of Modern Art, all of which had their hopes. The National Gallery went them one better by electing Dale its president in 1955, though, and the Dale Collection ended up in Washington, D.C.

Burroughs had done what he could for American art, which admittedly was not much. Harry B. Wehle, his longtime assistant who succeeded him as curator of paintings in 1934, had very little use for it. An elegant and courtly gentleman from Louisville, Kentucky, an accomplished ladies' man, and a fine scholar who wrote excellent catalogues of the museum's European paintings, Wehle preferred above all the art of the French eighteenth century; in the American field, he rather liked miniatures, particularly if they happened to represent good-looking New York girls.

Toward the end of the 1930s, increasingly strident protests by artists, critics, and dealers forced the Metropolitan trustees to reexamine their policy on American art. Stephen C. Clark, the director of the Singer Sewing Machine Company and a trustee of both the Museum of Modern Art and the Metropolitan, urged Herbert Winlock to adopt a more liberal policy toward purchases in this field. "It doesn't matter particularly if we acquire a certain number of mediocre or uninteresting, or more or less radical pictures," Clark wrote, "so long as their purchase can be justified on political grounds. They can hang on our walls for a while and then receive a decent burial in the cellar." The more liberal policy finally surfaced in 1937, when the trustees engaged a specialist in American art to advise on Hearn Fund purchases. The specialist was Lloyd Goodrich, a writer on modern art and a curator at the Whitney Museum.

Goodrich served for one year as adviser to the Metropolitan. He recommended a number of purchases and the trustees bought most of them— seventeen paintings in all, including works by Louis Eilshemius, Max Weber, Edward Hopper, Louis Bouché, and William Gropper. They were shown together in a special exhibition. Although purchases continued at a relatively high level in 1938 and 1939, so did the protests. The sculptor William Zorach, in a letter to *The Times*, castigated the museum's policy on American sculpture. From 1906 to 1931 purchases of American sculpture had been left entirely in the hands of Daniel Chester French, a trustee and an academic sculptor whose sympathies were limited to the work of his friends and pupils. Since French's death in 1931 no one had been buying sculpture. There was no special fund for it (the Hearn Fund was for paintings only), and no separate department—one of Zorach's complaints was that the Metropolitan relegated sculpture to the Decorative Arts Department. Another was that "certain trustees," according to Zorach, "object to a piece of museum sculpture's representing a figure of a woman weighing over 110 pounds."

"Why has the Hearn Fund been administered so miserably?" an editorial in *The Art Digest* demanded in 1939. "The roll of important American artists who are consistently refused admission to that once respected collection is as revealing of incompetent art judgement as the equally long roll of dreadful paintings by poor artists that are so gaily purchased every so often . . ." The sharpest attacks of all focused on the issue of abstract art, which seemed to claim more adherents every day but which still had not breached the Metropolitan's defenses. The abstract painter Stuart Davis charged in 1940 that the Metropolitan "suppresses modern and abstract art in its policies as effectively as would a totalitarian regime."

The Times' art critic Howard Devree joined the attack in 1940. Devree listed forty-six well-known American artists who were not represented in the Metropolitan (Hartley, Dove, Evergood, Feininger, Kuhn, Spencer, Stella, Sheeler, Macdonald Wright, etc.). He also suggested that the Metropolitan work out some sort of cooperative arrangement with the Whitney and perhaps also with the Museum of Modern Art, an arrangement similar to the one that had long existed between the Luxembourg and the Louvre in Paris, under which the works of leading artists passed, after their death, from the Luxembourg to the Louvre, which paid for them and thus provided the Luxembourg with funds to buy works by living artists.

Francis Taylor had been at the Metropolitan only a few weeks when the Devree article appeared. Somewhat to the surprise of those who knew his feelings on modern art, Taylor agreed with much of what Devree said. "I think the press has a very legitimate case against the Museum for the way the matter [of the Hearn Fund] has been handled in the past few years," Taylor wrote to Henry Kent (whose stated opinion on the matter was that "to buy the modern in haste is to repent at leisure"). Taylor told Roland Redmond, a trustee who was becoming more and more influential on the Metropolitan board, that the chronic surplus of unspent income in the Hearn Fund did not reflect a lack of purchasable paintings so much as it did "many years of bad management." Ivins agreed with him. In a 1940 report the curator of prints and counselor to the board argued cogently that a public museum should take the same attitude toward contemporary art that a public library took toward contemporary books, i.e., it should buy examples whether or not the trustees liked them, and it should be willing to take risks. The opportunity to do just that now arose.

When Gertrude Vanderbilt Whitney died in 1942, the Whitney Museum trustees were left in a state of concern about the future. Juliana Force, the director, was a brilliant and inspiring force in American art, but she operated somewhat extravagantly and did not like being confined by a budget. The Whitney, moreover, had again outgrown its Eighth Street quarters— the permanent collection now numbered approximately two thousand works of art. After some preliminary soundings, a meeting took place on November 11, 1942, between Francis Taylor and Frank L. Crocker, the Whitney's treasurer, at which they agreed tentatively to a relationship far more intimate than that between the Luxembourg and the Louvre. Taylor and Crocker proposed an outright merger under which the Whitney would move uptown to a new wing that would be built adjacent to the Metropolitan, and which would also include the Metropolitan's American paintings and sculpture. Some of the Whitney staff would also be absorbed, one Whitney trustee would go on the Metropolitan board, and the remaining Whitney trustees would serve as an advisory committee on American art. Although the wing would be known as the Whitney Museum of American Art, the Whitney collections would actually be turned over to the Metropolitan.

The tentative agreement was ratified by trustees of both museums early in 1943. The banns were posted, friends of both parties rejoiced, but a number of obstacles still delayed the happy union. No new construction could be started until after the war, for one thing. The Whitney trustees had agreed to pay for building the new wing—using for that purpose the entire $2,500,000 endowment left to them in Mrs. Whitney's will—but it was difficult to reach agreement on the design of the wing and almost impossible to estimate in advance what the postwar construction costs would be. Just at this moment, moreover, while Taylor and his board were deep in plans for their own postwar construction and rehabilitation (plans that had been drastically altered by the Whitney merger agreement), they received a stunningly unpleasant surprise. Robert Moses, the New York City Parks Commissioner, informed them that the Metropolitan itself would have to pay at least half the cost of any new construction after the war.

It had never occurred to the trustees that the city would not pay the basic construction costs. The city had always done so, the only exceptions being the American Wing which the de Forests had donated, and a small addition to it that was paid for partly by the city and partly by donations from the trustees. To be sure, there had not been any additions to the museum since the south extension on Fifth Avenue (Wing K), which had been authorized in 1914 and completed in 1926. The city had appropriated $300,000 in 1937 for converting the old Hall of Casts into an Arms and

Armor gallery, though, and the trustees had never doubted that the city would provide for their carefully thought-out postwar needs.

Robert Moses, one of the ablest public servants in the city's history but by no means a model of tact, took a certain satisfaction in setting them straight. Ever since becoming Commissioner of Parks in 1933, Moses had been rather a thorn in the trustees' side. As an ex-officio Metropolitan trustee he had insisted on being represented in meetings of the executive committee—something no other city official had ever requested. More recently, Moses had erupted with anger over the treatment shown to his friend Joseph Medill Patterson, publisher of *The Daily News*, whom he had recommended for one of two vacancies on the Metropolitan board of trustees. Patterson had written to the museum to ask what sort of duties and expenses would be expected of him, in the event that he were elected. He had received a rather cool reply from Lauder Greenway, Kent's successor as secretary, informing him that the museum could not give out such information. Patterson wrote back to say that in that case he would have to withdraw his name. Greenway replied that this would not be possible— once a nomination had been made, it could only be withdrawn by the person who made it. More amused than angry, Patterson thereupon notified the museum that in the unlikely event he was elected, he would decline to serve. To Moses, the whole ludicrous incident just proved that the Metropolitan trustees were antediluvian relics of another era. "The arrogance and conceit of those people were phenomenal," he recalled years later. "They really felt they were the lords of creation, and that nobody had the right even to question what they did." Moses exempted William Church Osborn from this denunciation, although even Osborn, he said, could be a bit pompous at times. When Osborn had run against Al Smith for the Democratic nomination for Governor of New York in 1918, Smith occasionally made fun of his more orotund pronouncements, and once referred to him as "William *Cathedral* Osborn." The quip got around, and Osborn never forgave him.

Moses had been instructed by Mayor La Guardia to consider all appropriations in the light of soaring postwar costs for all city departments. He not only felt justified in questioning what the Metropolitan trustees did, but he gave every indication that he richly enjoyed doing so. With customary bluntness he referred to the proposed new Whitney wing as "another wart" on the landscape of Central Park, and refused to approve the preliminary architectural plans. The Whitney trustees, meanwhile, had begun to feel that their original concept of a building that would reflect the Whitney's traditional warmth and informality was being overridden by the Metropolitan's penchant for grandeur. Many friends of the Whitney were urging that it remain where it was, perhaps as a downtown branch of the Metropolitan. The Metropolitan trustees, keenly aware by now of rising construction costs, worried that the Whitney's $2,500,000 endowment might not cover the costs of building and maintaining the wing. Each time the two boards seemed close to an agreement over the designs, some new snag arose and the building plans were again deferred.

Since 1942, however, Juliana Force had been serving as unofficial adviser on all Metropolitan purchases under the Hearn Fund. Her recommendations came mostly from the Whitney Annuals, and were generally accepted by the Metropolitan trustees. She had opposed the merger plan at first but had changed her mind, in part because she found that she and Taylor got on remarkably well. They were much alike in many ways—witty, outspoken, and strongly opinionated—and they did not try to minimize the difficulties of their relationship. One day when they were touring the Whitney Annual together, she asked how he thought the Metropolitan trustees would react to the pictures she had selected for them to buy. "I think they will puke," Taylor said. He backed her up without hesitation, though, and was no doubt delighted to be thus relieved of personal responsibility for modern American art.

Modern *American* art, however, was only part of the problem. The most distressing tendencies in American painting and sculpture—the abstractions and "distortions" that the Metropolitan trustees had sought most earnestly to ignore—reflected what appeared more and more to be the dominant trends of modern art in general. The trustees, heads of great corporations and leaders of men, were accustomed to being forthright and sure of their opinions; they could be reasonably forthright and sure about Italian paintings and Persian rugs and medieval enamels, but the strange forms and upsetting images of modern art made them very, very nervous.

In the museum's younger days the board had been more adventurous, accepting two Manets from Erwin Davis as early as 1889, buying Renoir's

Madame Charpentier and Her Children in 1907 and Cézanne's *La Colline des Pauvres* in 1913—though not without certain risks on the part of the curators. Prompted by the New York lawyer-collector John Quinn and by Louisine Havemeyer, Lizzie P. Bliss and several others, the museum had put on an exhibition of French Impressionist and Postimpressionist art in 1921—a show that drew down denunciations in several newspapers for its "degenerate" and "Bolshevik" inclusions, but which disappointed many others because it excluded all but the tamest examples. The trustees had been pleased to receive the Havemeyer Impressionists in 1928, but their sympathies for the moderns had not progressed much—if at all—since then. Quinn's frequent offers to lend his Postimpressionist pictures had all been rebuffed. Herbert Winlock used to say he was sorry he had ever left the field of Egyptology, where all the artists were dead. When offered the loan of a Picasso by the abstract painter George L. K. Morris, Harry Wehle looked pained and said, "If it's a pile of bones, the answer is no."

A minor soul-searching took place in 1934, when Alfred Barr of the Museum of Modern Art, in his catalogue of the Lizzie P. Bliss collection, noted that in the Metropolitan Museum there were "no works by Gauguin, Seurat, Signac, Toulouse-Lautrec, Henri Rousseau, Matisse, Derain, Picasso, Dunoyer de Segonzac, and Modigliani." Barr had erred in writing "works" when he meant "paintings"; he was promptly called to account by William Ivins, who pointed out that the Metropolitan owned one hundred and thirty-three prints and three drawings by the artists mentioned. But even Winlock was somewhat taken aback by Barr's statement. "As a matter of fact it was a great surprise to Mr. Blumenthal and myself to find that we actually had no paintings by these people," he wrote to Bryson Burroughs. "Do you not think it would be a good idea if we got some?"

It was during this same year of 1934, interestingly enough, that a joint committee was appointed by the Museum of Modern Art and the Metropolitan to consider "some form of relation" between them. Even then the idea was not a new one. In its original 1929 prospectus (written mostly by Alfred Barr), the Museum of Modern Art had announced that it "would in no way conflict with the Metropolitan Museum of Art, but would seek rather to establish a relationship to it like that of the Luxembourg to the Louvre." William Sloane Coffin, the Metropolitan's president then, had echoed the same notion at the opening of the Museum of Modern Art's new

building in 1931. "When the so-called 'wild' creatures of today are regarded as the conservative standards of tomorrow," Coffin had said, "is it
too much to hope that you will permit some of them to come to the Metropolitan Museum of Art, leaving space on your walls for the new creations
of the new day?" The joint committee of trustees that was formed in 1934
discussed several possible alternatives, including the suggestion by A. Con-
ger Goodyear, the Modern Museum's first president, that the Modern con-
fine itself to a contemporary span of fifty years, and that the Metropolitan
purchase from it works of art over fifty years old that the Modern had
owned for twenty years or more. Nothing concrete was decided, though,
and the joint committee eventually stopped meeting.

Soon after Francis Taylor took over at the Metropolitan, the overtures
began anew. In a 1941 letter to John Hay Whitney, the Modern Museum's
fourth president, Taylor expressed the hope "that these two institutions
may in the near future draw closer and closer to each other." The reply,
which came by return mail, was from Alfred Barr. "I want to tell you,"
Barr said, "how much I . . . look forward to realizing what we both want:
namely, to work out a sensible, intelligent, and friendly cooperation." Taylor had several conversations over the next few years with Barr and with
James Johnson Sweeney, who served for a time as director of the Modern
Museum, but again no decisions were forthcoming. Part of the problem this
time was Taylor, who had never made any secret of his hostility to a great
deal of modern art.

Taylor's attitude toward modern art, like everything else about Taylor,
was highly complicated. He did not dismiss or condemn it out of hand, as
some people accused him of doing. Taylor took modern art very seriously,
seeing in it a frightening reflection of the moral crisis that threatened all
humanity. While he could be unreservedly contemptuous of the nonsense
that was so often talked or written about contemporary painting and sculpture, and witheringly scornful of imitators who merely mimicked the forms
of Picasso and Matisse—"second-rate minds mouthing second-hand ideas,"
he called them—Taylor acknowledged the importance of the leading mod-
ernists. Picasso to him was a painter of "unearthly power," and "the towering genius of our day." He knew perfectly well that modern art was not
going to disappear conveniently if nice people refused to pay attention to
it, and for this reason he was genuinely interested in working out some

form of relationship with Alfred Barr and his colleagues. The Metropolitan had certain established standards. It bought works of art that its curators believed to have a permanent place in art history. It was *not* accustomed to buying experimentally, which was what one had to do when buying modern works. Why not, then, let the Museum of Modern Art and its talented staff do the experimenting, while the Metropolitan, applying its own standards, acquired from it those works that had best stood the test of time?

Taylor gradually swung a majority of the Metropolitan board to his view. He had the support of Osborn, the president, who owned some superb Postimpressionist pictures that would soon come to the museum, and also of Stephen C. Clark and Nelson A. Rockefeller, both of whom were also on the board of the Museum of Modern Art. Osborn retired in 1947, becoming honorary president. His successor was Roland L. Redmond, who strongly favored establishing a relationship with the younger museum and who also wished to formalize the semiofficial collaboration that had existed since 1943 with the Whitney. Redmond, a corporate lawyer, and Alfred Barr were the real architects of what came to be called the Three Museum Agreement. Signed by trustees of all three institutions in September 1947, it was to run for a term of five years, with every expectation that it would then be renewed and become permanent.

The document was a curious one. Legal form required definitions, and for the purposes of the agreement the term "modern art" was "deemed to include any painting, drawing, print or sculpture by a living artist and any such work by a deceased artist which is still significant in the contemporary movement in art." Classic art included "all other paintings, drawings, prints or sculpture which have become part of the cultural history of mankind." Both Redmond and Barr were perfectly aware that artists as long deceased as Poussin, Rembrandt, and even Phidias could still be considered "significant in the contemporary movement," but a legal document is a legal document, and everyone presumably knew what was meant by it. The significant points of the agreement, in any case, were more precise. Each museum recognized the others' primary interest in a certain area— the Metropolitan's in "classic art," the Museum of Modern Art's in European and American visual art of the present and recent past, the Whitney's in American art. In the interests of "rendering better service to the public and effecting economies," the Metropolitan would refrain from active buying of modern art. All three museums would lend freely to one another for exhibitions and for educational purposes. The coalition between the Whitney and the Metropolitan was confirmed. Furthermore, the Metropolitan agreed to "deposit with the Modern Museum such paintings, drawings, prints and sculpture . . . as it believes can be more appropriately exhibited at the Modern Museum," while the Modern Museum agreed to sell to the Metropolitan, for the sum of $191,000 payable in four annual installments, a total of forty works of art that both museums had decided would be better off there.

Some rather significant works of art changed hands as a result. Picasso's *Portrait of Gertrude Stein,* painted in 1906 and considered by Barr to be one of the greatest masterpieces of the twentieth century, came down to the Modern Museum, along with Maillol's large bronze *Chained Action.* The Picasso portrait was the sole picture mentioned specifically in Gertrude Stein's will; she considered it "the only reproduction of me which is always I, for me," and she had wanted it to go to the Metropolitan because she thought that there it would have a measure of immortality. (Miss Stein had once remarked, apropos the Museum of Modern Art, that one could either be a museum or be modern, but one could not be both.) Alice B. Toklas, her lifelong companion, was reportedly furious when she heard that the picture had gone to the Modern Museum. It came back to the Metropolitan when the Three Museum Agreement finally expired in 1952. The forty works of art the Modern had agreed to sell to the Metropolitan are still there, though, in some cases to Alfred Barr's intense regret. They include two Cézannes, three Matisse oils, two Rouaults, three Seurat drawings, five Maillol sculptures, and two very fine Picassos—*Woman in White,* and *La Coiffure.*

A *ménage à trois,* as the French never tire of informing us, is often stimulating but rarely peaceful. In no time at all the Three Museum Agreement began showing signs of strain. Barr was said to be resentful over the loss of the *Woman in White.* The Whitney Museum architects were squabbling with the Metropolitan architects over plans for the Whitney wing. The Metropolitan's rejection of several pictures recommended that year by Juliana Force led to her angry withdrawal in 1948 as their adviser on American art ("I am sure you will be able to find some expert whose point of view does agree with yours and your board's," she wrote to Taylor that February, just before she went into the hospital for a protracted stay). In the hope of resolving their various differences and clearing the air, Roland Redmond invited the key staff members of all three museums to dinner at the Brook Club, where in the most genteel surroundings the *ménage* rather noisily came apart.

The evening began pleasantly enough. Redmond, Taylor and Horace Jayne from the Metropolitan, Barr and James Thrall Soby from the Modern, Lloyd Goodrich and Herman More from the Whitney carried on a genial conversation until about ten in the evening, when Taylor launched into an attack on the purchasing policies of the Whitney. Taylor and Redmond had just returned from a trip around the country. They had visited a great many museums and galleries, had called on artists in their studios, and had come to the conclusion that the Whitney people did not know what was going on in American art. The Whitney (and by implication the Modern as well) had concentrated so much in recent years on abstract painting, they argued, that it had virtually ignored most of the other trends; the Whitney was forsaking its traditional policy and becoming a political force in art, encouraging the trends its curators liked and ignoring those they did not—a rather odd accusation by the director of the Metropolitan, which had been doing precisely the same thing for decades. Taylor said that everywhere he and Redmond went, they had been struck by the number of different tendencies at work in American painting and sculpture, and also by the number of artists who bitterly resented being left out of the Whitney Annuals.

A heated argument followed. Barr and Soby sided with Goodrich and More, and the two sides hammered away at each other until after two in the morning. Although they parted on fairly friendly terms, the evening proved to be a turning point. Goodrich and More decided as a result of it that there was no compelling reason to merge with an institution that was so hostile to their point of view. Juliana Force agreed—she was still in the hospital at the time, undergoing treatment for the cancer that would kill her a few months later. The Whitney trustees reached the same conclusion not long afterward. The advantages of the coalition, they decided, were not worth the loss of their museum's individual identity. They abandoned all plans to build on property adjoining the Metropolitan, and on September 30, 1948—just one year after the signing—the Whitney formally withdrew from the Three Museum Agreement.

What had thus shrunk to a two museum agreement between the Metropolitan and the Museum of Modern Art remained in effect until 1952. It was not helped along by Taylor, who could seldom resist honing his rhetorical knives on the subject of modern art. In a much-quoted article in the December 1948 *Atlantic*, Taylor wrote that "the contemporary artist has been reduced to the status of a flat-chested pelican, strutting upon the intellectual wastelands and beaches, content to take whatever nourishment he can from his own too meager breast." He charged that the new "Academy of the Left," in its zeal to secure total freedom for the artist, had merely "substituted the rubber girdle for the whalebone corset," and he expressed grave concern that the modernist critics, by refusing to apply to contemporary art the same rigorous standards that they applied to the arts of the past, were actually undermining artistic integrity and thus "debasing the one remaining currency of civilized man."

Taylor's gibes annoyed the trustees of the Modern Museum (which Taylor occasionally referred to as "that whorehouse on Fifty-third Street"), but what distressed them much more was the growing fear that they would lose out to the Metropolitan on future gifts and bequests. A trustees' revolt shook the Modern Museum in the early fifties. Some of the founders, who had gone all out for Postimpressionism in 1929, could not stomach the newer trends in art; they disliked many of the paintings that Barr and his staff were currently buying—paintings by Jackson Pollock, Mark Rothko, Franz Kline, and others of the generation that would be known as Abstract Expressionists. Personality conflicts led to resignations. Sam A. Lewisohn, a great collector in the Postimpressionist field, resigned from the Modern Museum board and became a Metropolitan trustee in 1950, and left the lion's share of his collection to the Metropolitan when he died the following year—it included Gauguin's *Ia Orana Maria*, Van Gogh's *L'Arlésienne*, and Seurat's oil sketch for *La Grande Jatte*. Stephen C. Clark, chairman of the Museum of Modern Art's board from 1939 to 1946 and an important collector in many areas including the Postimpressionist, transferred his primary allegiance back to the Metropolitan about the same time (he had resigned from the Metropolitan board in 1945 because Taylor, without

consulting him, had tried to hire a man on the Modern Museum's staff).
When Clark died in 1960 his collection was divided, half of it going to Yale
and the other half to the Metropolitan.

How many other potential Modern Museum benefactors, realizing that
their pictures might eventually go to the Metropolitan in any case, would
prefer to give them there directly? Had this thought perhaps influenced
Georgia O'Keeffe in 1949, when she gave to the Metropolitan the extremely
important collection of modern paintings, sculpture, and drawings assembled by her late husband, Alfred Stieglitz? (The Metropolitan had purchased and shown Stieglitz's photographs in the early days of the century,
and, thanks largely to William Ivins and A. Hyatt Mayor, Ivins' successor
as curator of Prints, both Stieglitz and O'Keeffe had remained friendly to
the Metropolitan ever since.) In the spring of 1952, at any rate, the Museum of Modern Art trustees notified Roland Redmond that they did not
wish to renew the agreement. After reviewing the past five years of their
collaboration, they said, "it did not seem to us that there were any real advantages in its continuation to either institution or to the community."

Today, most of those who were involved agree that matters probably
turned out for the best. All three museums began competing actively in the
field of modern art, with salutary results for American artists. The Whitney
eventually built its new quarters on land donated by and adjoining the
Museum of Modern Art, where it remained until it moved again in 1966
into Marcel Breuer's spectacular ziggurat on Madison Avenue at Seventy-
fifth Street. The Modern Museum has expanded in many directions, and so
has the Metropolitan. It is possible that the greater efficiency of coalition
might have resulted in less variety for the public.

Both Taylor and Redmond were keenly disappointed over the Whitney
breakup. Instead of sulking in their tent, however, they established a Department of American Art at the Metropolitan and hired Robert Beverley
Hale to run it. Hale, a teacher at the Art Students' League, knew a great
many artists and understood and sympathized with what they were doing.
Taylor gave him a free hand. After a fact-finding tour around the country,
Hale came to the conclusion that the most useful service the Metropolitan
could render would be to sponsor a series of open, competitive exhibitions
of American art, chosen by juries of American artists.

"American Painting Today," the first of these big shows, took place at the Metropolitan in 1950. Four regional juries made their selections from nine thousand entries, and more than three hundred works were shown. Although twenty-eight New York painters and sculptors boycotted the exhibition, charging that the juries were too conservative, *The Art Digest* hailed it as a "triumph of abstraction." As Hale wrote in the *Bulletin,* it proved that "the vast majority of our artists had ceased to be conservative," and that American art was no longer regional or even national. "What has happened, of course," Hale wrote, "is that the United States, like the rest of the world outside the Iron Curtain, has succumbed to the aesthetic revolution largely promoted in Paris at the turn of the century." The Metropolitan's subsequent jury shows—one of sculpture in 1951–1952 and one of prints and drawings in 1954—confirmed the trend, to such an extent that the diehard National Sculpture Society accused the museum of fostering "Communist art," and Congressman George A. Dondero (R.-Mich.), speaking in the House of Representatives in March 1952, included the Metropolitan among the more insidious disseminators of Communist propaganda.

The Metropolitan had established its Department of American Art at the precise moment when a group of New York artists, for the first time in history, were forging a native style that would have a wide international influence. Abstract Expressionism, as the new style came to be called, did not succeed at the museum without a struggle. Robert Hale saw it as the strongest emerging tendency in American art, but when he submitted examples to the purchasing committee there would be gales of laughter and gasps of disbelief. After a few fairly catastrophic sessions, Taylor and Hale decided that they could get nowhere with the full committee. Taylor's solution was to set up a three-man trustee advisory committee on American Art, which would be authorized to make purchases with income from the Hearn Fund. This was approved by the board in 1949. The first advisory committee consisted of Elihu Root, Jr. (who like his father before him served for many years as vice-president of the museum), Sam Lewisohn, the only trustee who was at all enthusiastic about Abstract Expressionism, and Walter C. Baker, a discerning collector of antiquities and drawings. They resolved at the outset not to buy on the basis of their individual likes and dislikes. According to Root, "if a large segment of the community interested in 'Art' esteemed the works of an artist, and desired to see them . . . [the committee] would buy and exhibit them."

Elihu Root, Jr.,—known to his friends as "Sec" Root, ever since the days when his father served as Secretary of State—was a kindly man whose hobby was painting. He took private lessons, and turned out competent landscapes and still lifes until his interest shifted in later years to female nudes (larger and larger, increasingly explicit nudes, some wearing high-heeled slippers or carrying a cocktail glass, all rather embarrassing for the family). Root liked Hale and did his best to help him, but whenever Hale brought in another abstract canvas he would cover his eyes with his hand and say, his shoulders quivering, "I can't look, Bob. If you think the museum should have it I'll go along, but I just can't look."

Gradually, over the years, Hale nevertheless came to feel that he was making progress. In 1952 he persuaded the trustees to exhibit the superb modern collection of Edward Wales Root, Elihu's brother, who taught a famous course in art appreciation at Hamilton College and who would leave his collection to the Munson-Williams-Proctor Institute in Utica. The following year the trustees actually commissioned a piece of modern sculpture—Richard Lippold's dazzling network of gold wire entitled *Variations Within a Sphere, No. 10: The Sun.* Hale bought a small Jackson Pollock out of his meager curator's fund, survived the trustees' astonishment and anger, and later traded it in as part payment on Pollock's great *Autumn Rhythm,* which the museum bought in 1959 after Hale had telephoned every trustee to plead for funds. By this time, however, a number of people had come around to thinking that Pollock and Willem de Kooning and Franz Kline might be something more than flat-chested pelicans.

No one can deny that modern art—both American and foreign—has received considerable attention at the Metropolitan in recent years. The museum established in 1967 a Department of Contemporary Art, headed by the most swinging of contemporary curators, Henry Geldzahler, and the museum's current director, who is accused of many things, cannot be accused of ignoring contemporary trends. The confusion and controversy of the present, in fact, makes some trustees nostalgic for the dear old days when Abstract Expressionism was just a dark, dripping cloud on the horizon, and when Bob Hale could be counted on to do the right thing, whatever it was.

Soon after the 1950 "American Painting Today" show at the Metropolitan, a group of artists decided to write an open letter to Roland Redmond to say what a fine job they thought Hale had done. Their leader telephoned Hale, explained what they had in mind, and then said that as none of them had much facility for phrasing things, would he mind drafting the letter himself? Hale obliged them. A few days later, Hale had a call from Taylor. The museum had received an awfully nice letter from a group of artists, Taylor said, and it deserved a reply. Since Hale knew the situation so well, would he mind drafting it? Hale drafted a reply to his own letter, Redmond redrafted and signed it, and everyone felt fine.

TWENTY-THREE

Not since the museum's fiftieth birthday in 1920 had there been such festivity at the Metropolitan. After four years of dust and disruption, the museum was getting ready in January 1954 to open ninety-five completely renovated galleries and six new period rooms. The three oldest wings of the building had been rebuilt from basement to roof, and provided at last with proper ventilation and alternating instead of direct current. New galleries connected the Morgan Wing with the north extension on Fifth Avenue; the old and inadequate lecture hall had given way to the Grace Rainey Rogers Auditorium, a modern theater seating seven hundred and fifty persons; a major reconstruction of the south Fifth Avenue wing had yielded new administration offices, new Greek and Roman galleries, a new Junior Museum, and a large public restaurant. The celebrations planned for the reopening of the picture galleries were to be preceded by the first meeting ever held in this country of the International Council of Museums, which would bring to the Metropolitan the leading art scholars and museum directors from a score of countries. Francis Taylor referred to the whole galaxy of events as the "balloon ascension"—the hopes of all friends of the Metropolitan being borne aloft to airy regions as yet uncharted.

All this had cost the museum a great deal of money. Bowing to Robert Moses, the trustees had accepted a new formula for municipal partnership under which New York City would pay no more than half the costs of construction and rehabilitation of the museum buildings, and none of the costs of installation. Moses had also stipulated that not more than $1,000,000 of the city's share would be included in the capital budget for any single year, which meant that the museum was forced to divide its long-range reconstruction program into several stages and undertake them one at a time. Stage One—the renovations completed in 1954—cost $9,600,000 in all, of which the city paid less than one third.

The museum had hoped to make up the balance out of special funds raised for this purpose by the seventy-fifth anniversary campaign. Thomas J. Watson, the campaign chairman, helped matters along by his own timely gift of IBM stock worth $49,000 (as a result of this and other Watson gifts, which came to more than $1,000,000, the reconstructed museum library now bears his name). Even so, the fund-raising campaign was a spectacular failure, achieving less than one fifth of its goal; the trustees were obliged to go into endowment funds for the rest. Thanks to astute postwar reinvestment of these funds by Roland Redmond, the president, and Devereux C. Josephs, the head of the trustees' finance committee—plus a million-dollar bequest in 1948 from Morgan's partner Thomas M. Lamont—they would be able to restore the endowment cuts within the next few years, while doubling and eventually tripling the market value of the museum's investments. Under the circumstances it was hard to feel too bitterly toward Robert Moses. The trustees had even gone along with Moses' repeated suggestions that they elect a woman trustee by electing *three* in 1952— Mrs. Ogden Reid, Mrs. Sheldon Whitehouse, and Mrs. Vincent Astor. Moses thought these choices showed a rather heavy reliance on the Social Register, but he had nothing but praise for the election two years later of Dorothy Shaver, the president of Lord and Taylor, whose energy and drive had helped to bring the Costume Institute to the Metropolitan.

The vast sums being spent on rehabilitation and modernization had not interfered with the more thrilling business of acquisition. Taylor and Redmond pushed through a constitutional amendment in 1947 that made it possible to move much more quickly on major purchases, and despite widening competition the museum became more and more dominant in the international art market, acquiring such treasures as Caravaggio's *The Musicians* (the first Caravaggio to enter the collection); Velazquez's stunning equestrian portrait of *Don Gaspar de Guzmán, Count Duke of Olivares; The Tribute Horse,* an early Sung landscape on silk that is one of the great masterpieces of Chinese painting; the lovely marble *Aphrodite* of the Medici type, a Hellenistic copy of a lost original but so marvelous a copy that its unveiling was featured on the front page of *The New York Times;* the silver

and parcel-gilt Antioch Chalice that Francis Taylor had once exhibited at
Worcester; and a very large and important group of medieval, ancient
Near Eastern, and classical works of art from the estate of the dealer Joseph
Brummer. The museum also took title in 1949 to sixty-three Old Masters from
the collection of Jules Bache, a wealthy stockbroker who had acquired
nearly all of them in six years of spectacular buying from Duveen and other
dealers. Bache was one of Duveen's most satisfactory clients—his purchases
from Duveen alone totaled more than $6,000,000. The pictures had been on
loan to the Metropolitan since 1943, and Bache wanted them to stay there,
but he also wanted them to be kept permanently together in "contiguous
galleries" bearing his name. It was the familiar dilemma. In 1936 the trustees
had been unwilling to accept the restriction, but when Bache died in 1944
they decided they had "no right" not to, inasmuch as the collection
included such supernovae as Rembrandt's *The Standard-Bearer,* Titian's
Venus and Adonis, Velazquez's portrait of *The Infanta Maria Theresa,*
Crivelli's *Madonna and Child,* Fragonard's *Le Billet Doux* (a portrait of the
artist François Boucher's daughter just before her marriage to M. de Caval-
lier, whose name is written on the note she holds in her hand), Watteau's
The French Comedians, which was once owned by Voltaire, and Goya's
portrait of *Don Manuel Osorio de Zuñiga,* a four-year-old boy in red
trousers, holding a pet magpie that is being watched intensely by two cats
in the background—judging from the sale of postcard reproductions of this
picture in the museum bookstore, it is the Metropolitan's most popular
painting. One year after the Bache gift, the trustees gathered in the incredibly rich harvest of the Edward and Mary Stillman Harkness bequest, the
culmination of Harkness gifts going back to 1912 and benefiting nearly
every department of the museum.

There were still a few gaps and thin spots in the collections. The Paintings Department had never managed to develop much strength in Italian
painting of the fourteenth and fifteenth centuries, although Maitland F.
Griggs's bequest in 1943 of thirteen rare and beautiful Italian primitives,
including Sassetta's magical little *Journey of the Magi,* had greatly improved its showing of the early Renaissance. The museum had lost the
modern era's most lavish collector of Italian paintings, Samuel H. Kress, to
the National Gallery in Washington, D.C. Ironically, Kress offered his
collection to the Metropolitan in the 1920s, when it consisted mostly of me-

diocre French Salon pictures, and was turned down cold. After that he
sought advice from Duveen and Agnew and bought Italian masters in
great quantity, but by the time the Metropolitan got around to making him
a trustee in 1936 it was too late—although Kress eventually gave the Metropolitan nine paintings, he had made up his mind to outshine Andrew
Mellon's benefactions to the National Gallery, which he nearly did with his
huge gift to it in 1939. The Metropolitan also lacked strength in German
paintings and in French paintings of the sixteenth, seventeenth, and eighteenth centuries, and it badly needed examples of European Renaissance
and post-Renaissance sculpture. The museum's curious habit of treating
sculpture as one of the decorative arts may have had something to do with
its relatively poor showing here, but it was also true that there had been a
number of harrowing near-misses in this field.

Back in 1937, before Taylor's time, Winlock had negotiated for a marble
Pietà attributed to Michelangelo (the ˙so-called *Palestrina Pietà*), until
Mussolini's government found out who the prospective buyer was and abruptly raised the price to $2,000,000. Negotiations collapsed, and Il Duce
eventually gave the statue to the Accademia Museum in Florence. In 1945,
the Metropolitan came agonizingly close to getting another and finer version of the same subject by Michelangelo. Myron C. Taylor, the Metropolitan trustee who was then in Rome as President Franklin D. Roosevelt's
personal envoy to the Vatican, learned that the Italian authorities might be
willing to issue an export permit for the *Rondanini Pietà*, which was being
offered for sale by its private owner. This was tremendously exciting news.
The unfinished *Rondanini Pietà* was Michelangelo's last work, the sculpture he had been working on when he died. Of the four versions of the
subject that he had carved in his long lifetime, this was the most spiritual;
compared to the striking realism of the Vatican *Pietà*, which he had done
when he was twenty-three, this last sculptural testament was nearly abstract, the figures so attenuated that the marble itself seemed transformed
into sheer, transcendent grief. All the Metropolitan's curators were asked to
give their opinions about it, and all of them strongly urged its purchase,
even if this meant giving up their own curatorial funds for years to come.

The negotiations were secret and extremely delicate. Myron Taylor had
been authorized to go as high as $500,000 for the sculpture. Payment was
to be made in New York, and if the necessary export permit did not come

through as promised within fifteen days the funds would then be blocked. Roberto Vimercati Sanseverino, the owner, held out for $550,000, and after much deliberation the trustees agreed to his figure. Everything appeared to be settled. A U.S. Navy cruiser stood by to carry the prize to New York. And then, at the last moment, Italian family troubles and Italian politics intervened. One of Sanseverino's brothers brought suit against him, charging that the statue, in which the entire family evidently had a stake, was being sold for less than its value. Two Communist deputies in the Italian Senate got wind of the suit, sniffed out the purchaser, and raised a loud hue and cry. As it happened, the new government of Premier Alcide de Gasperi had just come to power with a very narrow majority, threatened on the left by the strongest Communist party in Europe. De Gasperi was well aware of the storm that would break upon him if Michelangelo's last work went to America. He decided not to risk it. The Metropolitan was regretfully informed that "an insuperable obstacle" had arisen, negotiations ceased, and the *Rondanini Pietà* was subsequently sold, for the sum of $200,000, to the city of Milan.

Another heavy disappointment, five years later, involved the Giovanni Bologna sculptural group of *Samson Slaying the Philistine*—the same piece whose distinguished provenance had caused old George Blumenthal to side against it in 1939 because too many people had wanted to give it away. In spite of Blumenthal's adverse opinion on that occasion the trustees had agreed to buy the sculpture, but the outbreak of the Second World War had put an end to the negotiations. It was offered for sale again in 1949, and Taylor went over to England to see it. While there he talked with Leigh Ashton, the director of the Victoria and Albert, from whom he secured what he thought was a tacit understanding that if the Metropolitan refrained from bidding on a Bernini sculpture that had also come up for sale, then the Victoria and Albert would not oppose the sale of the Bologna to the Metropolitan. Evidently there was some misunderstanding, for the Victoria and Albert, once it had bought the Bernini, did oppose the sale of the Bologna, and then proceeded to buy the Bologna as well when the British government refused to give it an export permit. As a result of this contretemps, Taylor persuaded the directors of several U.S. museums to join him in formally protesting current British policies on national art treasures.

There were a number of important misses in Taylor's time. The Metropolitan did not bid on the Leonardo da Vinci from the Liechtenstein collection, the portrait of *Ginevra de' Benci* that is now in the National Gallery in Washington, D.C., because the price was too high—$5,000,000 —and because Theodore Rousseau, the paintings curator, although convinced that it was indeed by Leonardo, argued cogently that it was not in the same class with such later works of that master as the *Mona Lisa* or the *Lady With an Ermine* in Cracow. Taylor declined to press for a superb Toulouse-Lautrec café scene that is now in the Chester Dale collection in the National Gallery, nor did he argue strenuously for Rubens' magnificent *Marriage of Saint Catherine* that is now one of the treasures of the Toledo Museum, or for a Renoir *Girl With a Griffon* that a few Metropolitan trustees considered not only too expensive but also too voluptuously nude. His interest in the decorative arts had always been somewhat limited ("You and I are not the sort to *genuflect* before a highboy," he once told Lydia Powel), and his popularity with the Medieval Department suffered a catastrophic decline when he botched the purchase of the Rothschild *Cameo*. One of the greatest pieces of early Christian art to come on the market in this century, the *Cameo* was offered by Elie de Rothschild in 1952 for $100,000. The trustees authorized the purchase at that price, but Taylor, on a whim, offered only $75,000 and so offended the owner—one does not bargain with a Rothschild—that he decided to keep it instead. Taylor used to delight society people by telling them that he "hated art," and over the years one or two curators came to believe that he meant it.

On the whole, though, the misses faded into insignificance before the newly restored splendors of the collections. Not even the National Gallery, with all its rooms filled by Mellon and Kress, could overshadow the Metropolitan's encyclopedic range or the quality of its masterpieces. The Metropolitan, moreover, was proving to be even more national in scope than the National Gallery. It attracted nearly two million visitors in 1954 (well over two million, counting The Cloisters' attendance), as compared to the National's three quarters of a million. The Junior Museum was breaking new ground in museum education and work with school groups. Membership was rising steadily, and operating funds were getting a pleasant boost from the "Metropolitan Miniatures," a fund-raising idea thought up by Horace Jayne, which involved mail-order sales of small color facsimiles of works of art in the museum; the "Miniatures" were so popular that the museum could not handle the orders, and Taylor turned the job over to the Book-of-the-Month Club which sold more than eight million sheets of tiny reproductions between 1948 and 1958, when the program gave way to the equally popular "Metropolitan Seminars" booklets on art appreciation.

The mass public had discovered the Metropolitan, and vice versa. A revolution in popular culture was taking place, and Francis Taylor, the architect and exemplar of the new dynamic spirit animating the nation's greatest museum, was its undisputed leader. One could almost envisage him as the central figure in a baroque canvas by Tiepolo, aloft in a cloud-borne chariot, pulled by winged steeds representing the curatorial departments, with flights of cherubs holding his various honors and symbols—Taylor on the cover of *Time* in 1952; Taylor's own book *The Taste of Angels,* the first volume of a projected two-volume history of art collecting; scrolls and awards from learned societies and foreign governments; gourmet dinners and bottles of Richebourg—while a trio of airborne muses placed on his ample brow the gilded laurels of museology.

To most of the foreign savants and museum men who came in 1954 to the International Council of Museums meeting at the Metropolitan, Taylor appeared to be in his element. He welcomed them all with habitual gusto, told jokes and spouted witticisms in several languages, and at the climactic dinner in the museum's new public restaurant accepted with good grace the many unkind remarks about its purple and red decor that had been created, as the decorators liked to say, by the high-powered New York interior designer Dorothy Draper—Taylor had already started calling it the "Dorotheum." Only one or two of those present on that occasion could have predicted that he would leave the Metropolitan before the year's end.

He had spoken vaguely of resigning from time to time. After fourteen years as director he was "fed up," as he said, with many aspects of the job. He was sick of dealing with plumbing contractors and heating engineers and bureaucrats of the Board of Estimate. He was tired of coping with a staff of more than five hundred people spread out over seventeen and a half acres of floor space. He was also getting rather fed up with some of the trustees.

The Metropolitan's board of trustees was still the most exclusive club in

New York, populated at that time by such august figures as Henry Luce, Nelson Rockefeller, and Dwight David Eisenhower, the new president of Columbia University. Taylor approached them with a minimum of awe. When Eisenhower ran against Adlai Stevenson for the presidency in 1948, Taylor listened to their respective campaign speeches on the radio; the contrasting styles, he said, showed "the difference between a college president and an educated man." One day in the museum, a young staff lecturer, notebook in hand, was extolling to a group of visitors the marvels of Bruegel's *Harvesters* when she saw the director bearing down on her. With him was Robert Lehman, the museum's vice-president and the owner of the finest private art collection in America. Both men were red in the face and obviously angry. As they passed by the little group of art appreciators, Taylor suddenly stopped, seized the lecturer's notebook and pencil, scribbled something, then thrust it back at her and strode on. Glancing down at her pad, the shaken young woman saw that he had written "DAMN!" in large and furious capitals.

Dealing with the curatorial staff also presented frustrations. The war and the life expectancy tables had worked in Taylor's favor here, and he had been able to replace a number of old guard obstructionists with younger men of his own choosing like Rousseau, Winternitz (now curator of the Department of Musical Instruments), and Robert Hale. There were still some entrenched positions, however, and a good deal of continuing resistance to Taylor's efforts to modernize display techniques, enliven the exhibits, and generally to bring order out of chaos.

Horace Jayne resigned as vice-director in 1949, in part because of his inability to win from the curators the cooperation he needed in order to be effective. Taylor's choice to succeed him was Preston Remington, the curator of Renaissance and Modern Art, a man ideally unsuited to the job. Remington was a curator of the old school. He had studied architectural drawing at Harvard, and should really have been an interior designer; his installations were planned with matchless elegance and precision, and his predilection for "virile gray" backgrounds was legendary. The museum's painters and maintenance men used to have great sport with Remington's instructions, fondly discussing the relative merits of mouse-belly gray, elephant-breath gray, and other fine distinctions. A bachelor who dressed invariably in a well-cut dark suit, a narrow black silk tie and a starched col-

lar, Remington moved in the highest social circles and was responsible for
several important gifts to the museum, the most important being the Cath-
erine Wentworth bequest, in 1948, of antique French silver and an up-to-
the-minute legacy of $4,500,000. He took pains at all times to conceal his
hard work, preferring to appear as a gifted amateur, but the truth was that
he ran his large department with great efficiency and was highly respected
by his colleagues for his knowledge and his eye, and for these reasons he
seemed to Taylor eminently qualified for the job of vice-director. Unfortunately, Remington had a terrible time making the most minor decisions.
Dozens of questions crossed the vice-director's desk every day—questions
involving vacations, salaries, work schedules, and the like. Taylor did not
want to be bothered by these, and when Remington came to him for guidance he often received a tongue-lashing instead. Under this treatment, his
efficiency rapidly declined.

Many curators were frankly afraid of Taylor. They feared his biting wit,
his sudden rages, his unpredictableness. Taylor was much too subtle to engage in the usual management practice of playing one person off against
another. "He played you off against yourself," a curator once observed. "He
was wonderfully good to you if you were in trouble, lent you money out of
his own pocket and things like that, but if you were doing well he had to
cut you down periodically, undermine your confidence. And yet he was so
fascinating, so charming and amusing, that you never remembered the
need for caution in dealing with him, and you always forgave him afterward." Dietrich von Bothmer, a young classical scholar who had fled Nazi
Germany, fought in the American Army in the Pacific during the war, and
come to work at the Metropolitan afterward as assistant to Christine Alexander, Gisela Richter's successor in the Greek and Roman Department, felt
that Taylor harbored a basic contempt for scholarship and for scholarly curators. Taylor used to make a point of referring to von Bothmer's beloved
black-figured amphorae as *"vases de nuit"* (i.e., chamberpots). He also used
to complain, when advised of curatorial discontent, that everything got to
him via the "sour grapevine."

The Greek and Roman Department never forgave Taylor for allowing a
restaurant (the "Dorotheum") to obliterate their Roman sculpture court at
the south end of the building. Several other department heads resented
him for making them sell large quantities of surplus material. Taylor be-

lieved firmly that if an object was not on exhibition, on loan, or in active use by scholars the museum should get rid of it. In 1953 the trustees ordered a major housecleaning by all departments—the first since 1929—to dispose of such surplus material; some fifteen thousand objects were eventually sold at auction (the sales did not actually take place until 1956, two years after Taylor's resignation), including an Egyptian tomb chamber to the Boston Museum of Fine Arts and another, even finer one to the Brooklyn Museum, both of which the present curator deeply regrets. The Egyptian curator at that time was William C. Hayes, a magnificent scholar who shared with Taylor an oddly nonacquisitive streak. He agreed that his department had far too much material, and cooperated enthusiastically in selling off duplicates and other secondary items, but his attitude was somewhat unusual.

Curators who fought with Taylor and stood up to his verbal batterings usually won their points and his respect. Soon after the end of the war Taylor wanted Charles Wilkinson, the curator mainly responsible for the museum's archaeological excavations in the Near East, to go over to Egypt and close down the remaining operations there. Wilkinson thought it was too much of a job for one man and said so. He insisted that another curator in the Egyptian department go with him. Taylor grew angrier and angrier. At length he banged his fist on the table and shouted, "You know damn well that if *he* goes you'll just come back with another ton of archaeological study material."

"Francis, you go up to your paintings galleries," Wilkinson shot back, "and tell me whether nine tenths of what you see there isn't archaeological study material."

Taylor looked absolutely stunned. "By God, Charles, you're right," he said a moment later, and roared with laughter. As Wilkinson remarked afterward, it was hard to dislike a man who did that.

Taylor was deeply hurt when the museum's guards went out on strike in October 1953. It was the first labor dispute in the museum's history, and Taylor took it as a personal affront. He moved into the building and lived there for the two weeks that the strike lasted, during which the museum remained closed to the public. Looking gloomily out his office window one day, Taylor and Winternitz noticed that the men in the picket line outside were shivering. Forgetting his rancor, Taylor telephoned the museum restaurant and ordered coffee and hot buns served to the strikers—a gesture that may have had its influence on their coming to terms shortly thereafter.

In the end, though, the administrative burdens of the job probably counted less than personal considerations in Taylor's decision to quit. Taylor was tired of running the Metropolitan. He had worked extremely hard for fifteen years, his health had always been uncertain, and he did not want, as he once confided to Margaret Freeman of the Medieval Department, "to go out of here like poor Winlock, on a stretcher." The financial strain he had been under for many years was starting to ease a little, as his older children finished school and college, and Taylor longed for time to travel and to write—he had hundreds of notes for a second volume of his history of art collecting.

He had also begun to have doubts about the ultimate value of his work at the Metropolitan. Without question the museum had been transformed, had become truly public for the first time in its history, but what did the public actually draw from it? Every time he saw people meandering indiscriminately through the galleries, Taylor felt discouraged. "How lucky you are, having nothing on your walls that isn't worth looking at," he once told Harry Grier, a former Metropolitan staff member who had left to work in the Frick Collection (he is now its director). "Dammit, we've got them into the museum, but what do they look at?" Taylor said. "One thing after another—if they come to a fire hose they look at that, too." Museums should be able to instill a sense of quality, Taylor thought, and they should work constantly to narrow the breach that divides the artist from the public, and he was not at all sure that the Metropolitan, for all its booming attendance and glittering endowment, was doing those things as well as the Worcester Museum had done them when he was director there. It was just at this point that the Worcester Museum, whose director was leaving, made Taylor an immensely tempting offer.

When asked by a friend why, after leaving the Metropolitan, he had chosen to go back to the job he had held before, Taylor quipped that he was "too old to make new enemies." Actually, the Worcester offer coincided almost perfectly with Taylor's needs and desires. He would be allowed to spend a good part of each year traveling and writing. The staff and most of the trustees he had worked so well with were still there, so that there would be little or no administrative friction. The operating and purchase funds, while not spectacular, were better than adequate. After hesitating for several weeks, Taylor made up his mind in December 1954 to go back to Worcester.

The year that had begun so gloriously at the Metropolitan thus ended on a note of shock and sadness. Taylor called the curators into his office one by one, and told them individually of his decision. Later in the day he addressed a meeting of the whole staff in the auditorium. The guards, the maintenance men, the bookstore clerks, and all the others whose names Taylor always knew and whose families he often inquired after, could hardly believe it—any more than they could comprehend the news, a scant three years later, that Taylor had died suddenly in the Worcester hospital, at the age of fifty-four, after a minor operation from which he had seemed to be recovering normally. On the day Taylor died in 1957, one of the older Metropolitan guards stopped Lydia Powel in the main hall. "It isn't true," he said, the tears pouring down his cheeks. "It isn't true."

And yet, when it came to choosing a new director, the Metropolitan staff stressed almost unanimously that they did not want another Taylor. Their opinions were solicited by the committee of trustees formed to select candidates for the job, and nearly all of them gave the impression that they would welcome a quieter regime, an administration that was less given to large ideas and large projects and more concerned with the details of orderly housekeeping.

In the interregnum after Taylor's resignation, the trustees picked two curators to share administrative responsibility on a temporary basis. William C. Hayes of the Egyptian Department was put in charge of curatorial matters. He had no interest in becoming director and was never seriously considered for the post. The curator placed in charge of the building and the operational side of administration was James J. Rorimer. There was never the slightest doubt that Rorimer wanted to be director of the Metropolitan, and from the beginning he was high up on the trustees' list of candidates. During the six months of the committee's search, which covered more than a hundred possible nominees and several countries, Rorimer quietly made himself indispensable. He had studied the job as carefully and as thoroughly as he had once studied John D. Rockefeller, Jr., and when the time came there was really no choice at all.

TWENTY-FOUR

Francis Taylor and James Rorimer were both medievalists and they both liked to cook. Aside from that they had little in common, personally or professionally.

Trained and encouraged by his father, Rorimer had grown up with a craftsman's eye for materials and workmanship and a connoisseur's eye for quality. His contact with works of art was intense and immediate—when Rorimer examined an object, a fellow curator once remarked, "one felt that he had exhausted its every possibility, that he possessed it completely." The ideas contained or suggested by art objects, on the other hand, held relatively little interest for him, and he rarely expressed any strong opinions, as Taylor used to do so readily, about the function of museums as social institutions. It was possible to imagine Taylor's career having taken any number of different courses—he might have been a college president, for example—but no one could picture Rorimer anywhere but the Metropolitan Museum. Except for his army service he had never worked anywhere else. Rorimer lived, breathed, and thought the museum, and no one ever relished so thoroughly the job of director, which he surrounded with an almost childlike aura of mystery and intrigue.

The position of vice-director was abolished soon after Rorimer took over, Rorimer having made it clear that he wanted no such division of responsibility. This was hard on Preston Remington, Taylor's unfortunate choice to succeed Horace Jayne in that post. Remington went back to his old department as a "research curator," a rather bitter title for one whose influence in the museum had once been considerable; he died three years later. Although Rorimer did consent to hire an operating administrator (Joseph V. Noble, the man who later dethroned the Greek *Bronze Horse*), he was utterly unable to delegate any real authority within the museum, and because his own decisions were sometimes painfully slow in coming and usually shrouded in secrecy there were times when a kind of inertia seemed to settle over the place. Sterling Callisen, who served as dean of education under both Taylor and Rorimer, summed up the difference by saying that working for Taylor had been like being on a roller coaster, very exciting and full of dramatic ups and downs, while with Rorimer it was more like the Tunnel of Love—you never quite knew what was going on, or whether you would come out with a kiss or a black eye.

Several of the curators had lobbied hard for Rorimer's appointment as director. He knew the museum through and through, having worked there ever since he graduated from Harvard in 1927, and he had proved his administrative abilities at The Cloisters. Some of his strongest supporters were not personally fond of Rorimer, though, and the traits that had long bothered his colleagues were not lessened or made more tolerable by his elevation. Rorimer remained painfully sensitive about his Jewish background. His father had changed their name from Rohrheimer to Rorimer; another branch of the family in Cleveland had not changed it, and some people felt that the repercussions of what became a long-standing family dispute had contributed greatly to James Rorimer's social insecurity, and to the kind of inherent suspiciousness that led him, for example, to file a group of congratulatory messages on his appointment as the director of the Metropolitan under the heading "Axes to Grind." He took pains to conceal his ancestry, and feared for years that it would prevent him from achieving his lifelong ambition to become the director. His fears were not entirely unfounded. When Rorimer's election was still pending, the Metropolitan's vice-president, Robert Lehman, had urged the socially impeccable curator of paintings, Theodore Rousseau, to do all he could for him with the other trustees, adding, "I can't say these things because I'm a Jew." Even after becoming director, Rorimer remained acutely sensitive to the whole question, and the year before he died he would warn Henry Geldzahler, then a young assistant curator of American Paintings, never to let on to the trustees that he was Jewish.

Like many people who are socially ill at ease, Rorimer had developed compensatory traits. He could be annoyingly pompous and absurdly egotistical. Invited by Paul Sachs to come back and give a talk to the students in Sachs's museum course at Harvard, soon after he had graduated and gone to work for the Metropolitan, Rorimer told such indiscreet tales of doddering curators and superior wisdom on his own part that Sachs felt compelled to remind the students afterward that nothing they had heard was to be repeated outside class. William Ivins, in a letter to Winlock soon after the opening of the new Cloisters in 1938, described Rorimer as "brown, fat, important, rolling Byronic eyes and lollygagging about himself and his future." Ivins, Winlock, and several others on the staff took pleasure in deflating Rorimer's pretensions as an art scholar. He was not a true scholar in the sense that Ivins was. Rorimer knew works of art visually and intuitively, with the deep understanding of the connoisseur, and his intuitions often turned out to be correct, but there were other times when they led him astray. He found a considerable body of evidence to support his theory that the Unicorn Tapestries, no documentary records for which have ever been found, were woven to celebrate the marriage of Anne of Brittany and Louis XII of France in 1499. He was enormously proud of this finding—so much so that he named his two children Anne and Louis —and he may still be proved correct in it someday. Few contemporary scholars accept this explanation or Rorimer's methods of reaching it, however, and recent studies at the Metropolitan have cast doubt on the Anne-Louis theory. In some ways Rorimer was pathetically easy to deflate. Ivins and Winlock could do it with a well-timed use of the nickname "Jimsy," which he hated, but Rorimer often laid himself open to subtler slants. One day in the director's lunchroom, soon after his return from war service, Rorimer was holding forth on various subjects including the museum course at Harvard. He turned to Alan Priest, who had been a year ahead of him there, and said expansively, "Remember at Harvard, Alan, when you told me I shouldn't go into museum work?"

"I haven't changed my mind, James," Priest replied silkily.

The older curators resented Rorimer's habit, after he became director, of seeking out and befriending the younger men in their departments. He genuinely liked young people, and when he invited them to his home or to his office for a chat they invariably found him warm and sympathetic and endlessly informative.° Some of the department heads suspected, however, that this was Rorimer's little way of checking up on them. The older curators also resented it when Rorimer ended Taylor's practice of having them sit in on meetings of the purchasing committee. He explained this by saying he knew they would prefer to come in and speak their piece and then withdraw, thus sparing themselves the "embarrassment" of hearing the trustees argue; some curators did prefer it this way, but others assumed that Rorimer simply wanted to keep them in the dark as long as possible. They felt that power and influence was once again being concentrated in the board of trustees, and that their own professional standing was being subtly undermined as a result. A good many of them also believed that they could not depend on Rorimer's promises, and that they would receive little official recognition for the major achievements and acquisitions of their departments. Rorimer made all the important decisions, and he took most of the credit afterward. And in the long run, all this made surprisingly little difference. "James was the sort of man who pushed all his shortcomings out ahead of him like a big cowcatcher," a curator once remarked. Once you learned how to deal with the shortcomings you were free to appreciate his good points, which were very, very good indeed—superb taste, a genius for installation and display, and a total dedication to the museum.

The museum had never looked so well, inside and out, as it did under Rorimer. Each morning he would drive his Cadillac to work—a distance of three blocks or so—park in the parking lot behind the south wing, and walk slowly around the exterior of the building to see if anything needed painting or trimming or touching up. Then he went inside and did the same thing for the whole museum. Nothing escaped his eagle eye. If a pot of flowers had been moved he noticed, and if the flowers showed signs of wilting he noticed that, too, and gave orders to have them replaced. Dust on a display case or a label that had fallen over brought an immediate call to the curator in charge. Rorimer spent so much time out in the galleries that it was often difficult to get him on the telephone, and his feeling for the museum was fiercely possessive. Naive or careless visitors who touched

° It is significant that at least three of those in whom Rorimer took particular interest have become museum directors in their own right—Jack MacGregor at the DeYoung Museum in San Francisco, Richard Randall at the Walters Art Gallery in Baltimore, and Thomas P. F. Hoving at the Metropolitan.

the works of art were sometimes startled out of their wits by a thunderous
"Take your hands off that statue!"—from a medium-sized, dark-haired man
in a blue suit who turned out, if they dared to question his authority, to be
the director. At The Cloisters one day, he ordered a guard to remove two
teen-age boys from the room of the *Unicorn Tapestries,* then turned to the
reporter who was interviewing him and muttered, "They bring moths." As
between the public and the works of art, there was never any doubt where
Rorimer's primary allegiance lay.

"Putting the house in order" came to be Rorimer's trademark, but this
was far more than a matter of careful housekeeping. The museum had
grown so large that only an initiate could find his way about in it. Rorimer, far more successfully than Taylor, sought to guide the visitor and to
bring order out of chaos, and he did so not with signs and arrows but by
the placement of objects. The Greek column in front of the restaurant led
the visitor's eye toward Classical Antiquities, just as Queen Hatshepsut's
sphinx at the other end of the entrance hall led to Egypt and the Ancient
Near East. Over the years more and more galleries were transformed and
given new life. The throbbing, orange-red color he chose to paint the room
of Egyptian jewelry, the twelfth century stone doorway in the early medieval corridor to the left of the grand staircase, the seventeenth century
carved oak staircase by Grinling Gibbons with which he filled an awkward
small room in the Decorative Arts wing (with a fake door at the top to
make it look as though it went somewhere)—these were typical Rorimer
touches, with which he tried continually to evoke what he called "the character of an era." His conviction in matters of taste was so strong that he
did not hesitate to risk an occasional anachronism. The great seventeenth
century wrought-iron choir screen from the Cathedral of Valladolid, a gift
from the Hearst Foundation in 1956, is actually three centuries later than
most of the objects in the great medieval hall, but no one has ever quar-
relled with Rorimer's decision to install it there.

Nor could even his severest critics find much fault with Rorimer's installation of the Spanish Renaissance Patio of Velez Blanco, which had remained more or less forgotten in the basement, in two thousand numbered
blocks, since its removal twenty years before from George Blumenthal's
Park Avenue mansion. Taylor had tried at one time to get rid of the patio
by offering it to the government of a Latin-American republic. When the

trustees decided to go ahead with plans for a new library and service building, though, Rorimer saw to it that the plans included space for the Velez Blanco Patio, which became the central architectural element of the new addition in 1964. Construction was delayed for several weeks because Rorimer did not like the color of the bricks being used on the exterior of the library—he had the walls ripped down twice before the contractor came up with the correct tone.

Rorimer's involvement with the museum was exclusive and total. He sat on no other civic committees or boards of directors, took part in no extra-museum activities, and hardly ever left the building for lunch. He was in the museum all day Saturday and a good part of Sunday as well. He even met his wife in the museum—although Katherine Newton Serrell had left her job in the library and gone to work on the Index of Christian Art at Princeton by the time Rorimer got around to proposing to her in 1942. When the Rorimers entertained, they entertained people in the museum world, and when they went out to dinner the conversation had a way of getting around, sooner or later, to the Metropolitan Museum.

Rorimer was acutely attuned to all the activities that went on in that vast and labyrinthine colossus. Although his primary interest was in exhibition and display, he wanted to know what was going on at all times in each department, and somehow he managed to do so. No museum publication, not even a minor press release, could go out without his having read and approved it. Taylor had started the Department of Conservation when he brought Murray Pease from the Fogg Museum; Rorimer, who had been fascinated by chemistry since his childhood, worked closely with Pease and his successor, Kate C. Lefferts. He was ahead of most museum men in recognizing the value of X-ray and ultraviolet analysis as curatorial tools, although, as he once remarked, it was "madness" to depend so heavily on scientific analysis that you neglected the surer testimony of the experienced eye. "Get the collection in your eye," he would tell the younger curators— build up a visual memory so strong and so detailed that any new object can then be seen in relation to objects already in the museum. Rorimer himself kept notes on every work of art he had ever seen, and he never lost track of the important ones. "I've waited more than twenty years to flush a waiting treasure from its impenetrable surroundings," he once said. The proof of his patience was plain throughout the Metropolitan.

Rorimer also passed with honors the supreme test of the complete museum man—he got along splendidly with rich collectors. John D. Rockefeller, Jr.'s, trust in him never wavered, and The Cloisters is in one sense a testament to the friendship between these two dedicated perfectionists. Rorimer's social insecurities never seemed to interfere with his consummate tact when dealing with collectors or trustees. He maintained smooth relations with Stephen C. Clark, the touchy, strong-willed millionaire who left the Metropolitan board after a spat with Taylor in 1945, returned to it in 1950, and eventually gave the museum major works by Cézanne, Van Gogh, Renoir, Degas and Seurat, together with a $500,000 bequest that was used to air-condition the paintings galleries. For many years Rorimer bore smilingly the cross of Adelaide Milton de Groot, a far more difficult sort of collector than Stephen Clark. Miss de Groot had spent forty years of her life in Europe, painting hideous landscapes and buying second-rate pictures by the important French artists of her day. When she returned to New York in 1938, the Metropolitan, which at that time had no modern pictures to speak of, accepted the loan of her Dufys, Utrillos, Modiglianis, and Bonnards. They remained on view for several years, and helped to fill the gap left by the evacuation of art objects to the Stotesbury mansion in 1941. Soon after the war, though, the Metropolitan started to acquire first-rate pictures by the Postimpressionists and the School of Paris moderns, and Miss de Groot's pictures began to disappear into the storeroom. Miss de Groot was far from pleased. Rorimer or one of the younger paintings curators had to make monthly or even weekly pilgrimages of penance to her one-room apartment where she lived entirely alone, kept her furniture under plastic covers, and cooked her meals over a two-burner stove—she used to tell Rorimer that the way to boil an egg was in an empty orange juice can, because that way you used less water and did not have to buy a pot. She threatened regularly to remove all her pictures and give them to another museum, a step that might have come as a relief to the Paintings Department inasmuch as the money bequest that the museum had also been led to expect from her was earmarked for archaeological research, in which Miss de Groot had been interested as a child. The pilgrimages prevailed, however, and the museum eventually got the money.

By way of compensation, Rorimer was rewarded by another of those windfalls that periodically astonish Metropolitan trustees. In 1959 the museum found itself the residuary legatee in the estate of Mrs. Thomas Hammond Foulds, who had died in a Glens Falls, New York, hospital at the age of ninety-four. Mrs. Foulds had inherited a fortune from her father, a Glens Falls paper and lumber merchant. She married a mild-mannered dentist, and on their wedding trip they chanced to visit the Metropolitan's Egyptian excavations at Deir el-Bahri, as a result of which her husband became interested in Egyptology. He gave the museum $1,000 in 1921 and was elected a Fellow for Life. Four years later, Mrs. Foulds sent the Egyptian Department a check for $3,000, and in 1933, the year her husband died, she forwarded to the Egyptian curator a small scarab in his memory, but nothing more had been heard from her since then. Her legacy to the museum in 1959 came to $4,500,000.

The benefactors whom Rorimer so dutifully wooed reflected profound changes in the scale and pattern of art collecting in America. Americans no longer wanted the same sort of art objects that their fathers and grandfathers had admired. The trend to smaller, more informal houses and apartments had helped to limit the size and shape of desirable treasures—medieval tapestries, suits of armor, Renaissance furniture, and full-length English portraits were too cumbersome for bright modern interiors, and Old Master paintings were virtually unobtainable in any case, most of the important ones having come to rest in museums by this time. Impressionist and Postimpressionist pictures, now considered thoroughly safe, looked beautiful anywhere; since the Gabriel Cognacq sale in Paris in 1952 they had been getting more and more expensive, though, and the market for them was intensely competitive. With the exception of a few old-school connoisseurs like Robert Lehman, who continued brilliantly to add to the collection of Old Masters and Impressionists and decorative arts that his father had begun to build up about 1910, the newer American collectors were left with two alternatives: they could either start taking risks with contemporary art, or else they could look around for something other than paintings to collect. Those who turned to contemporary painting and sculpture—Nelson Rockefeller, for example—gravitated naturally into the orbit of the Museum of Modern Art or the Whitney Museum. Those who looked for something else usually found themselves, before long, on increasingly friendly terms with James J. Rorimer and his curators.

At the Metropolitan, the decorative arts flourished as they had in the old days under Morgan. Rorimer was naturally sympathetic to this department, which had encompassed nearly two thirds of the museum when he came to work for Joseph Breck, its curator, in 1927. Over the years it had been broken down into four separate departments—Medieval, Renaissance and Modern, Near Eastern, and the American Wing. "Ren and Mod" became a quaint memory when it was reconstituted in 1962 as the Department of Western European Arts under the guidance of John Goldsmith Phillips, a low-key but exceptionally able curator who had joined Breck's staff two years after Rorimer did. A new period of growth began, encouraged and abetted by such trustee-collectors as Irwin Untermyer, a retired Justice of the Appellate Court of New York and a lifelong collector of English furniture, porcelains, bronzes, and silver; R. Thornton Wilson (elected an honorary trustee in 1968), a New York banker who has devoted his retirement to rounding out the museum's collection of European ceramics—his regular appearances at the museum with a new piece of Meissen or Nymphenburg or Sèvres earned him the soubriquet of "One-a-Day Wilson"; and Charles B. Wrightsman, an Oklahoma oil baron who had built up in a little more than a decade, with the expert assistance of his wife Jayne, one of the world's leading collections of French eighteenth century furniture and decorative arts. It was Wrightsman who suggested moving the lovely little French shopfront from the Quai Bourbon (given by J. P. Morgan, Jr., in 1920) out of a dim corridor and into its present location, where it forms the entrance to an elegant room full of inlaid Sèvres porcelain furniture from the Hillingdon Collection. Since then, the Wrightsmans have given two complete period rooms of French furniture and a number of other gifts, and Wrightsman has become one of the most influential trustees on the board. Although the curatorial staff has been reasserting its authority somewhat since Rorimer died, an invitation to come down to the Wrightsman's "Louis Quinze Beach House" in Palm Beach or to go cruising on the Wrightsmans' yacht is an invitation that no staff member can wisely refuse.

Rorimer's taste, his perfectionism, and his tireless pursuit of works of art often turned out to be extremely expensive, but this never deterred him. The entire period was marked by great purchases in all departments, including such soaring masterworks as Raphael's red-chalk *Madonna of the*

Meadow drawing and Robert Campin's *Annunciation* altarpiece, one of the great landmarks of Western art, which is now at The Cloisters. So far as the general public was concerned, though, these acquisitions faded to insignificance in comparison with Rembrandt's *Aristotle Contemplating the Bust of Homer,* which the Metropolitan bought in 1961 for the record-breaking auction price of $2,300,000—a figure that for some time loomed so indelibly in the minds of viewers that the picture itself was difficult to see.

Rembrandt's *Aristotle* is in many ways the quintessential Metropolitan painting, a work that sums up the long continuity of New York collecting ambitions and ideals. It had always been an expensive picture. Commissioned in 1652 by Don Antonio Ruffo, a Sicilian grandee and art patron, it was delivered by the artist a year later along with a bill for five hundred florins—about $7,800. Ruffo complained that this was four times what he usually paid for Italian pictures of the same size, but he liked the painting immensely and from then on considered it one of his finest possessions. Ruffo may have suggested the subject, although it is more likely that he simply asked for a painting of a philosopher, and that Rembrandt conceived the ambitious scheme of portraying in one canvas the fountainhead of philosophy and the father of poetry.

The picture passed down through generations of Ruffos until a plague wiped out the family's male line in the eighteenth century. Sometime before 1815 it was sold and transported to England, where it passed through several collections and eventually crossed the Channel to join the fabulous Paris collection of Rodolphe Kann, a Frenchman who had been associated with Cecil Rhodes in South Africa. When Kann died in 1907 his entire collection was purchased by the young Joseph Duveen, who proceeded to sell the paintings at a smart profit to Benjamin Altman, Joseph P. Widener, and other Americans in the category that Bernard Berenson called the "squillionaires." No less than twenty-two of the Kann pictures ended up eventually in the Metropolitan, and the *Aristotle* would have come, too, if Altman had managed to buy it. Duveen, however, had sold this painting to Mrs. Collis P. Huntington, the railroad tycoon's merry widow. When she died in 1924, as we have seen, her son, Archer M. Huntington, gave up his own life interest in the Collis P. Huntington Collection and donated it outright to the Metropolitan. The *Aristotle* did not figure in this transaction, having been purchased by Mrs. Huntington after her husband had died; Archer is said to have contemplated giving it to the museum anyway, but he didn't, and a few years later he sold it back to Duveen, who promptly resold it to Alfred W. Erickson, the advertising executive, for $750,000. During the depths of the Depression in 1930 Erickson sold it back to the ever-obliging Duveen for $500,000; in 1936, having recouped his fortune, Erickson bought it a second time—for $590,000. Erickson died that same year, and a number of dealers and museum men had been paying gentlemanly court to his widow ever since.

Claus Virch, who was then an associate curator in the Paintings Department, learned through private channels in 1960 that Mrs. Erickson planned to put her entire collection up for auction. In the absence of Theodore Rousseau, the curator, who was in Europe at the time, Virch alerted the trustees. He said he thought the painting would probably bring about a million dollars. This seemed a fantastic sum to the trustees, who only fifteen years earlier had balked at spending more than half a million for Michelangelo's last work. Such an amount, they felt, could not come out of museum purchase funds. Several trustees volunteered to make private contributions, though, and an all-out effort to get the picture was decreed.

During the next twelve months Rousseau and Virch and their colleagues did a great deal of painstaking research. They studied the painting exhaustively, using X-ray analysis to make sure that the original paint, under its many layers of old varnish, was in good condition. They also asked themselves a number of searching questions, such as "What Are the Twelve Greatest Rembrandts in Existence?" and "Is This One of Them?" Their conclusions were all affirmative. The emotional depth of the painting, the world of intelligence and feeling and inner experience it conveyed, the manner in which Aristotle's sensitive hand touched the head of the poet, the way his eyes, veiled in half-shadow, contrasted with the clearly lighted, forcefully modeled nose and mouth and chin, the rendering of the philosopher's magnificent chain falling like a golden shower diagonally across the composition—all this seemed a distillation of Rembrandt's mature genius, an achievement comparable to *The Jewish Bride, The Night Watch,* or any of the artist's finest paintings in the Rijksmuseum in Amsterdam. The more

Rousseau and Virch studied the painting, the more convinced they were that no Rembrandt in America could compare with it.

The same general conclusions had been reached, meanwhile, by a number of other people. Serious interest in the painting was being shown by the Cleveland Museum of Art, a wealthy and fast-growing institution whose director, Sherman Lee, was appearing more and more often in competition with the Metropolitan. The Carnegie Institute was also interested, and was being backed in its bid by Pittsburgh's wealthiest benefactress, Mrs. Sarah Mellon Scaife. Baron Heinrich H. von Thyssen-Bornemisza, the Swiss industrialist, wanted it for his collection in Lugano. Other museums and private individuals were said to be marshaling their forces, and the international art world seethed with rumors and wisecracks. (An avant-garde syndicate was supposedly going to buy it for Marcel Duchamp, the crown prince of antiart, who had once proposed as a "readymade" work of art the use of a Rembrandt as an ironing board.) It was becoming amply clear in any case that the picture would bring considerably more than $1,000,000 —perhaps even more than the $1,116,400 that Andrew Mellon had paid the Soviet government in 1931 for Raphael's *Alba Madonna,* the top price ever commanded by any work of art up to then. In a moment of wishful thinking, Rousseau and Virch wondered whether the U.S. Government might not be persuaded to step in and forbid the picture's export, as European governments so often did in the case of their national treasures.

During the weeks preceding the sale, Rorimer was in his element. He loved the painting, which he had seen for the first time at the Century of Progress Exposition in Chicago in 1933, and he loved the atmosphere of intrigue that surrounded its sale. Even Rousseau did not always know what went on in the director's office regarding the *Aristotle* (Rorimer was always somewhat on his guard with Rousseau, an urbane and charming man who moved with great agility through all strata of the international *haut monde;* their relations were not improved by Rorimer's being asked once at a dinner party what he did, and, on replying that he was "with" the Metropolitan Museum, was told by his beaming interlocutress, "Oh, then you work for my friend Ted Rousseau, the director!") A few of the Metropolitan trustees were opposed to the purchase. They thought the resulting publicity would be bad for the museum, and they did not entirely understand

why the Metropolitan, which already owned thirty-one Rembrandts,° had
to spend so much money for another. Robert Lehman, Charles Wrightsman, Roland Redmond and others on the board knew the answer to that
one. As Redmond, the president, put it in a letter to Rorimer shortly before
the sale, "it is the really great pictures that make a collection . . . In the
long run the price will be forgotten but the picture won't."

The auction took place at the Parke-Bernet Gallery on the evening of
November 15, 1961. A group of trustees and friends met at the Rorimers'
apartment for dinner and went directly from there to the gallery on Madison Avenue at Seventy-seventh Street, where they found a large crowd waiting on the sidewalk. More than a thousand spectators, who had not managed to get tickets to the main auction room, would watch the proceedings
over closed-circuit television in three adjoining galleries. It had been
agreed that Rorimer himself would bid for the Metropolitan. He sat in
about the center of the room, wearing an immaculate dark blue suit and a
serene expression. Charles Wrightsman sat next to him. Rorimer felt sure
that if the price went above what the trustees had authorized him to bid,
he would almost certainly get a nudge that meant he could go up another
hundred thousand or so.

Wrightsman wanted to buy another of the Erickson pictures for his own
collection—Fragonard's exquisite painting of a young girl reading, called
La Liseuse. He lost it to Chester Dale, who bought it for the National Gallery for $875,000 (more than twice the price of any Fragonard sold up to
that time, and, for a very brief moment, more than any picture had *ever*
brought at a public auction). There was a momentary drop in the Metropolitan group's spirits as a result. A few minutes later, though, *Aristotle
Contemplating the Bust of Homer* took its place on the stand and the
crowd drew in its collective breath. Louis J. Marion, the Parke-Bernet's
veteran auctioneer, had an opening bid of $1,000,000 in his pocket. The
bidding went up from there, at $100,000 a clip. The dealer Saemy Rosen-
berg, bidding for the Cleveland Museum, stood just to the left of the auc-

---

° The Metropolitan has been re-evaluating its Rembrandts of late, and at last count
fourteen of them, including the well-known *Old Woman Cutting Her Nails,* have been
demoted to "Rembrandt?" This still leaves a lot of Rembrandt. Interestingly enough,
Aristotle is the only Rembrandt the museum has ever purchased, all the rest having
come in by gift or bequest.

tioneer's platform, plainly visible to everyone. No one seemed to notice Rorimer, whose previously arranged system of discreet winks and lapel-fingerings was so deceptive that the wife of one Metropolitan trustee in the audience suddenly gripped her husband's sleeve and said, "He's asleep, for God's sake! Bid another hundred thousand before it's too late!" But Rorimer was not asleep.

The agents for Baron Thyssen and the Carnegie Institute were also bidding, as was a man whose accents marked him unmistakably as a Texan, and whose wife was overheard to say to him at one point, "Keep bidding, sugar, or it'll go to some *public* place like a museum." The contest lasted four minutes in all. One by one the others dropped out, and it became a duel between Saemy Rosenberg and Rorimer. Rosenberg's last bid was $2,200,000. Rorimer winked once more. Louis Marion looked hard at Rosenberg, then back at Rorimer, and his gavel rang down. The entire audience rose to its feet, clapping and cheering.

The next few days brought hundreds of letters from the public—some with adverse comments on the price, some canceling their membership in the museum, but the overwhelming majority full of congratulations. A surprising number of correspondents said they thought the purchase was a great thing not only for the Metropolitan Museum but for New York, and several even suggested that the museum's determination to acquire the best would encourage future gifts and bequests; the Metropolitan now says this is exactly what happened. Attendance at the museum in 1961 was more than a million higher than it had been the year before, with most of the increase during the two months that the newly acquired *Aristotle* was on display. Each day curious throngs would gather before the prize, which was exhibited behind a velvet rope in the main hall, and if a certain proportion of visitors did not see precisely what made the picture worth its record-breaking price, no one seemed to begrudge the purchase.

The Metropolitan paid for its new Rembrandt mostly out of purchase funds after all. Private contributions were received from several trustees and from a number of proud citizens—one little girl sent in thirty-five dollars that she had saved in pennies—but the major part of the huge sum came from the Rogers, Dick, Pulitzer, and other funds long associated with Metropolitan grandeur. The museum, like Don Antonio Ruffo in 1653, was a little out of pocket for a time, but there were no regrets.

TWENTY-FIVE

The *Mona Lisa* slipped into the Metropolitan one cold February afternoon in 1963, in a precision-fitted suitcase. It was taken immediately downstairs to the safe in one of the Western European Arts storerooms, where for the next few days a brace of secret service men kept twenty-four-hour vigil outside the door, watching the safe on closed-circuit TV and keeping a constant check on the temperature and humidity readings, while upstairs in the medieval hall an army of curators, guards, riggers, administrators, conservators, lighting specialists, and more secret service men prepared for the picture's New York debut. Lorenzo di Credi's *Portrait of a Lady*, a painting almost identical in size, served as stand-in during these elaborate preparations. Not until a few hours before the official welcoming committee of United Nations diplomats, city fathers, and Metropolitan trustees began to gather in the restaurant for a gala dinner in her honor did Leonardo's celebrated lady, the second wife of an obscure fifteenth century Florentine official, travel upstairs to take her place on a velvet panel in the center of the great Valladolid Choir Screen. Her smile, behind bulletproof glass, was as enigmatic as ever.

The arrival of the world's most famous painting was a momentous and somewhat controversial event. A group of curators at the Louvre had threatened to resign when they learned that André Malraux, the French Minister for Cultural Affairs, planned to send the picture to America as a gesture of friendship toward President John F. Kennedy. The curators' objections had been overruled, as they sometimes are in Paris as well as in

340

New York. With every possible precaution taken to insure its safety en route, the painting had gone first to the National Gallery in Washington, D.C., where it received the obeisance of prominent politicians and enormous crowds during the four weeks it was on exhibition. The Metropolitan, which would also have it for four weeks, had prepared for large crowds. No one foresaw just how immense the New York attendance would be, however, or how fervent its devotions. Francis Taylor once said that the museum had become the parish house of the twentieth century; from February 7 to March 4, 1963, the Metropolitan was the mother church for the religion of art.

Day after day, the line would start to form on the front steps long before the museum opened at ten o'clock. By midmorning it stretched south for several blocks, inching forward imperceptibly, oblivious to rain, snow, sleet, or the occasional New York combination of all three. Guards maintained the ranks inside the museum, channeling them across the main hall, down the early Christian corridor to the right of the staircase (its walls turned black by the end of the first week), through the next gallery, and into the medieval hall where the *Mona Lisa* hung. The picture was flanked by two guards and watched from behind the choir screen by detectives. Another museum attendant exhorted the pilgrims to keep moving. No one was allowed to pause in front of the shrine, and once past it the anointed were funneled out through a side entrance into the museum parking lot. Nearly every day a few of them would go around to the front of the building and get into line again. Claus Virch, the associate curator, who spent a great deal of time in attendance upon the picture, once offered to hold a restless infant when his weary father came abreast of the painting. The father refused. "I want him to see it," he explained, "and then when he grows up I can tell him he saw it."

The crowds were swelled by an avalanche of schoolchildren. When the requests from school groups became too great to handle, Rorimer decided to open the museum an hour early each morning exclusively for them; the entire staff of gallery lecturers, working in rotation, could usually manage to shepherd about five hundred children through between nine and ten o'clock, but this was only a fraction of the school groups that sought admission—the rest were obliged to wait their turn in line. One day seventy young girls fainted, more or less simultaneously, in the main hall.

They had come together by bus from New Jersey, arriving at ten o'clock and waiting outside until nearly one thirty, in zero weather, before they got through the front door. The shock of coming into the warm building undid them, but they all recovered a few moments later and resumed their places in line.

There was something eerie about the line. Although many visitors wrote letters of complaint to the museum afterwards—the main grievance being the guards' repeated orders to "keep moving"—very little irritation or impatience was observed in the line during the entire four weeks. Virch and others often wondered what the strangely docile multitudes expected to see, and what they actually did see when they finally came face to face with the dim green goddess of the Louvre, whose "rosy and tender" coloring, remarked upon by Vasari, lay hidden behind layers of glass and centuries of varnish. Explanatory panels had been posted along the visitors' route, with photographic blowups of the eyes, the mouth, the hands, and the far distant landscape; in his essay for the special *Mona Lisa* catalogue, Theodore Rousseau had urged viewers to try to put out of their mind everything they had ever heard or read about the picture, and to approach it in terms of feeling rather than understanding. How many did so? How many saw only a watery blur labeled "famous painting," and took away, like the man's infant son, no more than the knowledge that they had seen it? Nearly a century of American museum ideals led up to that confrontation in the medieval hall, where more than a million people passed by the *Mona Lisa* during the month that it was on exhibition. For all the quasi-religious ardor with which they came to view the holy relic, what was the quality of their experience?

The question, which had haunted Taylor during his last years, went right back to the old issue of education. Like the great majority of American museums, the Metropolitan had been founded on the notion that art belonged, not to a cultivated elite, but to the public. In order to make proper use of its museums, though, the public had to be educated, given some insight into the complex inner life of a work of art—otherwise the experience remained on the level of mere curiosity seeking. Methods and techniques of museum education had not really changed much over the years. Gallery talks had been supplemented by tape recorders that could be carried about individually, and in the Metropolitan's Junior Museum children were encouraged to spin color wheels, observe shapes, and learn the ingredients of the egg-tempera medium, but for the majority of museum-goers art education was still limited to a few facts and dates and perhaps an anecdote or two (Leonardo's hiring musicians to keep Mona Lisa amused while he painted her, etc.). Time after time a new generation of administrators had found the Metropolitan's education program inadequate and obsolete, and, mindful of the need to justify municipal funds, had pleged renewed dedication to the cause of "popular instruction." In the nineteen sixties, though, the phenomenal increase of the museum-going public had given rise to an extremely ironic problem. The Metropolitan, it seemed, had succeeded only too well in attracting the mass public—had succeeded so overwhelmingly that the crowds themselves sometimes made it difficult if not impossible for anyone to enjoy the works of art. Modern mass culture was threatening to render the works of art inaccessible to the very public for whose benefit they were intended.

The need for new concepts in museum education occupied the thinking of a good many museum directors, and in this respect Rorimer came in for much criticism. The Metropolitan's Department of Education did not get from Rorimer the same intensely personal interest that he gave to other aspects of the museum. Today, however, when a number of people have begun to think that art education should become the responsibility of schools rather than the museums, Rorimer's scale of priorities is beginning to win new converts. Why, it is asked, should museums continue to ride on the backs of the public schoolchildren? Why should not the expert preservation and display of works of art provide its own justification? Sherman Lee of the Cleveland Museum has become the leading spokesman for a new conservatism that sees museums as institutions for educated men and women and not as community centers for the masses. At Cleveland the emphasis is on what Sherman Lee calls the primary things—conservation, exhibition, and scholarship. "Our first responsibility is to the object, and to the person who wants to respond to it in a private way," Lee has written. There are many who agree with him, and who look back with increasing respect to the example of James Rorimer.

The Metropolitan, however, has moved in quite another direction. History and geography have always helped to keep New York's museums in the front lines, ideologically speaking, and any apparent retreat from "popular instruction" and other pragmatic traditions would be met with cries of betrayal. Criticism of the Metropolitan, in fact, started to heat up again in the 1960s. Art critics complained that important loan shows often skipped New York because the Metropolitan no longer welcomed them. Many of the paintings galleries were closed during this period while air conditioning was being installed, but the critics argued that other spaces could have been made available and that the public interest was being spurned. American artists complained, as usual, that the Metropolitan was not doing enough about American art—the truth was that their pictures had become so expensive that the Hearn Fund income was no longer adequate for major purchases. Aesthetes objected to Theodore Rousseau's resurrection from storage, in the interest of seeing again what had once been wildly fashionable, of several old chestnuts of narrative painting such as Bastien-Lepage's *Joan of Arc* and Rosa Bonheur's *Horse Fair,* and they were appalled when the museum accepted as a gift and hung, in 1957, Paul Chabas's large canvas of a girl knee-deep in a Swiss lake, called *September Morn.* The Philadelphia broker and former tennis champion William Coxe Wright had offered the famous picture first to the Philadelphia Museum, which haughtily turned it down, but Rousseau argued that it had a certain niche in art history (a copy of it had been denounced as immoral by Anthony Comstock in 1913, which gave rise to the popular couplet, "Please don't think I'm bad or bold/ But where it's deep it's awful cold"), and that it deserved to be shown even though it now appeared the epitome of calendar art. Once a year, by previous arrangement, the Coxe Wrights reclaim "Miss Morn" for two months; it hangs in their house outside Philadelphia from Thanksgiving to Christmas, and presumably brings holiday cheer to all the family.

Ignoring the complaints of aesthetes and philistines, Rorimer stuck to his own values and worked longer and longer hours. Alan Priest, his most persistent critic inside the museum, once remarked that Rorimer *had* to work eighteen hours a day because it took him several hours to make a decision that anyone else would make in five minutes. Priest was becoming more waspish and more difficult each year. He had won a long wrangle to have his many gifts to the museum revalued at their current market price (he had acquired most of them at bargain rates during his trips to the Far East), so that they would add up to more than $50,000 and thus qualify him for the title of Benefactor °; his name appeared in 1960 on one of the marble plaques on the wall of the grand staircase—"just at eye level," as Priest noted approvingly. Both Taylor and Rorimer had seriously considered firing Priest, but Taylor always relented and Rorimer decided to wait it out until the *enfant terrible* reached retirement age. When that magic date came around in 1960, however, Priest refused to retire. He claimed that Edward Robinson had engaged him for life, and he retained a formidable female lawyer who appeared at the annual meeting of the museum corporation to insist that he be reinstated. It was not just one of Priest's little jokes, as some people thought at the time. Retirement for Priest meant the shattering of all his brilliantly contrived illusions about himself, illusions sustained for so many years by the whimsical style that was his substitute for youth. For the first time, perhaps, he was forced to realize that he had spent his intelligence in the effort to be a character, leaving undone nearly everything that he might once have achieved. His lawyer failed to impress the trustees, however, and Priest withdrew, in great bitterness, to Kyoto, where he spent the remaining years of his life. Gisela Richter, also retired and living in Rome, urged him to turn his literary gifts to the writing of books, as she herself had been doing for years. Priest would not hear of it. "I prefer," he said, "to look at the birds."

Not many of the Old Guard were left at the museum. John Phillips in Western European Arts, Stephen Grancsay in Arms and Armor, William H. Forsyth in the Medieval Department and a few others had been there long enough to remember Robinson and de Forest, but in the years since the Second World War a whole new generation had grown up with the museum. The shortage of trained curators that plagued many museums throughout the country did not particularly affect the Metropolitan, which could usually have its pick of the brightest young graduate students. New York University's Institute of Fine Arts, whose students spent at least one semester working in one of the Metropolitan's curatorial departments, had largely replaced Harvard as the primary source of new talent. But it was Princeton that produced Thomas Pearsall Field Hoving, the dazzlingly confident young scholar upon whom Rorimer had set his highest hopes for the future.

Rorimer's critics often failed to credit his talent for spotting and encour-

° Membership rates went up in 1964; it now costs $100,000 to be a Benefactor.

aging brilliance in younger men. He discovered Hoving in 1959, at the art history symposium that is held every spring at the Frick Museum and which is known among graduate students as the "meat rack"—the place where budding young scholars are exposed to seasoned university and museum men. Hoving, a tall, lean, and rather brash young Princetonian who gave the impression of having extraordinarily long arms, had just delivered a paper on certain antique sources of the Annibale Carracci frescoes in the Farnese Palace in Rome. Rorimer approached him afterward, and asked whether in his research he had come across any references to a large marble table designed by Vignola (second-in-command to Michelangelo, the architect of the palace), which had once dominated a large room in the Farnese Palace adjoining that which held the Carracci frescoes. Upon receiving a negative answer, Rorimer inquired whether Hoving would like to see it. Hoving had not the slightest idea whom he was talking to, but he remembers being immediately impressed by this quiet, rather stout man with penetrating brown eyes. They went to see the table, which turned out to be in the Marquand gallery of the Metropolitan (Phillips had acquired it in Italy that same year), and by this time Hoving realized that his host must be the director, but because he did not know who the director was he was still at somewhat of a disadvantage. They went back to Rorimer's office, where Hoving managed to sneak a look at an envelope in the "in" box and discovered his name.

Hoving's background and educational career were oddly reminiscent of Francis Henry Taylor's. The son of Tiffany & Company chairman Walter Hoving, he had grown up in well-to-do New York City surroundings and gone to the right Eastern schools (Buckley, Eaglebrook, Exeter—from which he was expelled after six months for slugging a teacher—and Hotchkiss), where he proved to be an intelligent but erratic student. As an undergraduate at Princeton he did little work until the end of his sophomore year, when a course in sculpture from the Renaissance to the present day caught his interest and led him to major in art and archaeology. He graduated *summa cum laude,* and after two years' service in the Marine Corps returned to Princeton for his graduate degree. Kurt Weitzmann, the eminent medievalist under whom he studied, thought that Hoving had the makings of a major scholar. He specialized in medieval studies, but his curiosity kept him open to other influences as well. Midway through the writing of his graduate thesis on Carolingian ivories, Hoving happened to see a show of Robert Rauschenberg's highly aggressive, pre-pop "red paintings" at the Egan Gallery in New York; the experience so thoroughly shook up all his ideas about art that he went back and rewrote his thesis.

Hoving came to work for the Metropolitan after receiving his doctorate from Princeton in 1959. Rorimer made him his assistant, and later sent him up to work at The Cloisters, where he continued to keep a fatherly eye on him. The following spring, Hoving and his wife joined the Rorimers on an extended trip through France, Spain, and Italy. Rorimer introduced him to the European dealers, collectors, museum men and university people, and took him through countless churches and galleries. "Pick out the three best things," he would say, everywhere they went. "Why did you pick that? What are your reasons?" It was the best sort of training, and it would prove invaluable in Hoving's subsequent acquisition for The Cloisters of such masterpieces as the *Annunciation* relief from the pulpit of a church in Arcetri, the Romanesque doorway from the Church of San Leonardo al Frigido, and the twelfth century ivory cross from Bury St. Edmunds.

There are some art scholars who believe that the Bury St. Edmunds cross is the most important purchase made by the Metropolitan in the last two decades—not excluding Rembrandt's *Aristotle*. The cross first came to the museum's attention in 1957, when the free-lance museum agent Harold Parsons wrote to Rorimer from Europe about a heterogeneous collection of objects in the collection of a certain Mr. Ante Topic-Mimara. Although Parsons said that the cross seemed almost "too good to be true," he believed firmly that it was genuine. Rorimer and Richard Randall, who was then curator of The Cloisters, were not so sure. Randall looked at it the following year and pronounced it "one of the worst forgeries (or best) that I have ever seen. Unquestionably wrong." The profusion of tiny figures carved into the small (twenty-four-inch) walrus ivory cross—one hundred and eight separate figures and more than sixty inscriptions in Latin and Greek—seemed incredible to Randall, as did the cross's excellent state of preservation, but what seemed even more incredible was the owner himself. Topic-Mimara, a Yugoslav who traveled under an Austrian passport and lived in Tangier, was a short, heavyset, round-faced character with rather unpleasant manners and a bewildering collection of good, bad, and indifferent objects that included a number of obvious forgeries. He had served with Tito in the war, and when he turned up in Germany right after the fall of Berlin he was wearing the uniform of a Yugoslav Field Marshal. With the aid of an American colonel, he somehow managed to purchase enough art objects to fill two railroad box cars, which he sent across war-ravaged Europe and then transshipped to Tangier. It was a curious operation about which he would say nothing at all, nor would he give out any information about the previous history of the objects in his collection.

Since 1958 the cross had been seen by most of the top museum men in the United States and Europe, several of whom had become convinced of its authenticity. Hoving heard about it in 1960 from Randall, who by then had moved to the Boston Museum of Fine Arts; Randall still believed that it was a fake, but the more he described it the more curious Hoving became. Hoving's special field in graduate school had been medieval ivories, and since then he had learned a great deal about art forgeries, which fascinated him. He wormed from Randall Topic-Mimara's name but not his address, and, having no idea how to get in touch with him, wrote a letter to the Austrian police because he had heard that they had a system for tracing anyone in Europe. Five days later Hoving got a worried letter from Topic-Mimara, whom the efficient Austrian police had traced to a Swiss hospital where he was recovering from a spinal operation. Hoving wrote back immediately, explaining that he would like to see the ivory cross. Topic-Mimara replied with the phrase that J. P. Morgan had come to know so well; the cross, he said, was something "unique in the world."

When Hoving actually saw the cross a few weeks later, in a bank vault in Zurich, his initial reaction was that for once the use of the old cliché was justified. The cross had the kind of monumentality that small, very great medieval works of art sometimes possess. After studying it for three days in the bank vault, Hoving guessed that it was probably twelfth century. He also judged it to be English, which would make it an extraordinary survival from the destruction wreaked on that country's monasteries and religious orders by Henry VIII, Cromwell, and other anti-Papists. Topic-Mimara would permit no photographs to be taken of it; his wife, an art scholar, was planning to publish a paper on the cross and he did not wish any pictures to appear before hers did. Hoving managed nevertheless to snap eight shots with his Minox when Topic-Mimara left the room momentarily. He showed these shortly afterward to Erich Steingraber, the leading

European authority on medieval art, and to Kurt Weitzmann at Princeton, both of whom confirmed his own belief that the cross was a very great and authentic work of art.

The British Museum was after it, however, and Harold Parsons, whom Topic-Mimara was using as his agent, feared that it would go to England. Topic-Mimara gave the British an option. The price was so high—well over half a million dollars—that the British Museum could not buy it without being specifically authorized to do so by an act of Parliament, but as Parsons said, some title-seeking, new-rich English magnate might very well prove vulnerable to suggestions from high places. Much to Hoving's dismay, the Metropolitan trustees proved recalcitrant. They did not like Topic-Mimara's refusal to reveal anything about the provenance of the cross. Rorimer himself was haunted by the memory that Walter Milliken of the museum in Minneapolis had once bought from a French dealer an ivory plaque that was instantly claimed by the Yugoslav government as property stolen from the Cathedral of Zagreb, and had been obliged to give it back. The trustees, moreover, could not quite get used to the idea of dealing with Ante Topic-Mimara. Here was this little Central European *person,* this fellow of questionable background, who met you in the lobby of the Hotel Sankt Peter in Zurich and took you to his bank vault, and then proceeded to dictate *terms!* He wanted the museum to buy the rest of his collection as well as the cross. He even suggested that the trustees fly over to Zurich to see it; they could afford to, he said. It was just not the way to do things.

Topic-Mimara would not budge on his price. The British didn't raise the price; their option expired on January 30, 1963. On January 31, having finally prevailed over the scruples of the trustees, Hoving handed Topic-Mimara a check, and Topic-Mimara, who had stipulated that the price was never to be revealed, handed over the cross. It reached the museum during the same week that Rorimer purchased Rembrandt's *Aristotle,* and it went on permanent exhibition that June at The Cloisters. Meanwhile, Hoving completed his intensive and remarkably brilliant research which dated it between 1181 and 1190, and offered convincing evidence that it had been carved for the powerful Abbot Samson of the monastery of Bury St. Edmunds, in Suffolk. "If one were to choose a single work of art of comparable scale in all the collections of the world that would most typify the art, the history, and the theology of the late Romanesque period in England," Hoving wrote in the *Bulletin*, "one could do little better than to select the Cloisters cross. It is the spirit and essence of its times."

Rorimer's pride in his protégé was clearly evident the following year, when he named Hoving curator of The Cloisters. By this time, though, Hoving had started to feel a trifle restless. His own ambitions had grown along with his curatorial talents. It was fairly obvious to him that the Metropolitan directorship was not likely to go twice in succession to a curator of The Cloisters. He also felt that it would be a good idea for him to work for a while in a smaller museum, where he would have to deal with a wide variety of objects, periods, and situations. This opportunity arose in 1965, when he was offered a job as director of the Wadsworth Atheneum, the oldest and one of the best of the country's art museums. He was about to accept it when New York's Mayor-elect John V. Lindsay asked him to run the city's Department of Parks. Hoving went into Rorimer's office the next day to ask for advice. Rorimer would give none, arguing sadly that either way it could only be resented.

It was very difficult for Rorimer to understand why anyone—much less Tom Hoving—would even consider working anywhere else but the Metropolitan. He was deeply hurt by Hoving's decision to become New York City's Commissioner of Parks, and during the next fifteen months he hardly seemed to notice that Hoving, with his Central Park "Happenings" and his imaginative planning for increased use of better-run parks, was generating more excitement and gathering more favorable publicity than anyone else in the Lindsay administration. The two men remained friends, though, and in May 1966 Hoving came to a meeting of the Metropolitan board in his new capacity as an ex-officio trustee. It seemed to him and to most of the others present that day that Rorimer was in splendid form. He sat on the edge of the board room table after the meeting, laughing and talking animatedly; he was full of plans and projects, and Arthur A. Houghton, Jr., who had been elected president when Roland Redmond stepped down from that position in 1964, thought he had never seen the sixty-year-old director looking so well. Rorimer died in his sleep that same night.

Once again the trustees appointed a committee to seek out, interview, and evaluate candidates for the top museum job in the country. Most of

the leading American museum directors were approached, and several of them made it clear that they would not accept the position under any circumstances—they wanted no part of New York or of the Metropolitan, which they considered too big to be manageable. John Lindsay's young Commissioner of Parks was also approached. At the beginning, though, he was not very high up on the list of prospective candidates. Hoving's galvanic career in city government did not exactly commend itself to some of the elder trustees. Kite-flying events, public paint-ins on a mile-long roll of paper, and the creative use of plastic foam might be all very well for Central Park, but hardly the sort of thing one wants to have in the museum, question of dignity and all that. Besides, Hoving was only thirty-six—a year younger than Francis Taylor had been when he came to the Metropolitan—and no one knew whether he even wanted the job.

Hoving wanted it. When he appeared before the trustees' screening committee he brought along some rough notes that he had jotted down beforehand on yellow legal paper, but he hardly even glanced at them during his extended peroration. He talked for two hours, outlining his ideas for the museum, and his grasp of both the long-range and the immediate problems made an effective impression. Arthur Houghton, the president, was a strong Hoving partisan from then on. Others on the board had come to believe that a new period of innovation and long-range planning was necessary, after the consolidation and careful management of the eleven Rorimer years. The pendulum had swung once again, youth and energy and fresh ideas were at a premium, and the soundest policy might well lie in the calculated risk. Gradually and with severe misgivings, the more conservative trustees allowed themselves to be persuaded. On December 20, 1966, Thomas P. F. Hoving became the youngest director in the Metropolitan's history.

TWENTY-SIX

Those who viewed with trepidation the appointment of Thomas P. F. Hoving have had their apprehensions confirmed. Those who supported it, both inside the museum and out, have been for the most part delighted by his performance. And a performance it undeniably has been, strongly reminiscent to some curators of the exciting days under Francis Taylor. Hoving has shown many of Taylor's strengths and weaknesses—great personal style, wit, a flair for dramatic exhibitions, unpredictability, and such a profusion of ideas that they tend to get in each other's way. The clarion call to education and uplift resounds once more throughout the museum, as it did under Taylor. Hoving has doubled the education department's staff and budget, and encouraged its young chairman, Harry S. Parker III, to innovate and experiment with new programs geared to break through the "unforgivable silence" that surrounds works of art. He has also promised to make the Metropolitan a great center of scholarly research, the "Harvard of museums." Hoving insists, moreover, that the Metropolitan must be more than a cultural generator where people can recharge their aesthetic batteries; it must be "a crusading force to see that quality and excellence is known more broadly," he has said, and it must bring about "a true and active enhancement of the quality of life in New York City."

Hoving's detractors charge that he is cheapening the museum, drowning it in a sea of publicity (Hoving himself once remarked that his middle initials stood for "P.ublicity F.orever"), or else using it—amazing thought—to further his political ambitions. The fine arts have never yet served in this country as a springboard to public office, but nothing appears impossible these days, and Hoving has said that he does not intend to remain at the Metropolitan very long. Some observers even see him as the leading example of a new, comprehensive type of artist, who uses the art museum and all its resources as raw materials with which to concoct gigantic and unprecedented works of art.

Not since the days of Cesnola, in any case, has the museum been so embroiled in controversy. Extravagant praise or violent abuse, or both, has attended most of Hoving's major exhibitions—from "In the Presence of Kings," the first, a striking display of art objects associated with royalty and drawn from nearly every department of the museum (it attracted such dense crowds that it was known among the staff as "In the Presence of Schoolchildren"), to "Harlem On My Mind," the environmental show with which Hoving sought to pay homage to black culture and ended by giving offense to Negroes, Jews, Puerto Ricans, Irish, liberals, reactionaries, artists, politicians, *The New York Times,* and several Metropolitan trustees. The latter occasion also gave rise to the defacing of ten Metropolitan paintings, including a Rembrandt, by an unknown vandal who scratched the letter "H" (for Harlem? or Hoving?) into their surfaces with a ballpoint pen, an act that sent shudders down the spine of every curator in protest-prone America.

Hoving's decision to establish a Department of Contemporary Art, headed by the controversial young curator Henry Geldzahler and covering not only paintings and sculpture but prints, decorative arts, and other aspects of contemporary design, has drawn down the wrath of traditionalist critics who see the Metropolitan's sole function as one of preserving the best of the past according to established and time-tested standards of quality. Art critics are notably uncertain of their own role these days, when rapidly changing concepts of art's nature and purpose continually undermine their laboriously acquired dogmas; some journalist reviewers have resorted at times, no doubt in extreme frustration, to the kind of shrill personal attacks on Hoving and Geldzahler that Clarence Cook once leveled against Cesnola. Unlike Cesnola, though, Hoving is merely amused by these diatribes. There is no cut-off date in the artistic imagination, he believes, and any museum that purports to be encyclopedic must collect and exhibit contemporary art, in spite of the risks that this involves. The question that was nearly decided another way by the three-museum agreement in 1947 has thus been resolved once and for all, in any event; at the Metropolitan contemporary art will seek to establish its value in direct comparison with the art of fifty centuries.

Contrary to many reports, Hoving has had relatively smooth relations with the board of trustees. Some of his actions and statements have naturally upset the old guard, but the most active members of the board (which expanded from twenty-eight to thirty-six members during his regime) have supported him when it counted most, and so has the new president, Arthur A. Houghton, Jr. Houghton, in fact, has actively encouraged Hoving's efforts to further curatorial independence—a rather touchy issue over the years. During the difficult interregnum following Rorimer's death, when Houghton took leave from the Steuben Glass Company and his other business interests to devote virtually all his time to the museum, he made it very clear to the staff that he was there to help in any way possible but that he had no intention of encroaching upon the curators' professional terrain. This was a change from the style of his predecessor, and it was soon put to the test. Learning that Theodore Rousseau and John Phillips had called a meeting of the curators to discuss and coordinate their ideas, some members of Rorimer's old administrative staff reacted as though a palace revolt had been declared. Word came down that such meetings were to cease immediately, which they did—until Rousseau had a talk with Houghton; after that they were reinstated, and the practice continues. The curators now get together to discuss *all* the works of art that each department has up for purchase, and they decide among themselves which works should get priority. Only the objects that have passed this joint curatorial scrutiny come before the trustees of the purchasing committee. The new system is a clear indication that the long, slow, and often interrupted evolution from a trustee-run museum to a thoroughly professional organization is now at last an established fact.

The climate of change and controversy that surrounds Hoving has not kept the Metropolitan from going about its pleasant old business of acquisition. Far from it. Some of the most spectacular acquisitions in many years have been made during Hoving's tenure: the Monet *Terrasse à St.-Adresse*, for which a group of trustees raised the sum of $1,411,200; five major, large-scale works of French and Italian eighteenth and nineteenth century sculpture, obtained through the good offices of Colonel C. Michael Paul, which filled a large gap in the collections and gave the Metropolitan the most important collection of French sculpture outside France; an incredible treasure of Greek gold and silver dating from the sixth century B.C., one of the most important acquisitions of Greek art in this or any other century. The museum may also have located the ivory Christ figure that belonged originally to the Cross of Bury St. Edmunds; at this writing Dr. Florens Deuchler, the renowned medieval scholar whom Hoving persuaded to come and run the Medieval Department and The Cloisters, is conducting extensive new investigations of the figure, and if his conclusions coincide with everyone's hopes the Cloisters cross will escalate in value beyond even the wildest dreams of Ante Topic-Mimara.

No single event in Hoving's Metropolitan career, however, is likely to surpass his success in winning back the goodwill of the late Robert Lehman, and with it the finest private art collection in existence. A Metropolitan trustee for twenty-seven years, Lehman knew more about art than all the other trustees combined. As an undergraduate at Yale he had catalogued the magnificent collection that his father had started to build about 1910, and when Philip Lehman died in 1926, and Robert took over as head of Lehman Brothers, the highly successful investment banking firm, he also took over the art collection which he continued to add to throughout his life. Unlike his cousin Herbert, who left the family firm to enter politics and served with great distinction as Governor of New York and later in the Senate, Robert Lehman scrupulously avoided the public eye. He was a bewilderingly complex and difficult man, autocratic in some matters and strangely indecisive in others; although friends and strangers alike called him "Bobby," the legends of his shyness were legion. Approached one day by a classmate who invited him to a fund-raising luncheon for Yale, Lehman, who had suffered deeply at college from the humiliations inflicted on Jews by Ivy League brokers' sons of that era, inquired somewhat plaintively whether he might not just send a check for $40,000 instead. His classmate gravely informed him that he could not get away so easily—the class expected half a million from him at the very least. "Oh, well, then," Lehman said sadly, "I might as well go to the lunch."

As is so often the case with great collectors, works of art became for Lehman both a solace and an incentive. He studied them with a scholar's

dedication, becoming as thoroughly grounded in art history as many curators, and acquiring in the process an encyclopedic knowledge of the art
market in this country and abroad. He compensated for the drying up of
the Old Master market by brilliant purchases in other fields. To the Italian,
Spanish, and Flemish paintings, Gothic tapestries, Renaissance bronzes and
other decorative arts that his father had acquired before the Depression,
Lehman added superb Impressionist works, medieval illuminations, and
even a few splendid Old Masters such as Rembrandt's portrait of *Gerard
de Lairesse,* but his most important contribution probably lay in the field
of drawings, which he bought lavishly and appreciated with a connoisseur's devotion.

Lehman came on the Metropolitan board in 1941—the same year that
George Blumenthal died. He became vice-president in 1948, and exerted a
quiet but profound influence over most of the important acquisitions and
decisions of the postwar era. In 1954, when his paintings returned from the
Colorado Springs Fine Arts Center where they had been sent for safekeep-
ing, along with many of the Metropolitan's, during the Korean emergency,
Lehman placed ninety of them on loan to the Metropolitan. Four adjoining
galleries were done over in Fortuny silk wall hangings and devoted exclusively to the Lehman pictures. Two years later, in 1956, these and other
works from the Lehman collection traveled to Paris for a special exhibition
at the Orangerie. It was the first time an American collection had ever
been shown there, and the French critics were duly impressed; "We would
like the purchases of our museums to be inspired by a taste as severe as
that which M. Robert Lehman today gives us dazzling evidence," one of
them wrote afterward. The paintings returned to the Metropolitan where
they remained for the next seven years, save for a brief period in 1959 when
they were exhibited at the Cincinnati Art Museum. Then, in 1961, Lehman
removed them. He reinstalled the collection in his father's former town
house on West Fifty-fourth Street, which he had had entirely redecorated
and arranged as a private museum. Lehman publicly denied that he was in
any way dissatisfied with the Metropolitan, but the art world assumed that
the museum, in losing a collection comparable and perhaps even superior
in scope and magnificence to those of Frick, Widener, or Mellon, had suffered an irreparable misfortune. This assumption was not diminished by
the election of Arthur Houghton as president of the museum in 1964. Leh-

man had been vice-president longer than anyone else, he wanted very much to be president, and he was openly bitter at being passed over when Roland Redmond stepped down.

That the misfortune proved to be reparable after all was due in large part to the persistence and tact of Theodore Rousseau, the paintings curator, who had recognized from the beginning the incomparable quality of the collection and who never ceased to work and hope for an accommodation. One of the directors of the Lehman family foundation remarked after Lehman's death that, for many years, "the only thread that linked him to the museum was Ted Rousseau." It was Hoving, however, who engineered the reconciliation. Two days after he became director of the Metropolitan, Hoving went downtown to the Lehman Brothers building at One William Street for what was to be a brief courtesy visit; it turned into a three-hour, wide-ranging conversation, at the close of which Lehman, who had been far from enthusiastic about Hoving's appointment as director, took his guest to the elevator and told him, "My fears are allayed—it's going to be fun to be a trustee of this institution again." Other conversations followed, the results of which were not at first evident. In 1967, though, Arthur Houghton was able to announce that the Metropolitan's board of trustees, in addition to having a president, had just acquired a chairman, whose name happened to be Robert Lehman. It was not quite clear whether the president was outranked by the chairman—the board had never *had* a chairman before—but it was very evident that Lehman, whose health was already failing, appreciated the honor.

Matters were still far from being settled at this point. Lehman had once told Claus Virch that he would never give his collection to the Metropolitan because he did not want it dispersed throughout the building as J. P. Morgan's had been. Even the Altman Collection had been stretched and spread out in ways that Benjamin Altman could hardly have envisioned, and Lehman's determination not to let this happen to the collection that he and his father had built led him to think in terms of establishing a private museum for it, as Henry Clay Frick had done. Hoving and Rousseau were equally determined to find some means of meeting the collector's undeniably stiff terms. The cat-and-mouse game proceeded according to its ancient rules, with all its attendant suspense, and ended finally in that happiest of outcomes, a victory for both contestants: the hunter gained his prize, the quarry won his immortality. Lehman died in the summer of 1969. Two months later, it was joyously revealed that the three thousand works of art in the Lehman Collection would indeed come to rest at the Metropolitan— in a separate wing of their own, suitably identified, and forever inviolate from contamination by alien objects. At the benefactors' dinner which formally inaugurated the museum's centennial celebrations that fall, the gift was hailed as the most lavish and important in the museum's history—a benefaction that raised the Metropolitan, in the words of Arthur Houghton, "from greatness to preeminence"—and Robert Lehman was acclaimed as the Metropolitan's greatest benefactor. Although the value of the collection had been estimated at $100,000,000, it was literally priceless, for there was no likelihood that such treasures could ever again be gathered together.

Grandiose plans for the museum's second century abound. Kevin Roche, John Dinkeloo and Associates, architectural successors to Eero Saarinen, have drawn up a master plan for the future expansion of the museum's eighteen departments and for a large-scale physical expansion of the museum. New wings will push westward into the hallowed turf of Central Park (although all the land from Fifth Avenue to the Park Drive and from 79th to 84th Streets was set aside for the museum in 1876 by state enabling legislation, Hoving and Roche are highly sensitive to feelings on this issue; their plans envisage public delights on the park side that should forestall criticism). One of the new structures will house the Temple of Dendur, Egypt's gift to America in return for U.S. aid in saving Abu Simbel and other Nubian monuments threatened by the Aswan High Dam (Hoving's rough sketch for the glass-enclosed temple was a major factor in the U.S. Government's decision to award the temple to New York's Metropolitan rather than to Washington, D.C.'s Smithsonian Institution). Kevin Roche's design for a matching wing on the south side of the museum helped to persuade Nelson A. Rockefeller in 1969 to present his vast collections of primitive art, thus fulfilling the long dream of Dudley T. Easby, Jr., who came to the Metropolitan in 1945 as Francis Taylor's chief legal adviser and who had been trying ever since, in his capacity as secretary to the board, to infect the trustees with his own passion for pre-Columbian art.

After a brief flirtation with pre-Columbian and other primitive objects in its earliest years, the Metropolitan decided that it had no use for them, and accordingly farmed them out on long-term loan to the Brooklyn Museum, the American Museum of Natural History, and other institutions. Easby, who had once served with Nelson Rockefeller in the government's Office of Inter-American Affairs, was painfully aware that in 1939 Rockefeller had offered funds to finance a Metropolitan archaeological expedition to Mexico, and that the offer had been turned down by Herbert Winlock. Winlock apparently thought that Mexican art did not warrant digging up. Although "primitive art" was and still is a meaningless term—Ruskin used to refer to Romanesque sculpture as primitive, and the word is applied even today to artists as sophisticated as Jan Van Eyck and Botticelli—interest in the art of African, pre-Columbian and other "primitive" cultures has risen notably since the 1930s, and Easby never wholly gave up hope that the Metropolitan might one day recall its loaned specimens and restore them to favor. Now they are all back—together with four thousand treasures from the Rockefeller collection. With the diplomatic assistance of Mrs. Vincent Astor, one of his most useful trustees, Hoving overcame the effects of Winlock's rejection and the Metropolitan swallowed in one great gulp the Museum of Primitive Art that Rockefeller had founded in 1957 to house his growing collection. For the first time, as a result, primitive objects will receive the attention and study of curators in a major art museum—under the delighted eyes of Dudley Easby, who resigned as secretary in 1969 to become the consultative chairman of the Metropolitan's new Department of Primitive Art.

C. Douglas Dillon, the investment banker and former Secretary of the Treasury who became the Metropolitan's new president on January 1, 1970 (Arthur Houghton moved up simultaneously to the position of chairman of the board), lends his financial expertise to the immense job of capital fund-raising in the future. All museums face severe financial problems today. The steadily worsening urban, educational, and welfare crises will inevitably cut down on public appropriations for cultural institutions; at the same time, potential changes in the federal tax laws could undermine the basis of private support on which the Metropolitan and other museums have for so long depended. The future benefactors of our art museums may then turn out to be the great private corporations, which so far have hardly been tapped by the museum fund-raisers. At any event it appears that after a century of growth and in spite of the fiscal storm signals, the

Metropolitan fully intends to go right on growing—which leads, of course, to more controversy.

The museum is too big already, many people argue. Too vast, too confusing, too full of paintings and objects and categories, and too full of people. Attendance now approaches six million a year (as against about two million at the Louvre), and the Sunday crowds often make it impossible to see the paintings. Why, it is asked, should the museum build new wings that will increase its gallery space by two thirds? Why not follow what appears to be the current social trend and start to decentralize—establish branches in all the boroughs, or even take over and rejuvenate some of the city's existing museums that are withering for lack of funds and public interest? Hoving and his coplanners are giving thought to these ideas. It is not likely, however, that the Metropolitan will do anything to discourage the mass public that it has so successfully attracted. Other museums may seek to limit their audience and to preserve their image as hushed temples and shrines of art, but not the Metropolitan. "I do not believe for a moment," Hoving has said "that there is anything but danger in the attitude, all too often indirectly and pusillanimously expressed, that quality should be reserved for a small, sophisticated elite."

And so the new century begins, in a sense, with the battle cries of the old. Hoving's words might have been spoken by Joseph H. Choate, and the ideals of education and uplift, though muted now and couched in subtler language, are not forgotten. It is surprising, in fact, how much of the past remains in the echoing corridors and stately galleries of the museum, where Van Dyck's elegant *Duke of Lennox* recalls the vanished New York of Henry Marquand, and where the traces of splashed acid on the torso of a Cypriote priest summon up General Cesnola's tribulations at the hands of his doubters. These benevolent ghosts remind us that museums, more perhaps than other institutions, insure the continuity of change, and that the Metropolitan has more to offer us than its works of art. What we will find there in the future depends, as it always has, upon our manner of looking and responding.

APPENDICES

Elective Trustees of the Metropolitan Museum of Art, 1870–1970

° *Founding Trustee.*

Adams, Edward Dean	1894–1931	Craig, Cleo F.	1953–1968
Aldrich, Malcolm P.	1951–	Trustee Emeritus	1968–
Alexander, Henry C.	1947–1948	Curtis, George W.	1870–1889
Trustee Emeritus	1968–	Dale, Chester	1952–1962
Andrews, William Loring	1878–1920	Davis, John W.	1947–1955
° Aspinwall, William H.	1870–1874	Davison, Daniel	1963–
Astor, Mrs. Vincent	1964–	Dean, Bashford	1927–1928
Astor, Mrs. W. Vincent	1952–	de Forest, Robert W.	1889–1931
(now Mrs. James W. Fosburgh)		° Detmold, Christian E.	1870–1874
Astor, William Waldorf	1876–1882	Dillon, C. Douglas	1951–1953;
Avery, Samuel P.	1872–1904		1965–
Baker, George F.	1909–1931	Dilworth, J. Richardson	1961–
Baker, Walter C.	1948–	° Dix, General John A.	1870–1874
Baldwin, Sherman	1963–1967	Dodge, William E., Jr.	1876–1903
° Barlow, Samuel L. M.	1870–1889	Drexel, Joseph W.	1881–1888
Bigelow, John	1887–1911	Eisenhower,	
Bingham, Harry Payne	1937–1955	General Dwight D.	1948–1953
Bishop, Heber R.	1882–1902	Fahnestock, Harris C.	1901–1914
Bliss, Cornelius N.	1931–1949	Field, Marshall	1931–1956
° Blodgett, William T.	1870–1875	Ford, Mrs. Henry II	1957–1960
Blum, John R. H.	1968–	(Anne McDonnell)	
Blumenthal, George	1909–1941	Fosburgh, Mrs. James W.	1952–
Brown, John Crosby	1895–1909	(elected under name of	
Brown, John Mason	1951–1956	Mrs. W. Vincent Astor)	
Brown, R. Manning, Jr.	1968–	Frelinghuysen, Peter H. B.	1968–
° Bryant, William Cullen	1870–1874	French, Daniel Chester	1903–1931
Bundy, Mrs. McGeorge	1968–	Frick, Henry Clay	1909–1919
Butler, Richard	1871–1893	Gardner, James W.	1957–1965
Cadwalader, John L.	1901–1914	Garland, James A.	1893–1900
Chauncy, Henry	1870–1872	Gifford, Walter S.	1945–1950;
° Choate, Joseph H.	1870–1917		1954–
° Church, Frederick E.	1870–1887	Gilbert, Cass	1934–1934
Clark, Stephen C.	1932–1945;	Gilpatrick, Roswell L.	1963–
	1950–1960	° Gordon, Robert	1870–1884
Cochran, Thomas	1932–1936	Gould, Charles W.	1915–1930
Coffin, William Sloane	1924–1933	° Green, Andrew H.	1870–1884
° Comfort, George Fiske	1870–1872	Griggs, Maitland F.	1935–1943
Cooke, Terence Cardinal	1969–	Halsey, R. T. Haines	1914–1942

John Taylor Johnston
1870-1889

Henry Gurdon Marquand
1889-1902

Frederick W. Rhinelander
1902-1904

John Pierpont Morgan
1904-1913

Robert W. de Forest
1913-1931

William Sloane Coffin
1931-1933

George Blumenthal
1933-1941

William Church Osborn
1941-1947

Roland L. Redmond
1947-1964

Arthur A. Houghton, Jr., 1964-1970
(Chairman of the Board, 1970-   )

C. Douglas Dillon
1970-

Robert L. Lehman
Chairman of the Board, 1967-1969

Louis Palma di Cesnola
1879-1904

Sir Caspar Purdon Clark
1905-1910

Edward Robinson
1910-1931

Herbert E. Winlock
1932-1939

Francis Henry Taylor
1940-1954

James J. Rorimer
1955-1966

Thomas P. F. Hoving
1967-

Henry Watson Kent

Joseph Breck

Bryson Burroughs

Gisela M. A. Richter

William M. Ivins, Jr.

Alan Priest

Bashford Dean

Guarding the museum: The pistol champions of 1931

Jacob S. Rogers   William H. Riggs   Mrs. H. O. Havemeyer

Benjamin Altman   Frank Munsey

The portraits (details of paintings and photographs) on pages 366 to 370 are from The Metropolitan Museum of Art's archives except for the following: The photographs of Arthur A. Houghton, Jr., C. Douglas Dillon and Herbert E. Winlock are by Fabian Bachrach; the photograph of Robert L. Lehman is by Blackstone Studio, Inc.; the photograph of Thomas P. F. Hoving is by T. A. Ellis; the photograph of Bryson Burroughs is by Underwood and Underwood Studios.

INDEX

DATE DUE

MAR 1 9 2013	
APR 1 4 2013	